Attention, Representation, and Human Performance

Attention, Representation, and Human Performance

Integration of Cognition, Emotion, and Motivation

Slim Masmoudi
David Yun Dai
Abdelmajid Naceur
Editors

Psychology Press
Taylor & Francis Group

New York   London

Psychology Press
Taylor & Francis Group
711 Third Avenue
New York, NY 10017

Psychology Press
Taylor & Francis Group
27 Church Road
Hove, East Sussex BN3 2FA

© 2012 by Taylor & Francis Group, LLC
Psychology Press is an imprint of Taylor & Francis Group, an Informa business

Printed in the United States of America on acid-free paper
Version Date: 20111007

International Standard Book Number: 978-1-84872-973-5 (Hardback)

Library of Congress Cataloging-in-Publication Data

Attention, representation, and human performance : integration of cognition, emotion, and motivation / [edited by] Slim Masmoudi, David Yun Dai, Abdelmajid Naceur.
    p. cm.
Includes bibliographical references and index.
ISBN 978-1-84872-973-5 (hardback)
    1. Cognitive psychology. 2. Emotions and cognition. 3. Motivation (Psychology) 4. Cognition. I. Masmoudi, Slim. II. Dai, David Yun. III. Naceur, Abdelmajid.

BF201.A88 2011
153--dc23   2011020517

Visit the Taylor & Francis Web site at
http://www.taylorandfrancis.com

and the Psychology Press Web site at
http://www.psypress.com

This little book is for
Imen Masmoudi
My wife and best friend
And the sons I adore Karim and Ahmed
I'll love you forever
And ever and ever
And ever and ever
And fifteen days more

SM

To Lily and my children Vivian and Victor

DYD

To Monia and my children Oumayma and Arij

AN

Contents

SECTION III   THE ROLE OF EMOTION AND MOTIVATION IN HUMAN PERFORMANCE

Preface

The field of psychological sciences has witnessed an increasing tendency toward specialization, even compartmentalization. At the same time, many intriguing psychological phenomena demand an understanding that entails integration of cognitive, emotional, and motivational processes situated in particular functional and social contexts. To combat compartmentalization, to formulate meaningful theories that can explain real-life behavioral and psychological phenomena, we put together this volume, in which a range of psychological problems is tackled from an integrative perspective.

This project was launched after two conferences held at the University of Tunis in 2007 and 2009, respectively, on the topic of integration of cognition, emotion, and motivation (CEM). Invited keynote speakers, such as George Sperling, Irving Biederman, David Yun Dai, Klaus Scherer, Jacques Tardif, Alan Baddeley, Art Markman, Johnmarshall Reeve, and Bernard Rimé, and many other presenters included scholars from all over the world. Particularly noteworthy is the fact these were rare occasions when English-speaking and French-speaking scholars came together to share their research programs and findings. Despite different research foci and methodologies, there was a strong consensus that we need to understand a psychological phenomenon in all its complexity, involving neural, psychological, and social dimensions; involving perception and conception and decision processes; involving motivation, emotion, and cognition in complex interaction. Put in the larger context of the emergence of integration efforts on many fronts of psychology and cognitive and affective neurosciences, the collection of the research work reported in this volume from the labs across the Atlantic Ocean and the Mediterranean Sea represents a unique contribution to the advance of the field.

With the "Introduction" providing an overview, the volume is divided into three parts: (a) *attention*, including sensory and perceptual processes that allow the person to catch the information from the world; (b) *representation*, including multiple formats of coding and abstracting information; and (c) *performance*, including enactive thought processes, skill execution, and problem solving. The organization of the three parts in this order represents our understanding of the increasing organized complexity at each level of cognition. As we move from Section I to Section III, we can see how higher-order processes build on and interact with lower-order processes and how motivation and emotion are also represented in a different manner depending on the level of cognitive processes under investigation.

"Section I, Attention," features Alan Baddeley's discussion of the role of emotion in the context of his now-classic theory of the cognitive apparatus. Frühholz and Grandjean provide an updated account of conscious and unconscious processing, informed by state-of-the-art neuroimaging research. Their discussion is followed by Mermillod's elaboration on an embodied cognition perspective as compared with an associative network perspective. In comparison, Gil and Droit-Volet's chapter has a more circumscribed focus. They give an intriguing account of their research on how processing of positive and negative emotions influence one's time perceptions.

"Section II, Representation," features diverse research interests, but with a common concern over how various types of information are encoded, represented, and constructed, depending on their valences of the information involved and the cognitive, emotional, and motivational states of the processing agent. Gilet and Jallais tackle the intricacies of how valence and arousal aspects of emotion have an impact on memory and cognitive processing. Batt and van Leeuwen look at how artists and nonartists mentally represent and process abstract arts versus representational arts. Sklad deconstructs retrospective opinions to show how they can be biased for cognitive, emotional, and motivational reasons. Morgavi and colleagues seek inspirations from young children's understanding of metaphors for the sake of building robots that are capable of generating new representations worthy of the term *understanding*. In "Section III, Performance," Russell, Dunbar, and Gobet attempt to elucidate the functional and adaptive value of religion in problem solving through the analysis of two distinct forms of emotion: euphoria and dysphoria. Clément incorporates the appraisal theories of emotion into the otherwise cognitive theory of problem solving, such that emotion serves an adaptive role of evaluating current situations in problem solving, such as an impasse. Bonnardel examines how different types of stimuli with distinct valences and associations differentially evoke inspirations in design ideation. Masmoudi proposes a decision model that is based on interaction of percepts, concepts, and decisions, on one hand, and of cognition, emotion, and motivation on the other, a model that is, he argues, more realistic than the ones based purely on logic and reason. The volume concludes with an epilogue by Dai and Sun, who use the CLARION architecture to frame their comments on each chapter as well as the unity and structure of mind that are implicated by the organization of the volume.

This volume is intended to reach out to basic and applied psychological researchers, cognitive and affective scientists, learning scientists, biologists, sociologists, neuropsychological researchers, and philosophers, who have an interest in an integrated understanding of the mind at work, particularly pertaining to explanations of real-life phenomena that have social and practical significance. A distinct feature of this volume is that most research involved is heavily built on neuropsychological evidence, while loyal to the experimental tradition with its focus on functional behavior in various situations and conditions that mimic or resemble real life. The viability of this approach to doing cutting-edge research that is relevant and applicable to many real-life phenomena should also make this body of research useful for a wide range of human endeavor, from education to industrial psychology.

This volume was made possible by the support of the University of Tunis, through the Faculty of Humanities and Social Sciences of Tunis and the Institute of Higher Education and Lifelong Learning; and of the National Center for Educational Innovation and Research in Education, which sponsored the two conferences mentioned, leading to this project. We would like to thank Irving Biederman and Johnmarshall Reeve, who served as reviewers of chapters for this volume. We are grateful also to Art Markman, Bernard Rimé, Catherine Meyor, Didier Grandjean, Guido Gendolla, Nathalie Bonnardel, Paula Niedenthal, and Rob Goldstone, who helped us review the extended abstracts of some chapters proposed to the Cem09 conference. Thanks are also due to Paul Dukes, a publishing editor of Psychology Press and his assistant, Lee Transue, for their efforts to facilitate this project. Finally, we thank our families for supporting our scholarly efforts and for the many sacrifices they have made for us.

SM, DYD, and AN

Contributors

Alan Baddeley, Department of Psychology, University of York, Heslington, York, United Kingdom

Roger Batt, Harvard University, Laboratory for Perceptual Dynamics, RIKEN BSI, Cambridge, Massachusetts, USA

Nathalie Bonnardel, Centre PsyCLÉ, Université de Provence, Aix-en-Provence Cedex 1, France

Evelyne Clément, Université de Rouen, Mont Saint Aignan Cedex, France

Paola Cutugno, Istituto di Elettronca e di Ingegneria dell'Informazione e delle Telecomunicazioni Consiglio Nazionale Ricerche, Genova, Italy

David Yun Dai, Department of Educational and Counseling Psychology, State University of New York, Albany, New York, USA

Sylvie Droit-Volet, Laboratoire de Psychologie Sociale et Cognitive, CNRS – UMR 6024, Université Blaise Pascal – UFR de psychologie, Clermont-Ferrand, France

Robin I. M. Dunbar, British Academy Centenary Research Project, Institute of Cognitive and Evolutionary Anthropology, and Explaining Religion Project, Institute of Social and Cultural Anthropology, University of Oxford, Oxford, United Kingdom

Sascha Frühholz, University of Geneva, Department of Psychology, Geneva, Switzerland

Sandrine Gil, CeRCA/MSHS, Poitiers, France

Anne-Laure Gilet, University of Geneva, Faculty of Psychology and Educational Sciences, Geneva, Switzerland

Fernand Gobet, Centre for the Study of Expertise, Department of Psychology, Brunel University, Uxbridge, Middlesex, United Kingdom

Didier Grandjean, University of Geneva, Department of Psychology, Geneva, Switzerland

Christophe Jallais, Laboratoire "Education, Cognition, Développement," Université de Nantes, France

Lucia Marconi, Istituto di Elettronca e di Ingegneria dell'Informazione e delle Telecomunicazioni Consiglio Nazionale Ricerche, Genova, Italy

Slim Masmoudi, Department of Psychology, University of Tunis, Tunisia

Martial Mermillod, Université Blaise Pascal, Clermont-Ferrand Cedex, France

Mauro Morando, Istituto di Elettronca e di Ingegneria dell'Informazione e delle Telecomunicazioni Consiglio Nazionale Ricerche, Genova, Italy

Giovanna Morgavi, Istituto di Elettronca e di Ingegneria dell'Informazione e delle Telecomunicazioni Consiglio Nazionale Ricerche, Genova, Italy

Yvan I. Russell, Centre for the Study of Expertise, Department of Psychology, Brunel University, Uxbridge, Middlesex, United Kingdom; British Academy Centenary Research Project, Institute of Cognitive and Evolutionary Anthropology and Explaining Religion Project, Institute of Social and Cultural Anthropology, University of Oxford, Oxford, United Kingdom

Marcin Sklad, Roosevelt Academy, Honors University College of Utrecht University, Middelburg, The Netherlands

Ron Sun, Cognitive Science Department, Rensselaer Polytechnic Institute, Troy, New York, USA

Cees van Leeuwen, Laboratory for Perceptual Dynamics, BSI RIKEN, Saitama, Japan

Introduction
Toward an Integrative Understanding of Cognitive, Emotional, and Motivational Processes

SLIM MASMOUDI

Recent scientific breakthroughs in the integration of cognition, emotion, and motivation (CEM) into the study of a wide range of human activities at multiple levels, from neural activity to functional behavior, have noteworthy implications for cognitive science, neuroscience, affective science, and psychological sciences in general. They have also significant implications for a wide range of professional fields, like education, sports, communication, business, and so on. Consider three pivots of cognitive processes: (a) attention, including sensory and perceptual processes that allow the person to catch the information from the world; (b) representation, including multiple formats of coding and abstracting information; and (c) performance, including enactive thought processes, skill execution, and problem solving that involves attention and representation. Much time and material resources were devoted to studying these components separately or jointly. However, only a small proportion of studies have been conducted on the integration of emotion and motivation in understanding these processes. This volume provides a sample of the recent research on the integration of CEM in understanding attention, representation, and performance in America, Africa, and Europe. It provides a concrete instance of the burgeoning link between cognitive psychology, neuroscience, cognitive science, and affective science. The research reported in the book demonstrates how an in-depth, interdisciplinary, and integrated approach to attention, representation, and human performance can shed light on long-standing problems in the cognitive and affective sciences, including emotion and working memory, time perception, neuronal synchronization, recognition of emotions, mood-semantic memory links, power of motivation, creative processes, self, religion, and emotion-problem-solving and decision processes.

A CEM COGNITIVE REVOLUTION

In an important way, the integration efforts are meant to overcome weaknesses in the classical information processing paradigm:

1. Thinking is understood as a set of logical inferential processes.
2. High-level cognitive processes are detached from perception and motor skills.
3. Knowledge is represented in terms of knowledge rules.
4. Processing is considered linear manipulation of symbols, despite the parallelism provided by McClelland's and Rumelhart's (McClelland & Rumelhart, 1981; see also McClelland, 1985, 1988) connectionism and distributed activation processes.
5. Hidden layers of processing in neural networks are based on mathematical computational units emphasizing the formalization of thought by a connectionism characterized by Hurley (1998) as a "mental sandwich" (p. 402).
6. It fails to reveal the pragmatic, complex, and dynamic nature of the cognitive processes, as being blinded by the mathematical statistical formalisms of mind.
7. It does not take into account the modulation effects of emotional and motivational processes on cognitive processes and vice versa.
8. It does not express cognition in terms of grounding perception, which is rooted in the sensory experience and action, in terms of counterintuitive decisional processes and in terms of conceptual structures acting as a bridge between perception and decision.

The integration efforts reported in this volume may be indicative of a new phase of the cognitive revolution. It represents a collective effort in the past decade or so at integrating diverse cognitive psychology and cognitive science arenas. In the past three phases of cognitive revolution (i.e., the three cognitive revolutions), Tolman's (1932, 1938, 1948) representational revolution (the 1930s), information-processing revolution (the 1950s), and distributed parallel processing revolution (the 1970s), research attention was drawn to components of the cognitive system underlying intellectual functioning, without careful consideration regarding how these components work in conjunction with noncognitive ones, such as the regulatory role of emotion. Currently, the pure cognitivism is no longer viable in light of the preponderance of neuropsychological and behavioral evidence (e.g., Damasio, 1999; Panksepp, 1998). Integration of the different components and dimensions of mind (i.e., the human mental processes, personality, and behavior) was becoming a new focus of research (Dai & Sternberg, 2004). Integration means explaining the nature of the different links and the interplay between the affective, conative, and cognitive processes. In short, we consider information processing in authentic task environments as inherently involving CEM aspects. So, we might consider this tendency toward integrated understandings as representing a new development that continues the time-honored tradition of the cognitive revolution in its focus on understanding of the mind as a central task of an interdisciplinary cognitive science, yet overcomes the limitations of its major premises (e.g., using the computer as a root metaphor of mind).

If we trace the evolution of research in an effort to integrate CEM, the following books provide a rich sample of related studies:

- *Motivation, Emotion, and Cognition: Integrative Perspectives on Intellectual Functioning and Development* (Dai & Sternberg, 2004)
- *Motivation and Emotion* (Gorman, 2004)
- *Cognition and Emotion* (Eich, Kihlstrom, Bower, Forgas, & Niedenthal, 2000)
- *Learning, Motivation, and Cognition: The Functional Behaviorism of Robert C. Bolles* (Bouton & Fanselow, 1997)
- *Integrative Views of Motivation, Cognition, and Emotion* (Dienstbier & Spaulding, 1994), including contributors such as Herbert A. Simon
- *Basic Processes of Learning, Cognition, and Motivation* (Cormier, 1986)
- *Altruistic Emotion, Cognition, and Behavior* (Eisenberg, 1986)
- *Handbook of Motivation and Cognition: Foundations of Social Behavior* (Higgins & Sorrentino, 1990; see also Sorrentino & Higgins, 2008).

Two other works have emerged, involved in the project of integration of CEM. These works are derived from two international conferences held in Tunisia under the label CEM: Cem07 (organized in 2007) and Cem09 (organized in 2009). These two conferences were the basis for the production of two books. The book *Cognition, Emotion and Motivation: Integrate—Better Explain Performance* (Naceur & Masmoudi, 2008; [original French title: *Cognition, Emotion et Motivation: Intégrer—Mieux expliquer la performance*]) stressed the importance of integrating the three dimensions in explaining human performance in different contexts. The book *From Percept to Decision: Integration of Cognition, Emotion and Motivation* (Masmoudi & Naceur, 2010; [original French title: *Du percept à la décision: Intégrer la cognition, l'émotion et la motivation*]) brought together multidisciplinary efforts around an emerging paradigm, percept-concept-decision (PCD), supporting the links between percepts, conceptual structures, and decisions and integrating CEM processes modulating these links. The present volume also builds on efforts initiated during these two conferences.

All these works and others set the stage for a new way to understand and study cognition and performance. These earlier efforts, however, have their own limitations. For example, although the volume edited by Dai and Sternberg (2004) attempted to combat compartmentalization in psychology and to generate cross talk among people of different theoretical and research traditions and affiliations, new neuropsychological research does not feature prominently in this volume. Another example is *Cognition and Emotion* by Eich and his colleagues (2000).

Although the book deals with issues that have a bearing on human performance, the focus of that book is mainly on effects of emotion on memory and social cognition, and the level of analysis does not encompass skilled human performance.

Recent neuropsychological research suggests that cognition (i.e., attention, representation, and related processes) is intricately related to emotion and motivation. For example, in "the first half second" of visual processing, the microgenesis (i.e., a short-term formation of a psychological process; Ögmen & Breitmeyer, 2006, p. 12) of perception is based on representations that are behaviorally relevant and phenomenally rich, using two to four fixations per second. These representations are modified or newly constructed by the visual system in a very short time, lasting from about 250 to 500 ms. Thereby, the highly dynamic underlying neural processes are updated several times per second. Evidence shows that separate pathways lead to conscious and unconscious representations, and behaviors are blended with emotions and motives (de Gelder, de Haan, & Heywood, 2001; Metzinger, 2000; Shapiro, 2001). LeDoux (1996) described two pathways of emotion processing, a short unconscious pathway involving the thalamus and the amygdala and a long conscious pathway involving the thalamus, the neocortex, and the hippocampus.

Emotion is considered as a function among seven functions of the visual system, via the responses of the visual system to facial emotional expressions (Ögmen & Breitmeyer; 2006). However, emotion is processed as a permanent component of the cognitive system in more intricate subsystems involving the pulvinar nucleus of the thalamus, the superior colliculus, the amygdala and cortex networks (Pessoa, 2010). The so-called affective attention plays a central role in perception and decision making (Holland & Gallagher, 1999; Seymour & Dolan, 2008). Motivation is also associated with emotion in the various levels of sensory processes. For example, the basolateral amygdala is involved in value representation and exhibits signals linked to reward expectancy (Sugase-Miyamoto & Richmond, 2005). Reward is highly associated with learning and decision making. These findings and others underpin an emergent theoretical framework in which various pathways connecting the first raw representations of environmental stimuli to internal cognitive representations are modulated by emotion and motivation. Reciprocally, feelings and motives can be generated by internal representations. In short, evidence is so compelling that we cannot think, study, and improve cognition without reference to emotion and motivation.

A NEW EMERGENT PARADIGM OF ATTENTION, REPRESENTATION, AND PERFORMANCE

In a chapter titled "Percept-Concept-Decision, Secrets of an Emotional and Motivated Progress" (Masmoudi, 2010, translated title from French), I showed that for a long time, the SPR (stimulus-processing-response, known as the information-processing paradigm) cognitive paradigm has ruled over the existing models of cognition. Although it seemed to be a useful scheme in studying various aspects of human cognition, it is becoming increasingly obsolete and unable to explain the richness and complexity of mental representations, dynamic aspects of situated cognition, and in particular the crucial effects of emotional and motivational modulation and regulation. By bringing together work to support this theoretical orientation, I proposed to move to a new paradigm, PCD (percept-concept-decision) (cf. Chapter 12; see also Masmoudi, 2010; Naceur, 2010), which represents the progress from the active mental representation of a stimulus to the decision made for action, through the various formats of concepts in mind (cf. the CLARION model discussed in Dai and Sun's "Epilogue," this volume). This new paradigm connects information processing to the various contexts of everyday life and takes into account the role played by emotion and motivation. Works and models from cognitive psychology and cognitive neuroscience discussed in this book support this new paradigm. I proposed that any expression of mind is a combination of cognitive processes, emotional processes, and motivational processes and should be studied as such, as shown in the following formula:

$$\text{Mind} = C_{PCD} \times E \times M \rightarrow \text{MIND} = \text{CEM}$$

The formula proposed is a conceptual tool in identifying and describing the various phenomena of the human mind. This formula, combined with the PCD paradigm, helps us to envision an integrated view of the mind, setting up strong links between CEM on the one hand and between PCD on the other.

As shown in Figure I.1, a first framework of the PCD paradigm can be proposed, including perception, conceptual structures, and decision making. In this general framework, conceptual structures are the knowledge core, directly connected to percepts, which are the instantaneous representations of the world. Decisions and choices, which effect performance and are informed in return by performance, stem from percepts and concepts. Based on the most recent work, the new PCD paradigm corrects and reformulates the SPR/IPO schema (stimulus-processing-response/input-processing-output) of the 1950s, known as the

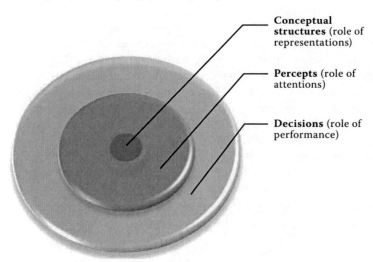

Conceptual structures (role of representations)

Percepts (role of attentions)

Decisions (role of performance)

Figure I.1   A general framework of the PCD paradigm and respective roles of attention, representation, and performance.

information-processing model (Broadbent, 1958; Miller, 1956). One of the main reasons why the SPR/IPO model has become obsolete is because it is unable to capture the pragmatic, complex, and dynamic nature of cognition in the various contexts of everyday life and the factors of initiation, maintenance, adaptation, and change in performance. The new PCD paradigm reflects the importance of perceptual and sensory processing in the construction of concepts, perceptual processing that is modulated by attentional processes. It also reflects the importance of conceptual representations in both generating an online percept and making a choice. However, this paradigm could not be a complete framework unless it includes the impact of emotional and motivational regulation and modulation.

Emotion and motivation are essential for the proper functioning of mind. According to Uric Neisser (1967), it was possible to say that cognition is involved in everything a human can do, that every psychological phenomenon is a cognitive phenomenon, but currently we should rather say that every psychological phenomenon is a CEM phenomenon.

There is a wide range of applications of the proposed formula and PCD paradigm. Consider areas like education, work, health, new technologies, and so on. Consider also all forms of learning in different physical, social, and symbolic environments and think about how to inspire teachers, content designers, pedagogues, and business leaders using methods and approaches based on PCD and CEM connections to enhance the quality of learning and the growth of learners. The PCD paradigm, with the motivational and emotional underpinnings fully infused in every phase of processing, should be a powerful framework for studying and understanding functioning of mind and performance.

The present volume focuses on various facets of attention, representation, and performance, such as perceptual formation, conceptual structures, and decision-making processes in judgment or problem solving. To tackle complex cognitive processes, the book organizes the research in terms of three levels of task complexity. At the basic level are chapters focused on attentional and perceptual processes. At the next level, several chapters look at the memory and cognitive representations that are richly textured in specific content areas and contexts. At the most complex level are chapters that focus on human performance, which involves enactive processes as well as basic attentional/perceptional components, and content-related representations and processes, all implicated in problem solving, creativity, decision making, and physical performance. At each level, specific designs and methodologies are used to reveal the physical (brain) and mental processes that entail not just "cold" computation but also "hot" activation and pathways (or blockages) and meaning-making acts.

THE INTEGRATION PROJECT OF COGNITION, EMOTION, AND MOTIVATION

Challenges of Integration

The present volume is motivated by explaining performance in light of the different links between CEM involved in the human attentional, representational, and decision-making cognitive systems. An overall theme for the book is that intellectual functioning is always situated in a functional context and thus inherently involves cognition as well as motivation and emotion. To integrate, we must face two types of challenges: conceptual ones and methodological ones. At a conceptual challenge level, scholars should adopt a new theoretical paradigm, like the PCD paradigm (see Chapter 12), that allows integrating the three dimensions and catches the central components and processes of the human cognitive system. More effort is made to integrate behavioral, neurological, and computer simulation data. Consequently, based on data that have emerged since the year 2000, any theoretical model or theory should take into account the connections and interplay between the prefrontal cortex on the one hand and structures involved in emotion and motivation, particularly subcortical limbic structures, on the other (Panksepp, 1998; Uylings, Feenstra, & Pennartz, 1999). Prefrontal cortex and limbic structures function as an integrative center of CEM through dynamic interactions between circuits involved in these structures. This integrative center is implicated in attention-perception, conceptual structures, and decision making. As for methodological challenges, scholars should adopt an advanced methodology based on a multimethod approach, toward a more adapted method of investigating CEM variables simultaneously. A multimethod approach means a combination of various methods, such as experimental design, neuroimaging techniques, nonreactive methods, questionnaires, and so on, in the aim of capturing the multifaceted, dynamic, and adaptive nature of human functioning. A multimethod approach is becoming increasingly necessary because of the nature of the theoretical integration of CEM processes and representations. The integrated study of different dimensions requires, at a methodological level, cross-validating and a cross-investigating research instruments and refined procedures (for a review of the multimethod approach, see Eid & Diener, 2006).

Evidence of the CEM Formulation of Mind: An Overview of the Ensuing Chapters

This book provides evidence of the CEM view of mind, through the study of attention, representation, and performance, and through 12 chapters and an epilogue written by authors from different fields of cognitive sciences and psychology, followed by a commentary. The volume is composed of three parts. In Section I, the contributors discuss the respective roles of emotion and motivation in attention and perception, with a focus on working memory, dynamical neural interactions of attention and emotion, cognitive and neural foundation of emotional processing, the interplay between emotional facial expressions and time perception, and finally differences between the perception of abstract and representational art in the context of neuroaesthetics. In Section II, the contributors investigate the interplay between cognitive representations, emotion, and motivation, with a focus on the relationships between mood and semantic memory; the interaction between motivation and opinion construction; the change of functional meaning, abstraction, and insight in children, considered as a creative cognitive process (integrating CEM), which can inspire an artificial system design of robots; and finally the interaction between cognition and emotion in religious representations. In Section III, the contributors discuss the different roles of emotion and motivation in human performance observed in problem solving, creative design, physical activity, and decision making.

Emotion and motivation are integrated into attention and perception through a hedonic detector in working memory, as discussed by Baddeley (Chapter 1). This detector is a hypothetical system that allows the positive or negative valence of objects or episodes in the internal or external environment to be evaluated. This mechanism plays a central role as it is used to determine future action. Depression is discussed in the context of this hedonic detector and is contrasted with the impact of anxiety on working memory. Baddeley suggests that anxiety impairs performance through disruption of the central executive component of working memory, while depression has its impact on a basic mechanism for motivation and action control.

Attentional and emotional processes are intimately connected in a recipro-cal manner. That is what Frühholz and Grandjean (Chapter 2) try to investigate. Referring to recent studies and based on evidence from recent neuroscientific approaches to model the neural network connectivity between specific functional brain systems, the authors show the dual effect of the attention-emotion interac-tion through a stimulus-driven influence of emotional stimuli on attentional mech-anisms and attentional top-down effects on emotional processing influencing the processing of emotional stimuli.

Mermillod (Chapter 3) argues that in the study of emotion, its genesis, nature, role, and control, it is very important to adopt an integrated viewpoint that com-bines psychological and neurobiological approaches. The author investigates the psychological and neural basis of emotional processing, taking into account its connections with cognitive processing. Particularly interesting is the contrast he draws between two models of cognition: embodied cognition and associate net-work, which have implications for how we conceptualize the integration of CEM.

With regard to recent work and strong data stemming from experimental inves-tigations, Gil and Droit-Volet (Chapter 4) discuss the impact of emotional facial expressions on processing of temporal information and time perception. Results reported by the authors show that the perception of emotional facial expressions induces temporal distortion observed in 3-year-old children and is a function of the perceived emotion: a temporal overestimation for the facial expressions of anger, fear, joy, and sadness and a temporal underestimation for the facial expres-sion of shame.

Starting with a definition of mood as a less-intense affective state than emo-tions but more durable and pervasive, and as a state that is always present in the background and thus less accessible to the conscience, Gilet and Jallais (Chapter 5) discuss the various effects of mood on information processing, particularly on perception and memory, with a special focus on semantic memory. The authors provide strong theoretical and empirical data that allow disentangling two com-petitive hypotheses: the valence hypothesis and the arousal hypothesis.

Within the field of neuroaesthetics, Batt and van Leeuwen (Chapter 6) give an overview of differences in the perception of abstract and representational visual art, particularly between artists and nonartists. The authors discuss this issue regarding the experience of cognition and emotion while viewing paintings and its impact on processing the various artistic elements.

In his chapter, Sklad (Chapter 7) discusses a range of cognitive and motivational theories, such as cognitive dissonance reduction theory, self-presentation theory, and self-consistency theory, explaining common errors of retrospective opinions. The author provides theoretical perspectives and empirical data, which confirm the central role of motivation in maintaining consistency of one's opinions in creating retrospective opinions and suggest that the type of the opinion's object may moderate this role.

In relation to this issue, but from both a developmental point of view and epigenetic robotics perspective, how and to what extent should knowledge construction and abstraction processes by children be considered as a creative process that could inform adaptive robotic models and intelligent system design? That is the question Morgavi, Marconi, Morando, and Cutugno (Chapter 8) try to answer. Theoretical work and empirical data are brought into play to map out the various thinking paths that resulted in some very interesting suggestions for the architecture of an adaptive and evolving robot. The authors show how important is the integration of multisensory perception, motivational and emotional drives, and the growing up of insights, which permits modeling the emergent self-organized behaviors.

Affective functioning is also investigated in relation to religious representation and experience. Russell, Dunbar, and Gobet (Chapter 9) discuss the crucial role of emotion, particularly euphoria and dysphoria, in religious experiences. The authors wonder whether euphoria and dysphoria have functional value. They propose that dysphoria is appropriate for learning procedural tasks, whereas euphoria is appropriate for social bonding and creative thinking.

Clément (Chapter 10) starts from the observation that many of the cognitive models of information processing, particularly goal-driven activities like problem solving, do not take into account the emotional dimension. She incorporates the appraisal theories into problem solving, according to which emotion serves an adaptive role of evaluating the current situation in problem solving. Based on these approaches, the author provides evidence that emotional states are activated in the face of critical events of the problem-solving activity. She discusses the various links between emotion and problem solving, bringing into the forefront the importance of integrating emotional components and cognitive processes in a goal-directed activity into a general model of higher-order human functioning.

Creative design is another goal-direct cognitive activity. Bonnardel (Chapter 11) describes the relationships between cognition and emotion in the context of creative design. The author discusses recent work on the topic and examines empirical data regarding whether positive and negative affect, conveyed through words or images, enhance new creative design ideas and facilitate the emergence of new inspiration.

Are our decisions rational or irrational? It is a very important question whose answer seems obvious to anyone who thinks that decision and reason go together, like many philosophers, who believe that the affect does not have an assignment on the rational. However, this question's answer is not obvious (Masmoudi, Chapter

12) based on recent work in cognitive neuroscience and cognitive psychology. I provide evidence that emotion and motivation interfere in the course of rational decision, making the decision process very personal and subjective, away from logical rules, and endowing it with a more adapted capacity to social and personal needs (Kahneman, 2003).

Taken together, the 12 chapters present a wide range of issues surrounding the key concepts of attention, representation, and performance and make a strong case for integrating efforts. It is our hope that ultimately an integrated, even unified, science of CEM will be made possible by our collective efforts, inspired by new ideas and supported by innovative technologies.

REFERENCES

Bouton, M. E., & Fanselow, M. S. (1997) *Learning, motivation, and cognition: The functional behaviorism of Robert C. Bolles*. Washington, DC: American Psychological Association.

Broadbent, D. E. (1958). *Perception and communication*. London: Pergamon.

Cormier, S. M. (1986). *Basic processes of learning, cognition, and motivation*. Mahwah, NJ: Erlbaum.

Dai, D. Y., & Sternberg, R. J. (Eds.). (2004). *Motivation, emotion, and cognition: Integrative perspectives on intellectual functioning and development*. Mahwah, NJ: Erlbaum.

Damasio, A. R. (1999). *The feeling of what happens: Body and emotion in the making of consciousness*. New York: Harcourt Brace.

de Gelder, B., de Haan, E., & Heywood, C. (Eds.). (2001). *Out of mind: Varieties of unconscious processes*. Oxford, UK: Oxford University Press.

Dienstbier, R. & Spaulding, W. D. (1994). *Integrative views of motivation, cognition, and emotion*. Volume 41 of the Nebraska Symposium on Motivation. Lincoln: University of Nebraska Press.

Eich, E., Kihlstrom, J. F., Bower, G. H., Forgas, J. P., & Niedenthal, P. M. (2000). *Cognition and emotion*. New York: Oxford University Press.

Eid, M., & Diener, E. (Eds.). (2006). *Handbook of multimethod measurement in psychology*. Washington, DC: American Psychological Association.

Eisenberg, N. (1986). *Altruistic emotion, cognition, and behavior*. Hillsdale, NJ: Erlbaum.

Gorman, P. (2004). *Motivation and emotion*. London: Routledge.

Higgins, E. T., & Sorrentino, R. M. (Eds.). (1990). *The handbook of motivation and cognition: Foundations of social behavior* (Vol. 2). New York: Guilford.

Holland, P. C., & Gallagher, M. (1999). Amygdala circuitry in attentional and representational processes. *Trends in Cognitive Sciences, 3*, 65–73.

Hurley, S. (1998). *Consciousness in action*. Cambridge, MA: Harvard University Press.

Kahneman, D. (2003). A perspective on judgment and choice: Mapping bounded rationality. *American Psychologist, 58*, 697–720.

LeDoux, J. E. (1996). *The emotional brain*. New York: Simon & Schuster.

Masmoudi, S. (2010). Percept–Concept–Décision, les secrets d'un cheminement émotif et motivé. In S. Masmoudi & A. Naceur (Eds.), *Du percept à la décision: intégration de la cognition, l'émotion et la motivation*. Brussels: Deboeck.

Masmoudi, S., & Naceur, A. (Eds.). (2010). *Du percept à la décision: Intégrer la cognition, l'émotion et la motivation*. Brussels: Deboeck.

McClelland, J. L. (1985). Distributed models of cognitive processes. In D. Olton, E. Gamzu, & S. Corkin (Eds.), *Memory Dysfunctions: An integration of animal and human research*. New York: New York Academy of Sciences.

McClelland, J. L. (1988). Connectionist models and psychological evidence. *Journal of Memory and Language, 27*, 107–123.

McClelland, J. L. & Rumelhart, D. E. (1981). An interactive activation model of context effects in letter perception: Part 1. An account of basic findings. *Psychological Review, 88*, 375–407.

Metzinger, T. (2000). *Neural correlates of consciousness*. Cambridge, MA: MIT Press.

Miller, G. A. (1956). The magical number seven plus or minus two: Some limits on our capacity for processing information. *Psychological Review, 63*, 81–97.

Naceur, A. (2010). Quand l'émotion perçoit et décide: Un paradigme se construit. In S. Masmoudi & A. Naceur (Eds.), *Du percept à la décision: Intégrer la cognition, l'émotion et la motivation*. Brussels: Deboeck.

Naceur, A., & Masmoudi, S. (Eds.) (2008). *Cognition, émotion et motivation: Intégrer— mieux expliquer la performance*. Tunis: Éditions du CNIPRE.

Neisser, U. (1967). *Cognitive psychology*. New York: Appleton.

Ögmen, H., & Breitmeyer, B. G. (2006). *The first half second: The microgenesis and temporal dynamics of nonconscious and conscious visual processes*. Cambridge, MA: MIT Press.

Panksepp, J. (1998). *Affective neuroscience: The foundations of human and animal emotions*. New York: Oxford University Press.

Pessoa, L. (2010). Emotion and cognition and the amygdala: From "what is it?" to "what's to be done?" *Neuropsychologia, 48*, 3416–3429.

Seymour, B., & Dolan, R. (2008). Emotion, decision making, and the amygdala. *Neuron, 58*, 662–671.

Shapiro, K. (2001). *The limits of attention: Temporal constraints on human information processing*. Oxford, UK: Oxford University Press.

Sorrentino, R. M., & Higgins, E. T. (Eds.). (2008). *Handbook of motivation and cognition across cultures*. San Diego, CA: Academic Press.

Sugase-Miyamoto, Y., & Richmond, B. J. (2005). Neuronal signals in the monkey basolateral amygdala during reward schedules. *Journal of Neuroscience, 25*, 11071–11083.

Tolman, E.C. (1932). *Purposive Behavior in Animals and Men*. New York: Century.

Tolman, E.C. (1938). The determinants of behavior at a choice point. *Psychological Review, 45*, 1–41.

Tolman, E.C. (1948). Cognitive maps in rats and men. *Psychological Review, 55*, 189–208.

Uylings, H. B. M., Feenstra, M., & Pennartz, C. M. A. (1999, August 23–27). Cognition, emotion and autonomic responses: the integrative role of the prefrontal cortex and limbic structures. *Proceedings of the 21st International Summer School of Brain Research*, held at the Royal Netherlands Academy of Sciences, Amsterdam, The Netherlands.

Section *I*

The Role of Emotion and Motivation in Attention and Perception

1

How Does Emotion Influence Working Memory?

ALAN BADDELEY

INTRODUCTION

*I*n the early years of the last century, psychology was regarded as comprising three related fields: *cognitive, orectic* (concerned with the emotions), and *conative* (concerned with the will). During the second half of the century, experimental research was increasingly dominated by cognitive psychology, influenced by the computer metaphor. Computers have provided a valuable model for understanding the processes and mechanisms involved in such cognitive capacities as perception, attention, and memory but, perhaps unsurprisingly, have so far proved less fruitful as analogies of emotion and the will. Consequently, while cognitive psychologists have become increasingly knowledgeable about how the brain processes information, we have made much less progress on the question of why the organism does one thing rather than another or indeed why it does anything at all.

Happily, in recent years there has been a resurgence of interest in bringing together studies of cognition and emotion and, subsequently, conation. This development has been influenced both by clinical evidence and by the development of neuroimaging, which now allows the detailed study of the role of the brain in emotion in healthy human participants. I would like to give an account of my own involvement in this enterprise and in particular to outline some speculations regarding how the study of emotion might be fitted in to the multicomponent model of working memory that has evolved from the original proposal by Graham Hitch and myself (Baddeley & Hitch, 1974). I begin with a brief account of my own long-standing interest in emotion deriving from work on performance in dangerous environments. I then give a brief account of attempts to study the important clinical emotions of anxiety and depression from a cognitive viewpoint; my account is strongly influenced by the work of my former colleagues at the Medical Research Council (MRC) Applied Psychology Unit (APU) in Cambridge. Finally, I describe an attempt to use the multicomponent working memory model as a way of integrating research in this area using a framework that I hope may prove helpful for studying the cognitive, clinical, and neurobiological aspects of the influence of emotion on cognition.

PERFORMANCE IN DANGEROUS ENVIRONMENTS

My interest in the experimental study of emotion arrived by accident. As an enthusiastic amateur scuba diver, I saw a promising way of allowing my employer, the U.K. MRC to subsidize a diving holiday in the Mediterranean. The Cambridge University Underwater Exploration Group has a tradition of summer expeditions, preferably with a theme (or excuse) that might help attract sponsorship. I proposed the theme of studying nitrogen narcosis, the drunkenness that air-breathing divers experience at depths of 100 feet or more. A number of my fellow divers were in the Officer Training Corps and were able to arrange for collaboration with the Royal Engineers, a branch of the British army that uses divers for harbor maintenance and which provided us with a suitable diving boat located in Famagusta, Cyprus. The boat had an echo sounder so that we could find a test site exactly 100 feet deep. I proposed to study manual dexterity using a very simple piece of equipment comprising a brass plate with rows of holes through which were screwed nuts and bolts. The subject's task was to move the nuts and bolts from one end of the plate to the other as rapidly as possible. I knew from a U.S. Navy study (Kiessling & Maag, 1962) carried out in a dry pressure chamber that performance should be impaired by narcosis, but it was not known whether the results would be the same under water as in a dry chamber. Our study showed that the effects of narcosis on land and under water were very different. Simply performing the task in shallow water substantially increased the time taken, while testing at 100 feet in the open sea led to a much greater narcosis effect than was found under dry chamber conditions.

Our findings resulted in an article (Baddeley, 1966) and funding for further expeditions, this time to Malta. One study, conducted at the much greater depth of 200 feet, compared the effect on performance when breathing air with that of a much less narcotic oxy-helium mixture. Again, we found an exaggerated effect of narcosis on manual dexterity when tested out at sea (Baddeley & Flemming, 1967). However, a demanding grammatical reasoning task showed an effect of narcosis that was broadly equivalent on land and under water. I return to this point further in the chapter.

The plot thickened yet further when an underwater experiment performed on a third expedition failed to find the expected interaction even with our manual dexterity task (Baddeley, de Figueredo, Hawkswell-Curtis, & Williams, 1968). The crucial difference appeared to be the dive setting. The first two dives had involved taking a boat out to sea and diving "into the blue"; the assurance that there really *was* the seabed 100 or 200 feet below still left divers used to diving from or near the shore distinctly anxious. This third study involved leaving the quay of an idyllic

Maltese fishing village through crystal clear water and following the bottom down until one reached the test station at 100 feet, surrounded by other divers studying fish or underwater vision. In this relaxing environment, the effect of narcosis under water was exactly that predicted from our dry pressure chamber study (Baddeley et al., 1968). We hypothesized that the exaggerated decrement at depth stemmed from the anxiety engendered in divers unfamiliar with open-sea diving. We later confirmed this in a fourth study in which we recorded both subjective and physiological indices of anxiety, testing subjects in much-less-benign waters off the Scottish coast (Davis, Osborne, Baddeley, & Graham, 1972). Divers were anxious and showed an enhanced narcosis effect under water.

Having lost my excuse for going to the Mediterranean, and having by now acquired a wife and family, it seemed a good point to move on. I did, however, maintain my interest in the relationship between cognition and emotion, doing a little work with parachutists (Idzikowski & Baddeley, 1987) and with people about to give a talk at the APU; the heart rate of these individuals proved to be virtually as high as that found in people about to jump out of an airplane for the first time (Idzikowski & Baddeley, 1983). Given the effects of the vagaries of British weather on parachuting studies, and the inadvisability of designing our program of visiting speakers around my experiment, this line of research lapsed.

A few years later, however, the opportunity arose to expand the research program of the APU, and we were able to persuade the MRC to fund a number of posts for research-oriented clinical psychologists interested in the possible application of cognitive psychology to their discipline. This development did not prove easy, as there were few clinicians with potential research interests in cognitive psychology. However, we eventually built up a first-rate group comprising Fraser Watts, Mark Williams, and John Teasdale, subsequently joined by Andrew Mathews, all of whom were experienced clinicians with an enthusiasm for cognitive psychology. The group flourished, founded the journal *Cognition and Emotion,* and published an influential book applying the concepts and methods of cognitive psychology to the study of anxiety and depression (Williams, Watts, MacLeod, & Mathews, 1988, 1997). It is the work of this group that dominates the next section, which is concerned with the effects of anxiety and depression on cognitive function, which unlike my own rather sporadic earlier work, gave rise to some very fruitful theorizing.

Fear, Anxiety, and Cognition

I use the term *fear* to refer to an emotional response to a specific object or threat and *anxiety* to refer to a general state of vigilance against possible threat. Using animal models, LeDoux (1996) explored in detail the neurobiological basis of the fear response, identifying two routes to action, one rapid, automatic, and feeding directly to the amygdala and the other indirect and operating through cortical mediation. He distinguished between *emotions,* which he regarded as physiological states, and their psychological counterparts, *feelings*, proposing that working memory plays an important, though unspecified, role in connecting the two.

Research on humans has principally involved either patients or volunteers selected for trait anxiety, in each case comparing their performance with that of a less-anxious control group. In the case of patients, two groups have been studied extensively, namely, those suffering from a general anxiety disorder (GAD) and patients suffering from phobias. A typical GAD patient will be nervous, having an exaggerated view even of minor threats, whether present in the environment or as news stories. The anxiety experienced by phobic patients on the other hand tends to result from learned fear of a specific object or situation, an unreasonable fear of spiders, for example, or in the case of agoraphobia, of going out in public places (Williams et al., 1988).

A prominent feature of anxiety is its impact on attentional bias, with anxious patients differentially sensitive to possible sources of threat. One way of showing this is through the emotional Stroop test in which the participant must name the color in which each of a series of words is presented, some of which are neutral and some phobia related. In one study (Watts, McKenna, Sharrock, & Trezise, 1986), spider phobics read a list containing both neutral and spider-related items, such as *web* and *hairy*, naming the ink color in which they were printed. In contrast to controls, they took longer to name the color of the spider items, presumably because they were distracted by the meaning of the word.

Another method of detecting the attentional effects of anxiety is through the dot probe method. This involves presenting two words, one above the other, followed by a dot located in the upper or lower word position. Participants must name the upper word and respond as rapidly as possible to the dot by pressing a button. An anxious and a nonanxious group were tested using a mix of neutral and high-threat words. All participants responded most rapidly when the dot followed the named word in the upper location, with anxious subjects responding more rapidly than controls. If a threat word had appeared in the lower location however, the anxious group responded more slowly to the upper dot, while the controls did not. This suggests that anxiety had biased attention toward the threat word (MacLeod, Mathews, & Tata, 1986). Enhanced biasing effects have been shown during temporary periods of high anxiety, such as surrounds important academic examinations (MacLeod & Mathews, 1988), and even following a brief stress such as that induced by failing to solve an unsolvable anagram problem (Mogg, Mathews, Bird, & MacGregor-Morris, 1990).

Further research has indicated that an effect of emotion can be detected even when the emotional word is masked to a point at which participants are unable to report that any word was presented (Öhman & Soares, 1994). This suggests that the effect may be preattentive, perhaps operating via the direct route to the amygdala proposed by LeDoux (1996). Although the effects described are robust, there remains some controversy regarding the extent to which they reflect the earlier *detection* of emotional words, operate through an impaired capacity to *withdraw attention* from such items, or possibly both (Fox, 1994; Fox, Russo, Bowles, & Dutton, 2001).

Eysenck and colleagues have studied the influence of anxiety on more complex cognitive tasks, principally based on individual differences within the normal population, using questionnaire methods to identify groups with high and low levels of trait anxiety. A study of prose comprehension, for example, found that under low attentional load conditions, no difference between groups occurred. As cognitive load increased, the high-anxiety subjects made more regressive eye movements, perhaps to compensate for brief attentional lapses. When this was prevented by presenting the words one at a time, the anxious group resorted to a greater degree of subvocalization of the material being read. When rehearsal was also prevented by articulatory suppression requiring the participant to repeatedly utter a word such as "dog," a clear decrement in comprehension was found in the anxious group (Calvo, Eysenck, Ramos, & Jimenez, 1994). Eysenck accounted for his results in terms of what is sometimes termed the *worry hypothesis*. Impairment occurs because the anxious participant's executive processing is interrupted by the need to check sources of potential threat, hence reducing the amount of attention available for the task in hand, resulting in lapses of attention. To some extent, these can be offset by strategies such as rereading or holding material in the phonological loop, but if both these are denied, performance will suffer (Eysenck, 1992; Eysenck & Calvo, 1992).

Cognition and Depression

While depressed patients are often anxious, their most prominent symptoms are somewhat different from those of patients with GAD or phobias. They tend to complain of memory problems, to be apathetic, and to ruminate on their limitations, shortcomings and misfortunes, often becoming locked into dysfunctional negative thought patterns (Williams et al., 1997). Experimental studies also show a different pattern from that shown in anxiety patients. When tested using the emotional Stroop or dot probe tasks, most studies fail to find a biasing effect for negative words such as that observed in the case of anxiety. A review of this literature by Mogg and Bradley (2005) observed that the few studies in which attentional effects are detected tend to involve self-related negative words presented after longer delays than are typical of demonstrations of anxiety effects. There is virtually no evidence for preattentive negative processing in depression.

In contrast to anxiety, however, there are clear effects of depression on long-term memory (LTM). First, depressed patients often complain of memory problems and perform poorly on tasks such as free recall (Cronholm & Ottosson, 1961; Potts, Camp, & Coyne, 1989). Further research, however, suggests that this stems from a lack of initiative in organizing the material, rather than directly resulting from a memory impairment, with the effects tending to disappear when the material becomes more structured and is tested by methods such as recognition that are less reliant on the organizational capacity of the rememberer (Hertel & Rude, 1991; Watts, 1993; Weingartner, Cohen, Murphy, Martello, & Gerdt, 1981). This does not, of course, mean that the memory problems of depressed patients are not genuine; it does, however, suggest that they are not a direct function of the depressive state but are secondary to other symptoms such as apathy.

Another phenomenon of potentially great clinical significance is that of mood-congruent retrieval. This is a context-dependency effect whereby patients in a depressed mood tend to remember negatively toned memories rather than positive. The effect of this of course is to make the patient even more depressed, causing yet more negative memories to be retrieved. One of the principal features of the cognitive approach to the treatment for depression is to try to break into this negative

TABLE 1.1   Summary of the Major Differences Between Anxiety and Depression

Fear and Anxiety	Depression
Major preattentional and attentional disruption of cognition	Weaker purely postattentional effects
Effect on learning principally due to distraction	Disruption of learning attributable to lack of initiative
Little evidence of mood-congruent disruption of retrieval	Major mood congruency
Evolutionary context clear	Evolutionary context controversial

cycle, helping patients to restructure their self-view and to develop strategies for avoiding a recurrence of this vicious circle (Beck, 1976). Mood dependency has been demonstrated many times using both patients (Clark & Teasdale, 1985) and healthy participants under mood induction (Teasdale, Taylor, & Fogarty, 1980). There have in addition been some reported demonstrations of *mood dependency*, which, unlike congruency effects, occur even with neutral material, provided the emotional state at encoding and retrieval is equivalent. However, in contrast to emotional congruency effects, there have been many failures to replicate mood dependency demonstrations (see Blaney, 1986, for a review).

Table 1.1 summarizes the comparative influence on cognition of anxiety and depression. One might expect there to be considerably more overlap between the cognitive effects of the two states, given that depressed patients are often anxious. There appears to be no generally accepted interpretation for this apparent paradox (see Mogg & Bradley, 2005, for further discussion). One possibility may be that the source of anxiety is different in the two cases, with anxiety patients typically leading to a focus on a potential *external* threat, while depressed patients may be more *internally* oriented.

Underpinning the contrast between anxiety and depression is the question of their evolutionary significance. In the case of fear and anxiety, it is clearly valuable for an organism to be alert to possible sources of threat, with the clinical anxiety disorders seen as the malfunctioning of an important evolutionary mechanism. While this view of anxiety is widely accepted, there is no equivalent agreement on the evolutionary value of depression. There is, however, no shortage of candidate explanations. Freud (1917/1986) interpreted depression as a form of displaced anger at the loss of a love object. Behaviorist interpretations explain depression in terms of lack of social reinforcement (Coyne, 1976; Lewinsohn, 1975), while Seligman's (1975) theory of learned helplessness sees depression as a response to an insoluble problem whereby uncontrollable negative events come at unpredictable times. The most influential theory, however, is Beck's (1976) cognitive theory, which explains depression in terms of the learning of dysfunctional negative self-schemas in early childhood, to which the patient reverts under stress. Beck (1976) has developed an effective method of cognitive therapy that involves the gradual acquisition of more positive and constructive self-representations, aided by the therapist.

However, although Beck's work has certainly had a very positive influence on treatment, his theory has been criticized on a number of fronts (Williams et al.,

1997). First, it is suggested that the negative self-schemas shown by depressed patients are a result rather than the cause of the depression since they seem to vanish once the patient ceases to be depressed. This does not simply reflect successful learning of a new self-scheme as it is found regardless of method of treatment. Second, Beck's purely environmentalist interpretation says nothing about genetic factors, the effects of drugs, or endogenous fluctuation in level of depression, sometimes on a seasonal or occasionally on a daily basis. All of these suggest an important biologically based component to depression.

In an attempt to provide a theoretical link between the multicomponent working memory model and emotion, I have reviewed both the psychological and biological evidence (Baddeley, 2007). While the worry hypothesis provided a simple way of incorporating the effects of anxiety within a multicomponent working memory model, interpretation of the effects of depression was more problematic. A possible solution then presented itself in a rather strange way.

I had been taking pills for a minor complaint. These had the unfortunate side effect of giving me indigestion in the early hours of the morning, when I would wake up to rather dismal ruminations. We were about to make a major house move, and my gloomy forebodings often concerned buying and selling houses, something that it is not unreasonable to worry about, although I do not remember such gloom associated with past moves. The move, however, went well; the removal men were extremely helpful, and I gave them a somewhat, but not greatly, generous, tip. Next morning, I awoke to ruminations as to whether this might have insulted them. One night, my wife recommended that I take a kind of macrobiotic yogurt last thing at night; the indigestion went away, although I still woke up, on this occasion wondering why I was *not* depressed. I speculated that my previous gastric symptoms had resembled the visceral symptoms that characterize anxiety, causing me to search for a possible source of that anxiety, and with my central executive still half-asleep, to accept what subsequently were clearly unreasonable interpretations. As I realized in due course, I was reinventing Damasio's (1994, 1998) somatic marker hypothesis.

Damasio proposed the somatic marker hypothesis to account for a subgroup of patients with orbital-frontal lesions who appeared to be cognitively unimpaired and yet led chaotic lives. Why should that be? Damasio (1994) suggested that such patients have lost the capacity to make appropriate life decisions, decisions that depend on the ability to evaluate the positive and negative features of the options at hand. He suggested that this evaluation is based on motivational/emotional signals that are fundamentally visceral in nature, although these can in addition be mediated by learned preferences.

This view has much in common with the ideas proposed in the 18th century by David Hume (1739/1978), who suggested "Reason is and ought to be the slave of passions, and can never pretend to any other office save to serve and obey them" (p. 415), suggesting that the world is characterized by objects and options, all of which have positive or negative valences that are based on "the capacity of the emotions to reflect the prospect of pain or pleasure from any object."

Like LeDoux, Damasio distinguished between physiological emotions and psychological feelings. As in the case of LeDoux, Damasio suggested that working memory plays a role in this link. He did not, however, appear to have applied his concept to depression. So, how might the somatic marker hypothesis enable my nocturnal "insight" to be turned into a theory of depression?

THE HEDONIC COMPARATOR HYPOTHESIS

The account of the emotions and feelings presented by Hume and by Damasio could be described as a *valenced world hypothesis*. Aspects of the world possess a positive or negative valency, either intrinsically or as a result of learning, and these are used to determine our actions. We are guided through the world through a combination of "negative alarm bells" and "beacons of incentive" (Damasio, 1994). Such valences are not limited to the immediate environment but occur at a wide range of levels, from the immediate temptation offered by a piece of chocolate, to the long-term goals that determine our major life choices. Given the complexity that these multiple levels imply, there is an obvious need for a relatively sophisticated choice mechanism, a role that both Damasio and LeDoux attributed to working memory.

How might such a capacity be fitted into the multicomponent model that I myself use? First, there is need for a temporary storage system that is capable of combining and maintaining information from a range of sources, including both the environment and LTM. The obvious candidate for this within the current model is the episodic buffer (Baddeley, 2000). This is assumed to provide a temporary store based on a multidimensional code that allows access from LTM, from the visuospatial and verbal subsystems, and from perception (Baddeley, 2000, 2007). It is also assumed to be accessible through conscious awareness. This is not a necessary characteristic for a valenced world hypothesis, particularly when responses are rapid, as in the case of reaction to sources of danger. Access to conscious awareness is, however, necessary for those situations in which decisions are the result of careful deliberation. There is one very necessary further component that is currently absent from the multicomponent model, namely, a valence evaluation system. To respond to the positive and negative valences in the world, we need a hedonic detector that may be used actively as a comparator, weighing the hedonic evidence and allowing one choice to be made rather than another.

The Hedonic Detector

Which characteristics should our hedonic detection system possess?

1. It should be sensitive to both positive and negative valences.
2. It should be possible to focus the detector on a specific target, or scan across a range of potential targets, which
3. It should be able to average, after which
4. The outcomes may be stored, allowing
5. Comparison across outcomes within working memory.

It would also be desirable for our comparator to have a number of crucial features, including

1. A neutral point, such that items to one side evoke a positive response, and to the other a negative.
2. The neutral point should be relatively stable but not be rigidly fixed. Something that is positive in one context, such as a piece of chocolate when hungry, should potentially be negative in another, such as having just gorged on chocolate or when on a strict diet.
3. The system should be sensitive to detect relatively minor advantages if necessary, but
4. It should not be too unstable;
5. It should be linked to a system with storage capacity and
6. To a mechanism capable of discriminating among options.

The Hedonic Detector and Depression

How might our new working memory component help in providing an account of depression? A crucial feature of the system is its neutral point. If the detector is set at a point at which the degree of positive valence necessary to move beyond neutral is high, then the world will seem a more negative place than it will for another person whose threshold for positivity is set lower. It is reasonable to suggest that such differences may be influenced genetically, producing either a gloomy and melancholic view of life or a Pollyanna-ish optimism. Such a setting of the neutral point may be assumed to be determined biologically, as may the sensitivity and volatility of the hedonic system. This biological influence is presumably responsible for the genetic component of depression and for its liability in some patients to fluctuate diurnally, seasonally, or indeed unpredictably. The likelihood that this system is neurochemically controlled also provides a framework for incorporating evidence concerning the influence of pharmacological treatment on mania and depression.

The detector is of course also assumed to be sensitive to environmental factors. Given the death of a spouse, for example, many of the situations that were previously pleasurable joint ventures will no longer be the same, making the future seem gloomy, leading to mood-dependent recollection of negative experiences such as loneliness and dejection and in turn leading the bereaved into a potentially deepening depressive cycle.

As Gilbert, Pinel, Wilson, Blumberg, and Wheatley (1998) have demonstrated, we are very bad at hedonically evaluating future events. Anticipating the future is difficult, given that it is likely to involve an expanding set of future choice points, each potentially influenced by prior decisions. Given this degree of complexity, we tend to settle on one or two of the more prominent features. In doing so, we tend to neglect the many potential modulating factors. In one study, Gilbert et al. (1998) studied a group of academics who were 1 year away from a decision on their job tenure. They were asked to predict their feelings 1 year after the decision if it were positive and if it were negative. Not surprisingly, there were major differences in the two sets of predictions. However, when followed up a year later, the failed tenure people were considerably less unhappy than they had anticipated and the successful rather less content.

As Gilbert et al. (1998) pointed out, there are many unanticipated options that begin to appear as we react to our situation, generating new and unanticipated developments. Furthermore, we are equipped with a formidable array of mechanisms for protecting our self-esteem. These include denying responsibility for failure (Zuckerman, 1979), forgetting failure while remembering success (Crary, 1966), being skeptical of criticism (Wyer & Frey, 1983), and attributing any such criticism to prejudice (Crocker & Major, 1989). While such self-serving processes can be criticized as providing a false picture of one's self, they do play an important role in potentially reducing the danger of lapsing into a ruminative depressive cycle. A lack of such defenses may be one factor that makes some of us more prone to depression than others.

It appears to be the case, therefore, that in practice the hedonic system has a built-in bias to see the world through somewhat rose-tinted spectacles. Consequently, a number of studies have shown that depressed people often evaluate negative situations more accurately than healthy controls (Taylor & Brown, 1999). This positive bias is likely to have two advantages. The first, as mentioned, is to maintain stability in the face of minor setbacks. If, however, the world is indeed continuously negative, then it will tend to overcome the slight positive bias, hence allowing appropriate action to be taken. The second advantage relates to the energizing effect of positive affect, the attraction of Damasio's beacons of incentive, in contrast to the ruminative apathy that accompanies depression. Even in a negative environment, reacting positively to the few remaining beacons is likely to be more productive than inertia.

I therefore suggest (Baddeley, 2007) that depression may represent the malfunctioning of a crucial motivational system necessary for coping in a complex world. The system is assumed to be influenced genetically, pharmacologically, and environmentally, through both the positive and negative aspects of the environment encountered. This system is assumed to reflect a mechanism for valence detection coupled with storage, evaluative, and decision processes. How might such a mechanism be fitted into the multicomponent working memory model?

As previously suggested, a hedonic comparator needs a storage mechanism by which information can be held and compared. The only component of working memory that could fulfill this function is the episodic buffer, a multidimensional storage system that is able to link with both the subsystems of working memory and LTM. This system also has the desirable capacity of being accessible through conscious awareness, hence providing part of the mechanism of deliberation that accompanies important reflective conscious decisions, such as which of two houses to buy or whether to marry someone. This implies that the comparator has to operate in a manner that is accessible to both the buffer and the central executive, as shown in Figure 1.1. As we now assume that the buffer itself is a passive storage system (Allen, Baddeley, & Hitch, 2006; Baddeley, Hitch, & Allen, 2009), presumably there needs to be an active source of hedonic evidence that occurs before entering the buffer. This is indicated in Figure 1.1 by three arrows. Arrow a is concerned with positive hedonic information, Arrow b with negative, and Arrow c with evidence of danger, resulting in a fear response. Is an entry into the episodic buffer necessary for a hedonic response? Apparently this is not necessary

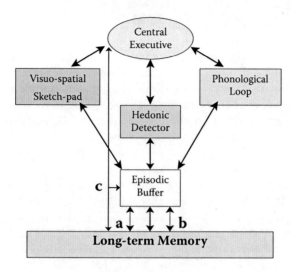

Figure 1.1   The current working memory model adapted to account for the flow of hedonic information through the system. Arrow a represents positive valance, Arrow b represents negative, and Arrow c represents threat information. (Based on Baddeley, A. D. *Working memory, thought and action.* Oxford, UK: Oxford University Press, 2007, Figure 15.1.)

in the case of fear, which as LeDoux (1996) has demonstrated, appears to have a rapid and direct route to the amygdala in addition to a slower cortical route. It may well be the case that positive and negative valence are also able to influence performance with minimal, or possibly even no, conscious reflective involvement, as when absentmindedly picking up and eating a piece of chocolate.

How could one test this broad hypothesis? It certainly does not lead to a simple prediction that will validate or invalidate the proposal. In this respect, it does not differ from the original multicomponent model of working memory, which has continued to serve as a theoretical framework rather than a detailed model. We have deliberately left options open, allowing them subsequently to be developed into more precise and predictive models of specific components of the system. A good example is provided by the case of the phonological loop, in which the original loose verbal proposal has subsequently led to the development of a range of much more specific mathematical and computational models (Burgess & Hitch, 1992, 1999, 2006; Henson, 1998; Page & Norris, 1998).

One hint regarding both the possible way ahead and potential pitfalls is provided by the further research generated by Damasio's somatic marker hypothesis. This has met with a mix of support and controversy. There is certainly sufficient support for the idea that a combination of the frontal lobes and the amygdala plays an important role in emotional judgment and choice. Somewhat less successful has been the attempt to decide whether the somatic markers are indeed somatic, using patients who have damage to one or more sources of information from the viscera and related systems (Craig, 2002; Heims, Critchley, Mathias, Dolan, & Cipolotti, 2004; North & O'Carroll, 2001). There are two possible reasons for this lack of clear support. The first concerns the fact that somatic information is transmitted through a number of different routes, with the result that it is unlikely that all of these were completely abolished in any of the patient groups. The second concerns the role of learning and the probability that many valences, although perhaps originally somatically based, may now be stored at a higher cortical level, hence allowing the system to operate in the absence of visceral cues.

A more serious problem for the hedonic detection hypothesis concerns the practical problem of how to measure the output of the detector. One possibility might be to use the task that has been developed by Damasio's group to investigate the operation of the somatic markers experimentally, namely, the Iowa Gambling Test (IGT). This involves presenting participants with four packs of cards. Two have high-payoff and high-cost cards that start by being profitable and then rapidly decline, while the other two packs give more modest but continuously positive returns. Most people confronted with this task begin with the high-payoff but higher-cost packs and gradually switch to the modestly positive alternatives. Damasio and colleagues studied patients with a classical frontal lobe lesion; despite apparently unimpaired cognition, these patients nevertheless led chaotic lives and began with the initially high-payoff packs and continued despite ever-heavier losses. Damasio's group used this task extensively, demonstrating similar effects in other groups and linking them to emotional differences between the groups using the electrodermal response (Bechara, Damasio, Damasio, & Anderson, 1994; Bechara, Damasio, Tranel, & Damasio, 1997).

There are two reasons for rejecting this as an appropriate way of testing the hedonic detector hypothesis, both stemming from its comparative complexity. While there have been some successful replications (Bowman & Turnbull, 2004), there have also been failures and claims that the effects observed might reflect the demands placed on the central executive by such a complex decision task (Hinson, Jameson, & Whitney, 2002, 2003). Bechara, Damasio, Tranel, and Anderson (1998) claimed to have refuted the executive load interpretation. However, their rejection was based on a single measure of working memory, delayed matching to sample, a task taken to reflect working memory in the animal literature but not regarded as an adequate measure of human working memory. Indeed, it would be unwise to rely on any single measure of executive processing (Baddeley, 2007). A second reason why the IGT is not suitable for testing the hedonic detector hypothesis stems from the fact that it measures the capacity to *acquire* hedonic information; as such, it is a learning task, whereas the hedonic detector hypothesis requires a measure of the capacity to evaluate existing valences.

We have therefore developed a simple task in which the participant is shown a sequence of stimuli comprising words, faces, or pictures and is required to make a hedonic judgment using a rating scale. In an attempt to test the sensitivity of this method, we have carried out a number of experiments in which we attempted to move the neutral point of the hedonic detector by manipulating mood, proposing that if we were able to shift the neutral point, then items that were previously slightly positive would register as slightly negative. Our results were encouraging, suggesting that this simple method may prove valuable in further exploring the hedonic detector hypothesis (Baddeley, Banse, Huang, & Page, in press).

Does the proposed theoretical framework offer an explanation of the results of my previous atheoretical diving experiments? In the case of the screwplate results in which anxiety and narcosis interacted, a plausible account was provided by Eysenck's worry hypothesis (Eysenck & Calvo, 1992). Anxiety results in constantly checking the environment, drawing attention away from a task that has already become more difficult as a result of intoxication. Then, why does this not apply to the grammatical reasoning task? This can readily be explained by Lavie's (1995) demonstration that distraction may be reduced in high-load tasks, which focus attention on the task in hand, leaving little spare capacity for peripheral stimuli. Our demanding reasoning test certainly required full attention, whereas an activity less attentionally demanding such as manipulating nuts and bolts would be likely to leave attention free to be captured by potentially disruptive threatening thoughts (Lavie, 1995, 2005). I must confess, however, that I myself have no immediate plans to test this hypothesis in the cold and murky waters off Scotland.

In conclusion, I suggest here, and in earlier work (Baddeley, 2007), that working memory plays a role in the transfer of information from physiologically based emotions into psychologically based feelings. I have illustrated this in terms of two clinically important emotional states, anxiety and depression. Anxiety reflects the functioning or malfunctioning of a threat detection system that may disrupt cognition through the capacity of threat-related material to interrupt the operation of the central executive. Clinical depression, on the other hand, is assumed to reflect the malfunction of a hedonic detector system that underpins our capacity to make motivated choices within a positively and negatively valenced environment.

REFERENCES

Allen, R. J., Baddeley, A. D., & Hitch, G. J. (2006). Is the binding of visual features in working memory resource-demanding? *Journal of Experimental Psychology: General, 135,* 298–313.

Baddeley, A. D. (1966). Influence of depth on the manual dexterity of free divers: A comparison between open sea and pressure chamber testing. *Journal of Applied Psychology, 50,* 81–85.

Baddeley, A. D. (2000). The episodic buffer: A new component of working memory? *Trends in Cognitive Sciences, 4,* 417–423.

Baddeley, A. D. (2007). *Working memory, thought and action.* Oxford, UK: Oxford University Press.

Baddeley, A., Banse, R., Huang, Y., & Page, M. (In Press). Working memory and emotion: Detecting the hedonic detector. *Journal of Cognitive Psychology.*

Baddeley, A. D., de Figueredo, J. W., Hawkswell-Curtis, J. W., & Williams, A. N. (1968). Nitrogen narcosis and performance underwater. *Ergonomics, 11,* 157–164.

Baddeley, A. D., & Flemming, N. C. (1967). The efficiency of divers breathing oxy-helium. *Ergonomics, 10,* 311–319.

Baddeley, A. D., & Hitch, G. J. (1974). Working memory. In G. A. Bower (Ed.), *Recent advances in learning and motivation* (Vol. 8, pp. 47–89). New York: Academic Press.

Baddeley, A. D., Hitch, G. J., & Allen, R. J. (2009). Working memory and binding in sentence recall. *Journal of Memory and Language, 61,* 438–456.

Bechara, A., Damasio, A. R., Damasio, H., & Anderson, S. W. (1994). Insensitivity to future consequences following damage to human prefrontal cortex. *Cognition, 50,* 7–15.

Bechara, A., Damasio, H., Tranel, D., & Anderson, S. W. (1998). Dissociation of working memory from decision making within human prefrontal cortex. *Journal of Neuroscience, 18,* 428–437.

Bechara, A., Damasio, H., Tranel, D., & Damasio, A. R. (1997). Deciding advantageously before knowing the advantageous strategy. *Science, 275,* 1293–1295.

Beck, A. T. (1976). *Cognitive therapy and the emotional disorders.* New York: International Universities Press.

Blaney, P. H. (1986). Affect and memory: A review. *Psychological Bulletin, 99,* 229–246.

Bowman, C. H., & Turnbull, O. H. (2004). Emotion-based learning on a simplified card game: The Iowa and Bangor Gambling Tasks. *Brain and Cognition, 55,* 277–282.

Burgess, N., & Hitch, G. J. (1992). Toward a network model of the articulatory loop. *Journal of Memory and Language, 31,* 429–460.

Burgess, N., & Hitch, G. J. (1999). Memory for serial order: A network model of the phonological loop and its timing. *Psychological Review, 106,* 551–581.

Burgess, N., & Hitch, G. J. (2006). A revised model of short-term memory and long-term learning of verbal sequences. *Journal of Memory and Language, 55,* 627–652.

Calvo, M. G., Eysenck, M. W., Ramos, P. M., & Jimenez, A. (1994). Compensatory reading strategies in test anxiety. *Anxiety, Stress and Coping, 7,* 99–116.

Clark, D. M., & Teasdale, J. D. (1985). Constraints on the effects of mood on memory. *Journal of Personality and Social Psychology, 48,* 1595–1608.

Coyne, J. C. (1976). Depression and the response of others. *Journal of Abnormal Psychology, 85,* 186–193.

Craig, A. D. (2002). How do you feel? Interoceptors: The sense of the physiological condition of the body. *Nature Reviews, 3,* 655–666.

Crary, W. G. (1966). Reactions to incongruent self-experiences. *Journal of Consulting Psychology, 30,* 246–252.

Crocker, J., & Major, B. (1989). Social stigma and self-esteem: The self-protective properties of stigma. *Psychological Review, 96,* 608–630.

Cronholm, B., & Ottosson, J. O. (1961). Memory functions in endogenous depression. Before and after electroconvulsive therapy. *Archives of General Psychiatry, 5,* 193–199.

Damasio, A. R. (1994). *Descartes' error: Emotion, reason, and the human brain.* New York: Putnam.

Damasio, A. R. (1998). The somatic marker hypothesis and the possible functions of prefrontal cortex. In A. C. Roberts, T. W. Robbins, & L. Weiskrantz (Eds.), *The prefrontal cortex* (pp. 36–50). New York: Oxford University Press.

Davis, F. M., Osborne, J. P., Baddeley, A. D., & Graham, I. M. F. (1972). Diver performance: Nitrogen narcosis and anxiety. *Aerospace Medicine, 43,* 1079–1082.

Eysenck, M. (1992). *Anxiety: The cognitive perspective.* Hove, UK: Erlbaum.

Eysenck, M. W., & Calvo, M. G. (1992). Anxiety and performance—the processing efficiency theory. *Cognition and Emotion, 6,* 409–434.

Fox, E. (1994). Attentional bias in anxiety: A defective inhibition hypothesis. *Cognition & Emotion, 8,* 165–195.

Fox, E., Russo, R., Bowles, R. J., & Dutton, K. (2001). Do threatening stimuli draw or hold visual attention in subclinical anxiety? *Journal of Experimental Psychology: General, 130,* 681–700.

Freud, S. (1986). Mourning and melancholia. In J. Coyne (Ed.), *Essential papers on depression* (pp. 48–63). New York: New York University Press.

Gilbert, D. T., Pinel, E. C., Wilson, T. D., Blumberg, S. J., & Wheatley, T. P. (1998). Immune neglect: A source of durability bias in affective forecasting. *Journal of Personality and Social Psychology, 75,* 617–638.

Heims, H. C., Critchley, H. D., Mathias, C. J., Dolan, R. J., & Cipolotti, L. (2004). Social and motivational functioning is not critically dependent on autonomic responses: Neuropsychological evidence from patients with pure autonomic failure. *Neuropsychologia, 42*, 1979–1988.

Henson, R. N. A. (1998). Short-term memory for serial order. The start-end model. *Cognitive Psychology, 36*, 73–137.

Hertel, P. T., & Rude, S. S. (1991). Depressive deficits in memory: Focusing attention improves subsequent recall. *Journal of Experimental Psychology: General, 120*, 301–309.

Hinson, J. M., Jameson, T. J., & Whitney, P. (2002). Somatic markers, working memory, and decision making. *Cognitive, Affective and Behavioural Neuroscience, 2*, 341–353.

Hinson, J. M., Jameson, T. J., & Whitney, P. (2003). Impulsive decision making and working memory. *Journal of Experimental Psychology: Learning, Memory and Cognition, 29*, 298–306.

Hume, D. (1739/1978). *A treatise of human nature*. Oxford, UK: Oxford University Press.

Idzikowski, C., & Baddeley, A. D. (1983). Waiting in the wings: Apprehension, public speaking and performance. *Ergonomics, 26*, 575–583.

Idzikowski, C., & Baddeley, A. D. (1987). Fear and performance in novice parachutists. *Ergonomics, 30*, 1463–1474.

Kiessling, R. J., & Maag, C. H. (1962). Performance impairment as a function of nitrogen narcosis. *Journal of Applied Psychology, 46*, 91–95.

Lavie, N. (1995). Perceptual load as a necessary condition for selective attention. *Journal of Experimental Psychology: Human Perception and Performance, 21*, 451–468.

Lavie, N. (2005). Distracted and confused: Selective attention under load. *Trends in Cognitive Science, 9*, 75–82.

LeDoux, J. E. (1996). *The emotional brain*. New York: Simon & Schuster.

Lewinsohn, P. M. (1975). The behavioral study and treatment of depression. In R. Henson, R. M. Eisler, & P. M. Miller (Eds.), *Progress in behaviour modification* (pp. 19–64). New York: Academic Press.

MacLeod, C., & Mathews, A. (1988). Anxiety and the allocation of attention to threat. *Quarterly Journal of Experimental Psychology, 40A*, 653–670.

MacLeod, C., Mathews, A., & Tata, P. (1986). Attentional bias in emotional disorders. *Journal of Abnormal Psychology, 95*, 15–20.

Mogg, K., & Bradley, B. P. (2005). Attentional bias in generalised anxiety disorder versus depressive disorder. *Cognitive Therapy and Research, 29*, 29–45.

Mogg, K., Mathews, A., Bird, C., & MacGregor-Morris, R. (1990). Effects of stress and anxiety on the processing of threat stimuli. *Journal of Personality and Social Psychology, 59*, 1230–1237.

North, N. T., & O'Carroll, R. E. (2001). Decision making in patients with spinal cord damage: Afferent feedback and the somatic marker hypothesis. *Neuropsychologia, 39*, 521–524.

Öhman, A., & Soares, J. J. F. (1994). "Unconscious anxiety": Phobic responses to masked stimuli. *Journal of Abnormal Psychology, 103*, 231–240.

Page, M. P. A., & Norris, D. (1998). The primacy model: A new model of immediate serial recall. *Psychological Review, 105*, 761–781.

Potts, R., Camp, C., & Coyne, C. (1989). The relationship between naturally occurring dysphoric moods, elaborative encoding, and recall performance. *Cognition and Emotion, 3*, 197–205.

Seligman, M. E. P. (1975). *Helplessness: On depression, development and death*. San Francisco: Freeman.

Taylor, S. E., & Brown, J. D. (1999). Illusion and well-being: A social psychological perspective on mental health. In R. F. Baumeister (Ed.), *The self in social psychology* (pp. 43–66). Philadelphia: Psychology Press.

Teasdale, J. D., Taylor, R., & Fogarty, S. J. (1980). Effects of induced elation and depression on the accessibility of memories of happy and unhappy experiences. *Behaviour Research and Therapy, 18*, 339–346.

Watts, F. N. (1993). Problems of memory and concentration. In C. G. Costello (Ed.), *Symptoms of depression* (pp. 113–140). New York: Wiley.

Watts, F. N., McKenna, F. P., Sharrock, R., & Trezise, L. (1986). Colour naming of phobia-related words. *British Journal of Psychology, 77*, 97–108.

Weingartner, H., Cohen, R. M., Murphy, D. L., Martello, J., & Gerdt, C. (1981). Cognitive processes in depression. *Archives of General Psychiatry, 38*, 42–47.

Williams, J. M. G., Watts, F. N., MacLeod, C., & Mathews, A. (1988). *Cognitive psychology and emotional disorders.* New York: Wiley.

Williams, J. M. G., Watts, F. N., MacLeod, C., & Mathews, A. (1997). *Cognitive psychology and emotional disorders* (2nd ed.). Chichester, UK: Wiley.

Wyer, R. S., & Frey, D. (1983). The effects of feedback about self and others on the recall and judgments of feedback-relevant information. *Journal of Experimental Social Psychology, 19*, 540–559.

Zuckerman, M. (1979). *Sensation seeking: Beyond the optimal level of arousal.* Hillsdale, NJ: Erlbaum.

2

Dynamical Interactions of Attention and Emotion
A Cognitive Neuroscience Approach Through Neural Network Connectivity

SASCHA FRÜHHOLZ and DIDIER GRANDJEAN

INTRODUCTION

*I*magine you find yourself at some crowded place anywhere in a big city. You move around and perceive a lot of information on the things that happen around you, and there is other information that you simply do not recognize or process consciously. There is, for example, a bulk of cars that quickly rush by, and you have to strongly concentrate while you attempt to cross the street. At the same time, you do not realize the anxious child next to you who fearfully hesitates to cross the street. You also meet a lot of other people, some of them just pass by, and with others you start some small interactions. Some of these individuals might smile in a friendly manner at you, but one person might approach you with an angry expression since the person might have just lost his or her job and therefore is extremely agitated. Besides these visual impressions, you also encounter a multitude of sounds. For example, you might hear a group of people laughing and celebrating since they just passed a challenging exam, but you may also hear a scream of another person just around the corner or a dog barking somewhere nearby but you cannot exactly locate where it originates.

So, what can we learn from these daily situations? We think these examples have three important implications. First, the outside world is full of information, but our cognitive system is only able to process a limited amount of this information at a time. We have to focus our attention on the information that is currently most important to adapt our behavior to the context. While you cross the street, you just neglect the anxious child since the cars capture all of your attention. Second, emotional events might be more attractive than neutral events. Walking up the street, you just ignore the majority of people who pass by, but you simply cannot ignore the person with the angry expression, the frightening sound of the scream, or the barking dog. However, the potential of emotional events to attract attention also depends on how strongly one currently focuses on another event. Remember, you just neglected the anxious expression of the child because you strongly focused on the cars. Third, attentional focusing on relevant information as well as attraction of attention by emotional events are adaptive since they can guide human behavior to avoid painful harm or to approach reward from the environment. For example, if the barking sound of the dog is slowly approaching, you are well advised to immediately find a safe place.

Taken together, these few examples should have demonstrated that both attentional and emotional processing are strongly associated since one process can influence the other. Recent neuroscientific investigations on attentional and emotional processing have revealed many interesting insights in the interplay between attentional and emotional processing (Compton, 2003; Corbetta & Shulman, 2002; Vuilleumier & Driver, 2007). From the viewpoint of attentional processes, we know much about a dorsal frontoparietal attention system (Hopfinger et al., 2000) that acts in a goal-directed manner. This system helps us to accomplish a primary task by focusing on task-relevant stimuli or stimulus features by means of top-down modulation information flow in the brain system. This top-down control could, for example, inhibit the processing of emotional information when it is not relevant for the primary task (Compton et al., 2003). However, in some cases the impact of irrelevant information is quite strong, such that this novel information can strongly attract attention by means of different mechanisms. Such a system should be able to detect salient and relevant events that are currently not in the focus of attention and has been described as a "circuit breaker" (Corbetta & Shulman, 2002) localized in the ventral parietal and frontal cortex. Such salient events could be novel stimuli, which attract attention, compared to repeatedly encountered stimuli, for which the brain already shows habituation.

Emotional stimuli are another good example of these salient events, and the advantage of such a relevance detector is especially evident for harmful and threatening events. However, emotional stimuli and regions involved in processing emotionally meaningful stimuli are not well captured by the circuit-breaking system in the model of Corbetta and Shulman (2002). Apart the from ventral brain system in the parietal and frontal cortex that processes novel events, there seem to be specific brain regions that encode the emotional value of stimuli. Especially, brain regions belonging to the limbic system, and most prominently the amygdala (Sander et al., 2003) or the orbitofrontal cortex (Sander et al., 2005; Vuilleumier et al., 2002), process the emotional quality of stimuli and seem to enhance their perceptual processing by feeding this emotional information to sensory cortices (LeDoux, 1996; Vuilleumier, 2005) using temporo-occipital anatomical pathways described by fiber tractography (see Catani et al., 2003). This enhanced decoding could actually occur independent of the attentional focus (Grandjean et al., 2005; Vuilleumier et al., 2001), supporting the evidence of a specific emotional circuit breaker in addition to the brain system encoding stimulus saliency proposed by Corbetta and Shulman (2002).

Thus, though attentional and emotional processing are mostly accomplished by different brain regions, their functional mechanisms are nevertheless closely intermingled. One of these processes can support or influence the other depending on the requirements of the context. In this chapter, we review empirical studies dealing with the functional interactions between emotional and attentional processing. We first introduce evidence suggesting that emotional stimuli can be rapidly detected and processed without depending much on attentional and cognitive resources. This priority of processing of emotional stimuli might strongly guide attentional orienting since emotional stimuli might guide the attentional system to relevant stimuli related to our concerns, goals, and needs. Furthermore, we discuss the reversed influence of attentional processes on the processing of emotional stimuli. We finish this chapter by introducing and summarizing some recent evidence about the relationships between emotion and attention as revealed by new connectivity modeling approaches. These approaches now allow us to evaluate the spatial and temporal connectivity patterns in a distributed emotion-attention network.

IS EMOTION PROCESSING
INDEPENDENT OF ATTENTION?

Empirical evidence suggests that emotional stimuli strongly gain priority in processing, and this phenomenon occurs even without voluntarily attending these stimuli. Especially, the processing of negative stimuli is assumed to be strongly automatic since the instantaneous decoding of emotional signals such as danger or threat should have proven evolutionarily advantageous to prevent impending harm (e.g., Ohman, 2002). The human brain might, therefore, have developed a specific brain mechanism with a crucial role for the amygdala to rapidly decode negative signals (LeDoux, 1996; Ohman & Mineka, 2001; Vuilleumier, 2005). Especially, it has been suggested that the amygdala mediates the fast encoding of the emotional value based on coarse sensory information received either via a subcortical route involving the superior colliculi and pulvinar thalamus (LeDoux, 1996) or from primary sensory cortices (Vuilleumier, 2005) or other or higher-order sensory cortices (Pessoa, 2005). Consequently, emotional stimuli seem to be able to drive brain activity and behavior in a preattentive manner. That means that the human brain is able to detect emotional stimuli and change the behavior accordingly even without conscious awareness of the emotional stimulus (de Gelder et al., 1999; Morris et al., 1999; Murphy & Zajonc, 1993) or if the person is engaged in another demanding primary task unrelated to the emotional stimulus (Compton et al., 2003; Vuilleumier et al., 2001). This provides evidence that emotional processing occurs nearly effortlessly, and studies reported early influences of emotional stimuli during the course of processing undermining the prioritized access of emotional stimuli to the cognitive system.

Evidence for an early influence of emotional stimuli comes from electrophysiological investigations employing methods such as electroencephalography (EEG), magnetoencephalography (MEG), or intracranial recordings, which provide a high temporal resolution to delineate the brain responses to emotional stimuli. Facial expressions of emotion have been found to modulate brain response as early as about 80–100 ms after stimulus onset (Eimer & Holmes, 2002; Grandjean et al., 2009; Pizzagalli et al., 1999; Pourtois et al., 2004; Streit et al., 2003), and a first differentiation between emotional expressions seems to occur at about the same latency or a few milliseconds later (Batty & Taylor, 2003; Liu et al., 1999). Pleasant and especially unpleasant pictures seem to influence the temporal dynamics of stimulus processing at the same early stage of processing, beginning at about 100 ms after stimulus onset (Carretie, 2004; Schupp, 2003), whereas the emotional value of words might be encoded as early as 100–140 ms (Ortigue et al., 2004), but usually affects event-related potentials (ERPs) beyond 200 ms (Kissler et al., 2006; Schacht & Sommer, 2009). Finally, the recognition of the emotional tone from prosodic features in verbal and nonverbal speech is encoded as early as 150–200 ms after stimulus onset (Paulmann & Kotz, 2008; Paulmann et al., 2010; Spreckelmeyer et al., 2009; Wambacq et al., 2004). Using intracranial recordings, we have shown that the amygdala is even sensitive to anger and fear in vocal expressions in a time period directly after stimulus onset until about 150 ms, whereas sadness and happiness showed modulations as early as 250 ms after stimulus onset (Grandjean et al., 2009).

Altogether, these studies demonstrated an early encoding of the emotional value of stimuli, The emotional significance of biological emotional cues (faces, prosody) seems to be encoded earlier than from symbolic cues (words) and from behavioral-relevant emotions (anger, fear) earlier than for other emotional stimuli (sadness, happiness). Furthermore, these early effects were found both over different cortical scalp regions (Batty & Taylor, 2003; Eimer & Holmes, 2002; Liu et al., 1999; Pizzagalli et al., 1999) and in subcortical areas such as the amygdala (Streit et al., 2003). Many of these regions sometimes also demonstrate late responses in addition to these early brain responses (Krolak-Salmon et al., 2004; Schupp et al., 2004). Nonetheless, the early brain responses to emotional stimuli are evidence for their prioritized processing.

This prioritized processing can also be demonstrated by experimental designs in which we can trace the influence of emotional stimuli on brain and behavioral responses although participants are unable to consciously perceive the emotional stimulus. Studies using an affective priming paradigm have shown that unconsciously encoded emotional stimuli used as primes can subsequently influence evaluative judgments of neutral or meaningless targets according to the valence of the primes (Murphy & Zajonc, 1993). Other studies tried to examine brain responses to unconsciously encoded emotional stimulus itself by using experimental or brain lesion-dependent inabilities to perceive the emotional stimulus. In the former case, studies have shown that the amygdala is still sensitive to subliminally presented fearful expression (Williams et al., 2006), fearful eyes (Whalen et al., 2004), or fear-conditioned faces (Esteves et al., 1994). In the case of brain-lesioned subjects, studies with hemianopic patients have shown that detection of emotional expressions in the blind hemifield is above chance (de Gelder et al., 1999) and can influence the processing of emotional faces in the intact hemifield (de Gelder et al., 2005). Furthermore, emotional stimuli can be better detected in the inattended hemifield of patients suffering from visual neglect (Vuilleumier & Schwartz, 2001). In the same brain-damaged patients, inattention to stimuli can be reduced by the emotional tone of human voices (Grandjean et al., 2008). This decreased auditory extinction is assumed to be related to the integrity of subcortical (such as the putamen) and cortical regions (e.g., orbitofrontal cortex [OFC] and amygdala) (see Vuilleumier et al., 2004). We discuss these results more extensively in the next section. Interestingly, in normal subjects different connectivity patterns of the amygdala with other brain regions seem to demark this unconscious and conscious processing of emotional stimuli. Williams and colleagues (2006) found strong negative coupling of sensory cortical and subcortical pathways to the amygdala during conscious perception of fear. This most likely reflects reentrant projection from the amygdala to sensory cortices, whereas during subliminal encoding of fear the amygdala exhibited a positive coupling to regions in the subcortical pathway.

This fast decoding of emotional stimuli on conscious and unconscious levels of stimuli presentations might render emotional stimuli to be processed in a mandatory and entirely stimulus-driven manner. Whenever there is a nearby emotional stimulus able to affect the sensory system, the brain might be obliged to register this stimulus. Indeed, facial expressions have been shown to elicit amygdala activity although they were outside the focus of attention (Vuilleumier et al., 2001; Williams et al., 2005). Similarly, emotional prosodic cues (Grandjean et al., 2005; Sander et al., 2005) are able to elicit brain activity even when outside the focus of attention. However, this sensitivity to emotional information outside the focus of attention also strongly depends on individual differences, such as trait-level anxiety (Bishop, Duncan, & Lawrence, 2004) or the individual sensitivity to punishment and reward (Behavioral Inhibition Scale [BIS] score; Sander et al., 2005). It also depends on the amount of cognitive load that is currently focused on the primary task while emotional stimuli are presented outside the focus of attention (Pessoa et al., 2002, 2005).

At least, if the primary task involves only an intermediate rather than a high level of attentional resources, emotional stimuli can be encoded even when presented outside the focus of attention (Pessoa et al., 2005). Thus, emotional stimuli need some amount of cognitive and attentional resources, but this amount might be considerably decreased compared to the processing of neutral stimuli. The processing of emotional stimuli might be preattentive in this sense since they draw less on attentional resources when they have to be detected in an array of different stimuli (Eastwood et al., 2003; Ohman et al., 2001), encoded when outside the focus of attention (Compton et al., 2003; Vuilleumier et al., 2001; Williams et al., 2005), or categorized even when contextual distracters interfere with them (Fruhholz et al., 2009a, 2009b). This prioritized encoding of emotional stimuli might be of general advantage since adaptive behavior strongly depends on detecting and processing the relevant information in our environment. Therefore, emotional stimuli might be a powerful guide to orient the attentional focus to the most meaningful information in our environment, leading to adaptive and accurate responses according to the behavioral context. Emotional stimuli are embedded in the spatial and temporal context of other stimuli; the next section traces different possibilities of emotional stimuli influencing attentional orienting. However, there also are limits to the capability of emotional stimuli to attract attention and sometimes it is inappropriate according to the requirements of the situation. In the next section, we show how attentional requirements, in turn, can modulate the processing of emotional stimuli. Both emotional influences on attention and attentional influences on emotional processing are organized in a distributed network of specific brain regions. We especially highlight the dynamics in this brain network to exert these bidirectional influences.

HOW EMOTIONAL PROCESSING INFLUENCES ATTENTIONAL ORIENTING

As we mentioned in the introduction, the human cognitive system has a limited capacity, but the outside world is full of information. Therefore, the cognitive system and the human brain have to make a selection of the information that is most meaningful and most relevant for our current behavior in a specific context. However, sometimes relevant information occurs outside our current focus of attention and of which we are currently not aware. Although this information might not be relevant for our current primary task, it can be relevant for our general well-being, especially when it is a threatening or dangerous event. This emotionally relevant information might strongly attract our attention and force the brain to interrupt the current primary task. This reorienting process acts as the circuit-breaking unit (Corbetta & Shulman, 2002) described, and emotional stimuli are powerful in nonvoluntarily guiding the attentional focus to meaningful information and spatial locations.

For the last case of spatial location, imagine that you are presented with emotional information at one spatial location and with neutral information at another location. For example, the scream that you hear while you walk up the street comes from a side street on your right side, while the world on your left just goes its normal way. The emotional information should attract your attention and should facilitate subsequent object processing at this specific location since this location is tagged with emotional meaning.

In one of our studies, we auditorily presented emotional prosodic information that appeared more lateralized to one ear and neutral prosody lateralized to the other ear. We found that participants could detect visual targets faster at a spatial location that matched the former location of the emotional prosodic stimulus (Brosch et al., 2008). This cross-modal facilitation of visual target recognition by emotional prosodic stimuli seems to be mediated by early stages of processing, as reflected by a modulation of the visual P1 component. The P1 is an early ERP component emerging around 100 ms after stimulus onset, and the cross-modal facilitation effect on the P1 component seems to be located in the striate and extrastriate visual cortex (Brosch et al., 2009).

Similarly, facial expression presented at a specific spatial location can facilitate target detection at locations matching the location of emotional expressions. Again, these facilitation effects revealed early temporal modulations in target processing

(Pourtois et al., 2004) and were located to the occipital and parietal cortex (Pourtois et al., 2006). Therefore, emotional stimuli can strongly attract and hold spatial attention (Fox et al., 2002; Georgiou et al., 2005; Pourtois et al., 2004, 2006).

This is also evident in patients suffering from brain lesions that induce symptoms of impaired orienting to specific areas in extrapersonal space. As we mentioned, neglect is a syndrome often seen after right hemispheric lesion, especially in the parietotemporal cortex, which leads to a nonvoluntary inattention to contralesional space. Furthermore, the simultaneous presentation of information to contra- and ipsilesional space leads to an extinction of information in contralesional space. However, emotional stimuli can significantly reduce the number of missed items in contralesional space. When these neglecting patients are presented with emotional prosodic stimuli to the left simultaneously to neutral prosodic information to the left ear, we have shown that this emotional prosodic information is less often missed compared to a simultaneous presentation of neutral prosody to both ears (Grandjean et al., 2008), and the same effects were achieved with emotional pictures (Vuilleumier & Schwartz, 2001).

Therefore, emotional compared to neutral stimuli can enhance their probability of being detected and encoded even during limited capacities of the attentional system. Such detections of emotional stimuli during limited attentional capacities have also been shown by studies using the attentional blink paradigm. Studies have shown that a second target in a series of rapid presentations of stimuli is often missed when presented shortly after a first target (Marois et al., 2000). The processing of the first target is assumed to utilize most of the attentional resources, impairing the processing of the second target. However, studies have shown that if the second target is of an emotional quality, it is less likely missed compared to neutral second targets. This effect critically depends on the intact activity of the amygdala (Anderson & Phelps, 2001). The amygdala, therefore, acts as a detector of relevant emotional information that can influence activity in sensory cortices to enhance the perceptual processing of meaningful information and to orient the attentional system to this meaningful information.

These studies provided evidence that emotional information can act as guidance for attentional orientation. Furthermore, once emotional information is detected, the attentional system seems to strongly engage with this emotional information. Remember, we described the fast detection of stimuli at spatial locations formerly cued by emotional spatial information. These studies have also shown that it is more difficult to reorient attention to another location once the attentional system is captured by the location of an emotional stimulus. Targets presented at an opposite location of the emotional stimulus are usually detected more slowly since the attentional system has some difficulty to disengage from emotional stimuli (Brosch et al., 2008, 2009; Georgiou et al., 2005; Pourtois et al., 2004, 2006). This focus on emotional stimuli can delay and impair orienting away from emotional stimuli to engage with other stimuli. Emotional stimuli might act as a temporarily attentional "magnet," making it difficult to process other information, at least in the same sensory modality. For the latter case of the same sensory modality, studies reported that detecting a masked visual target is greatly impaired if preceded by emotional cues of the same *visual* modality, but visual target detection is better for targets preceded by an *auditory* emotional cue (Zeelenberg & Bocanegra, 2010).

Fenske and Eastwood (2003) have also shown that negative expressions can constrict the focus of attention such that other nearby facial expressions are less likely processed and influence the processing of the task-relevant facial expressions. Thus, once attention is captured by emotional information, the focus is restricted on this information and is, at least for a short period, strongly attached to the emotional stimulus, making it difficult to reorient attention to other stimuli or stimulus features. Furthermore, this attention focus on emotional stimuli is again dependent on individual differences such that individuals with specific emotional disorders more strongly engage to emotional stimuli compared to normal subjects (Bishop, Duncan, Brett, & Lawrence, 2004; Bishop, Duncan, & Lawrence, 2004; Bishop et al., 2007; Mathews & MacLeod, 2005; Mathews et al., 2004), and this "attachment" seems to be mediated by activation levels of the amygdala (Bishop, Duncan, & Lawrence, 2004; Bishop et al., 2007).

The amygdala therefore seems to have a critical role in tagging sensory stimuli with an emotional value and consequently forcing the attentional system to orient to this meaningful emotional information. It has been suggested that the amygdala sends this information to sensory cortices to enhance the perceptual processing of meaningful information (LeDoux, 1996; Vuilleumier, 2005). Anatomically, the amygdala is well connected with primary and secondary visual cortices (Amaral et al., 2003) but also shows anatomical connection to auditory cortical regions (Amaral & Price, 1984). Evidence for a functional connection between brain regions during spatial cuing comes from recent functional magnetic resonance imaging (fMRI) studies.

For example, Mohanty and colleagues (2009) found that cues predicting the spatial location and the angry valence of a face involved increased functional coupling between the amygdala and both regions in a frontoparietal spatial attention network as well as in the fusiform gyrus. Activity in the fusiform gyrus might reflect anticipatory activation in face-sensitive areas for an upcoming emotionally meaningful event such as an angry face. This anticipatory effect is similar to enhanced perceptual processing of the emotional stimulus itself.

This enhanced sensory processing of emotional stimuli has already been shown to critically depend on the integrity (Vuilleumier et al., 2004) and activity in the amygdala (Sabatinelli et al., 2005). As mentioned, Williams and colleagues (2006) have shown a positive reentrant signal from the amygdala to the visual sensory cortex is necessary so that fearful facial expressions can come to conscious levels of awareness.

Besides spatial attention, emotional stimuli might facilitate object- and feature-based attention, and these effects might again depend on feed-forward signals from the amygdala. With respect to object-based attention, the amygdala seems sensitive to fearful expressions when presented with a neutral object superimposed by facial expressions independent of whether the object or the expression was attended (Anderson et al., 2003). Despite these object-based attentional processes, the amygdala seems also to be necessary to guide the attention to specific features of emotional objects. For example, the eye and the mouth regions of the human face seem to be extremely important for reading emotion from facial expressions. Amygdala lesions might lead to impairment to spontaneously orient attention to these stimulus features, which usually facilitates emotion recognition from faces (Adolphs et al., 2005). Amygdala lesions have also been shown to lead to impaired emotional prosody recognition (Scott et al., 1997; Sprengelmeyer et al., 1999), but the data are not consistent (Adolphs & Tranel, 1999; Anderson & Phelps, 2002). Moreover, other brain structures might be more important for attending to emotional prosodic features, such as the basal ganglia. The basal ganglia are important for analyzing the temporal structure of auditory events (Nenadic et al., 2003). Emotional prosodic stimuli have a specific temporal acoustic pattern (Banse & Scherer, 1996), which seems difficult to decode by patients with damage to the basal ganglia (Breitenstein et al., 2001; Peron et al., 2010).

In summary, emotional stimuli such as facial expressions or emotional prosodic cues should be powerful stimuli to attract attention independent of the current focus of attention. This capturing of attention acts as a circuit breaker, and we have hypothesized that some brain structures, such as the amygdala, might be a crucial nexus that mediates this stimulus-driven guidance of attentional orienting. This is a highly adaptive mechanism given the fact that some emotional stimuli, such as a threat or danger or reward, are essential for successful behavior not only in specific contexts but also for our long-term well-being. As emotional stimuli are powerful stimuli to drive attention in a bottom-up fashion, we might, in turn, infer that top-down attentional processes during processing of emotional stimuli are less influential compared to these bottom-up effects. In the next section, we outline brain possibilities and mechanisms of top-down attentional influences on emotional processing.

HOW ATTENTION CAN INFLUENCE EMOTIONAL PROCESSING

Imagine the case that any emotional event is nonvoluntarily attracting your attention or any emotional event is processed mandatorily on a subliminal level. The angry man who you encounter on the street, the scream, and the barking dog involuntarily attract your attention. This capturing of attention might be adaptive in many situations, as discussed. But, there might be specific situations in your daily life for which it is rather inefficient to be attracted by any emotional event in your environment, especially in situations when you have to accomplish a primary task that needs all of your attentional resources. Remember again, while crossing the street you might probably do better by not taking notice of any other event that is not primarily related to your crossing of the street. Or, imagine you suffer from severe anxiety regarding spiders. To successfully recover from this disorder, one has to learn to regulate this overwhelming emotional distress, which is often induced by hyperreactivity in the amygdala. You have to learn to reorient attention to nondisturbing emotional stimuli. This inhibition of emotional processing and voluntary reorienting of the attentional focus is a fundamental property of the frontal cortex (Bishop, Duncan, Brett, et al., 2004; Fruhholz et al., 2010). In the examples, the attentional system, specifically the frontal cortex, has the function to direct attention away from the emotional stimulus or to inhibit the attentional attraction of emotional stimuli.

In other cases, however, one has to voluntarily direct attention to rather than away from emotional stimuli or stimulus features. This focusing of attention to emotional stimuli is especially necessary for an elaborated processing of these stimuli. This elaborated processing could not be well accomplished by the fast orienting to and encoding of emotional stimuli mediated by the amygdala since this fast processing is coarse in many cases. This fast decoding does not clearly and uniquely discriminate between different emotions as it mainly represents the general arousing property of the stimulus (Zald, 2003). Beyond the first detection of emotionally arousing stimuli, the discrimination between different emotional valences is often necessary. This is often required by specific circumstances since different emotional stimuli and even different negative emotional stimuli imply different adaptive responses in relation to the context (i.e., fear and anger). Therefore, beyond a fast decoding of emotional stimuli, it is sometimes necessary to process emotional stimuli in more detail to identify, categorize, and name the specific emotional stimuli. This is strongly evident for emotional stimuli that are inherently less emotionally distinctive, such as mild expressions of surprise (Kim et al., 2004), or when emotional stimuli are presented in distracting emotional contexts that introduce ambiguities during the categorization of these stimuli (Fruhholz et al., 2009a, 2009b).

Thus, the modulatory influence of attention on emotional processing can appear in three different modes. First, attention is voluntarily directed to emotional stimuli or stimulus features; second, attention has to be maintained on a primary task while inhibiting the influence of task-irrelevant emotional information. Finally, sometimes it is necessary to voluntarily be directed away from emotional stimuli or stimulus features.

For the first case, we have shown that emotional compared to neutral prosody seems to be mandatorily processed independent of the focus of attention. We found activation in the amygdala (Sander et al., 2005) and in a region in the mid-right superior temporal cortex (Grandjean et al., 2005). This last brain region is an intermediate part of three functionally interconnected regions in the superior temporal cortex (Kriegstein & Giraud, 2004) that have been shown to be sensitive to human voices (Belin et al., 2000). More interestingly, by directing attention to the emotional value of the prosodic stimulus, we found activation in the orbitofrontal cortex (Sander et al., 2005) and in the inferior frontal cortex (Bach et al., 2008; see also Ethofer et al., 2009; Schirmer & Kotz, 2006; Wildgruber et al., 2005), while other studies reported also activation in the posterior superior temporal cortex (Ethofer et al., 2006; Wildgruber et al., 2005). These signal increases in the frontal cortex during attention to the emotional value of a stimulus are often accompanied by signal decreases in the amygdala (Hariri et al., 2000, 2003). This indicates some negatively correlated signals between the frontal and limbic regions during different attentional states in the presence of emotional stimuli. Voluntarily attending to emotional stimuli and accomplishing a higher-order cognitive task such as elaborated stimulus processing and categorization of emotional stimuli might be mediated by regions in the frontal cortex (Lange et al., 2003). The simultaneous decrease of amygdala activity might be an index of attenuated emotional processing to keep the attentional focus on the primary task. This adaptive brain mechanism seems to be slightly impaired in neurotic or anxious subjects (Fruhholz et al., 2010) and is critically impaired in patients with emotional disorders (Bishop, Duncan, Brett, et al., 2004; Mayberg, 1997). Anatomical evidence actually suggested a suppressive role of the frontal cortex onto the amygdala via inhibitory interneurons (e.g., Lang & Pare, 1998). Connectivity modeling approaches on the frontoamygdala connectivity revealed a suppressor effect of frontal cortex on the amygdala (Etkin et al., 2006) and enhanced connectivity on frontal regions if required by the task context (Blair et al., 2007).

Not only the suppression of emotional processing might be required by specific task contexts, but also sometimes the primary task engages much of one's attentional resources so that emotional stimulus processing is almost completely attenuated. This is the second mode described. While increasing the attentional load of a primary task, Pessoa and colleagues (2005) have shown that amygdala activity to simultaneously presented emotional stimuli was only significant under low attentional load of the primary task, again suggesting an inhibitory influence of frontal regions on limbic structures during higher demands on attentional resources. Therefore, increasing the attentional demand of a primary task can attenuate or abolish the processing of emotional stimuli. This seems, at first sight, to be contrary to the central role of emotional stimuli to break the current circuit of the attentional focus as we discussed. But sometimes, this can have an adaptive function. When the emotional value of a stimulus is extremely aversive, it can be an adaptive strategy to redirect the attention away from this stimulus to reduce its aversive impact.

We have described that emotional stimuli can strongly capture and hold the spatial attentional focus. However, extreme aversive stimuli such as aversively conditioned stimuli can have an opposite effect such that they facilitate shifting attention away from rather than to these stimuli (Stormark & Hugdahl, 1997). This is the third mode that we described about orienting attention away from emotional stimuli. An extremely emotional aversive stimulus is somatic pain, and the level of distress is considerably influenced by the attentional state in relation to this somatosensory stimulus. Voluntarily directing attention away from this aversive stimulus can strongly attenuate the aversiveness of pain. Again, to regulate the impact of pain stimulation, medial frontal regions seem to attenuate activity of regions in the "medial pain system," such as the anterior insula, thalamus, or midbrain structures. The last regions encode the aversive quality of pain when engaged with a highly demanding cognitive task (Bantick et al., 2002). They also encode the aversive quality of pain during placebo administration. This was shown by a connectivity analysis between the medial frontal cortex and the medial pain system. The frontal cortex influenced the pain encoding brain regions by means of this top-down regulation (Eippert et al., 2009).

Altogether, during cognitive tasks that either involve selective attention to a primary task or to specific emotional features, there seem to be strong relationships between limbic structures coding the emotional value of stimuli and regions, especially in the frontal cortex, involved in accomplishing a primary task or to influence emotional processing in limbic structures. Accordingly, Stein and colleagues (2007) empirically identified a complex amygdala-cortical network using structural equation modeling (SEM). SEM is one among other statistical methods for path analyses and allows researchers to generate directional hypotheses about the information flow between interconnected brain regions. Different directional network models of the amygdala as a central structure to receive and send information can then be compared to empirical brain time series data. A parsimonious model that fits the empirical data the best can then be taken as the winning model with the highest validity. By iteratively generating and fitting SEM models to fMRI data during processing of emotional facial expressions, Stein et al. (2007) identified bidirectional influences of various frontal regions on amygdala activity during a higher-order cognitive task. They found, for example, a positive influence of OFC, but a negative influence of the dorsal medial frontal cortex on amygdala activity. The amygdala, in turn, is positively connected with the subgenual anterior cingulate cortex as part of the ventral medial frontal cortex. Beside the well-known rich anatomical connection of the amygdala with many other brain regions (Amaral & Price, 1984; Ghashghaei & Barbas, 2002), this study by Stein and colleagues highlighted the importance of new analytical methods that directly provide evidence for a functional relationship between regions for emotional and attentional processing and help to refine functional networks of emotional processing in relation to different attentional modes.

MODELING THE INTERACTION OF EMOTION AND ATTENTION

In the introduction, we outlined brain networks belonging to a core attentional and to a core emotional system of stimulus processing. General top-down attentional systems that control for goal-directed behavior are primarily located in the dorsal frontal and parietal brain regions, keeping the attentional system focused on a specific primary task. On the other hand, limbic brain structures such as the amygdala and the orbitofrontal cortex encode the emotional value of stimuli and primarily seem to act in a stimulus-driven manner since they automatically code the emotional value of stimuli independent of the current attentional focus. More specifically, emotional stimuli can strongly capture the focus of attention such that they disrupt ongoing tasks. This function resembles the circuit-breaking system described by Corbetta and Shulman (2002), comprising regions in the ventral frontal and parietal system detecting the sudden appearance of a novel event. However, this proposed model lacks some new evidence from emotional processing, but it can be easily extended more ventrally to the limbic system, which detects especially the presence of emotional and behaviorally relevant stimuli.

Recent connectivity modeling studies already have provided evidence for a functional interconnection between regions belonging to the attentional and the emotional circuit and highlighting the central role of the amygdala as a *source* as well as a *target* of attentional processes. Mohanty et al. (2009) found that the amygdala as a source can enhance sensory processing in the fusiform gyrus and spatial attentional processing in the parietal cortex by increased functional coupling with these brain regions. If required by attentional task demands, frontal regions can, in turn, inhibit emotional processing in the amygdala as a target region. This is indicated by negative top-down connectivity from frontal regions onto the amygdala (Etkin et al., 2006; Stein et al., 2007). Therefore, emotional and attentional systems show a highly interconnected and reciprocal connectivity by which the dynamics in this network depend on the specific task requirements.

Taylor and Fragopanagos (2005) used a neural network modeling approach by implementing the complex neural emotion-attention system in an artificial neural network model. This model comprised reciprocally connected dorsal and ventral attentional circuits and limbic circuits involving the amygdala and the orbitofrontal cortex. Especially, the amygdala receives fast sensory input for an early tagging of the emotional value, which can strongly influence attentional circuits in a bottom-up manner. However, frontal systems also have top-down influences on limbic structures in this model. The OFC was excitatorily connected to ventral circuit-breaking systems and inhibitorily connected to a dorsal attention circuit. With this general emotion-attention network, Taylor and Fragopanagos (2005) were able to simulate and replicate findings of many behavioral and brain activations from various studies on emotional and attention relationships. By adding study-specific details to this general emotion-attention framework, they were able to replicate empirical findings for emotional target detection (Yamasaki et al., 2002), implicit processing of facial expression during a demanding primary cognitive task (Pessoa et al., 2002), and the emotional attentional blink effect (Anderson & Phelps, 2001).

Beyond using artificial neural networks to explore the dynamic interaction between brain regions involved in emotional and attentional processing, new methods emerged lately for analyzing brain physiological data to reveal the underlying information flow between different brain regions. These methods allow researchers to go beyond simply detecting brain activity for emotional stimuli. These new methods enable us to directly generate hypotheses about the functional connectivity between these brain regions, which can be empirically tested with the recorded brain data. For example, in many of our former studies we found a variety of brain regions sensitive to emotional prosody, such as several regions in the superior temporal cortex (Grandjean et al., 2005; Sander et al., 2005), the amygdala (Bach et al., 2008; Sander et al., 2005), the orbitofrontal cortex (Sander et al., 2005), the inferior frontal cortex (Bach et al., 2008), the occipital and parietal cortex (Sander et al., 2005), or the subcortical brain nuclei (Bach et al., 2008). Some of these regions were independent of the attentional focus, like activation in the superior temporal cortex and in the amygdala, whereas the OFC and inferior frontal cortex became active only during endogenously attending the emotional prosodic stimulus. These activations have let us speculate about the dynamic interconnection between these brain regions such that the superior temporal sulcus (STS) and amygdala became primarily active and feeding information to frontal brain regions only if it was required by the task (Sander et al., 2005). Although this proposed model of information flow fits well with a recent model of auditory emotional prosody recognition (Schirmer & Kotz, 2006), it is still speculative since there is no direct empirical evidence for this assumption.

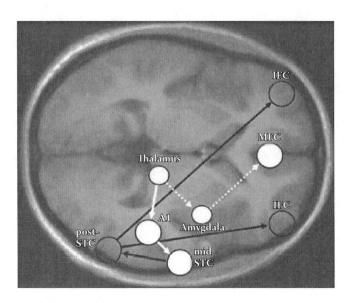

Figure 2.1 Network model of different subcortical (thalamus), medial (amgydala), and superior temporal regions (A1/primary auditory cortex, mid [mid-STC] and posterior superior temporal cortex [post-STC]) as well inferior frontal brain regions (medial [MFC] and lateral inferior frontal cortex [IFC]) involving different functional pathways for the decoding of emotional prosody. White arrows indicate bottom-up stimulus processing, and black arrows indicate top-down influences on stimulus processing. The dotted white arrows indicate an implicit processing pathway of information outside the focus of attention. (Adapted from Wildgruber, D., Ethofer, T., Grandjean, D., & Kreifelts, B. A cerebral network model of speech prosody comprehension. *International Journal of Speech-Language Pathology,* *11*, 277–281, 2009.)

Initial evidence for interregional information flow during emotional prosody encoding comes from a study done by Ethofer and colleagues (2006) using a dynamic causal modeling approach to determine intrinsic information flow between the STS and inferior frontal cortex. The authors found that during emotional prosody recognition, the most likely model involved activity in the STS that is fed forward in a parallel way to the bilateral inferior frontal cortex. Based on these connectivity results and based on the results from other studies (Grandjean et al., 2005; Sander et al., 2005), we proposed a model of brain connectivity of regions involved in emotional prosody recognition (Wildgruber et al., 2009; see Figure 2.1). We assumed that emotional signal from vocal prosody affects the brain system as early as on thalamic auditory relay nuclei, and this signal spreads in an implicit ventral pathway comprising the amygdala and the ventral parts of the frontal cortex, whereas the other explicit pathway transfers emotional prosodic information to the middle superior temporal cortex via primary auditory cortices, especially in the right hemisphere. Both former pathways are purely stimulus driven since these pathways are activated whenever the brain is exposed to emotional prosody independent of the focus of attention. During endogenous orienting to emotional prosody such as during elaborated stimulus processing, signal from the middle part of the superior temporal cortex further spreads to the posterior superior temporal cortex and subsequently to both inferior frontal cortices. In future studies, we will try to validate these connectivity models by using functional and effective connectivity approaches to obtain empirical evidence for these theoretical models.

So far, we discussed functional connectivity between emotional prosody recognition on a modular brain level, taking in account only mass neural activation in large-scale spatial neural networks. However, single cells as well as local cell populations can build transiently connected assemblies by phase synchronization of ongoing oscillatory activity within these cell populations (Engel et al., 2001). The human brain usually shows an oscillatory brain activity, and these oscillations appear in different frequencies, from slow to very fast oscillations. Different brain areas can show oscillations in different frequency ranges, but sometimes these brain areas can synchronize their oscillations. The phenomenon of neuronal synchronization has been conceptualized as the minimal requirement, for two different close or distant neuronal assemblies, to be able to exchange information and therefore subserves emergent psychological functions. Fries (2005) proposed the communication through coherence (CTC) model for modeling the interaction between different neuronal populations. The computation of neuronal synchronization is based on the difference of the phase of the signals in the time-frequency domain for two or more brain regions. The involvement of different brain regions in the processing of emotional auditory information should be investigated using this type of method based on neuronal signals recorded directly within the cerebral tissue for different clinical purposes in humans or in animal models. The measure of neuronal synchronizations could be the best way to address the questions related to distributed neuronal networks subserving a specific function, such as emotional prosody detection, discrimination, or identification.

CONCLUSIONS

We outlined the interaction between emotional and attentional processing. We described that emotional information can strongly influence attentional orienting since emotional stimuli carry meaningful information that is most often essential for adaptive behavior. Moreover, we also described possible ways that attention, in turn, can influence emotional processing. Sometimes, we have to accomplish a primary task that needs all of our attention, and the fast and conscious decoding of emotional information is not always immediately necessary and sometimes even counterproductive. In specific situations, it is also more convenient for our well-being to direct our attention away from emotional information, such as in the case of uncomfortable pain or a hypersensitivity to emotional information, as seen for many emotional disorders.

This hypersensitivity to emotional stimuli in people suffering from emotional disorders highlights the importance to take the interindividual sensitivity to emotional stimuli into account. One of the next challenges of interdisciplinary research between psychology and neuroscience will be to better understand how these interindividual differences are implemented in specific frontolimbic interactions and how life experiences and cultural features shape the interactive (dys-)functioning of neural networks.

Many recent studies have examined the neural networks that are involved in emotional processing itself and in relationship to attentional orienting, and we made some good progress in drawing the picture of this neural network. However, we only recently began to understand the neural temporal and spatial dynamics in the connections between these brain regions in terms of the principles and mechanisms of how these regions connect, how they might exchange information, and how they influence each other by excitatory and inhibitory connections to produce adaptive behavioral outcome. We have argued and there is recent evidence that the amygdala is a central brain structure that might be involved in a primary brain system for the fast decoding of emotional information. This fast decoding can influence sensory and spatial processing by modulating connections to sensory brain regions that code objects and spatial locations. This mechanism works accurately when our attentional system is not occupied by an important primary task. In the last case, however, a second system might come into play that might exert an inhibitory influence on this fast emotional decoding system. Especially, frontal brain regions have been shown to directly inhibit this primary brain system of emotional decoding if stressed by the requirements of the task.

So, imagine again you are situated at some crowded place anywhere in a big city. It is 9:55 a.m., and in 5 minutes you have a job interview at a famous company. You are in a hurry, and unfortunately you lost any orientation. Your primary task now is to quickly get back some sense of direction and to arrive at the company in time. Therefore, you hurry straight ahead along the street since it seems to be the right direction. But suddenly, as you pass the next side street you hear a scream from the right, and it strongly attracts your attention since somebody seems to cry for help. You stop for a short moment, and the conflict you experience now between your primary task to go on and the insisting scream is doubled in your brain. So, which wins? The amygdala, which drives the attention to the scream and prevents you from going on, or the frontal cortex, which is responsible for maintaining the goal-directed primary task: quickly rush to the company?

REFERENCES

Adolphs, R., Gosselin, F., Buchanan, T. W., Tranel, D., Schyns, P., & Damasio, A. R. (2005). A mechanism for impaired fear recognition after amygdala damage. *Nature, 433,* 68–72.

Adolphs, R., & Tranel, D. (1999). Intact recognition of emotional prosody following amygdala damage. *Neuropsychologia, 37,* 1285–1292.

Amaral, D. G., Behniea, H., & Kelly, J. L. (2003). Topographic organization of projections from the amygdala to the visual cortex in the macaque monkey. *Neuroscience, 118,* 1099–1120.

Amaral, D. G., & Price, J. L. (1984). Amygdalo-cortical projections in the monkey (*Macaca fascicularis*). *Journal of Comparative Neurology, 230,* 465–496.

Anderson, A. K., Christoff, K., Panitz, D., De Rosa, E., & Gabrieli, J. D. (2003). Neural correlates of the automatic processing of threat facial signals. *Journal of Neuroscience, 23,* 5627–5633.

Anderson, A. K., & Phelps, E. A. (2001). Lesions of the human amygdala impair enhanced perception of emotionally salient events. *Nature, 411*, 305–309.

Anderson, A. K., & Phelps, E. A. (2002). Is the human amygdala critical for the subjective experience of emotion? Evidence of intact dispositional affect in patients with amygdala lesions. *Journal of Cognitive Neuroscience, 14*, 709–720.

Bach, D. R., Grandjean, D., Sander, D., Herdener, M., Strik, W. K., & Seifritz, E. (2008). The effect of appraisal level on processing of emotional prosody in meaningless speech. *NeuroImage, 42*, 919–927.

Banse, R., & Scherer, K. R. (1996). Acoustic profiles in vocal emotion expression. *Journal of Personality and Social Psychology, 70*, 614–636.

Bantick, S. J., Wise, R. G., Ploghaus, A., Clare, S., Smith, S. M., & Tracey, I. (2002). Imaging how attention modulates pain in humans using functional MRI. *Brain, 125*, 310–319.

Batty, M., & Taylor, M. J. (2003). Early processing of the six basic facial emotional expressions. *Brain Research: Cognitive Brain Research, 17*, 613–620.

Belin, P., Zatorre, R. J., Lafaille, P., Ahad, P., & Pike, B. (2000). Voice-selective areas in human auditory cortex. *Nature, 403*, 309–312.

Bishop, S. J., Duncan, J., Brett, M., & Lawrence, A. D. (2004). Prefrontal cortical function and anxiety: Controlling attention to threat-related stimuli. *Nature Neuroscience, 7*, 184–188.

Bishop, S. J., Duncan, J., & Lawrence, A. D. (2004). State anxiety modulation of the amygdala response to unattended threat-related stimuli. *Journal of Neuroscience, 24*, 10364–10368.

Bishop, S. J., Jenkins, R., & Lawrence, A. D. (2007). Neural processing of fearful faces: Effects of anxiety are gated by perceptual capacity limitations. *Cerebral Cortex, 17*, 1595–1603.

Blair, K. S., Smith, B. W., Mitchell, D. G., Morton, J., Vythilingam, M., Pessoa, L., et al. (2007). Modulation of emotion by cognition and cognition by emotion. *NeuroImage, 35*, 430–440.

Breitenstein, C., Van Lancker, D., Daum, I., & Waters, C. H. (2001). Impaired perception of vocal emotions in Parkinson's disease: Influence of speech time processing and executive functioning. *Brain and Cognition, 45*, 277–314.

Brosch, T., Grandjean, D., Sander, D., & Scherer, K. R. (2008). Behold the voice of wrath: Cross-modal modulation of visual attention by anger prosody. *Cognition, 106*, 1497–1503.

Brosch, T., Grandjean, D., Sander, D., & Scherer, K. R. (2009). Cross-modal emotional attention: Emotional voices modulate early stages of visual processing. *Journal of Cognitive Neuroscience, 21*, 1670–1679.

Carretie, L., Hinojosa, J. A., Martin-Loeches, M., Mercado, F., & Tapia, M. (2004). Automatic attention to emotional stimuli: Neural correlates. *Human Brain Mapping, 22*, 290–299.

Catani, M., Jones, D. K., Donato, R., & Ffytche, D. H. (2003). Occipito-temporal connections in the human brain. *Brain, 126*, 2093–2107.

Compton, R. J. (2003). The interface between emotion and attention: A review of evidence from psychology and neuroscience. *Behavioral and Cognitive Neuroscience Reviews, 2*, 115–129.

Compton, R. J., Banich, M. T., Mohanty, A., Milham, M. P., Herrington, J., Miller, et al. (2003). Paying attention to emotion: An fMRI investigation of cognitive and emotional Stroop tasks. *Cognitive Affective & Behavioral Neuroscience, 3*, 81–96.

Corbetta, M., & Shulman, G. L. (2002). Control of goal-directed and stimulus-driven attention in the brain. *Nature Reviews Neuroscience, 3*, 201–215.

de Gelder, B., Morris, J. S., & Dolan, R. J. (2005). Unconscious fear influences emotional awareness of faces and voices. *Proceedings of the National Academy of Sciences of the United States of America, 102,* 18682–18687.

de Gelder, B., Vroomen, J., Pourtois, G., & Weiskrantz, L. (1999). Non-conscious recognition of affect in the absence of striate cortex. *Neuroreport, 10,* 3759–3763.

Eastwood, J. D., Smilek, D., & Merikle, P. M. (2003). Negative facial expression captures attention and disrupts performance. *Perception & Psychophysics, 65,* 352–358.

Eimer, M., & Holmes, A. (2002). An ERP study on the time course of emotional face processing. *Neuroreport, 13,* 427–431.

Eippert, F., Bingel, U., Schoell, E. D., Yacubian, J., Klinger, R., Lorenz, J., et al. (2009). Activation of the opioidergic descending pain control system underlies placebo analgesia. *Neuron, 63,* 533–543.

Engel, A. K., Fries, P., & Singer, W. (2001). Dynamic predictions: Oscillations and synchrony in top-down processing. *Nature Reviews Neuroscience, 2,* 704–716.

Esteves, F., Dimberg, U., & Ohman, A. (1994). Automatically elicited fear: Conditioned skin conductance responses to masked fearful expressions. *Cognition & Emotion, 8,* 393–413.

Ethofer, T., Anders, S., Erb, M., Herbert, C., Wiethoff, S., Kissler, J., et al. (2006). Cerebral pathways in processing of affective prosody: A dynamic causal modeling study. *NeuroImage, 30,* 580–587.

Ethofer, T., Kreifelts, B., Wiethoff, S., Wolf, J., Grodd, W., Vuilleumier, P., et al. (2009). Differential influences of emotion, task, and novelty on brain regions underlying the processing of speech melody. *Journal of Cognitive Neuroscience, 21,* 1255–1268.

Etkin, A., Egner, T., Peraza, D. M., Kandel, E. R., & Hirsch, J. (2006). Resolving emotional conflict: A role for the rostral anterior cingulate cortex in modulating activity in the amygdala. *Neuron, 51,* 871–882.

Fenske, M. J., & Eastwood, J. D. (2003). Modulation of focused attention by faces expressing emotion: Evidence from flanker tasks. *Emotion, 3,* 327–343.

Fox, E., Russo, R., & Dutton, K. (2002). Attentional bias for threat: Evidence for delayed disengagement from emotional faces. *Cognition & Emotion, 16,* 355–379.

Fries, P. (2005). A mechanism for cognitive dynamics: Neuronal communication through neuronal coherence. *Trends in Cognitive Sciences, 9,* 474–480.

Fruhholz, S., Fehr, T., & Herrmann, M. (2009a). Early and late temporo-spatial effects of contextual interference during perception of facial affect. *International Journal of Psychophysiology, 74,* 1–13.

Fruhholz, S., Fehr, T., & Herrmann, M. (2009b). Interference control during recognition of facial affect enhances the processing of expression specific properties—An event-related fMRI study. *Brain Research, 1269,* 143–157.

Fruhholz, S., Prinz, M., & Herrmann, M. (2010). Affect-related personality traits and contextual interference processing during perception of facial affect. *Neuroscience Letters, 469,* 2, 260–264.

Georgiou, G. A., Bleakley, C., Hayward, J., Russo, R., Dutton, K., Eltiti, S., et al. (2005). Focusing on fear: Attentional disengagement from emotional faces. *Visual Cognition, 12,* 145–158.

Ghashghaei, H. T., & Barbas, H. (2002). Pathways for emotion: Interactions of prefrontal and anterior temporal pathways in the amygdala of the rhesus monkey. *Neuroscience, 115,* 1261–1279.

Grandjean, D., Sander, D., Lucas, N., Scherer, K. R., & Vuilleumier, P. (2008). Effects of emotional prosody on auditory extinction for voices in patients with spatial neglect. *Neuropsychologia, 46,* 487–496.

Grandjean, D., Sander, D., Pourtois, G., Schwartz, S., Seghier, M. L., Scherer, K. R., et al. (2005). The voices of wrath: Brain responses to angry prosody in meaningless speech. *Nature Neuroscience, 8,* 145–146.

Grandjean, D., Tamarit, L., Sander, D., Vuilleumier, P., Seeck, M., & Scherer, K. R. (2009). *Human amygdala responses to emotional prosody: Early and late local field potential components*. Poster presentation at the 39th annual meeting of the Society for Neuroscience, Chicago, Illinois. October 17–21.

Hariri, A. R., Bookheimer, S. Y., & Mazziotta, J. C. (2000). Modulating emotional responses: Effects of a neocortical network on the limbic system. *Neuroreport, 11*, 43–48.

Hariri, A. R., Mattay, V. S., Tessitore, A., Fera, F., & Weinberger, D. R. (2003). Neocortical modulation of the amygdala response to fearful stimuli. *Biological Psychiatry, 53*, 494–501.

Hopfinger, J. B., Buonocore, M. H., & Mangun, G. R. (2000). The neural mechanisms of top-down attentional control. *Nature Neuroscience, 3*, 284–291.

Kim, H., Somerville, L. H., Johnstone, T., Polis, S., Alexander, A. L., Shin, L. M., et al. (2004). Contextual modulation of amygdala responsivity to surprised faces. *Journal of Cognitive Neuroscience, 16*, 1730–1745.

Kissler, J., Assadollahi, R., & Herbert, C. (2006). Emotional and semantic networks in visual word processing: Insights from ERP studies. *Progress in Brain Research, 156*, 147–183.

Kriegstein, K. V., & Giraud, A. L. (2004). Distinct functional substrates along the right superior temporal sulcus for the processing of voices. *NeuroImage, 22*, 948–955.

Krolak-Salmon, P., Henaff, M. A., Vighetto, A., Bertrand, O., & Mauguiere, F. (2004). Early amygdala reaction to fear spreading in occipital, temporal, and frontal cortex: A depth electrode ERP study in human. *Neuron, 42*, 665–676.

Lang, E. J., & Pare, D. (1998). Synaptic responsiveness of interneurons of the cat lateral amygdaloid nucleus. *Neuroscience, 83*, 877–889.

Lange, K., Williams, L. M., Young, A. W., Bullmore, E. T., Brammer, M. J., Williams, S. C., et al. (2003). Task instructions modulate neural responses to fearful facial expressions. *Biological Psychiatry, 53*, 226–232.

LeDoux, J. E. (1996). *The emotional brain*. New York: Simon & Schuster.

Liu, L., Ioannides, A. A., & Streit, M. (1999). Single trial analysis of neurophysiological correlates of the recognition of complex objects and facial expressions of emotion. *Brain Topography, 11*, 291–303.

Marois, R., Leung, H. C., & Gore, J. C. (2000). A stimulus-driven approach to object identity and location processing in the human brain. *Neuron, 25*, 717–728.

Mathews, A., & MacLeod, C. (2005). Cognitive vulnerability to emotional disorders. *Annual Review of Clinical Psychology, 1*, 167–195.

Mathews, A., Yiend, J., & Lawrence, A. D. (2004). Individual differences in the modulation of fear-related brain activation by attentional control. *Journal of Cognitive Neuroscience, 16*, 1683–1694.

Mayberg, H. S. (1997). Limbic-cortical dysregulation: A proposed model of depression. *Journal of Neuropsychiatry and Clinical Neurosciences, 9*, 471–481.

Mohanty, A., Egner, T., Monti, J. M., & Mesulam, M. M. (2009). Search for a threatening target triggers limbic guidance of spatial attention. *Journal of Neuroscience, 29*, 10563–10572.

Morris, J. S., Ohman, A., & Dolan, R. J. (1999). A subcortical pathway to the right amygdala mediating "unseen" fear. *Proceedings of the National Academy of Sciences of the United States of America, 96*, 1680–1685.

Murphy, S. T., & Zajonc, R. B. (1993). Affect, cognition, and awareness: Affective priming with optimal and suboptimal stimulus exposures. *Journal of Personality and Social Psychology, 64*, 723–739.

Nenadic, I., Gaser, C., Volz, H. P., Rammsayer, T., Hager, F., & Sauer, H. (2003). Processing of temporal information and the basal ganglia: New evidence from fMRI. *Experimental Brain Research, 148*, 238–246.

Ohman, A. (2002). Automaticity and the amygdala: Nonconscious responses to emotional faces. *Current Directions in Psychological Science, 11*, 62–66.

Ohman, A., Flykt, A., & Esteves, F. (2001). Emotion drives attention: Detecting the snake in the grass. *Journal of Experimental Psychology: General, 130*, 466–478.

Ohman, A., & Mineka, S. (2001). Fears, phobias, and preparedness: Toward an evolved module of fear and fear learning. *Psychological Review, 108*, 483–522.

Ortigue, S., Michel, C. M., Murray, M. M., Mohr, C., Carbonnel, S., & Landis, T. (2004). Electrical neuroimaging reveals early generator modulation to emotional words. *NeuroImage, 21*, 1242–1251.

Paulmann, S., & Kotz, S. A. (2008). Early emotional prosody perception based on different speaker voices. *Neuroreport, 19*, 209–213.

Paulmann, S., Seifert, S., & Kotz, S. A. (2010). Orbito-frontal lesions cause impairment during late but not early emotional prosodic processing. *Social Neuroscience, 5*, 59–75.

Peron, J., Grandjean, D., Le Jeune, F., Sauleau, P., Haegelen, C., Drapier, D., et al. (2010). Recognition of emotional prosody is altered after subthalamic nucleus deep brain stimulation in Parkinson's disease. *Neuropsychologia, 48*, 1053–1062.

Pessoa, L. (2005). To what extent are emotional visual stimuli processed without attention and awareness? *Current Opinion in Neurobiology, 15*, 188–196.

Pessoa, L., Japee, S., & Ungerleider, L. G. (2005). Visual awareness and the detection of fearful faces. *Emotion, 5*, 243–247.

Pessoa, L., McKenna, M., Gutierrez, E., & Ungerleider, L. G. (2002). Neural processing of emotional faces requires attention. *Proceedings of the National Academy of Sciences of the United States of America, 99*, 11458–11463.

Pizzagalli, D., Regard, M., & Lehmann, D. (1999). Rapid emotional face processing in the human right and left brain hemispheres: An ERP study. *Neuroreport, 10*, 2691–2698.

Pourtois, G., Grandjean, D., Sander, D., & Vuilleumier, P. (2004). Electrophysiological correlates of rapid spatial orienting towards fearful faces. *Cerebral Cortex, 14*, 619–633.

Pourtois, G., Schwartz, S., Seghier, M. L., Lazeyras, F., & Vuilleumier, P. (2006). Neural systems for orienting attention to the location of threat signals: An event-related fMRI study. *NeuroImage, 31*, 920–933.

Sabatinelli, D., Bradley, M. M., Fitzsimmons, J. R., & Lang, P. J. (2005). Parallel amygdala and inferotemporal activation reflect emotional intensity and fear relevance. *NeuroImage, 24*, 1265–1270.

Sander, D., Grafman, J., & Zalla, T. (2003). The human amygdala: An evolved system for relevance detection. *Reviews in the Neurosciences, 14*, 303–316.

Sander, D., Grandjean, D., Pourtois, G., Schwartz, S., Seghier, M. L., Scherer, K. R., et al. (2005). Emotion and attention interactions in social cognition: Brain regions involved in processing anger prosody. *NeuroImage, 28*, 848–858.

Schacht, A., & Sommer, W. (2009). Emotions in word and face processing: Early and late cortical responses. *Brain and Cognition, 69*, 538–550.

Schirmer, A., & Kotz, S. A. (2006). Beyond the right hemisphere: Brain mechanisms mediating vocal emotional processing. *Trends in Cognitive Sciences, 10*, 24–30.

Schupp, H. T., Junghofer, M., Weike, A. I., Hamm, A. O. (2003). Emotional facilitation of sensory processing in the visual cortex. *Psychological Science, 14*, 7–13.

Schupp, H. T., Ohman, A., Junghofer, M., Weike, A. I., Stockburger, J., & Hamm, A. O. (2004). The facilitated processing of threatening faces: An ERP analysis. *Emotion, 4*, 189–200.

Scott, S. K., Young, A. W., Calder, A. J., Hellawell, D. J., Aggleton, J. P., & Johnson, M. (1997). Impaired auditory recognition of fear and anger following bilateral amygdala lesions. *Nature, 385*, 254–257.

Spreckelmeyer, K. N., Kutas, M., Urbach, T., Altenmuller, E., & Munte, T. F. (2009). Neural processing of vocal emotion and identity. *Brain and Cognition, 69*, 121–126.

Sprengelmeyer, R., Young, A. W., Schroeder, U., Grossenbacher, P. G., Federlein, J., Buttner, T., et al. (1999). Knowing no fear. *Proceedings Biological Science/The Royal Society, 266*, 2451–2456.

Stein, J. L., Wiedholz, L. M., Bassett, D. S., Weinberger, D. R., Zink, C. F., Mattay, V. S., et al. (2007). A validated network of effective amygdala connectivity. *NeuroImage, 36*, 736–745.

Stormark, K. M., & Hugdahl, K. (1997). Conditioned emotional cueing of spatial attentional shifts in a go/no-go RT task. *International Journal of Psychophysiology, 27*, 241–248.

Streit, M., Dammers, J., Simsek-Kraues, S., Brinkmeyer, J., Wolwer, W., & Ioannides, A. (2003). Time course of regional brain activations during facial emotion recognition in humans. *Neuroscience Letters, 342*, 101–104.

Taylor, J. G., & Fragopanagos, N. F. (2005). The interaction of attention and emotion. *Neural Networks, 18*, 353–369.

Vuilleumier, P. (2005). How brains beware: Neural mechanisms of emotional attention. *Trends in Cognitive Sciences, 9*, 585–594.

Vuilleumier, P., Armony, J. L., Clarke, K., Husain, M., Driver, J., & Dolan, R. J. (2002). Neural response to emotional faces with and without awareness: Event-related fMRI in a parietal patient with visual extinction and spatial neglect. *Neuropsychologia, 40*, 2156–2166.

Vuilleumier, P., Armony, J. L., Driver, J., & Dolan, R. J. (2001). Effects of attention and emotion on face processing in the human brain: An event-related fMRI study. *Neuron, 30*, 829–841.

Vuilleumier, P., & Driver, J. (2007). Modulation of visual processing by attention and emotion: Windows on causal interactions between human brain regions. *Philosophical Transactions of the Royal Society of London B Biological Sciences, 362*, 837–855.

Vuilleumier, P., Richardson, M. P., Armony, J. L., Driver, J., & Dolan, R. J. (2004). Distant influences of amygdala lesion on visual cortical activation during emotional face processing. *Nature Neuroscience, 7*, 1271–1278.

Vuilleumier, P., & Schwartz, S. (2001). Beware and be aware: Capture of spatial attention by fear-related stimuli in neglect. *Neuroreport, 12*, 1119–1122.

Wambacq, I. J., Shea-Miller, K. J., & Abubakr, A. (2004). Non-voluntary and voluntary processing of emotional prosody: An event-related potentials study. *Neuroreport, 15*, 555–559.

Whalen, P. J., Kagan, J., Cook, R. G., Davis, F. C., Kim, H., Polis, S., et al. (2004). Human amygdala responsivity to masked fearful eye whites. *Science, 306*, 2061.

Wildgruber, D., Ethofer, T., Grandjean, D., & Kreifelts, B. (2009). A cerebral network model of speech prosody comprehension. *International Journal of Speech-Language Pathology, 11*, 277–281.

Wildgruber, D., Riecker, A., Hertrich, I., Erb, M., Grodd, W., Ethofer, T., et al. (2005). Identification of emotional intonation evaluated by fMRI. *NeuroImage, 24*, 1233–1241.

Williams, L. M., Das, P., Liddell, B. J., Kemp, A. H., Rennie, C. J., & Gordon, E. (2006). Mode of functional connectivity in amygdala pathways dissociates level of awareness for signals of fear. *Journal of Neuroscience, 26*, 9264–9271.

Williams, M. A., McGlone, F., Abbott, D. F., & Mattingley, J. B. (2005). Differential amygdala responses to happy and fearful facial expressions depend on selective attention. *NeuroImage, 24*, 417–425.

Yamasaki, H., LaBar, K. S., & McCarthy, G. (2002). Dissociable prefrontal brain systems for attention and emotion. *Proceedings of the National Academy of Sciences of the United States of America, 99*, 11447–11451.

Zald, D. H. (2003). The human amygdala and the emotional evaluation of sensory stimuli. Brain Research. *Brain Research Reviews, 41*, 88–123.

Zeelenberg, R., & Bocanegra, B. R. (2010). Auditory emotional cues enhance visual perception. *Cognition, 115*, 202–206.

3

Investigating the Psychological and Neural Basis of Emotional Processing

MARTIAL MERMILLOD

INTRODUCTION

*T*he study of emotions is expanding rapidly in the fields of psychology, the cognitive sciences, and cognitive neurosciences. This interest is amply justified by the theoretical and clinical consequences of this area of research. As a result, many authors have tried, and are still trying, to identify based on psychological and behavioral indicators the psychological mechanisms involved in emotion. At the same time, our knowledge of the neurobiological bases of emotional processes is continuing to grow. It seems that an approach to emotions from the perspective of functional neuroanatomy might help extend our understanding of these neurobiological factors and provide evidence that will either confirm or invalidate theories that are purely psychological in nature. Conversely, behavioral data taken from the psychological domain may make it possible to orient the hypotheses and help in the interpretation of the neurobiological results. It now seems essential to adopt a perspective that combines the psychological and neurobiological approaches if we are to attempt to resolve the many questions relating to the genesis, nature, role, and control of emotions.

Emotions are in no way a new area of theoretical investigation. Darwin (1872), one of the pioneers in the scientific analysis of emotions, identified three principles underpinning emotional behavior. First, certain emotional expressions seem to correspond to archaic behaviors of use for the survival of the individual or the species. Next, emotional mental states are thought to be associated with specific behaviors as a result of repeated association throughout evolution. Finally, according to the principle of "antithesis," contrasting mental states may produce contrasting emotional expressions (e.g., the state of sadness, which produces a physical "limpness," contrasts with the state of joy, which, on the contrary, restores vigor).

Based on these three principles, Darwin also proposed a number of guidelines for the scientific analysis of behavior. He assumed, for example, that the neuro-muscular mechanisms involved in the facial expression of emotions are subject to evolution at the phylogenetic level. He thought that these facial expressions were directly linked to the individual's emotional experience and that they could, through a process of associative learning, become manifest even in the absence of the environmental conditions of stimulation to which they are adapted. The expression of these emotions would play a fundamental role in the communica-tion processes, and because they are in part genetically determined, they should be identical in different cultures. Although naïve and subject to criticism in many areas, this initial approach had the virtue of opening the path toward a scientific study of emotions.

For his part, James (1884) proposed an original and counterintuitive approach to emotions: the peripheral approach. While the majority of philosophers and sci-entists held that emotions are a disorder of consciousness that induces instability in the organism, James, in contrast, suggested that neurovegetative manifestations are responsible for the disorder of consciousness. In other words, human beings are thought of as a "reverberation chamber" in which physical changes, however subtle, reverberate until they reach the level of the conscious experience of emotion.

This original perspective has given rise to a number of current theoretical approaches. Opposing James's peripheral approach, Cannon (1927) proposed a more central theory of emotions based on various scientific and experimental facts. He emphasized that the total separation of the viscera and the central nervous sys-tem does not lead to any absolute alteration of emotional behavior. Furthermore, changes at a visceral level take longer to occur than the emotional experience itself. Finally, identical visceral changes may be associated with completely different emotional states, and inducing a specific visceral change will not necessarily result in the production of the emotion that is habitually associated with it. Supported by these experimental arguments, the experimental physiological approach proposed by Cannon made it possible to anchor the study of emotions within a scientific framework. This opposition between a visceral and abstractive approach to emo-tions can still be observed in modern theoretical trends: the theory of appraisal and the embodiment theory.

THE PSYCHOLOGY OF EMOTIONS

Appraisal Theory

In the psychological field, two complementary theories have fueled the debate concerning emotional processing. The key proposal made in the cognitive models of emotions is that they are the result of the perceived meaning of situations (e.g., Mandler, 1984). These models therefore focus on the process involved in apprais-ing emotional meaning. According to these models (e.g., Arnold, 1960; Ellsworth & Scherer, 2003; Lazarus, 1968; Mandler, 1984; Scherer, 1984a, 1984b, 1999; Smith & Ellsworth, 1985), individuals constantly appraise the situations in which they find themselves in terms of relevance and importance to themselves. Within this framework, emotions would be triggered and become differentiated through the subjective appraisal of the meaning conveyed by a situation, object, or event. In particular, this appraisal would involve an assessment of whether the stimuli may prove to be positive or negative for the individual and the way in which the associated benefits or disadvantages may make themselves felt.

Even though the various appraisal theories derive from different academic and historical traditions, they share a certain consensus with regard to the various dimensions of appraisal. The classical approach, based on the pioneering work of Arnold (1960) and Lazarus (1968), suggests that individuals use a fixed set of dimensions or criteria to appraise the situations that they encounter (e.g., Frijda, 1986; Scherer, 1984b; Smith & Ellsworth, 1985). These criteria can be assigned to four different classes: the intrinsic characteristics of the objects or events, such as their novelty (or change) as well as the pleasure or aversion associated with them (or valence); the meaning of the event as a function of the individual's goals and needs; the individual's ability to influence or face up to the consequences of the event, including the attribution of the agent (was the event caused by the individual him- or herself or by someone else, or is it the result of interpersonal circumstances?); the compatibility of the event with social or personal standards and values.

It is then the specific profiles resulting from the appraisal made based on these different criteria that determine the nature of the experienced emotion. However, in most cases, these criteria have been identified by asking subjects to remember a specific emotional experience or by inducing emotions in them in an experimental context and then questioning them about the appraisal processes they employed (Scherer, 1999). Subjects are therefore generally required to undertake conscious, complex processes to remember or infer the nature of the appraisals they have made with regard to a given situation or event.

This research therefore raises a certain number of methodological problems. First, it does not permit any fine-grained dissociation between the antecedents of the emotional experience and its content and does not make it possible to address the dynamics of the appraisal process directly (by determining, for example, whether the various criteria are applied sequentially or in parallel; Frijda, 1986). Second, one may question whether cognitive appraisals as elaborate as those revealed by this method can be performed automatically and unconsciously in the few hundredths of a second it takes to generate certain emotional states. This research method has therefore sometimes led to the erroneous conclusion that the appraisal processes are necessarily intentional and conscious. However, the emotional experience might also result from simple, basic, automatic processes that are then further elaborated at the cognitive level. A number of critics (Izard, 1971) have therefore suggested that this type of method might be effective when it comes to revealing conscious, high-level cognitive processes, but that it cannot be used to address many of the appraisal processes that are likely to be performed outside the field of consciousness. It is therefore necessary to consider the possibility that appraisal may cover various levels of complexity, and that certain emotions may be triggered by nonintentional, unconscious, and possibly also noncognitive factors.

Thus, almost all the authors who have worked within this theoretical tradition now accept that the processing necessary to assess whether the meaning of an external situation is dangerous or pleasant for the individual may be, at least in certain cases, global, automatic, fast, and unconscious to ensure that the organism is prepared to respond appropriately. However, it is necessary to consider much more elaborate cognitive appraisals (and far more flexible and varied behavioral patterns) when considering complex emotions such as vanity, nostalgia, pity, or remorse. The number, nature, and scale of these appraisals vary as a function of the number and type of the emotions that each of the theories attempts to explain. Furthermore, a number of authors working within this theoretical tradition do not exclude the possibility that very simple cognitive appraisals, in particular with reference to the valence of these objects or events, may take place even before the objects or events have been identified, thus contributing to the rapid allocation of attentional resources (e.g., Clore & Ortony, 2000; Scherer, 1984b). Nevertheless, these appraisals are far from the main focus of cognitive appraisal in these theoretical models.

Embodiment Theory

The theories of embodied cognition appear to be completely at odds with the associative network theories, such as that put forward by Bower (1981, 1991). The mechanism for the propagation of activation proposed by Bower (1981) is based on the idea that memory consists of a network of interconnected associative nodes. According to this model, the presentation of an emotional stimulus activates the knowledge node that represents it, and this activation is then propagated through the lexical and semantic network to all the nodes that correspond to targets that are similar in terms of their appraisal.

In contrast, the approaches based on embodied cognition hold that the high-level cognitive processes are rooted in an embodied cognition located within the motor (Gallese, 2005), perceptual (Barsalou, 1999), and emotional systems (Niedenthal, 2007). These theories suppose, for example, that the fact of thinking of an action should bring about the partial activation of the motor states originally involved in the performance of this action. As far as emotional information is concerned, this would involve the partial reactivation of the neural states that occur when an individual experiences an emotion. Although this type of imitative behavior, which is present at birth (Meltzoff & Moore, 1989), could include all types of bodily movement, the most convincing evidence relates to the facial expressions of emotion.

For example, in a study conducted by Wallbott (1991), the participants were asked to categorize emotions in response to the presentation of a series of photographs, during which they were filmed without knowing it. A few weeks later, they were asked to watch the video recordings and judge which emotion from the first session they were decoding at the time. The results showed that the individuals were capable of identifying their mimicked emotions based on fairly subtle cues (the expressions on their own faces) of which they were unconscious. This imitative process is therefore performed in a relatively automatic and involuntary way below the threshold of consciousness (Strack, Martin, & Stepper, 1988).

Within this perspective, it seems justifiable to ask what the value of such a mechanism might be. Two main functions are suggested in the literature. First, it might permit rapid learning in a similar way to the learning of new actions through imitation (Gallese et al., 1996; Gallese, Keysers, & Rizzolatti, 2004). Second, it might be responsible for social contagion, that is, the induction of congruent emotional states in other people. As a consequence, it seems possible that this imitative process might be involved in empathy and social cooperation (e.g., Decety & Chaminade, 2003). The observation and the motor imitation of other people's facial expressions would enable us to identify their intentions and understand the reasons for their emotional reactions. They would thus act as a guide both in everyday social interactions and in uncertain situations (i.e., in the case of ambiguous facial expressions).

The basal ganglia are archaic structures responsible for the processing of emotion. Nevertheless, their role in the integration of the limbic, associative, and sensorimotor processes is still undefined. This integrative function primarily interests the proponents of embodied cognition (Niedenthal et al., 2010). It should be remembered that these conceptions of cognition consider that cognitive processing is intrinsically associated with each perceptual (or sensorimotor) modality and is therefore opposed to an amodal approach to cognitive processes. Most argued that the sensorimotor and emotional states that occur during perception, action, and introspection could be partially or fully captured by the associative areas of the brain (Damasio, 1994). However, to date, there is no formal evidence to exclude the possibility that traces of this process of integration might be found in the basal ganglia. A variety of theories have been proposed, such as Damasio's theory of somatic markers or Gallese's theory of mirror neurons (Gallese et al., 2004) in addition to Decety's concept of intersubjectivity (Decety & Chaminade, 2003). These theories presuppose the reactivation of the underlying neuronal states specific to the experience of each emotion and, consequently, the integration of the three functional components.

In line with the embodiment theory, many authors have revealed different patterns of activation of the facial muscles that are specific to the treatment of different emotional facial expressions (EFEs). For example, Dimberg and colleagues (Dimberg & Petterson, 2000; Dimberg & Thunberg, 1998) have shown that the rapid observation of angry or joyful faces produces electromyographic responses in the corresponding regions of the observer's zygomaticus major and corrugator supercilii. Moreover, the literature suggests that imitation not only consists of matching the visual aspects of other people's behavior but also generates the corresponding introspective (i.e., affective, emotional) aspects (Adolphs, 2002; Hess & Blairy, 2001). Recent neuroscientific studies have suggested that imitation and its neuronal correlates, as components of a mechanism that underpins the identification and understanding of facial expressions (Carr et al., 2003; Gallese et al., 2004), constitute a fundamental basis for the process of empathy (Sonnby-Borgstrom, 2002) and do so as of a very young age (Meltzoff & Moore, 1989). As far as the involved neuroanatomical substrates are concerned, it seems unlikely that these high-level cognitive and emotional functions are based on structures as archaic as the basal ganglia, even though this still has to be demonstrated and despite the fact that the basal ganglia have close links with more highly evolved cortical structures.

COGNITIVE NEUROSCIENCE STUDIES

As part of an interdisciplinary approach to emotions, we now present a number of neuroanatomical models of emotions to illustrate the need to bring together the debates relating to functional questions in the psychological field and those relating to neuroanatomical questions in the field of neurobiology.

LeDoux's Model (1996)

In many respects, LeDoux's model (1996) can be considered as a further development of the Papez circuit (Papez, 1937). Papez was one of the first authors to propose a neuroanatomical model of the experience and expression of emotions. According to this author, the term *emotion* covers two aspects: a mode of action that matches the emotional expression and a mode of feeling that relates to the emotional experience or subjective feeling. In this, Papez was in agreement with Cannon (1927), who suggested that the phenomenon of expressing and experiencing emotions might be dissociated in humans. According to Cannon (1927), when an emotionally charged event is perceived, the input from the nervous system is divided into two distinct channels at the thalamus; one part of this input is thought to reach the hypothalamus, which then generates the expressive aspect of emotion (peripheral vegetative manifestations), while the other part reaches the cortex, where it gives rise to the subjective emotional experience. The innovative new feature in Papez's model (1937) was that it no longer considered that there is a single emotional "center" (the thalamus): Emotion does not result from the activity of a specific structure in the brain but from the activation of a complex network of interconnected brain regions. Based on anatomical, clinical, and experimental data, the model suggested, in effect, that the reciprocal connections between the hypothalamus, the anterior thalamic nuclei, the hippocampus, the cingulate gyrus, and the parahippocampal gyrus act as the principal mediator of emotional behavior acting via the cerebral cortex.

More precisely, Papez (1937) suggested that emotion can be generated in two ways: According to him, the first of these originates in the cortex and leads, via the hippocampus, to the hypothalamus. It then propagates to the anterior thalamic nuclei and on to the cortex of the cingulate gyrus (or parahippocampal gyrus). The many neural projections from the cingulate gyrus to other cortical regions are then responsible for the emotional tone of various cognitive functions. The second originates in the anterior thalamic nucleus and also leads to the hypothalamus—but without passing through the cortex—and has the task of producing a fast but sketchy response to an emotional stimulus. LeDoux (1996) suggested that the notion of the limbic system, as proposed by Papez, needs to be modified to adequately take account of the neural bases of emotion. While certain structures are involved in nonemotional functions, other structures that do not form part of the limbic system have since been acknowledged to play an important role in the processing of emotions. LeDoux therefore suggested that even though the memory functions of the hippocampus can be significantly modulated by the emotional connotations of the stimuli, they are not an essential link in the emotional

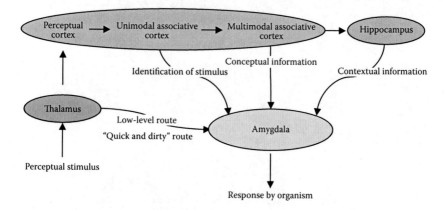

Figure 3.1   LeDoux's model (1996).

circuits. There would therefore appear to be a sufficiently large functional distinction between the memory and emotional structures for them to be considered as
different systems.

LeDoux's (1996) model therefore proposed two main channels. The first, the
mediobasal channel, is thought to correspond to the Papez circuit, whereas the
second connects the ventromedial hypothalamus to the dorsomedial thalamus, the
fronto-orbital cortex, and the temporal cortex. Furthermore, LeDoux paid special attention to the role of the amygdala in the processing of emotion since this
is thought to permit the appraisal of the emotional meaning of both perceptual
information and abstract thoughts. The amygdala is therefore thought to control
the expression of certain emotional reactions. Furthermore, LeDoux's model sup-
poses that there are two perceptual routes leading to the amygdala. According
to the model, the first, high-spatial-precision route is mediated by complex cortical areas (in particular, the ventral visual channel), whereas the second, fast, but
degraded ("quick-and-dirty"), route propagates directly from the thalamus, which
is the central point for the integration of perceptual information, to the amygdala.
The function of this second route is therefore to act as a sort of "backup system"
that short-circuits the more highly evolved but slower cortical processes through
reflex actions and by rapidly alerting the organism in the presence of an immediate
danger in the direct perceptual environment (Figure 3.1).

From Perception to Emotion

Based on work conducted by LeDoux (1996), a number of studies in the fields of
psychology and neuroimaging have attempted to understand the complexity of the
neuroanatomical circuits involved in the processing of emotions and the processing
of danger in particular. First, the low-level route in LeDoux's model might, as far as
the processing of visual information is concerned, originate in the lateral geniculate
nucleus of the thalamus, more particularly at the level of the magnocellular pathways. In effect, the human primary visual system breaks down spatial frequency
information as it passes from the retina through to the striate cortex (or primary

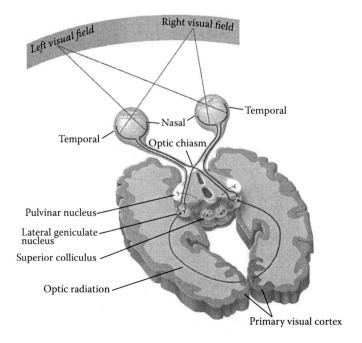

Figure 3.2 The human visual system. (From Webvision. Home page. http://webvision. med.utah.edu.)

visual cortex or V1) via the lateral geniculate nuclei (Figure 3.2), where the magnocellular and parvocellular pathways become dissociated (Hubel & Wiesel, 1977).

The properties of these two visual pathways exhibit asymmetrical spatiotemporal characteristics. The nonmyelinized parvocellular pathways are chromatic and transport all the spatial frequencies that constitute the image more slowly. In contrast, the myelinized magnocellular pathways are achromatic and transport low spatial frequencies quickly (cf. Figure 3.3).

Furthermore, the trajectory for the integration of the visual information is thought to be coarse to fine (Bullier, 2001; Marendaz, Rousset, & Charnallet, 2003; Ivry & Robertson, 1998; Mermillod, Guyader, & Chauvin, 2005; Peyrin, Mermillod, Chokron, & Marendaz, 2006). In other words, the faster information sourced from the low spatial frequencies (LSF) (Figure 3.4) (magnocellular pathways) would provide an outline view of the structure of the image and permit an initial perceptual categorization that would then be fine-tuned by the local information taken from the high spatial frequencies (HSF), which are extracted later (parvocellular pathways). Within the framework of LeDoux's model, the magnocellular pathways are thus the ideal candidate for a quick-and-dirty route to the amygdala.

A number of neuroimaging studies have been conducted to test LeDoux's model (1996) in humans and, in particular, to test the existence of a direct subcortical pathway between the amygdala and the primary visual system. For example, Vuilleumier et al. (2003) used a functional magnetic resonance imaging (fMRI) experiment to reveal the existence of a hemodynamic response in the subcortical

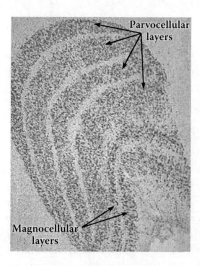

Figure 3.3   The lateral geniculate nucleus. (From Webvision. The primary visual cortex. March 30. http://webvision.med.utah.edu/VisualCortex.html#introduction.)

Figure 3.4   Example of stimuli from the Karolinska Directed Emotional Faces database. From left to right (low to high spatial frequencies): broad spatial frequency face, <8 CpI, 8–16 CpI, 16–32 CpI, 32–64 CpI and >64 CpI.

pathway involving the superior colliculus and the amygdala via the pulvinar when subjects were presented with faces expressing fear compared to neutrality filtered at low versus high spatial frequencies. These results therefore suggested that the transmission of the signal associated with the facial expressions of fear might short-circuit the primary visual cortex by taking a subcortical route that transports the low spatial frequency information very quickly (Figure 3.1). These studies also showed that images of faces filtered at high spatial frequencies resulted only in a low level or no activation of the amygdala, and that the signal produced by these faces seemed to take the ventral route (primary visual cortex or V1, then occipito-temporal cortex).

Within this perspective, the work conducted by Vuilleumier et al. (2003) made it possible to imagine that there are associations between the signal properties and the circuitry employed that have different cognitive functionalities: the purpose of an "LSF/magnocellular pathway" association would lie in the rapid emotional categorization of faces, whereas an "HSF/parvocellular pathway" coupling would be responsible for the accurate identification of faces. Unfortunately, the poor temporal resolution provided by fMRI (of an order of several seconds) does not make it possible to determine whether the amygdala as well as the superior colliculus and the pulvinar were activated before or after the elaborate cortical processing performed in the ventral route.

To overcome the problem of the temporal resolution offered by fMRI, de Gelder, Vroomen, Pourtois, and Weiskrantz (1999) conducted a number of studies using evoked potentials (EPs), which suggested the possibility that the amygdala may be directly activated in patients with hemianopsia (patients with a lesion on one side of the primary visual cortex who thus perceive only the contralateral half of the visual field) with a V1 lesion when exposed to EFEs in the blind half-field. Other EP studies have attempted to show the primacy of the processing of LF information over HF information in response to the presentation of both EFE (Eimer & Holmes, 2002; Holmes, Winston, & Eimer, 2005; Pourtois, Dan, Grandjean, Sander, & Vuilleumier, 2005; Pourtois, Thut, Grave de Peralta, Michel, & Vuilleumier, 2005) and complex emotional stimuli such as pictures taken from the International Affective Picture System (IAPS; Alorda et al., 2007). Unfortunately, the electroencephalography (EEG) techniques on which the event-related potential (ERP) are based consist of taking a surface recording of the electrical activity (or magnetic activity in the case of magnetoencephalography, MEG) in the brain. These techniques therefore suffer from major problems in terms of spatial resolution, in particular with regard to the subcortical structures involved in the processing of emotions.

In parallel with these neuroimaging techniques, a number of behavioral studies have nevertheless suggested the importance of the low spatial frequencies in EFE processing in healthy subjects (Mermillod, Droit-Volet, Devaux, Schaefer, & Vermeulen, 2010; Schyns & Oliva, 1999) as well as in the fields of psychopathology (Deruelle et al., 2008) and connectionist modeling (Mermillod et al., 2009; Mermillod, Bonin, Mondillon, Alleysson, & Vermeulen, 2010). Work into "blindsight" conducted within this line of research has revealed that patients with hemianopsia unconsciously perceive the emotional content of faces presented in the blind visual field (de Gelder et al., 1999; Pegna et al., 2004). Such work provides a new, indirect argument in favor of the existence of the low route proposed by LeDoux (1996), but again, however, without constituting formal proof of the existence of this route.

In effect, there is an alternative hypothesis that suggests that the neuroanatomical bases of blindsight might lie in residual connections in V1 (either ipsilateral or contralateral to the lesion). At present, therefore, the hypothesis that such a low route exists is based on the convergence of data taken from the fields of neuroanatomy, neuroimaging psychology, neuropsychology, and psychopathology, without any of these, however, providing any direct, formal proof of the existence of this route.

Subcortical Structures and Emotions

The work undertaken by LeDoux (1996) suggests that the amygdala is an important component of the system responsible for the acquisition, storage, and expression of fear. The amygdala consists of different neural centers (Figure 3.5), including the basolateral nuclei, which receive projections from the high-level, associative sensory cortical areas of the temporal lobe and the insula. In their turn, these

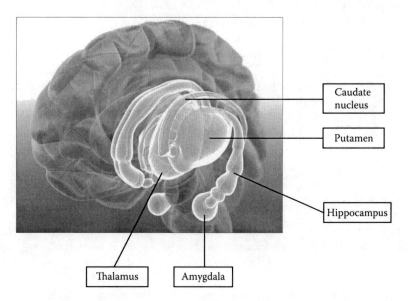

Figure 3.5   The basal ganglia.

basolateral nuclei project to the limbic associative cortex, the prefrontal cortex, and the hippocampal formation. The basolateral nuclei also project via the ventral amygdala pathway to the dorsal medial nucleus of the thalamus, which projects to the prefrontal associative cortex. The basolateral nuclei therefore project to the basal nucleus of Meynert, which consists of cholinergic neurons that exhibit a diffuse projection to the cortex. Finally, they also project to the central nuclei of the amygdala. In Ledoux's model, the function of the basolateral nuclei is therefore to evaluate the emotional meaning of sensory stimuli and to memorize these stimuli. The central nuclei receive visceral sensory afferents from the solitary and parabrachial nuclei as well as from the basolateral nuclei of the amygdala. They project, via the ventral amygdala pathway, to the dorsal motor nucleus of the vagus nerve (X) and to the other parasympathetic nuclei of the brain stem as well as to the lateral hypothalamus. The corticomedial nuclei receive projections from the olfactory bulb. They, in turn, project to the olfactory bulb as well as to the ventromedial nucleus of the hypothalamus via stria terminalis.

Ledoux's (1996) work has emphasized the importance of the amygdala in the processing of fear. It has been confirmed by a large number of studies conducted in the cognitive neurosciences that have revealed the importance of the amygdala in the *recognition* of fear (see Adolphs, 2002, for a review of this issue). The amygdala is also thought to be necessary to *experience* the sensation of fear (Calder, Lawrence, & Young, 2001). Nevertheless, new data point to a broader-based involvement of the amygdala. It has been suggested that it might be called on in all the ambiguous situations that might constitute a direct or indirect threat to the organism (Breiter et al., 1996; Whalen et al., 2001).

Since then, other scientific articles have supported the idea that the amygdala might be involved in the processing of the six primary EFE (fear, disgust, anger, joy, surprise, and sadness) under certain conditions of presentation (Fitzgerald, Angstadt, Jelsone, Nathan, & Phan, 2006; Winston, O'Doherty, & Dolan, 2003; Yang et al., 2002). While a considerable volume of work has been devoted to the role of the amygdala in the processing of emotions, the amygdala is clearly not the only subcortical structure involved in the regulation of emotions. In effect, the basal ganglia constitute a network of subcortical structures that are necessary for the regulation of emotion (Figure 3.5).

Among these structures, the caudate nucleus as well as the head of the caudate nucleus and nucleus accumbens seem to be particularly closely involved in the approach/avoidance process. These structures form the reward system (Kawagoe, Takikawa, & Hikosada, 1998; Parkinson, Cardinal, & Everitt, 2000; Schultz, 2002). A meta-analysis performed by Phan et al. (2002) suggested that these subcortical areas are highly involved in the detection of the valence of stimuli and, as a consequence, in the primary approach/avoidance behaviors. However, Davidson (1994) differentiated this primary approach/avoidance sensation from the more highly developed notion, which is cortical in nature and is thought to be controlled by the orbitofrontal cortex, which therefore might have the role of regulating this type of primitive, subcortical process (and constitute what is sometimes referred to as the "reptilian brain"). However, things could be a lot more complicated than they appear. It is thought that the striatum, which contains the caudal nucleus, the putamen, and the fundus (a network of neural fibers that connects the ventral part of the caudal nucleus to the putamen) is not only involved in the processing of emotion. The work conducted by Yelnik et al. (2007) showed that this structure, like all the basal ganglia, comprises three functional components: limbic (i.e., emotional), associative (i.e., cognitive), and sensorimotor.

Explaining this characteristic of the basal ganglia represents a real challenge at both the fundamental and applied levels. At the fundamental level, the task is to understand why life has evolved, even at the level of its most archaic neuronal structures, in a way that brings together the three functional components (sensorimotor, associative, and limbic) within one and the same set of neurons. Does this integration of the three components permit a faster, more effective integration of the signals coming from the direct perceptual environment? Might these integrative processes be associated with rudimentary social communication mechanisms such as understanding other people's emotions and providing an appropriate response to these emotions? Could these processes constitute the neural basis of empathy, or is this function rounded in more highly developed processes located at the cortical level?

The integration of these three functional structures at the level of the basal ganglia clearly raises the question of the involvement of these anatomical structures in the embodiment processes described. One initial hypothesis could be that embodiment is closely associated with the sensorimotor, limbic, and associative integration performed in the basal ganglia. Nevertheless, these archaic structures of the central nervous system might be too primitive to be involved in processes such as empathy or social emotions. It therefore seems more likely that they are at the origin of far more primitive approach/avoidance, alerting, or aggression-related behaviors. Thus, Olsson et al. (2005) showed that extremely archaic structures such as the amygdala might be involved in primitive behaviors such as racism, for example. More complex behaviors (such as empathy) that are associated with embodiment might therefore have originated in more highly developed areas of the encephalus, such as the somatosensory cortex or the prefrontal cortex.

At the applied level, the awareness of the functional components of the basal ganglia will make it possible to develop new neurosurgical techniques for the treatment of severe psychopathologies such as Parkinson's disease, refractory chronic depression, involuntary convulsive disorders, and obsessive-compulsive disorders (cf. Mermillod et al., 2008, for further details).

Cortical Structures and the Processing of Emotions

Neuropsychological data taken from a large sample of patients have revealed that the somatosensory cortex, the right anterior supramarginal gyrus, the insula, and the left frontal operculum all play a crucial role in tasks requiring the recognition of the six basic EFEs (Adolphs et al., 2000). Despite this, a complementary finding by Adolphs et al. (1996) has shown that lesions of the visual perceptual areas (in particular, the areas of the right visual cortex) result in deficits in the recognition of EFE (fear, for example). It is clear that the observed deficits are not based on the same cognitive functions (perceptual deficit relating to the visual cortex and deficit thought to relate more to the experience of emotion due to lesions of the somatosensory cortex). Adolphs et al. (2000) therefore suggested that the somatosensory cortex might act as a neuroanatomical substrate for the experience of emotion. This proposal has received support from Winston et al. (2003), who showed that both the somatosensory cortex and the ventromedial prefontal cortex are involved in tasks requiring the explicit judgment of the feeling of emotion, whereas the amygdala was found to react to EFE whatever the nature of the task.

This involvement of highly developed cortical structures in the experiencing of emotions has been confirmed by the work performed in primates by Gallese et al. (1996), which revealed the activation of "mirror neurons" in the premotor cortex (and, more specifically, area F5 in monkeys) during the recognition of actions performed by others. Similar phenomena might be at work in the perception of motor actions performed by others or in empathy. For example, an fMRI study conducted by Carr et al. (2003) has revealed the activation of the ventral premotor cortex, the amygdala, and the insula both during the passive observation of EFE and during the intentional imitation of these EFE. The study undertaken by Wicker et al. (2003) confirmed these results by showing that the cortical areas activated during the perception of a third-party feeling disgust after being exposed to an unpleasant smell are identical to those activated when the participants themselves were exposed to the same unpleasant smells. Wicker et al. (2003) reported an activation of the anterior part of the insula and, to a lesser extent, the anterior cingulate cortex. Finally, a study by van der Gaag, Minderaa, and Keysers (2007) has revealed an activation of the prefrontal cortex (inferior frontal gyrus) and the inferior parietal cortex during a task involving the observation or intentional mimicry of EFE (smile, fear, disgust, and neutral) but not in a control condition in which the participants had to puff out their cheeks. The use of a control condition in this final

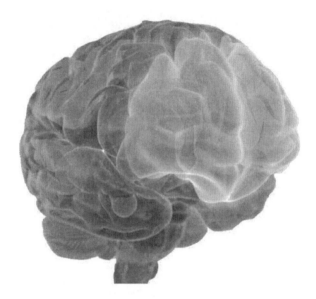

Figure 3.6   The frontal, prefrontal, and orbitofrontal cortex (light gray).

experiment showed that the simple programming of movements is not sufficient to explain these patterns of activation.

Moreover, complex cortical areas are also involved in the processing of emotions. Thus, the prefrontal cortex (Figure 3.6) has the role of regulating executive functions, that is, the management of action as a function of an individual's goals within his or her environment. However, the area of the prefrontal cortex that is most closely involved in the control of emotion is the orbitofrontal cortex. The orbitofrontal cortex occupies the backmost section of the frontal cortex, just behind the ocular orbit (from which it gets its name). Unlike the somatosensory cortex, the orbitofrontal cortex does not appear to be involved in the simulation and embodiment processes. Nevertheless, the orbitofrontal cortex plays a predominant role in the mechanisms responsible for emotional control and decision making (Kringelbach, 2005). More specifically, and unlike the subcortical structures of the reward system (ventral tegmental area and nucleus accumbens), the orbitofrontal cortex appears to be associated with the cognitive planning of action within the approach/avoidance process. In other words, the orbitofrontal cortex is thought to possess a more complex level of cognitive association than the primitive associative mechanisms that are at work in the subcortical structures of the reward system, thus giving it a predominant role in anticipation of actions and emotional control (Bechara et al., 1994).

While the medial section of the orbitofrontal cortex seems to be devoted to the process involved in approaching reinforcing stimuli, its lateral section appears to be devoted to the avoidance of aversive stimuli. Similarly, the anterior part of the orbitofrontal cortex seems to be responsible for the processing of stimuli (of a conceptual nature) of a higher level of abstraction than those processed in the posterior part, which, instead, appears to be involved in the reinforcement of simple perceptual stimuli (Kringelbach & Rolls, 2004). In addition, neuropsychological data show that lesions to the orbitofrontal cortex induce uninhibited behavior, such as excessive emotional reactions, compulsive purchasing behavior, or hypersexuality, as well as inappropriate social behaviors that may result in social exclusion. A variety of neuropsychological tests have thus shown that patients who have suffered a lesion to the orbitofrontal cortex are not able to inhibit behaviors associated with an aversive stimulus if a conditioned response has been associated with this stimulus in the past. This failure of the mechanism responsible for the elimination of the conditioned response is a fairly clear indication of the regulatory function assumed by the orbitofrontal cortex in the approach/avoidance processes at work in the reward circuit. Nevertheless, at present, the primary function of the frontal lobes is thought to be associated with the regulation of emotional behaviors rather than the processes at work in embodied cognition.

CONCLUSION

The aim of this chapter was to present two different theoretical approaches to the processing of emotion framed within a historical perspective and to point out the links between these theoretical approaches and the data provided by the cognitive neurosciences, while also taking account of the interdisciplinary aspects of this research. Current work undertaken in the field of the cognitive neurosciences suggests that cognitive appraisal theories relate mainly, although not exclusively, to associative cortical areas associated with the recognition, appraisal, and integration of emotional stimuli in networks of conceptual or social knowledge. As far as the theories of embodied cognition are concerned, a large number of neuroimaging studies have given us an insight into the elegance of the model, that is, the explanatory potential of a process that makes it possible to explain different levels of processing, ranging from the primary psychological response to a dangerous stimulus to complex high-level processes such as empathy.

With regard to archaic emotional processing such as the primary response to a dangerous stimulus, the work reported in current scientific literature suggests that this type of behavior is controlled by the sensorimotor and emotional integration of primitive, subcortical neuronal structures such as the amygdala. Of course, these structures would not be *exclusively* subcortical in nature since they permanently interact with the complex cortical structures involved in the cognitive and social regulation of behavior (the frontal lobes, among others). The elegance of the theoretical model of embodied cognition lies, in particular, in the fact that this process of sensorimotor and emotional integration, when transposed to highly developed cortical areas such as the somatosensory cortex, might make it possible to explain far more complex and highly evolved behaviors such as empathy. In other words, one and the same principle for the sensorimotor integration of emotional stimuli could be responsible, depending on the level of neural development in question, for behaviors as varied as fear (and by extension, phobia, cf. outgroup phobia), aggression (cf. also domination if the regulation processes integrated at the frontal lobes are taken into account), as well as far more highly developed processes associated with complex cortical areas of integration, such as empathy.

ACKNOWLEDGMENTS

This work was supported by a grant ANR-06-BLAN-0360-01 and ANR-BLAN08–1_353820 from the French National Research Agency (ANR).

REFERENCES

Adolphs, R. (2002). Recognizing emotion from facial expressions: Psychological and neurological mechanisms. *Behavioral and Cognitive Neuroscience Reviews, 1*, 21–62.

Adolphs, R., Damasio, H., Tranel, D., & Damasio, A. R. (1996). Cortical systems for the recognition of emotion in facial expressions. *The Journal of Neuroscience, 16*, 7678–7687.

Adolphs, R., Damasio, H., Tranel, D., Cooper, G., & Damasio, A. R. (2000). A role for somatosensory cortices in the visual recognition of emotion as revealed by 3-D lesion mapping. *The Journal of Neuroscience, 20*, 2683–2690.

Alorda, C., Serrano-Pedraza, I., Campos-Bueno, J. J., Sierra-Vázquez, V., & Montoya, P. (2007). Low spatial frequency filtering modulates early brain processing of affective complex pictures. *Neuropsychologia, 45*, 3223–3233.

Arnold, M. B. (1960). *Emotion and personality. Vol. 1. Psychological aspects.* New York: Columbia University Press.

Barsalou, L. W. (1999). Perceptual symbol system. *Behavioral and Brain Sciences, 22*, 577–660.

Bechara, A., Damasio, A. R., Damasio, H., & Anderson, S. W. (1994). Insensitivity to future consequences following damage to human prefrontal cortex. *Cognition, 50*, 7–15.

Bower, G. H. (1981). Mood and memory. *American Psychologist, 36*, 129–148.

Bower, G. H. (1991). Mood congruity of social judgments. In J. Forgas (Ed.), *Emotion and social judgments* (pp. 31–53). Oxford, UK: Pergamon.

Breiter, H. C., Etcoff, N. L., Whalen, P. J., Kennedy, W. A., Rauch, S. L., Buckner, R. L., et al. (1996). Response and habituation of the human amygdala during visual processing of facial expression. *Neuron, 17*, 875–887.

Bullier, J. (2001). Integrated model of visual processing. *Brain Research Reviews, 36*(2–3), 96–107.

Calder, A. J., Lawrence, A. D., & Young, A. W. (2001). Neuropsychology of fear and loathing. *Nature Reviews Neuroscience, 2*, 352–363

Cannon, W. B. (1927). The James-Lange theory of emotion: A critical examination and an alternative theory. *American Journal of Psychology, 39*, 10–124.

Carr, L., Iacoboni, M., Dubeau, M. C., Mazziotta, J. C., & Lenzi G. L. (2003). Neural mechanisms of empathy in humans: A relay from neural systems for imitation to limbic areas. *Proceedings of the National. Academy of Science of the United States of America, 100*, 5497–5502.

Clore, G. L., & Ortony, A. (2000). Cognitive neuroscience of emotion. In R. D. Lane & L. Nadel (Eds.), *Cognitive neuroscience of emotion* (pp. 24–61). New York: Oxford University Press.

Damasio, A. (1994). The brain binds entities and events by multiregional activation from convergence zones. In H. Gutfreund & G. Toulouse (Eds.), *Biology and computation: A physicist's choice* (pp. 749–758). River Edge, NJ: World Scientific.

Darwin, C. (1872). *The expression of the emotions in man and animals.* London: John Murray.

Davidson, R. J. (1994). On emotion, mood, and related affective constructs. In P. Ekman & R. J. Davidson (Eds.), *The nature of emotion: Fundamental questions* (pp. 51–55). New York: Oxford University Press.

Decety, J., & Chaminade, T. (2003). Neural correlates of feeling sympathy. *Neuropsychologia*, *41*, 127–138.

De Gelder, B., Vroomen, J., Pourtois, G., & Weiskrantz, L. (1999). Non-conscious recognition of affect in the absence of striate cortex. *NeuroReport*, *10*, 3759–3763.

Deruelle, C., Rondan, C., Salle-Collemiche, X., Bastard-Rosset, D., & Da Fonséca, D. (2008). Attention to low- and high-spatial frequencies in categorizing facial identities, emotions and gender in children with autism. *Brain & Cognition*, *66*, 115–123.

Dimberg, U., & Petterson, M. (2000). Facial reactions to happy and angry facial expressions: Evidence for right hemisphere dominance. *Psychophysiology*, *37*, 693–696.

Dimberg, U., & Thunberg, M. (1998). Rapid facial reactions to emotional facial expressions. *Scandinavian Journal of Psychology*, *39*, 39–45.

Eimer, M., & Holmes, A. (2002). An ERP study on the time course of emotional face processing. *NeuroReport*, *13*, 427–431.

Ellsworth, P. C., & Scherer, K. R. (2003). *Appraisal processes in emotion*. New York: Oxford University Press.

Fitzgerald, D. A., Angstadt, M., Jelsone, L. M., Nathan, P. J., & Phan, K. L. (2006). Beyond threat: Amygdala reactivity across multiple expressions of facial affect. *Neuroimage*, *30*, 1441–8.

Frijda, N. (1986). *The emotions*. Cambridge, UK: Cambridge University Press.

Gallese, V. (2005). 'Being like me': Self-other identity, mirror neurons, and empathy. Perspectives on imitation: From neuroscience to social science: Vol. 1: *Mechanisms of imitation and imitation in animals* (pp. 101–118). Cambridge, MA: MIT Press.

Gallese, V., Fadiga, L., Fogassi, L., & Rizzolatti, G. (1996). Action recognition in the premotor cortex. *Brain*, *119*, 593–609.

Gallese, V., Keysers, C., & Rizzolatti, G. (2004). A unifying view of the basis of social cognition. *Trends in Cognitive Science*, *8*, 396–403.

Hess, U., & Blairy, S. (2001). Facial mimicry and emotional contagion to dynamic emotional facial expressions and their influence on decoding accuracy. *International Journal of Psychophysiology*, *40*, 129–141.

Holmes, A., Winston, J. S., & Eimer, M. (2005). The role of spatial frequency information for ERP components sensitive to faces and emotional facial expression. *Cognitive Brain Research*, *25*, 508–520.

Hubel, H. D., & Wiesel, T. N. (1977). Ferrier lecture: Functional architecture of macaque monkey visual cortex. *Proceedings of the Royal Society of London [Biology]*, *98*, 1–59.

Ivry, R. B., & Robertson, L. C. (1998). *The two sides of perception*. Cambridge, MA: MIT Press.

Izard, C. (1971). *The face of emotion*. New York: Appleton-Century-Crofts.

James, W. (1884). What is an emotion? *Mind*, *9*, 188–205.

Kawagoe, R., Takikawa, Y., & Hikosada, O. (1998). Expectation of reward modulates cognitive signals in the basal ganglia. *Nature Neuroscience*, *1*, 411–416.

Kringelbach, M. L. (2005). The orbitofrontal cortex: Linking reward to hedonic experience. *Nature Reviews Neuroscience*, *6*, 691–702.

Kringelbach, M. L., & Rolls, E. T. (2004). The functional neuroanatomy of the human orbitofrontal cortex: Evidence from neuroimaging and neuropsychology. *Progress in Neurobiology*, *72*, 341–372.

Lazarus, R. S. (1968). Emotions and adaptation: Conceptual and empirical relations. In W. J. Arnold (Ed.), *Nebraska Symposium on Motivation* (Vol. 16, pp. 175–270). Lincoln: University of Nebraska Press.

LeDoux, J. E. (1996). *The emotional brain: The mysterious underpinnings of emotional life*. New York: Simon & Schuster.

Mandler, G. (1984). *Mind and body: Psychology of emotion and stress*. New York: Norton.

Marendaz, C., Rousset, S., & Charnallet, A. (2003). Reconnaissance des scènes, des objets et des visages: Modèles théoriques et neuropsychologiques. In A. Delorme & M. Fluckiger (Eds.), *Perception et réalité*. Montreal: Gaëtan Morin Editeur.

Meltzoff, A. N., & Moore, M. K. (1989). Imitation in newborn infants: Exploring the range of gestures imitated and the underlying mechanisms. *Developmental Psychology, 25,* 954–962.

Mermillod, M., Bonin, P., Mondillon, L., Alleysson, D., & Vermeulen, N. (2010). Coarse scales are sufficient for efficient categorization of emotional facial expressions: Evidence from neural computation. *Neurocomputing, 73,* 2522–2531.

Mermillod, M., Droit-Volet, S., Devaux, D., Schaefer, A., & Vermeulen, N. (2010). Are coarse scales sufficient for fast detection of visual threat? *Psychological Science, 21,* 1429–1437.

Mermillod, M., Galland, F., Mondillon, L., Durif, F., Chéreau, I., & Jalenques, I. (2008). Troubles Psychiatriques et stimulation cérébrale profonde: Perspectives de recherche clinique et fondamentale. In S. Campanella & E. Streel (Eds.), *Psychopathologie et neurosciences: Questions actuelles* (pp. 231–260). Brussels: De Boeck.

Mermillod, M., Guyader, N., & Chauvin A. (2005). The coarse-to-fine hypothesis revisited: Evidence from neuro-computational modeling. *Brain & Cognition, 57,* 151–157.

Mermillod, M., Vuilleumier, P., Peyrin, C., Alleysson, D., & Marendaz, C. (2009). The importance of low spatial frequency information for recognizing fearful facial expressions. *Connection Science, 21,* 75–83.

Niedenthal, P. M. (2007). Embodying emotion. *Science, 316,* 1002–1005.

Niedenthal, P. M., Mermillod, M., Maringer, M., & Hess, U. (2010). The simulation of smiles (SIMS) model: Embodied simulation and the meaning of facial expression. *Behavioral and Brain Sciences, 33,* 417–433.

Olsson, A., Ebert, J. P., Banaji, M. R., & Phelps, E. A. (2005). The role of social groups in the persistence of learned fear. *Science, 309,* 785–787.

Papez, J. W. (1937). A proposed mechanism of emotion. *Archives of Neurology and Psychiatry, 79,* 217–224.

Parkinson, J. A., Cardinal, R. N., & Everitt, B. J. (2000). Limbic cortical-ventral striatal systems underlying appetitive conditioning. *Progressive Brain Research, 126,* 263–285.

Pegna, A. J., Khateb, A., Lazeyras, F., & Seghier, M. L. (2004). Discriminating emotional faces without primary visual cortices involves the right amygdala. *Nature Neuroscience, 8,* 24–25.

Peyrin, C., Mermillod, M., Chokron, S., & Marendaz, C. (2006). Effect of temporal constraints on hemispheric asymmetries during spatial frequency processing. *Brain & Cognition, 62,* 214–220.

Phan, K. L., Wager, T., Taylor, S. F., & Liberzon, I. (2002). Functional neuroanatomy of emotion: A meta-analysis of emotion activation studies in PET and fMRI. *Neuroimage, 16,* 331–348.

Pourtois, G., Dan, E. S., Grandjean, D., Sander, D., & Vuilleumier, P. (2005). Enhanced extrastriate visual response to bandpass spatial frequency filtered fearful faces: Time course and topographic evoked-potentials mapping. *Human Brain Mapping, 26,* 65–79.

Pourtois, G., Thut, G., Grave de Peralta, R., Michel, C., & Vuilleumier, P. (2005). Two electrophysiological stages of spatial orienting towards fearful faces: Early temporo-parietal activation preceding gain control in extrastriate visual cortex. *Neuroimage, 26,* 149–163.

Scherer, K. R. (1984a). Emotion as a multicomponent process: A model and some cross-cultural data. In P. Shaver & L. Wheeler (Eds.), *Review of personality and social psychology* (Vol. 5, pp. 37–63). Beverly Hills, CA: Sage.

Scherer, K. R. (1984b). On the nature and function of emotion: A component process approach. In K. R. Scherer & P. Ekman (Eds.), *Approaches to emotion* (pp. 293–328). Hillsdale, NJ: Erlbaum.

Scherer, K. R. (1999). Appraisal theories. In T. Dalgleish & M. Power (Eds.), *Handbook of cognition and emotion* (pp. 638–663). Chichester, UK: Wiley.

Schultz, W. (2002). Getting formal with dopamine and reward. *Neuron, 36,* 241–263.

Schyns, P. G., & Oliva, A. (1999). Dr. Angry and Mr. Smile: When categorization flexibly modifies the perception of faces in rapid visual presentations. *Cognition, 69,* 243–265.

Smith, C. A., & Ellsworth, P. C. (1985). Patterns of cognitive appraisal in emotion. *Journal of Personality and Social Psychology, 48,* 813–838.

Sonnby-Borgstrom, M. (2002). Automatic mimicry reactions as related to differences in emotional empathy. *Scandinavian Journal of Psychology, 43,* 433–443.

Strack, F., Martin, L. L., & Stepper, S. (1988). Inhibiting and facilitating conditions of the human smile: A nonobstrusive test of the facial feedback hypothesis. *Journal of Personality and Social Psychology, 54,* 768–777.

van der Gaag, C., Minderaa, R., & Keysers, C. (2007). The BOLD signal in the amygdala does not differentiate between dynamic facial expressions. *Social Cognitive and Affective Neuroscience, 2,* 93–103.

Vuilleumier, P., Armony, J. L., Driver, J., & Dolan, R. J. (2003). Distinct spatial frequency sensitivities for processing faces and emotional expressions. *Nature Neuroscience, 6,* 624–631.

Wallbott, H. G. (1991). Recognition of emotion from facial expression via imitation? Some indirect evidence for an old theory. *British Journal of Social Psychology, 30(Part 3),* 207–219.

Whalen, P. J., Shin, L. M, McInerney, S. C., Fischer, H., Wright, C. I., & Rauch, S. L. (2001). A functional MRI study of human amygdala responses to facial expressions of fear vs. anger. *Emotion, 1,* 70–83.

Wicker, B., Keysers, C., Plailly, J., Royet, J.-P., Gallese, V., & Rizzolatti, G. (2003). Both of us disgusted in my insula: The common neural basis of seeing and felling disgust. *Neuron, 40,* 655–664.

Winston, J. S., O'Doherty, J., & Dolan, R. J. (2003). Common and distinct neural responses during direct and incidental processing of multiple facial emotions. *NeuroImage, 20,* 84–97.

Yang, T. T., Menon, V., Eliez, S., Blasey, C., White, C. D., Reid, A. J., et al. (2002). Amygdalar activation associated with positive and negative facial expressions. *Neuroreport, 13,* 1737–1741.

Yelnik, J., Bardinet, E., Dormont, D., Malandain, G., Ourselin, S., Tandé, D., et al. (2007). A three-dimensional, histological and deformable atlas of the human basal ganglia. I. Atlas construction based on immunohistochemical and MRI data. *NeuroImage, 34,* 618–638.

4

How Do Emotional Facial Expressions Influence Our Perception of Time?

SANDRINE GIL and SYLVIE DROIT-VOLET

THE TEMPORAL DYNAMIC OF THE SOCIAL INTERACTION AND THE ROLE OF FACIAL EXPRESSIONS: INTRODUCTION

*T*he effectiveness of social interaction mainly rests on the capacity of two interlocutors to share time; to coordinate, for example, their rate of speech; or to answer the requests of one or the other at an appropriate moment, neither too early nor too late. Social interaction thus fits into a temporal dynamic, which requires of each individual the uninterrupted processing of temporal information (Chambon, Droit-Volet, & Niedenthal, 2008; Chambon, Gil, Niedenthal, & Droit-Volet, 2005; Droit-Volet & Gil, 2009; Droit-Volet & Meck, 2007). Our objective is to study this social time, more precisely, time perception, in social interactions.

Within the framework of social interactions, facial expressions provide information about the emotions and the intentions of others (Keltner & Haidt, 2001; Keltner & Kring, 1998; Russell & Fernandez-Dols, 1997). Facial expressions thus convey efficiently important indices for understanding the state of the others and for inferences regarding action readiness (Darwin, 1872/1998; Ekman, 1982, 1999; Frijda, 1986; Ledoux, 1996). The question is: Does our perception of time change with the perception of various facial expressions? For example, does time seem to pass more slowly in the presence of an angry person than in the presence of a person not expressing any particular emotion? To answer this question, we have conducted a series of experiments examining the impact of the perception of facial expressions on time perception. We thus present initially the theoretical framework, then the method used, and finally the main results found.

THE PROCESSING OF TEMPORAL INFORMATION IS BASED ON AN INTERNAL CLOCK

There is considerable evidence that human beings, like any other animals, have an internal mechanism for measurement of time, operating like a genuine clock. According to the dominant model of the internal clock proposed by Gibbon, Church, and Meck (1984), the internal clock is composed of three elements: (1) a time base, (2) a switch, and (3) an accumulator (Figure 4.1). The time base (the pacemaker) runs like a pulse generator, sending pulses to the accumulator via the switch. More precisely, at the beginning of a stimulus to be timed, the switch closes, allowing pulses to be transferred during the timed interval. At the end of the stimulus period, the switch opens, interrupting the flow of pulses. The duration judgment (that is, subjective time) depends on the number of accumulated pulses: The greater the number of pulses, the longer the stimulus duration is considered to be.

Owing to this internal mechanism, individuals are able to estimate time in a precise manner and from an early age (Droit-Volet, Clément, & Wearden, 2001; Droit-Volet & Wearden, 2001, 2002). However, our perception of time is sometimes prone to distortions; we have all experienced the feeling that time seems to be shorter or longer than it is in reality. Among the processes likely to disturb the mechanism of the internal clock, two main processes have been highlighted: (1) an attention-based process and (2) an arousal-based process. According to the attentional models of time (Zakay, 1989, 1992; Zakay & Block, 1996), the fewer the attentional resources that are allocated to the passage of time, the shorter the time seems to be. Indeed, when attention is distracted away from the processing of time,

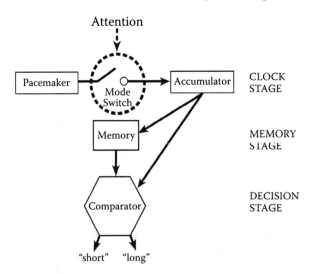

Figure 4.1   The temporal information-processing model. (From Gibbon, J., Church, R. M., & Meck, W. Scalar timing in memory. *Annals of the New Academy of Sciences, 423*, 52–77, 1984. With permission.)

the switch-closing latency is prolonged or the switch flickers during the stimulus duration. Consequently, pulses are lost, and the stimulus duration is judged to be shorter than it is objectively. A large number of studies have reported an underestimation of time when attention is diverted away from time (Coull, Vidal, Nazarian, & Macar, 2004; Fortin, 2003; Gautier & Droit-Volet, 2002; Zakay, 2005). On the other hand, empirical findings have shown that an increase in the level of arousal increases the speed of the pacemaker. For a given amount of time, the pacemaker runs faster, more pulses are collected in the accumulator, and stimulus duration is judged to be longer. A substantial body of research has effectively shown time overestimation due to arousal, involving arousal modifiers such as body temperature (for a review, see Wearden & Penton-Voak, 1995); repetitive stimuli such as clicks or visual flickers (Droit-Volet & Wearden, 2002; Penton-Voak, Edwards, Percival, & Wearden, 1996; Treisman & Brogan, 1992; Wearden, Norton, Martin, & Montford-Bebb, 2007); and pharmacological substances (Carrasco, Redolat, & Simon, 1998; Cheng, Ali, & Meck, 2007; Maricq, Roberts, & Church, 1981; Matell, Bateson, & Meck, 2006; Meck, 1996).

METHOD OF STUDY: THE TEMPORAL BISECTION TASK

To study the effect of emotional facial expressions on time perception, we used the temporal bisection task. This time perception task is commonly employed in human studies (e.g., Allan & Gibbon, 1991; Delgado & Droit-Volet, 2007; Droit-Volet, Clément, & Fayol, 2008; Droit-Volet, Meck, & Penney, 2007; Droit-Volet & Rattat, 2007; Lustig & Meck, 2001; Penney, Gibbon, & Meck, 2000; Wearden, 1991a, 1991b; Wearden, Todd, & Jones, 2006), as well as in animal studies (e.g., Church & Deluty, 1977; Meck, 1983; Miki & Santi, 2005; Orduna, Hong, & Bouzas, 2007). In our experiments, this temporal task is composed of two phases: (1) a training phase and (2) a test phase. During the training phase, two standard durations, one short (400 ms) and one long (1,600 ms), are presented in the form of a neutral stimulus, in fact an oval that appears in the center of the computer screen. Then, these two standard durations are each presented four times, in a random order. The subject has to learn how to discriminate them while pressing on a response key. For example, a press on the "K" key is correct following the short standard duration, and a press on the "D" key is correct after the long standard duration, these two keys being counterbalanced across subjects. In the test phase, the two standard durations as well as five intermediate values (600, 800, 1,000, 1,200, 1,400 ms) are presented in the form of faces, which express a specific emotion or neutrality (Figure 4.2). The neutral faces are used here as a control condition. In this test phase, the subject receives the same instructions as in the training phase, namely, to indicate on the appropriate key if the presentation duration of the face corresponds to the short or to the long standard duration.

In the temporal bisection task, one calculates the proportion of long responses for each stimulus duration. Then, as one can see in Figure 4.3, we calculate a

Anger   Fear   Happiness
Non-Duchenne smile

Neutral

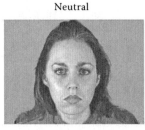

Disgust   Sadness   Shame

Figure 4.2 Example of the emotional facial expressions tested. (From Beaupré, M. G., & Hess, U. Cross-cultural emotion recognition among Canadian ethnic groups. *Journal of Cross-Cultural Psychology, 26,* 355–370, 2005. With permission.)

difference index (d scores) for each stimulus duration. The d corresponds to the difference between the proportion of long responses for the emotional faces and the neutral ones. A d value significantly greater than 0 thus reflects an overestimation of time for emotional expressions compared to neutral faces, whereas a d significantly lower than 0 reflects an underestimation of time.

TIME DISTORTIONS VARY AS A FUNCTION OF EMOTIONAL FACIAL EXPRESSIONS

Figure 4.3 presents d scores plotted against stimulus durations for each emotional facial expression that we have tested (anger, fear, happiness, sadness, disgust, and shame) and for each age group (5- and 8-year-olds and adults).

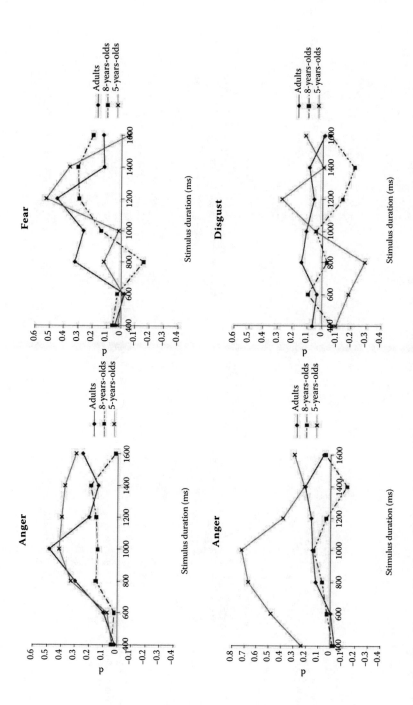

Figure 4.3   The *d* scores plotted against the probe durations for each tested emotional facial expression and for each age group (the 5- and 8-year-olds and the adults). *Continued*

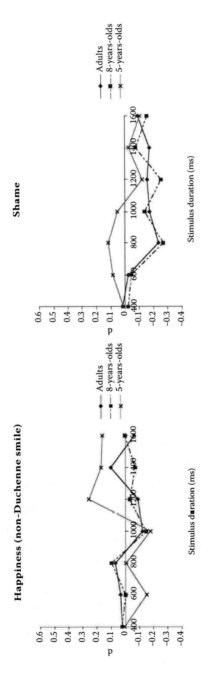

Figure 4.3 (*Continued*)   The *d* scores plotted against the probe durations for each tested emotional facial expression and for each age group (the 5- and 8-year-olds and the adults).

The Facial Expressions of Anger, Fear, Happiness, and Sadness Involve an Overestimation of Time

As shown in Figure 4.3, the d is significantly greater than 0 for the faces expressing anger and fear. The presentation duration of these emotional faces is thus overestimated compared to that of a neutral face. Moreover, this overestimation appears for all age groups; in a previous study, this effect was reported for children as young as 3 years of age (Gil, Niedenthal, & Droit-Volet, 2007).

Statistical analyses, based on the model of the internal clock, suggested that this overestimation of time would be due to an increase in the pacemaker rate. When the pacemaker runs faster, more pulses are accumulated, and the duration is considered to be longer. This effect is consistent with the results of studies showing that anger and fear are particularly arousing emotions (Calder, Keane, Lawrence, & Manes, 2004; Phelps & Ledoux, 2005). In this vein, the perception of anger or fear would increase, in an automatic way, the level of arousal of the organism to prepare it to react to a dangerous event as quickly as possible. In the presence of an angry face announcing the possibility of a threat, the clock rates would thus increase in an automatic manner. Indeed, the more rapidly time elapses, the quicker the organism is ready to react, to flee, or to attack.

Within the framework of evolutionary theories of emotions (Darwin, 1872/1998; Ekman, 1982), we can suggest that time distortions involved by the perception of a facial expression of anger or fear give an account of an early adaptive function of the emotions, preparing the organism to action in the service of survival. This idea is consistent with studies showing that threatening stimuli or stressful situations induce an overestimation of time (Angrilli, Cherubini, Pavese, & Manfredini, 1997; Handcock & Weaver, 2005; Langer, Wapner, & Werner, 1961; Meck, 1983; Noulhiane, Mella, Samson, Ragot, & Pouthas, 2007; Watts & Sharrock, 1984).

An overestimation of time has also been observed with the presentation of facial expressions of happiness and sadness (Droit-Volet, Brunot, & Niedenthal, 2004; Effron, Niedenthal, Gil, & Droit-Volet, 2006), regardless of the age of the subject, although overestimation appears to a greater extent for anger and fear than for happiness and sadness. However, as Figure 4.3 shows, the overestimation of time did not appear in the present study for the happiness condition, as it did in previous studies (Droit-Volet et al., 2004; Effron et al., 2006). In fact, in prior studies, happy faces exhibited a Duchenne smile (true smile), whereas in this study it was a non-Duchenne smile (false smile). The former smile is distinguished from the latter by the contraction of both the zygomaticus major and the orbicularis oculi muscles (see Figure 4.4) (Duchenne, 1862/1990; Ekman, 1989). The non-Duchenne smile corresponds to a fake smile, a social smile, whereas the Duchenne smile is related to the experience of enjoyment (Ekman, Davidson, & Friesen, 1990; Soussignan, 2002; Surakka & Hietanen, 1998). In a complementary study using both Duchenne and non-Duchenne smiles, results revealed effectively that an overestimation of time is only observed with the presentation of a true smile (nonpublished data, 2007). This result supports the idea that only Duchenne smiles imply affiliation behaviors (Mehu, Grammer, & Dunbar, 2007; Papa & Bonanno, 2008). Concerning sadness, this emotion is generally recognized as less arousing,

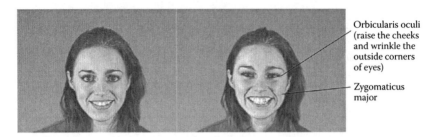

Figure 4.4   Example of a happy face with a non-Duchenne smile (left) or a Duchenne smile (right). (From Beaupré, M. G., & Hess, U. Cross-cultural emotion recognition among Canadian ethnic groups. *Journal of Cross-Cultural Psychology, 26*, 355–370, 2005. With permission.)

inducing a general slowing of the individual (Russell, 1980; Schwartz, Weinberger, & Singer, 1981). However, the perception of an expression of sadness is different from experiencing sadness. Some theorists suggest that a sad expression informs the perceiver that the perceived individual needs help (Fridlund, 1997). In this vein, we can suppose that the perception of a sad face increases the level of arousal of the perceiver to give assistance.

An additional finding in our results was a developmental change in the effects of the facial expressions on temporal performance for anger and sadness. Indeed, the magnitude of the temporal overestimation appears larger in 5-year-old children than in the older subjects. Part of this difference may arise from the appearance with age of a social control of emotions. Indeed, the acquisition of rules concerning emotional expressivity forms an integral part of the acquisition of social rules (Cole, 1986). Several studies show that during development, the child learns how to dissimulate some prejudicial emotional expressions. In our Western countries, the child would thus learn how to mask his or her anger, which is considered to be pejorative (Saarni & von Salisch, 1993; Underwood, 1997), and how to mask sadness, which would reveal vulnerability (Saarni, 1979). In short, with development, the facial expressions of anger and sadness would have a lower impact on time perception due to the acquisition of social rules. Nevertheless, it remains to be determined if this reduction in temporal distortions results from a process of inhibition of an automatic internal clock acceleration or from a process of an attentional filter.

The Facial Expression of Disgust Does Not Involve Any Time Distortion

As can be seen in Figure 4.3, with the bisection task the emotional facial expression of disgust does not cause any temporal distortion, regardless of the age of the subjects. We can explain the absence of this effect by the fact that the perception of disgust in others does not induce preparation for an immediate action enabling the organism to avoid imminent danger. Consequently, even though disgust is considered to be a high-arousal emotion, in this case the organism is not required to respond to an imminent threat. Thus, there would be no increase in the level of arousal accelerating the internal clock.

On its basic definition, disgust is strongly linked with contamination, with the rejection of something bad for health (Darwin, 1872/1998; Haidt, McCauley, & Rozin, 1994; Rozin & Fallon, 1987). In other words, it seems that the source of the emotion is particularly important for disgust. By this account, the facial expression of disgust appears not to be a stimulus relevant enough to affect the internal clock. Nevertheless, Angrilli and colleagues (1997), presenting disgusting pictures, such as a mutilated body, in a reproduction task, observed an overestimation of time consistent with a clock-related effect. Our research team, presenting disgusting food pictures in a bisection task, observed an underestimation of time consistent with an attention-related effect (Gil, Rousset, & Droit-Volet, 2009). It is thus interesting to note that, for the same emotion, time distortions vary as a function of the significance of the stimulus.

The Facial Expression of Shame Involves an Underestimation of Time

In the adults and the 8-year-old children, the facial expression of shame did not cause an overestimation but an underestimation of time. According to the internal clock model, such underestimation of time would be due to attentional-based processes. Indeed, shame is regarded as a self-conscious emotion, involving a reflexive attitude toward oneself (Haidt, 2003; Izard, 1971). We can thus suppose that shame faces attract attentional resources to the detriment of duration processing. The emotions of anger, fear, happiness, sadness, and disgust are primary emotions, appearing early in life because they have a biological basis as the result of evolution (Darwin, 1872/1998; Ekman, 1984; Izard, 1977; Tomkins, 1962). Shame is a secondary emotion that develops later with social interactions and the internalization of social rules (Lagattuta & Thompson, 2007; Tangney & Dearing, 2002). For this reason, underestimation for shame is not observed in younger children. In an additional study, we showed that 5-year-old children do not recognize the facial expression of shame (Figure 4.5), and that the recognition of the facial expression of shame was required to produce a time distortion. Consequently, the facial expression of shame had no significant impact on time perception in the younger children, who did not recognize the expression of shame (Droit-Volet & Gil, 2009; Gil & Droit-Volet, 2011b).

CONCLUSION

Our studies show that the perception of an emotional facial expression involves a temporal distortion. Moreover, our findings highlight that the direction (over-underestimation) and the amplitude of these temporal distortions depend on the adaptive function of each emotion. The effect of emotional facial expressions on subjective time would be thus closely related to the role of emotions in action (Frijda, 1986). It would now be important to test other temporal tasks, longer ranges of durations, and other kinds of emotional stimuli (e.g., Droit-Volet, Mermillod, Cocenas-Silva, & Gil, 2010; Gil & Droit-Volet, 2011a; Grommet, Droit-Volet, Gil, Hemmes, Baker, & Brown, 2011). The topic of social time thus represents a new and fascinating research domain.

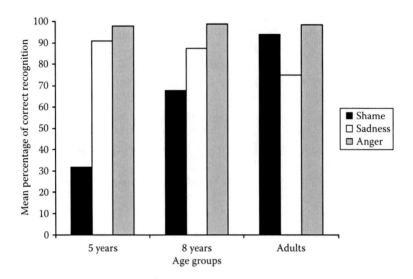

Figure 4.5   Mean percentage of correct responses in an emotional facial recognition task for 5- and 8-year-old children as for adults. (From Gil, S., & Droit-Volet, S. Time perception in presence of ashamed faces in children and adults. *Scandinavian Journal of Psychology,* 2011b.)

REFERENCES

Allan, L. G., & Gibbon, J. (1991). Human bisection at geometric mean. *Learning and Motivation, 22,* 39–58.

Angrilli, A., Cherubini, P., Pavese, A., & Manfredini, S. (1997). The influence of affective factors on time perception. *Perception & Psychophysics, 59,* 972–982.

Beaupré, M. G., & Hess, U. (2005). Cross-cultural emotion recognition among Canadian ethnic groups. *Journal of Cross-Cultural Psychology, 26,* 355–370.

Calder, A. J., Keane, J., Lawrence, A. D., & Manes, F. (2004). Impaired recognition of anger following damage to the ventral striatum. *Brain, 127,* 1958–1969.

Carrasco, C., Redolat, R., & Simon, V. M. (1998). Time estimation in minimally abstinent smokers. *Human Psychopharmacology, 13,* 543–549.

Chambon, M., Droit-Volet, S., & Niedenthal, P. M. (2008). The effect of embodying the elderly on time perception. *Journal of Experimental Social Psychology, 44,* 672–678.

Chambon, M., Gil, S., Niedenthal, P. M., & Droit-Volet, S. (2005). Psychologie sociale et perception du temps: L'estimation temporelle des stimuli sociaux et émotionnels. *Psychologie Française, 50,* 167–180.

Cheng, R.-K., Ali, Y. M., & Meck, W. (2007). Ketamine "unlocks" the reduced clock-speed effects of cocaine following extended training: Evidence for dopamine-glutamate interactions in timing and time perception. *Neurobiology of Learning and Memory, 88,* 149–159.

Church, R. M., & Deluty, M. Z. (1977). Bisection of temporal intervals. *Journal of Experimental Psychology Animal Behavior Process, 3,* 216–228.

Cole, P. M. (1986). Children's spontaneous control of facial expression. *Child Development, 57,* 1309–1321.

Coull, J. T., Vidal, F., Nazarian, B., & Macar, F. (2004). Functional anatomy of the attentional modulation of time estimation. *Science, 303,* 1506–1508.

Darwin, C. (1998). *The expression of the emotions in man and animals*. Oxford, UK: Oxford University Press. (Original work published 1872)

Delgado, M. L., & Droit-Volet, S. (2007). Testing the representation of time in reference memory in the bisection and the generalization task: The utility of a developmental approach. *The Quarterly Journal of Experimental Psychology, 60,* 820–836.

Droit-Volet, S., Brunot, S., & Niedenthal, P. M. (2004). Perception of the duration of emotional events. *Cognition and Emotion, 18,* 849–858.

Droit-Volet, S., Clément, A., & Fayol, M. (2008). Time, number and length: Similarities and differences in bisection behavior in children and adults. *The Quarterly Journal of Experimental Psychology, 61,* 1827–1846.

Droit-Volet, S., Clément, A., & Wearden, J. H. (2001). Temporal generalization in 3- to 8-year-old children. *Journal of Experimental Child Psychology, 80,* 271–288.

Droit-Volet, S., & Gil, S. (2009). The time-emotion paradox. *Journal of Philosophical Transactions of the Royal Society, B (Biological Sciences), 364,* 1943–1953.

Droit-Volet, S., & Meck, W. H. (2007). How emotions colour our time perception. *Trends in Cognitive Sciences, 11,* 504–513.

Droit-Volet, S., Meck, W., & Penney, T. (2007). Sensory modality effect and time perception in children and adults. *Behavioural Processes, 74,* 244–250.

Droit-Volet, S., Mermillod, M., Cocenas-Silva, R., & Gil, S. (2010). The effect of expectancy of a threatening event on time perception in human adults. *Emotion, 10,* 908–914.

Droit-Volet, S., & Rattat, A. C. (2007). A further analysis of temporal bisection behavior in children with and without reference memory: The similarity and the partition task. *Acta Psychologica, 125,* 240–256.

Droit-Volet, S., & Wearden, J. H. (2001). Temporal bisection in children. *Journal of Experimental Child Psychology, 80,* 142–159.

Droit-Volet, S., & Wearden, J. H. (2002). Speeding up an internal clock in children? Effects of visual flicker on subjective duration. *The Quarterly Journal of Experimental Psychology, 55B,* 193–211.

Duchenne, G. B. A. (1990). *The mechanism of human facial expression* (R. A. Cuthbertson, Ed. and Trans.). Cambridge, UK: Cambridge University Press. (Original work published 1862)

Effron, D., Niedenthal, P. M., Gil, S., & Droit-Volet, S. (2006). Embodied temporal perception of emotion. *Emotion, 6,* 1–9.

Ekman, P. (1982). *Emotion in the human face*. New York, Pergamon Press.

Ekman, P. (1984). Expression and the nature of emotion. In K. Scherer and P. Ekman (Eds.), *Approaches to emotion* (pp. 287–306). Hillsdale, NJ: Erlbaum.

Ekman, P. (1989). The argument and evidence about universals in facial expressions of emotion. In H. Wagner & A. Manstead (Eds.), *Handbook of psychophysiology: The biological psychology of emotions and social processes* (pp. 143–164). London: Wiley.

Ekman, P. (1999). Basic emotions. In T. Dalgleish and M. Power (Eds.), *Handbook of cognition and emotion* (pp. 301–320). Sussex, UK: Wiley.

Ekman, P., Davidson, R. J., & Friesen, W. V. (1990). The Duchenne smile: Emotional expression and brain physiology II. *Journal of Personality and Social Psychology, 2,* 342–353.

Fortin, C. (2003). Attentional time-sharing in interval timing. In W. H. Meck (Ed.), *Functional and neural mechanisms of interval timing* (pp. 235–260). Boca Raton, FL: CRC Press.

Fridlund, A. (1997). The new ethology of human facial expressions. In J. Russell & J. Fernandez-Dols (Eds.), *The psychology of facial expression* (pp. 103–129). Cambridge, UK: Cambridge University Press.

Frijda, N. H. (1986). *The emotions*. New York: Cambridge University Press.

Gautier, T., & Droit-Volet, S. (2002). Attention and time estimation in 5- and 8-year-old children: A dual-task procedure. *Behavioral Processes, 58*, 57–66.

Gibbon, J., Church, R. M., & Meck, W. (1984). Scalar timing in memory. *Annals of the New Academy of Sciences, 423*, 52–77.

Gil, S., & Droit-Volet, S. (2011a). Time flies in the presence of angry faces, depending on the temporal task used! *Acta Psychologica, 136*, 354–362.

Gil, S., & Droit-Volet, S. (2011b). Time perception in presence of ashamed faces in children and adults. *Scandinavian Journal of Psychology, 52,* 138–145.

Gil, S., Niedenthal, P. M., & Droit-Volet, S., (2007). Anger and temporal perception in children. *Emotion, 7*, 219–225.

Gil, S., Rousset, S., & Droit-Volet, S. (2009). How liked and disliked food affect time perception. *Emotion, 9*, 457–463.

Grommet, E. K., Droit-Volet, S., Gil, S., Hemmes, N. S., Baker, A. H., & Brown, B. (2011). Time estimation of fear cues in human observers. *Behavioural Processes*.

Haidt, J. (2003). The moral emotions. In R. J. Davidson, K. R. Scherer, & H. H. Goldsmith (Eds.), *Handbook of affective sciences* (pp. 852–870). Oxford, UK: Oxford University Press.

Haidt, J., McCauley, C., & Rozin, P. (1994). Individual differences in sensitivity to disgust: A scale sampling seven domains of disgust elicitors. *Personality and Individual Differences, 16*, 701–713.

Handcock, P. A., & Weaver, J. L. (2005). On time distortion under stress. *Theoretical Issues in Ergonomics Science, 6*, 193–211.

Izard, C. E. (1971). *The face of emotion*. East Norwalk, CT: Appleton-Century-Crofts.

Izard, C. E. (1977). *Human emotions*. New York: Plenum Press.

Keltner, D., & Haidt, J. (2001). Social functions of emotions. In T. Mayne & G. Bonanno (Eds.), *Emotions: Current issues and future directions* (pp. 192–213). New York: Guilford Press.

Keltner, D., & Kring, A. M. (1998). Emotion, social function, and psychopathology. *Review of General Psychology, 2*, 320–342.

Lagattuta, K. H., & Thompson, R. A. (2007). The development of self-conscious emotions: Cognitive processes and social influences. In J. L. Tracy, R. W. Robins, & J. P. Tangney (Eds.), *The self-conscious emotions: Theory and research* (pp. 91–113). New York: Guilford.

Langer, J., Wapner, S., & Werner, H. (1961). The effect of danger upon the experience of time. *American Journal of Psychology, 74*, 94–97.

Ledoux, J. E. (1996). *The emotional brain*. New York: Simon and Schuster.

Lustig, C., & Meck, W. H. (2001). Paying attention to time as one gets older. *Psychological Sciences, 12*, 478–484.

Maricq, A. V., Roberts, S., & Church, R. M. (1981). Methamphetamine and time estimation. *Journal of Experimental Psychology: Animal Behavior Processes, 7*, 18–30.

Matell, M. S., Bateson, M., & Meck, W. H. (2006). Single-trials analyses demonstrate that increases in clock speed contribute to the methamphetamine-induced horizontal shifts in peak-interval timing functions. *Psychopharmacology, 188*, 201–212.

Meck, W. H. (1983). Selective adjustment of speed of internal clock and memory processes. *Journal of Experimental Psychology: Animal Behavior Processes, 9*, 171–201.

Meck, W. H. (1996). Neuropharmacology of timing and time perception. *Cognitive Brain Research, 3*, 227–242.

Mehu, M., Grammer, K., & Dunbar, R. I. M. (2007). Smiles when sharing. *Evolution and Human Behavior, 28*, 415–422.

Miki, A., & Santi, A. (2005). The perception of empty and filled time intervals by pigeons. *The Quarterly Journal of Experimental Psychology, 58*, 31–45.

Noulhiane, M., Mella, N., Samson, S., Ragot, R., & Pouthas, V. (2007). How emotional auditory stimuli modulate time perception. *Emotion, 7*, 697–704.

Orduna, V., Hong, E., & Bouzas, A. (2007). Interval bisection in spontaneously hypertensive rats. *Behavioural Processes, 10,* 107–111.

Papa, A., & Bonanno, G. A. (2008). Smiling in the face of adversity: The interpersonal and intrapersonal functions of smiling. *Emotion, 8,* 1–12.

Penney, T. B., Gibbon, J., & Meck, W. H. (2000). Differential effects of auditory and visual signals on clock speed and temporal memory. *Journal of Experimental Psychology: Human Perception and Performance, 26,* 1770–1787.

Penton-Voak, I. S., Edwards, H., Percival, A., & Wearden, J. H. (1996). Speeding up an internal clock in humans? Effects of click trains on subjective duration. *Journal of Experimental Psychology, 3,* 307–320.

Phelps, E. A., & Ledoux, J. E. (2005). Contributions of the amygdala to emotion processing: From animal models to human behavior. *Neuron, 48,* 175–187.

Rozin, P., & Fallon, A. E. (1987). A perspective on disgust. *Psychological Review, 94,* 23–41.

Russell, J. A. (1980). A circumplex model of affect. *Journal of Personality and Social Psychology, 39,* 1161–1178.

Russell, J. A., & Fernandez-Dols, J. M. (1997). *The psychology of facial expression.* Cambridge, UK: Cambridge University Press.

Saarni, C. (1979). Children's understanding of display rules for expressive behavior. *Developmental Psychology, 15,* 424–429.

Saarni, C., & von Salisch, M. (1993). The socialization of emotional dissemblance. In M. Lewis & C. Saarni (Eds.), *Lying and deception in everyday life* (pp. 106–125). New York: Guilford Press.

Schwartz, G. E., Weinberger, D. A., & Singer, J. A. (1981). Cardiovascular differentiation of happiness, sadness, anger, and fear following imagery and exercise. *Psychosomatic Medicine, 43,* 343–364.

Soussignan, R. (2002). Duchenne smile, emotional experience, and autonomic reactivity: A test of the facial feedback hypothesis. *Emotion, 2,* 52–74.

Surakka, V., & Hietanen, J. K. (1998). Facial and emotional reactions to Duchenne and non-Duchenne smiles. *International Journal of Psychophysiology, 29,* 23–33.

Tangney, J. P., & Dearing, R. L. (2002). *Shame and guilt.* New York: Guilford Press.

Tomkins, S. S. (1962–1963). *Affect, imagery, consciousness* (Vols. 1 and 2). *The positive affects.* New York: Springer.

Treisman, M., & Brogan, D. (1992). Time perception and the internal clock: Effects of visual flicker on the temporal oscillator. *European Journal of Cognitive Psychology, 4,* 41–70.

Underwood, M. K. (1997). Top 10 pressing questions about the development of emotion regulation. *Motivation and Emotion, 21,* 127–146.

Watts, F. N., & Sharrock, R. (1984). Fear and time estimation. *Perceptual and Motor Skills, 59,* 597–598.

Wearden, J. H. (1991a). Do humans possess an internal clock with scalar timing properties? *Learning and Motivation, 22,* 59–83.

Wearden, J. H. (1991b). Human performance on an analogue of an internal bisection task. *The Quarterly Journal of Experimental Psychology, 43B,* 59–81.

Wearden, J. H., Norton, R., Martin, S., & Montford-Bebb, O. (2007). Internal clock processes and the filled duration illusion. *Journal of Experimental Psychology: Human Perception and Performance, 33,* 716–729.

Wearden, J. H., & Penton-Voak, I. S. (1995). Feeling the heat: Body temperature and the rate of subjective time revisited. *The Quarterly Journal of Experimental Psychology, 48B,* 129–141.

Wearden, J. H., Todd, N. P. M., & Jones, L. A. (2006). When do auditory/visual differences in duration judgements occur? *The Quarterly Journal of Experimental Psychology, 59,* 1709–1724.

Zakay, D. (1989). Subjective time and attentional resource allocation: An integrated model of time estimation. In I. Levin & D. Zakay (Eds.), *Time and human cognition* (pp. 365–397). Amsterdam: North-Holland.

Zakay, D. (1992). The role of attention in children's time perception. *Journal of Experimental Child Psychology, 54*, 355–371.

Zakay, D. (2005). Attention et jugement temporel. *Psychologie Française, 50*, 65–79.

Zakay, D., & Block, R. A. (1996). The role of attention in time estimation processes. In M. A. Pastor and J. Artieda (Eds.), *Time, internal clocks and movement* (pp. 143–164). Amsterdam: Elsevier.

Section *II*

Representation and Processing and the Role of Emotion and Motivation

5

Mood's Influence on Semantic Memory
Valence or Arousal?

ANNE-LAURE GILET and CHRISTOPHE JALLAIS

INTRODUCTION

*F*or years emotion and cognition have been considered as two distinct areas of research. Indeed, the attention was primarily given to the cognitive aspects of human functioning. Models of semantic memory were based on architecture and processes that were supposed to be insensitive to the (emotional) context. However, there has recently been renewed interest in the study of emotions, and their relationships with cognition appeared. Nonetheless, it seems necessary to be precise about what we mean by *affect, emotion,* and *mood*. Generally, *affect* is used as a more general term referring to *emotion* as well as *mood* (Bower & Forgas, 2000; Forgas, 1995, Exp. 3). There seems to be a consensus on the fact that *emotions* involve a subject–object relationship. Emotions are generally brief and are triggered in response to an object or a specific easily identifiable situation (Bower & Forgas, 2000). Moreover, because of their intensity, emotions usually interrupt the cognitive activities of an individual. On the other hand, a *mood* is a much less specific and more general state. Mood refers to a less-intense state but a durable and a pervasive one, always present in the background and thus less accessible to the conscience (Forgas, 1995). In addition, unlike emotions, moods do not disrupt the behavior of subjects, mainly because of their lower intensity (Ellis & Moore, 1999; Hänze & Hesse, 1993). Nevertheless, the distinction between emotion and mood poses some difficulties. Indeed, both emotional states maintain special relationships: Emotions often drain a state of latent mood that persists even beyond the effect of emotions itself.

As moods seem to be more enduring and less conscious than emotions, researchers investigated mainly the consequences of mood states on cognitive functioning. The development and the refinement of mood induction procedures in laboratory settings have prompted the intensification of research investigating cognitive consequences of both negative and positive mood states as well as the mechanisms underlying such effects (e.g., Gilet, 2008; Martin, 1990).

This chapter thus examines the influence of induced mood states on the information processing of nonemotional information. In the first part of this chapter, we present main theoretical hypotheses and models as well as some empirical evidence in favor of (1) the influence of mood as a global feeling and (2) the influence of valence (i.e., positive vs. negative mood). In the second part of this chapter, we review some empirical evidence indicating that a valence-based framework may not be the proper one. Indeed, a growing body of research concurs that another dimension of mood, namely arousal, may be responsible for the effects previously attributed to emotional valence variations.

Mood Influences Memory and Cognitive Processes

The primary interest of earlier studies on emotion and cognition was to better understand memory biases associated with naturally occurring negative moods. Consequently, the first models were initially developed in the context of memory research and more specifically emotion-congruent biases associated with depression or anxiety, such as the mood-congruent effect by which congruent information is better memorized than noncongruent information (e.g., Blaney, 1986; Colombel, Gilet, & Corson, 2004).

One of the most influential models developed to account for these effects is probably the mood-memory network model (Bower, 1981). Bower proposed that emotion nodes are integrated into the semantic network. Emotional nodes, like other nodes, are then activated due to the spread of activation within the network. Accounting for the effects of depressed mood (often generalized to negative mood) on memory, this first model also offered an interesting framework for the study of the influence of mood whatever its valence on memory processing. Together with the development of mood induction procedures in laboratory settings (e.g., Gilet, 2008; Martin, 1990), research investigating cognitive consequences of both negative and positive mood states as well as the mechanisms underlying such effects have further developed.

In an attempt to explain the growing body of empirical findings showing the influence of mood on cognitive functioning and, more precisely, on memory, researchers have developed theoretical propositions and models of emotion–cognition interaction. These theories can be classified along two general hypotheses that are presented separately here (see Corson, 2002, for a review).

Mood Influences Memory Performance Regardless of Its Valence

According to the view that mood influences memory performance regardless of its valence, mood states affect and regulate the amount of attentional resources allocated to cognitive tasks (e.g., Ellis & Ashbrook, 1988; Ellis & Moore, 1999). A depressive or negative mood state will cause memory deficits frequently observed by reducing the available resources due to ruminations or task-irrelevant and personal thoughts. More recently, these assumptions have been extended to positive mood, suggesting that positive mood leads to similar deficits as negative mood by also fostering the activation of irrelevant thoughts (Ellis & Moore, 1999). According to this perspective, mood, whatever its valence, is associated with indirect similar effects. Negative as well as positive moods are thought to impair cognitive processing and performance due to an overload of working memory. Many studies offered support for this theoretical approach, showing that performance and the occurrence of task-irrelevant thoughts are negatively correlated (e.g., Ellis, Ottaway, Varner, Becker, & Moore, 1997; Ellis, Varner, Becker, & Ottaway, 1995), and that positive as well as negative mood states favor the production of task-irrelevant thoughts or task-irrelevant processing, leading to deleterious effects on participants' performance (e.g., Ellis, Thomas, McFarland, & Lane, 1985; Oaksford, Morris, Grainger, & Williams, 1996; Seibert & Ellis, 1991).

Valence Matters: Positive and Negative Moods Lead to Different Effects

Another view of mood influences on memory concerns models that propose that mood acts directly on information processing. The nature of the moods per se is then thought to modify the involved cognitive processes. According to the affect-as-information hypothesis (Schwarz & Clore, 1983, 1988, 2003), positive and negative moods tend to result in different processing styles. Negative mood, which indicates that the environment poses a problem and might be a source of potential dangers, motivates people to change their situation. Negative mood is then thought to be associated with a systematic elaboration of information and greater attention to details. As a result, people would adopt systematic and detail-oriented processing based on bottom-up processes (e.g., Bless, Clore, et al., 1996). Superiority of negative mood has thus been highlighted in studies requiring strategic processes or fostering analytic processing of information (Hesse & Spies, 1996).

Support for this hypothesis has been found in studies examining the effects of mood variations on the false memory effect. In two experiments, Storbeck and Clore (2005) investigated the influence of induced positive and negative moods on the production of false memory using the Deese-Roediger-McDermott (DRM) paradigm (Roediger & McDermott, 1995). In this paradigm, participants are presented with lists of words associated with a nonpresented one (i.e., the critical lure that is frequently recalled or recognized together with studied words in a subsequent memory test). Following the affect-as-information hypothesis, the authors predicted that positive mood rather than negative mood should foster the false memory effect. Their results showed that false recall of critical lure was significantly reduced for participants in negative mood in comparison to participants in positive or neutral moods. This greater accuracy associated with negative mood provided empirical evidence that negative mood fosters the use of an analytic and detail-oriented mode of processing.

On the other hand, positive mood is thought to signal that the environment or situation is safe and benign, thus reducing an individual's motivation to improve his or her situation. Consequently, individuals in a positive mood may be more likely to rely on their general knowledge structures and on the use of simple heuristics in information processing (e.g., Clore & Huntsinger, 2007; Huntsinger, Sinclair, & Clore, 2009; Huntsinger, Sinclair, Dunn, & Clore, 2010; Park & Banaji, 2000). The activation of these general knowledge structures also allows individuals to enrich available information, create potentially useful inferences, and promote a new organization of conceptual relations in semantic memory (Bless & Fiedler, 2006; Bless, Schwarz, & Wieland, 1996). In a large body of work, Isen (see Isen, 2000, for a review) relatedly argued that positive mood leads people to see relatedness and interconnections among concepts stored in memory, thus facilitating more inte-grated cognitive organization—an organization that promotes flexibility, innova-tion, and creative thinking (Isen, 1999; Isen & Daubman, 1984; Isen, Daubman, & Gorgoglione, 1987; Isen, Daubman, & Nowicki, 1987; Isen, Johnson, Mertz, & Robinson, 1985; Lee & Sternthal, 1999). These arguments are also consistent with suggestions that positive mood, while creating a more complex cognitive context, leads to better integration of information in memory and a broader range of cogni-tion (Bolte, Goschke, & Kuhl, 2003; Fredrickson, 1998; Fredrickson & Branigan, 2005; Jallais & Corson, 2008).

This influence of positive mood on knowledge organization was highlighted in many experimental situations: Subjects in positive mood categorized more easily atypical exemplars as members of a category (Isen & Daubman, 1984) or produced more first unusual and diverse associates than subjects in neutral mood in response to neutral inductors (Isen et al., 1985). In two experiments, the authors showed that participants in a positive mood produce more first unusual and diverse associates than participants in a neutral mood in response to neutral inductors. These results suggest that patterns of association changed under positive mood are also consis-tent with suggestions that positive mood, while creating a more complex cognitive context, leads to a better integration of information in memory and greater flex-ibility. In line with this, Phillips, Bull, Adams, and Fraser (2002) provided evidence that induced positive mood, contrary to neutral mood, enhanced performance on a creative test (i.e., fluency task). Similarly, in a study using a creative word problem-solving task, Rowe, Hirsh, and Anderson (2007) showed that participants under a positive mood correctly solved more problems than participants in a neutral or neg-ative mood. The authors suggested that positive mood promotes greater access for semantic associations, which is consistent with the hypothesis of greater flexibility and a change in the patterns of semantic associations under a positive mood state.

Related to this, positive mood is also thought to have direct effects on the spreading activation in semantic memory by increasing the permeability of the network (Hänze & Hesse, 1993). Hänze and Hesse suggested that positive mood has a direct effect on the nature of the cognitive processes. More specifically, they made the assumption that positive mood facilitates the spread of activation in the semantic network. In their experiment, subjects (in positive and neutral moods) were asked to make lexical decisions on the target that was either highly or weakly associated to primes presented 200 ms before. The authors obtained a significant "mood" × "relatedness" interaction for high but not for low associative strength. Hänze and Hesse (1993) concluded that mood has a direct effect on the spreading activation in semantic memory independently of the emotional valence of the processed material by improving the permeability of the network, leading to the enrichment of the cognitive organization. Consistent with this, Bäuml and Kuhbandner (2009) illustrated the powerful effect of positive mood on the spread of activation in semantic memory using a directed forgetting paradigm. More specifically, the authors showed that induced positive mood, contrary to induced negative mood, eliminated the intentional forgetting of previously studied words.

In summary, the research previously presented has thus mainly investigated the effects of mood considering only its *valence* (positive vs. negative). However, besides the opposition positive-versus-negative mood valence, other distinctions could be highlighted. Many studies have shown that other dimensions of mood may affect cognitive processing. More precisely, research on the specific effects of *arousal* on memory (Clore & Storbeck, 2006; Eysenck, 1976; Revelle & Loftus, 1992) leads us to consider these results differently. As arousal has not been systematically examined or measured in the studies previously described, one cannot rule out the possibility that the effects observed are due to variations in the level of arousal rather than due to valence. Arousal, consequently, may be the underlying mechanism in studies examining valence effects. The distinction between valence and arousal is particularly relevant because mood induction procedures commonly used in studies have shown their effectiveness in producing changes in both the valence and arousal dimensions of mood (Gayle, 1997; Jallais & Gilet, 2010).

AND WHAT ABOUT THE IMPACT OF AROUSAL?

Defining Arousal: Facing Complexity

Studies on affect have shown that another dimension of mood, together with valence, best characterizes the structure of affect, namely, *arousal*. Valence and arousal are then generally treated as two independent dimensions (Watson & Tellegen, 1985; Yik, Russell, & Feldman-Barrett, 1999). This two-dimensional model of affect is supported by data in neuroscience. Much research showed that valence and arousal are underpinned by different brain circuits (Anders, Lotze, Erb, Grodd, & Birbaumer, 2004; Kensinger, 2004; Kensinger & Schacter, 2006; Nielen et al., 2009). Even so, and in contrast to the definition of valence, which is a hedonic value of a mood state varying along a pleasant–unpleasant, agreeable–disagreeable, or a positive–negative continuum (e.g., Feldman-Barrett, 2004; Kensinger & Schacter, 2006; Revelle & Loftus, 1992), the definition of arousal remains problematic; the ambiguity around the concept of arousal is especially evident in psychophysiological literature. It is then difficult to consider arousal as a general and unitary concept (Barrett, Mesquita, Ochsner, & Gross, 2007; Heller, 1993; Heller, Nitschke, & Lindsay, 1997). Arousal should not be regarded as equivalent to affect intensity (Barrett & Russell, 1999), and for some authors, arousal refers to either the intensity of an event ranging from very calming, relaxing to highly exciting (e.g., Kensinger & Schacter, 2006; Russell, 1980) or the perception of arousal associated with an emotional experience (e.g., Feldman, 1995). Affect is also sometimes defined as a level of vigilance or activation (Duffy, 1957; Humphreys & Revelle, 1984; Revelle & Loftus, 1992). However, a clear distinction between arousal and activation can be made: Arousal and activation are controlled by two separate but interacting neural systems (Pribam & McGuinness, 1975). Nevertheless, the distinction between the two dimensions of valence and arousal is relevant regarding the extent of their relative influence on participants' behavior.

Arousal Influences Cognitive Activities and Information Processing

Having been neglected in studies investigating the effects of mood, arousal has become the object of interest of a growing number of studies in psychology since the late 1990s (see Storbeck & Clore, 2008, for a review). Arousal effects have been shown in many different experimental situations, such as perception and the discrimination of colors (Ziems & Christman, 1998); processing and evaluation of advertisements (e.g., Gorn, Pham, & Sin, 2001); perception of heights (e.g., Stefanucci & Storbeck, 2009); perception of time (Angrilli, Cherubini, Pavese, & Manfredini, 1997; Noulhiane, Mella, Samson, Ragot, & Pouthas, 2007); spatial memory (Brunyé, Mahoney, Augustyn, & Taylor, 2009); affective priming (Hinojosa, Carretie, Mendez-Bertolo, Miguez, & Pozo, 2009); or information processing. For example, a high level of arousal is thought to foster superficial processing (Shapiro, MacInnis, & Park, 2002) or to facilitate the emergence of automatic behavior (Eysenck, 1976). It is also in this context that Hänze and Meyer (1998) proposed that the increased permeability of the semantic network observed associated with positive mood is partly due to a high level of arousal that fosters the spread of activation within the semantic network.

While some researchers manipulated independently valence and the level of arousal (low vs. high), others have decided to focus on the potential effects of specific moods or discrete emotions (Levine & Pizzaro, 2004). These studies yielded interesting differences or similarities between mood states of the same valence depending on their level of arousal (e.g., Bodenhausen, Sheppard, & Kramer, 1994; Levine & Burgess, 1997). For example, anxiety, anger, sadness, and fear may lead to different behaviors in judgment tasks (Keltner, Ellsworth, & Edwards, 1993); decision making and risk perception (Lerner & Keltner, 2000; Raghunathan & Pham, 1999); investigators' crime-related judgments (Ask & Granhag, 2007); or a lexical decision task (Corson, 2006, Exp. 2).

In a series of priming experiments, Corson (2006) investigated the influence of induced mood states varying along valence and arousal on information processing. In the second experiment, the author showed that both anger and fear (high arousal) facilitated lexical decisions for semantically related prime targets in contrast to sadness (low arousal). This result indicates that anger and fear on one side and sadness on the other trigger different types of information processing. The author suggested that anger and fear foster the spread of activation within the semantic network, whereas sadness favors a more analytic type of information processing. Mood states of the same valence (e.g., anger and sadness) may have distinct effects as any mood conveys information beyond valence, such as the level of arousal. Similarly, Bodenhausen and colleagues (1994), investigating the impact of negative affect on social judgment, showed that induced sadness promotes the use of an analytic, detail-oriented mode of processing, whereas anger induction leads participants to process information on a shallow or automatic mode. If sadness (negative valence, lower arousal) triggered a type of processing identical to that fostered by the negative mood usually induced, anger (negative valence, higher arousal) fostered the heuristic or global mode of processing commonly associated with positive mood states (e.g., happiness or joy). This last result suggests that mood states of opposite valence may have similar effects as they share the same level of arousal. More recently, electroencephalogram (EEG) studies reported evidence that the same areas (left prefrontal cortex) are activated under both happiness and anger mood states (see Carver & Harmon-Jones, 2009).

Likewise, it has been suggested that motivational-related approach and avoidance behaviors are independent of valence, leading to evidence that both happiness and anger moods are approach oriented, whereas serenity and sadness are avoidance oriented (e.g., Baas, De Dreu, & Nijstad, 2008; Carver & Harmon-Jones, 2009). Further research is still needed to investigate more thoroughly the influence of these motivational aspects of mood states on memory.

Disentangle Valence and Arousal Effects on Information Processing

In an attempt to disentangle valence and arousal effects on memory, a growing body of research examines the relative impact of positive and negative moods associated with a lower or higher arousal level, creating four mood states by crossing positive and negative valence with high and low levels of arousal (Brunyé et al., 2009; Corson, 2006; Corson & Verrier, 2007; Gilet & Jallais, 2011). For example, Corson (2006, Exp. 3) investigated the influence of two positive moods (serenity and happiness) and two negative moods (sadness and anger) with a low or high level of arousal on the automatic priming of primes and targets associatively or semantically related. These results showed that only positive and negative moods with a high level of arousal facilitated lexical decisions. Moods with a low level of arousal did not lead to any facilitation. Moods of opposite valence (happiness and anger) but with similar high levels of arousal were likely to produce the same effect, highlighting that the level of arousal more than valence may account for the facilitation effects observed that were previously attributed to positive mood.

The same kinds of results were found with false memories (Corson & Verrier, 2007). According to the literature on false memories, two mechanisms can be responsible for the tendency to produce false memories: the item-specific processing (or verbatim) or the relational processing (or gist) during encoding (Brainerd & Reyna, 2005; Hunt & Einstein, 1981). These two mechanisms are thought to have opposite influences on the production of false memories: Relational processing (i.e., encoding items in relation to others in memory) is thought to foster false memories, whereas item-specific processing of information (i.e., encoding specific and distinctive elements of items) is thought to reduce false memories (Smith & Hunt, 1998). If some studies showed the influence of valence on false memories (Storbeck & Clore, 2005), Corson and Verrier (2007) highlighted the importance of the level of arousal in mood states. The researchers investigated the influence of induced happiness and serenity (positive moods with higher and lower levels of arousal, respectively), anger and sadness (negative moods with higher and lower levels of arousal, respectively) on the production of false memory using the DRM paradigm (Roediger & McDermott, 1995). The authors predicted that high-arousal moods rather than low-arousal moods should promote the false recollection of critical lures. Consistent with their prediction, the results showed that participants induced in happiness and anger falsely recalled significantly more critical lures than participants induced in sadness and serenity. Whatever the participant's mood valence, false memories were more frequent in a high-arousal mood (i.e., happiness and anger) than in a low-arousal mood (i.e., serenity and sadness). Taken together, these results argue against the hypothesis that positive mood fosters the propagation of the activation within the network or increases the permeability of the network (Hänze & Meyer, 1998; Isen, 1999). These results rather suggest that higher levels of arousal associated with mood are primarily responsible for these effects rather than the valence. Mechanisms originally described to account for the influence of positive mood on memory may thus be true for high-arousal mood states whatever their valence.

In line with these studies, we investigated the relative influence of valence and arousal on the unusualness of word associations. In particular, we were interested in whether moods with a high level of arousal differed systematically in their effects on word associations than moods with a low level of arousal. As in experiments previously mentioned, valence and arousal factors were crossed, making it possible to consider positive moods with high (happiness) and low (serenity) levels of arousal as well as negative moods with high (anger) and low (sadness) levels of arousal. If the positive valence of mood is responsible for the unusualness of word associations, happy (high-arousal) and serene (low-arousal) groups should show a greater number of unusual first associates than sad and angry groups. However, if arousal is responsible for the unusualness of word associations, happy and angry (high-arousal) groups should show higher means of first unusual associates than sad and serene groups (low arousal).

In our study, 70 undergraduate students (M = 19.46, SD = 3.53) were randomly assigned to one of the four mood conditions: 19 participants in the positive-mood, low-arousal (serenity) condition; 17 participants in the positive-mood, high arousal (happiness) condition; 17 participants in the negative-mood, low-arousal (sadness) condition; and 17 participants in the negative-mood, high-arousal (anger) condition. Valence was assessed with the Brief Mood Introspection Scale (BMIS; Mayer & Gaschke, 1988) and arousal with the matrix from Eich and Metcalfe (1989) before and after the mood induction phase.

Following the mood inductions, performed using a composite technique that associates music and guided imagery (Mayer, Allen, & Beauregard, 1995), participants were asked to write down their first associate to each of the 48 nonemotional inducers proposed (e.g., thick/*épais*, trousers/*pantalon*). Following Isen and colleagues (1985), we used two measures of unusualness. Participants' responses were scored for uniqueness by referring to the word association norms provided by an additional group of 148 undergraduate students (M = 21.90, SD = 4.59). For the

TABLE 5.1   Unusualness of Word Associations for
Participants in Happy (n = 19), Angry (n = 17), Sad (n = 17),
or Serene (n = 17) Mood

Unusualness Criterion	Happy		Angry		Sad		Serene	
	M	SD	M	SD	M	SD	M	SD
First criterion[a]	17.10	6.22	15.17	5.21	12.58	4.22	11.64	4.40
Second criterion[b]	20.00	6.21	18.00	5.39	15.47	5.12	13.64	5.20

[a] Defined in terms of the frequency of the most frequent associate (i.e., is "unusual" if the associate has a score that is 5% or less of the total score of the most frequent associate).

[b] Defined independently of the popularity of the most frequent associate (i.e., is "unusual" if the associate is given by 2.5% or fewer of the participants).

first criterion, a response was considered unusual if it had a score that was 5% or less of the total score of the most frequent associate. For instance, the word *cuisine* was cited in response to the word *casserole* by 56 participants of the 148 respondents. Consequently, any word given by 3 or fewer participants was scored as an unusual response to *cuisine*. This measure provided a different criterion for each word. For the second measure, a response was considered unusual if it was given by 2.5% or fewer of the respondents. Because there were 148 respondents, for this measure, a score of 4 or less was the criterion for the label "unusual."

Table 5.1 provides mean numbers of unusual associates by the mood induction groups. Word associations were examined using a one-way analysis of variance with valence (positive, negative) and arousal (high, low) as between-subject factors. The results revealed a main effect of arousal for the first measure, $F(1, 66) = 11.27$, $MSE = 30.55$, $p < .01$, $\eta^2{}_p = .15$, and for the second measure, $F(1, 66) = 10.79$, $MSE = 26.19$, $p < .01$, $\eta^2{}_p = .14$. In addition, neither the main effect of valence nor the valence × arousal interaction was significant for both the first and the second measure (all $F < 1$).

As expected, analyses revealed the effect of arousal on word associations, with high-arousal moods (happy and angry groups) leading to significantly more unusual first associates than low-arousal moods (sad and serene groups) for each of the two criteria, $t(68) = 3.39$, $p < .01$, Cohen's $d = 0.82$ and $t(68) = 3.34$, $p < .01$, $d = 0.81$, respectively. In addition, participants in positive moods (happy and serene conditions) did not give more unusual associates than participants induced in negative moods (anger and sad conditions) for each of the two measures ($t < 1$). These results replicated results we obtained in a previous study using the same word association task but with another mood induction procedure, namely, the autobiographical recall (Gilet & Jallais, 2011).

In our two recent studies, participants under high-arousal conditions gave less-common associates than participants under low-arousal conditions, indicating that a broader range of concepts is activated by the presentation of the inducers. Consequently, our results suggest that higher-arousal mood states foster the spread of activation within the network, leading to increased availability of concepts that makes low associates as available as the most frequent ones. In line with Corson and Verrier (2007), the results of these studies bring new evidence that arousal by fostering the spread of activation in memory increases relatedness between concepts that can either facilitate the production of unusual associates or create confusion between studied and nonstudied items and thus enhance the probability of false memories. This interpretation is also consistent with findings from previous studies that showed that high levels of arousal lead to superficial processing (Shapiro et al., 2002) or to the facilitation of automatic behavior (Eysenck, 1976).

Our findings confirm and extend those reported by Isen et al. (1985), who showed that positive mood, contrary to negative mood, enhanced the production of unusual associates. But, they also argue against the valence-based hypothesis that suggests that positive mood, contrary to negative mood, triggers a greater propagation of the activation within the network or increases its permeability involving changes in the organization of concepts in memory so that the relatedness among concepts is then more easily perceived and obvious (Hänze & Meyer, 1998; Isen, 1999).

CONCLUSION

The issue of the influence of mood on information processing has been investigated for a long time. First, empirical evidence from the study of naturally occurring mood states (i.e., depression or anxiety) led researchers to suggest that the influence of mood results in mechanisms related to cognitive consequences of mood rather than to the mood per se. Subsequent theories have commonly focused on positive and negative mood states with respect to their specific effects on the execution of cognitive processes. However, this valence-based hypothesis has been challenged not only by research on discrete emotions, but also by recent research investigating the effects of other dimensions of mood.

Indeed, recent debate in the literature has focused on whether valence or arousal is responsible in the processing styles associated with mood states. In this chapter, we reviewed a large body of research suggesting that arousal may be the underlying or confounding factor in studies investigating the effect of mood. Research provided new evidence that moods of different valence but with similar levels of arousal are likely to foster the same effects. Research would benefit from investigating further the impact of arousal levels and specific moods on knowledge organization in semantic memory. Nevertheless, this chapter highlights the importance of taking into account factors such as arousal to better understand how our moods influence our cognitive processing as well as our behaviors.

REFERENCES

Anders, S., Lotze, M., Erb, M., Grodd, W., & Birbaumer, N. (2004). Brain activity underlying emotional valence and arousal: A response-related fMRI study. *Human Brain Mapping, 23*, 200–209.

Angrilli, A., Cherubini, P., Pavese, A., & Manfredini, S. (1997). The influence of affective factors on time perception. *Perception and Psychophysics, 59*, 972–982.

Ask, K., & Granhag, P. A. (2007). Hot cognition in investigative judgments: The differential influence of anger and sadness. *Law and Human Behavior, 31,* 537–551.

Baas, M., De Dreu, C. K., & Nijstad, B. A. (2008). A meta-analysis of 25 years of mood-creativity research: hedonic tone, activation, or regulatory focus? *Psychological Bulletin, 134,* 779–806.

Barrett, L. F., Mesquita, B., Ochsner, K. N., & Gross, J. J. (2007). The experience of emotion. *Annual Review of Psychology, 58,* 373–403.

Barrett, L. F., & Russell, J. (1999). The structure of current affect: Controversies and emerging consensus. *Current Directions in Psychological Science, 8,* 10–14.

Bäuml, K.-H., & Kuhbandner, C. (2009). Positive moods can eliminate intentional forgetting. *Psychonomic Bulletin and Review, 16,* 93–98.

Blaney, P. H. (1986). Affect and memory: A review. *Psychological Bulletin, 99,* 229–246.

Bless, H., Clore, G. L., Schwarz, N., Golisano, V., Rabe, C., & Wolk, M. (1996). Mood and the use of scripts: Does a happy mood really lead to mindlessness? *Journal of Personality and Social Psychology, 71,* 665–679.

Bless, H., & Fiedler, K. (2006). Mood and the regulation of information processing and behavior. In J. P. Forgas (Ed.), *Affect in social cognition and behavior* (pp. 65–84). New York: Psychology Press.

Bless, H., Schwarz, N., & Wieland, R. (1996). Mood and the impact of category membership and individuating information. *European Journal of Social Psychology, 26,* 935–959.

Bodenhausen, G.-V., Sheppard, L. A., & Kramer, G.-P. (1994). Negative affect and social judgment: The differential impact of anger and sadness. *European Journal of Social Psychology, 24,* 45–62.

Bolte, A., Goschke, T., & Kuhl, J. (2003). Emotion and intuition: Effects of positive mood and negative mood on implicit judgments of semantic coherence. *Psychological Science, 14,* 416–421.

Bower, G. H. (1981). Mood and memory. *American Psychologist, 36,* 129–148.

Bower, G. H., & Forgas, J. P. (2000). Affect, memory, and social cognition. In E. Eich (Ed.), *Counter-points: Cognition and emotion* (pp. 87–167). New York: Oxford University Press.

Brainerd, C. J., & Reyna, V. F. (2005). *The science of false memory.* New York: Oxford University Press.

Brunyé, T. T., Mahoney, C. R., Augustyn, J. S., & Taylor, H. A. (2009). Emotional state and local versus global spatial memory. *Acta Psychologica, 130,* 138–146.

Carver, C.-S., & Harmon-Jones, E. (2009). Anger is an approach-related affect: Evidence and implications. *Psychological Bulletin, 135,* 183–204.

Clore, G. L., & Huntsinger, J. R. (2007). How emotions inform judgment and regulate thought. *Trends in Cognitive Sciences, 11,* 393–399.

Clore, G. L., & Storbeck, J. (2006). Affect as information for social judgment, behaviour, and memory. In J. P. Forgas, K. D. Williams, & W. van Hippel (Eds.), *Hearts and minds: Affective influences on social cognition and behavior* (pp. 123–142). New York: Psychology Press.

Colombel, F., Gilet, A.-L., & Corson, Y. (2004). Implicit mood congruent memory bias in dysphoria: Automatic and strategic activation. *Cahiers de Psychologie Cognitive/ Current Psychology of Cognition, 22,* 607–634.

Corson, Y. (2002). Variations émotionnelles et mémoire: Principaux modèles explicatifs [Main models of effects of emotional variations on memory]. *L'année Psychologique, 102,* 109–149.

Corson, Y. (2006). Emotions and propagation of activation in semantic memory. *Canadian Journal of Experimental Psychology/Revue canadienne de psychologie expérimentale, 60,* 127–147.

Corson, Y., & Verrier, N. (2007). Emotions and false memories: Valence or arousal? *Psychological Science, 18*, 208–211.

Duffy, E. (1957). The psychological significance of the concept of "arousal" or "activation." *Psychological Review, 64*, 265–275.

Eich, E., & Metcalfe, J. (1989). Mood dependent memory for internal versus external events. *Journal of Experimental Psychology: Learning, Memory, and Cognition, 15*, 443–455.

Ellis, H.-C., & Ashbrook, P. W. (1988). Resource allocation model of the effects of depressed mood states on memory. In K. Fiedler & J. Forgas (Eds.), *Affect, cognition and social behavior* (pp. 25–44). Toronto: Hogrefe.

Ellis, H.-C., & Moore, B. A. (1999). Mood and memory. In T. Dalgleish & M. J. Power (Eds.), *Handbook of cognition and emotion* (pp. 193–211). Chichester, UK: Wiley.

Ellis, H.-C., Ottaway, S. A., Varner, L.-J., Becker, A. S., & Moore, B. A. (1997). Emotion, motivation and text comprehension: The detection of contradictions in passages. *Journal of Experimental Psychology: General, 126*, 131–146.

Ellis, H.-C., Thomas, R.-L., McFarland, A.-D., & Lane, J. W. (1985). Emotional mood states and retrieval in episodic memory. *Journal of Experimental Psychology: Learning, Memory, and Cognition, 11*, 363–370.

Ellis, H.-C., Varner, L.-J., Becker, A. S., & Ottaway, S. A. (1995). Emotion and prior knowledge in memory and judged comprehension of ambiguous stories. *Cognition and Emotion, 9*, 363–382.

Eysenck, M. W. (1976). Arousal, learning, and memory. *Psychological Bulletin, 83*, 389–404.

Feldman, L.-A. (1995). Valence focus and arousal focus: Individual differences in the structure of affective experience. *Journal of Personality and Social Psychology, 69*, 153–166.

Feldman-Barrett, L. (2004). Feelings or words? Understanding the content of self-report ratings of experienced emotion. *Journal of Personality and Social Psychology, 87*, 266–281.

Forgas, J. (1995). Mood and judgment: The affect infusion model (AIM). *Psychological Bulletin, 117*, 39–66.

Fredrickson, B. L. (1998). What good are positive emotions? *Review of General Psychology, 2*, 300–319.

Fredrickson, B. L., & Branigan, C. (2005). Positive emotions broaden the scope of attention and thought-action repertoires. *Cognition & Emotion, 19*, 313–332.

Gayle, M.-C. (1997). Mood-congruency in recall: The potential effect of arousal. *Journal of Social Behavior and Personality, 12*, 471–480.

Gilet, A.-L. (2008). Procédures d'induction d'humeurs en laboratoire: Une revue critique [Mood induction procedures: A critical review]. *L'Encéphale, 34*, 233–239.

Gilet, A.-L., & Jallais, C. (2011). Valence, arousal, and word associations. *Cognition and Emotion, 25*, 740–746.

Gorn, G., Pham, M.-T., & Sin, L.-Y. (2001). When arousal influences ad evaluation and valence does not (and vice versa). *Journal of Consumer Psychology, 11*, 43–55.

Hänze, M., & Hesse, F. W. (1993). Emotional influences on semantic priming. *Cognition & Emotion, 7*, 195–205.

Hänze, M., & Meyer, H. A. (1998). Mood influences on automatic and controlled semantic priming. *American Journal of Psychology, 111*, 265–278.

Heller, W. (1993). Neuropsychological mechanisms of individual differences in emotion, personality, and arousal. *Neuropsychology, 7*, 476–489.

Heller, W., Nitschke, J.-B., & Lindsay, D.-L. (1997). Neuropsychological correlates of arousal in self-reported emotion. *Cognition & Emotion, 11*, 383–402.

Hesse, F.-W., & Spies, K. (1996). Effects of negative mood on performance: Reduced capacity or changed processing strategy? *European Journal of Social Psychology, 26*, 163–168.

Hinojosa, J. A., Carretie, L., Mendez-Bertolo, C., Miguez, A., & Pozo, M. A. (2009). Arousal contributions to affective priming: Electrophysiological correlates. *Emotion, 9*, 164–171.

Humphreys, M. S., & Revelle, W. (1984). Personality, motivation, and performance: A theory of the relationship between individual differences and information processing. *Psychological Review, 91*, 153–184.

Hunt, R. D., & Einstein, G. (1981). Relational and item-specific information in memory. *Journal of Verbal Learning and Verbal Behavior, 20*, 497–514.

Huntsinger, J. R., Sinclair, S., & Clore, G. L. (2009). Affective regulation of implicitly measured stereotypes and attitudes: Automatic and controlled processes. *Journal of Experimental Social Psychology, 45*, 560–566.

Huntsinger, J. R., Sinclair, S., Dunn, E., & Clore, G. L. (2010). Affective regulation of stereotype activation: It's the (accessible) thought that counts. *Personality and Social Psychology Bulletin, 36*, 564–577.

Isen, A. M. (1999). Positive affect. In T. Dalgleish & M. J. Power (Eds.), *Handbook of cognition and emotion* (pp. 521–539). New York: Wiley.

Isen, A. M. (2000). Some perspectives on positive affect and self-regulation. *Psychological Inquiry, 11*, 184–187.

Isen, A. M., & Daubman, K. A. (1984). The influence of affect on categorization. *Journal of Personality and Social Psychology, 47*, 1206–1217.

Isen, A. M., Daubman, K. A., & Gorgoglione, J.-M. (1987). The influence of positive affect on cognitive organization: Implications for education. In R. Snow & M. Farr (Eds.), *Aptitude, learning, and instruction: Affective and conative factors* (pp. 143–164). Hillsdale NJ: Erlbaum.

Isen, A. M., Daubman, K. A., & Nowicki, G. P. (1987). Positive affect facilitates creative problem solving. *Journal of Personality and Social Psychology, 52*, 1122–1131.

Isen, A. M., Johnson, M. M., Mertz, E., & Robinson, G. F. (1985). The influence of positive affect on the unusualness of word associations. *Journal of Personality and Social Psychology, 48*, 1413–1426.

Jallais, C., & Corson, Y. (2008). Influence d'inductions d'humeurs positive et négative sur la structure des scripts [Impact of positive and negative moods inductions on the structure of scripts]. *Psychology Française, 53*, 81–95.

Jallais, C., & Gilet, A.-L. (2010). Inducing changes in arousal and valence: Comparison of two mood induction procedures. *Behavior Research Methods, 42*, 318–325.

Keltner, D., Ellsworth, P. C., & Edwards, K. (1993). Beyond simple pessimism: Effect of sadness and anger on social perception. *Journal of Personality and Social Psychology, 64*, 740–752.

Kensinger, E. A. (2004). Remembering emotional experiences: The contribution of valence and arousal. *Reviews in the Neurosciences, 15*, 241–251.

Kensinger, E. A., & Schacter, D.-L. (2006). Processing emotional pictures and words: Effects of valence and arousal. *Cognitive, Affective and Behavioral Neuroscience, 6*, 110–126.

Lee, A. Y., & Sternthal. (1999). The effects of positive mood on memory. *Journal of Consumer Research, 26*, 115–127.

Lerner, J. S., & Keltner, D. (2000). Beyond valence: Toward a model of emotion-specific influences on judgement and choice. *Cognition & Emotion, 14*, 473–493.

Levine, L. J., & Burgess, S. L. (1997). Beyond general arousal: Effects of specific emotions on memory. *Social Cognition, 15*, 157–181.

Levine, L. J., & Pizzaro, D. A. (2004). Emotion and memory research: A grumpy overview. *Social Cognition, 22*, 530–554.

Martin, M. (1990). On the induction of mood. *Clinical Psychology Review, 10*, 669–697.

Mayer, J. D., Allen, J. P., & Beauregard, K. (1995). Mood inductions for four specific moods: A procedure employing guided imagery vignettes with music. *Journal of Mental Imagery, 19*, 151–159.

Mayer, J. D., & Gaschke, Y. N. (1988). The experience and meta-experience of mood. *Journal of Personality and Social Psychology, 55*, 102–111.

Nielen, M. M. A., Heslenfeld, D. J., Heinen, K., Van Strien, J. W., Witter, M. P., Jonker, C., et al. (2009). Distinct brain systems underlie the processing of valence and arousal of affective pictures. *Brain and Cognition, 71*, 387–396.

Noulhiane, M., Mella, N., Samson, S., Ragot, R., & Pouthas, V. (2007). How emotional auditory stimuli modulate time perception. *Emotion, 7*, 697–704.

Oaksford, M., Morris, F., Grainger, B., & Williams, J. M. G. (1996). Mood, reasoning, and central executive processes. *Journal of Experimental Psychology: Learning, Memory, and Cognition, 22*, 476–492.

Park, J., & Banaji, M. R. (2000). Mood and heuristics: The influence of happy and sad states on sensitivity and bias in stereotyping. *Journal of Personality and Social Psychology, 78*, 1005–1023.

Phillips, L. H., Bull, R., Adams, E., & Fraser, L. (2002). Positive mood and executive function: Evidence from Stroop and fluency tasks. *Emotion, 2*, 12–22.

Pribam, K. H., & McGuinness, D. (1975). Arousal, activation, and effort in the control of attention. *Psychological Review, 82*, 116–149.

Raghunathan, R., & Pham, M.-T. (1999). All negative moods are not equal: Motivational influences of anxiety and sadness on decision making. *Organizational Behavior and Human Decision Processes, 71*, 56–77.

Revelle, W., & Loftus, D. A. (1992). The implications of arousal effects for the study of affect and memory. In S.-A. Christianson (Ed.), *The handbook of emotion and memory: Research and theory* (pp. 113–149). Hillsdale, NJ: Erlbaum.

Roediger, H., & McDermott, K. (1995). Creating false memories: Remembering words not presented in lists. *Journal of Experimental Psychology: Learning, Memory, and Cognition, 21*, 803–814.

Rowe, G., Hirsh, J. B., & Anderson, A. K. (2007). Positive affect increases the breadth of attentional selection. *Proceedings of the National Academy of Sciences of the United States of America, 104*, 383–388.

Russell, J.-A. (1980). A circumplex model of affect. *Journal of Personality and Social Psychology, 39*, 1161–1178.

Schwarz, N., & Clore, G. L. (1983). Mood, misattribution, and judgments of well-being: Informative and directive functions of affective states. *Journal of Personality and Social Psychology, 45*, 513–523.

Schwarz, N., & Clore, G. L. (1988). How do I feel about it? The informative function of affective state. In K. Fiedler & J. P. Forgas (Eds.), *Affect, cognition, and social behavior* (pp. 44–62). Toronto: Hogrefe.

Schwarz, N., & Clore, G. L. (2003). Mood as information: 20 years later. *Psychological Inquiry, 14*, 296–303.

Seibert, P.-S., & Ellis, H.-C. (1991). Irrelevant thoughts, emotional mood states, and cognitive task performance. *Memory and Cognition, 19*, 507–513.

Shapiro, S., MacInnis, D.-J., & Park, C. W. (2002). Understanding program-induced mood effects: Decoupling arousal from valence. *Journal of Advertising, 31*, 15–26.

Smith, R. E., & Hunt, R. D. (1998). Presentation modality affects false memory. *Psychonomic Bulletin and Review, 5*, 710–715.

Stefanucci, J. K., & Storbeck, J. (2009). Don't look down: Emotional arousal elevates height perception. *Journal of Experimental Psychology: General, 138*, 131–145.

Storbeck, J., & Clore, G. L. (2005). With sadness comes accuracy; with happiness, false memories. *Psychological Science, 16*, 785–791.

Storbeck, J., & Clore, G. L. (2008). Affective arousal as information: How affective arousal influences judgments, learning, and memory. *Social and Personality Psychology Compass, 2*, 1824–1843.

Watson, D., & Tellegen, A. (1985). Toward a consensual structure of mood. *Psychological Bulletin, 98*, 219–235.

Yik, M. S. M., Russell, J., & Feldman-Barrett, L.-A. (1999). Structure of self-reported current affect: Integration and beyond. *Journal of Personality and Social Psychology, 77*, 600–619.

Ziems, D., & Christman, S. (1998). Effects of mood on color perception as a function of dimensions of valence and arousal. *Perceptual and Motor Skills, 87*, 531–535.

6

Neuroaesthetics and the Art of Representation

ROGER BATT and CEES VAN LEEUWEN

THE DEVELOPMENT OF NEUROAESTHETICS

A Brief Background

The aesthetic experience of art is a complex, cognitive function that remains poorly understood, despite humankind's long-standing interest in the topic. Over 2,000 years ago, Plato became one of the first to describe aesthetics relative to human perception. In defining beauty as "that which is pleasing to the eye and ear," he fundamentally introduced the idea that the nature of art can be explored through the experience of the perceiver (Plato, 390 BC/2006). This concept was not explicitly developed, however, until Kant's *Critique of Esthetic Judgment* elaborated on the possibility of using empirical cognitive evidence to examine the phenomenon of beauty (Kant, 1790). Wundt (1874) and Fechner (1876) were among the first to pioneer studies in experimental aesthetics, using simple visual stimuli to methodically explain judgments of pleasure and preference. More recent behavioral studies found that symmetry (Frith & Nias, 1974), good Gestalts (Arnheim, 1954), and salience of structural organization (Locher, 2003) correlate with aesthetic preference. It was not until the 1990s, however, that developments in imaging technology provided the means to practically explore the neuroanatomical correlates of aesthetic experience.

Many of the earliest imaging studies in neuroaesthetics have continued to focus on judgments of beauty and the way aesthetic preference can differentially activate discrete regions of the brain. Results have shown that preferences for visual art can cause variations in a wide range of functional areas. Cela-Conde et al. (2004), for example, showed that there is greater activation in the left dorsolateral prefrontal cortex for paintings considered beautiful. Kawabata and Zeki (2004) found differences in the occipital prefrontal cortex and motor cortex when rating objects as beautiful, ugly, or neutral. Vartanian and colleagues (2005) illustrated that activation in the bilateral occipital gyri, left cingulated sulcus, and bilateral fusiform gyri increased in response to increasing preference for the artwork. Di Dio (2007), moreover, found that the insulate is more active when viewing "objectively beautiful" classical sculptures, while the amygdala is more active when viewing "subjectively beautiful" sculptures. Several other studies demonstrated further differences in the activation of the cingulate (Paradiso et al., 1999); left precuneus (Paradiso et al., 1999); right and left insula (Teasdale et al., 1999); visual cortex (Lane et al., 1997); right inferior frontal gyrus (Lane et al., 1997); and left caudate nucleus (Lane et al., 1997) when viewing paintings of varying emotional valence—a measure that is likewise associated with preferential ratings and appraisal of the artwork.

The Perception of Art as a Process

Although these results collectively establish correlates between localized neural activity and overall aesthetic judgment, they do not address much of the rest of the *process* of aesthetic evaluation. When images are viewed in everyday life, perception is oriented toward the process of object identification. When artists create works of art, however, they motivate a response to the stylistic and structural properties of their works, as well (Cupchik, Shereck, & Spiegel, 2009). Shklovsky (1917/1988) accordingly described how "the purpose of art is to impart sensation of things as they are perceived and not as they are known" (p. 20). Adopting an aesthetic approach may therefore necessitate a shift away from semantic categorization toward the stylistic properties of artwork. These stylistic properties comprise simple objective qualities that elicit more fundamental visual-cortical responses than high-order evaluation. It was initially speculated, for example, that visual simplicity is fundamental to aesthetic experience, but Berlyne (1970, 1971, 1974) demonstrated that visual complexity enhances aesthetic pleasure to a particular threshold, after which aesthetic pleasure begins to decline. Zeki and Marini (1998), likewise, found that the prefrontal dorsolateral cortex (PDC) is more active when participants view abnormally colored stimuli (Zeki & Marini, 1998). Although they did not test this in an aesthetic context, they speculated that this may relate to the emotional impact of the fauvists' experimentation with color, and Cela-Conde et al. (2004) hypothesized that there is a perceptive node for aesthetics in the PDC predicated on the manipulation of color and form. Observers with an artistic background appear to be particularly skilled at evaluating the formal qualities of a scene before projecting semantic categories. Eye movement studies, for example, have shown that, compared to novices, trained artists focus more attention on form and color features of complex scenes (Vogt, 1999; Vogt & Magnussen, 2005, 2007).

Different styles of art are distinguished relatively consistently according to variations in these formal characteristics and offer broader comparisons of artistic perception than the appraisal of beauty, which allows for only case-by-case analysis. Psychological models of aesthetic experience indicate that artistic understanding is in part an output of stylistic processing (Leder et al., 2004; Parsons, 1987), and several behavioral studies have shown that subjects' appreciation of paintings varies according to contextual information about artistic style (Cupchik et al., 2009; Leder, Carbon, & Ripsas, 2006; Millis, 2001; Russell, 2003). Similarities and differences in the cognitive processing of various artistic styles can therefore provide encompassing information on the nature of art and the way it is perceived.

EXPLORING THE "ABSTRACT AND THE REPRESENTATIONAL"

Until now, only few studies have been conducted to determine neuroanatomical variations based specifically on artistic genres, specifically "abstract" and "representational" artwork. From the perspective of art history, abstract and representational are not formal styles of art, but they are deemed as such for the purposes of many studies in neuroaesthetics (including our own) to describe these two categories based on clearly distinct visual qualities. Several studies, for example, have demonstrated a higher activation in the left frontal lobe (Lengger et al., 2007); bilateral temporal lobes (Lengger et al., 2007); temporoparietal junction (Fairhall & Ishai, 2008); prefrontal cortex (Fairhall & Ishai, 2008); and visual cortex (Fairhall & Ishai, 2008) during the perception of representational paintings compared to abstract paintings. Nicki and Gale (1977) also observed a decrease in cortical arousal in subjects without artistic backgrounds when viewing abstract works at higher levels of complexity (in accordance with the U-shaped function of complexity proposed by Berlyne). Although these studies addressed the influence of artistic style on aesthetic experience, their focus has nonetheless remained on discrete differences in localization. Spatially precise results acquired with techniques such as functional magnetic resonance imaging (fMRI) and positron emission tomography (PET) examined *where* specific mechanisms of artistic processing take place, but often overlooked more global characteristics of functional integration that can reveal *how* and *why* artistic information is interpreted the way that it is (Bressler, 2002).

"Style and Spectral Power": Findings by Batt et al. (2010)

Approaching the where, how, and why artistic information is interpreted in the manner of Batt and coworkers' (2010) study, "Style and Spectral Power," we used electroencephalography (EEG) to examine whether localized differences in the processing of abstract and representational art are likewise seen in more global measures of functional integration. The oscillatory dynamics of EEG recordings encompass a standard range of frequencies (delta, 1–3 Hz; theta, 4–7 Hz; alpha, 7–13 Hz; beta, 13–30 Hz; and gamma, 30–50 Hz), which are direct manifestations of synchronization over a region of the scalp centered on an electrode. The spectral power of these frequencies can be evaluated using methods such as fast Fourier transform (FFT) (e.g., Dijk, Hayes, & Czeisler, 1993; Fitzgibbon et al., 2004; Grillon & Buchsbaum, 1986; Luber et al., 2004; Musial et al., 1998; Stosnik, Krishnan, & O'Donnell, 2007) and phase synchrony analysis (e.g., Bhattacharya, 2009; Bhattacharya & Petsche, 2002, 2005; Sauseng et al., 2005), yielding information about the functional processes occurring across distant cortical areas. As a result, they offer more "global" analyses of functional integration than discrete measures of localization. Several studies have accordingly used EEG to illustrate global, state-dependent differences in artistic processing across specific conditions.

Bhattacharya and Petsche used a mixed 2 × 2 factorial design to compare frequency variations between artists and nonartists during performances of visual perception and imagery (Bhattacharya & Petsche, 2002, 2005; Bhattacharya, 2009; Sauseng et al., 2005). They revealed enhanced EEG phase synchrony in the beta and gamma bands among various brain regions of artists (compared to nonartists) during perception and in the delta band during imagery of paintings (Bhattacharya & Petsche, 2002). They also noted decreased phase synchrony in the alpha band of artists during both tasks. Bhattacharya (2009) later confirmed the enhanced phase synchrony in low-frequency bands (particularly the theta band in the bilateral prefrontal regions) in artists compared to nonartists during imagery tasks. Collectively, these results suggest that synchrony in high-frequency bands reflects the bottom-up processing of visual attributes, particularly in artists during the perception of paintings (Bhattacharya & Petsche, 2005), whereas the enhanced synchrony in low-frequency bands during imagery reflects the higher involvement of long-term visual memory (Bhattacharya, 2009). These results indicated that contrasting neurophysiological mechanisms of aesthetic processing in artists and nonartists are reflected in the distinct phases of EEG recordings. Within the same experiment, however, brain scientists did not address the contrasting ways in which artists and nonartists perceived different styles of art.

Our recent study, therefore, addressed this issue by examining the way global, functional mechanisms of aesthetic processing vary between artists (with at least 3 years of university-level training in visual art) and nonartists (with no formal training in visual art) in response to artistic styles (Batt et al., 2010). The experiment was expanded to a mixed 2 × 2 × 2 factorial design. "Subject type" (artists/nonartists) was treated as a between-subject variable, while "style" (abstract/representational) and "task" (visual perception/mental imagery) were manipulated within subjects. Participants were presented with the same set of artistic and naturally colored pictures divided into two groups: 20 pictures of abstract paintings and 20 pictures of classic representational paintings. For each stimulus, subjects were asked to carry out three primary tasks: (1) visual perception: looking at the painting presented on the screen; (2) mental imagery: looking at a blank screen and imagining the painting just shown before; and (3) behavioral analysis: evaluating the amount of time they focused on nine different factors when looking at the painting. Although the order of the paintings was randomized across the subjects, the sequence of these tasks was the same for each of the 40 paintings. During the performance of both visual perception and mental imagery, spontaneous EEG signals were recorded continuously by 19 Ag-AgCl electrodes distributed over the scalp according to the International EEG 10/20 System (Jasper, 1958). FFT was applied to normalized segments to calculate the integrated spectral powers (μV^2) within delta, theta, alpha, beta, and gamma bands at each of the 19 electrodes. At the end of each trial, subjects used a keyboard to answer a set of nine questions, rating on a scale of 1–6 (1 indicating very little time and 6 indicating much of the time) how much time they focused on various factors (i.e., aesthetic appeal, color, form/shapes, emotional impact, meaning, recognizable objects, details, the painting as a whole) when viewing the painting.

The specific aims of our study were as follows: (a) to examine whether global differences in the processing of abstract and representational paintings are reflected in EEG frequency variations; (b) to determine whether these style-related differences, if any, varied consistently between artists and nonartists during visual perception and mental imagery; and (c) to correlate the findings with behavioral data that further examined the neurophysiological mechanisms underlying these possible differences. By analyzing these global, functional processes in the perceiver, we hoped to further reveal how and why these artistic styles uniquely have an impact on aesthetic experience. This is the first study, to our knowledge, to compare cortical rhythms across these multimodal conditions and correlate them with behavioral data, thus providing one of the only comprehensive overviews of differences in the perception of abstract and representational visual art.

From these results, the following broad observations can be made:

1. Global differences in the processing of abstract and representational paintings were reflected in frequency variations of the theta and alpha bands.
2. The theta band power was significantly higher in artists, especially for tasks involving abstract art.
3. The alpha band power was significantly higher in nonartist for tasks involving abstract art.
4. These changes in theta and alpha power were reflected in distinct regions of the brain.
5. These changes were also correlated with distinct ratings from the behavioral data.

These findings collectively allude to the different ways abstract and representational art are globally processed under various conditions.

Regardless of the specifics, it is foremost important to note that significant differences exist in the theta and alpha bands across conditions. Although relatively general, this observation is important because it suggests that there are processing differences between abstract and representational styles on a global, functional level (as opposed to the discrete locations addressed in previous studies (Fairhall & Ishai, 2008; Lengger et al., 2007). Once this was preliminarily established, it enabled us to consider what these global frequency differences may specifically entail. Because the recording of spectral power provides only a broad and diffused indicator of cortical activity, however, the exact processes underlying these differences were left heavily to speculation based on what previous studies have found these frequency variations to indicate. It has previously been shown, for example, that signals in the delta band are heavily influenced by eye movements (such as blinks and saccades), while recordings in the gamma band are prone to vary with muscle movement activity (Bhattacharya & Petsche, 2002). The difficulty of controlling these artifacts may, in part, be the reason that no significant patterns were seen across conditions in either of these bands. The lack of any significant patterns in the beta waves may be due to the fact that low-amplitude beta waves are often associated with active concentration and "busy" thinking (Aftanas et al., 2004), which are fairly broad cortical processes that are unlikely to notably differ between the eight conditions that were tested.

Activity in the theta and alpha bands, on the other hand, has been attributed to cognitive processes that may explain the significant variations observed across conditions in our recordings. Several studies, for example, have associated increased activity in the theta band with top-down processing mechanisms, such as the recall of information stored in long-term memory and the evaluation of the affective significance of a stimuli (Li et al., 2009; Sauseng et al., 2005). Therefore, the higher theta band power in artists (relative to nonartists) may result from an increased amount of top-down processing. According to Bhattacharya and Petsche (2005), there are three steps involved in the visual processing of art: (1) extraction, (2) organization, and (3) the addition of meaning. The last step involves significant top-down processing and may be accentuated in artists due to their familiarity with evaluating art and interpreting its meaning based on the extensive artistic vocabulary stored in their long-term memories. In artists, the higher theta band activity in tasks involving abstract art (compared to those involving representational art) may result from an increased reliance on visual art patterns and associations stored in long-term memory to make sense of the less-definitive subject matter. In artists, the increased theta activity during visual perception compared to mental imagery (for both artistic styles) may result from the extensive top-down processes that are required to convert the image from working memory to long-term memory (Bhattacharya & Petsche, 2002). Also, when artists are first presented with a painting during the visual perception task, it presumably takes more top-down processing to find some meaning in the novel stimuli, whereas in the mental imagery task, they can rely more on the meaning they may have already ascribed to the piece.

In contrast to the theta band, the activity of the alpha band has been attributed to bottom-up processing mechanisms. Several studies have shown, more specifically, that alpha band activity is associated with the binding of elementary visual attributes into a coherent ensemble (Bhattacharya & Petsche, 2002). Therefore, in nonartists, the higher alpha band activity for tasks involving abstract art (compared to tasks involving representational art) appears to be associated with an increase in bottom-up processing. In other words, nonartists appear to focus more on extraction and organization of visual features when processing abstract art, rather than higher-order meanings and associations. Unlike artists, nonartists do not have extensive experience evaluating the higher-level meaning of art, so when they are presented with abstract pieces, it seems logical that they would focus more on finding basic visual features. It has also been shown that during performances of higher mental tasks, alpha activity often decreases, which may explain the correlation between decreased alpha activity and increased abstraction observed by Nicki and Gale (1977) (although we cannot directly compare results, as they did not distinguish between artists and nonartists). Therefore, the alpha activity in artists is slightly lower for tasks involving abstract art (compared to those involving representational art) since the "higher" top-down processing required for abstract art correlates with a suppression of alpha activity.

In addition to the global differences observed in the processing of abstract and representational art, the spectral recordings indicated several localized distinctions between conditions. It is important to note that the following observations are based on preliminary data and serve merely as conjecture. In artists, the theta activity was most significant in the right frontal lobes (particularly F4 and F8) during all four conditions. This would not be surprising, given that the right frontal lobe has repeatedly been shown to play a dominant role in creative activities (Cupchik et al., 1994; Grill-Spector et al., 1998; Lane et al., 1997). Compared to the other brain regions, therefore, top-down processing activities are most heavily localized in artists' frontal lobes, and the overall increase in top-down processing for abstract art is reflected by a proportional increase in these frontal regions. During the processing of abstract art in artists and nonartists, the respective increases in theta and alpha activity are most significant in the right temporoparietal cortex (i.e., T4, T6, and P4). Using simple visual stimuli, Fokin et al. (2008) similarly showed that the temporoparietal cortex was more activated by chaotic arrangements of dots, whereas the occipital lobe was more activated by highly ordered arrangements. They also showed that the frontal lobe was responsible for evaluating the degree of randomness in these stimuli. Although Fokin did not note any sort of hemispheric dominance, the increased right hemispheric activity in these regions that we found during the processing of abstract art may be associated with the evaluation of the apparent "randomness" of this style (regardless of whether it is handled through top-down or bottom-up mechanisms).

The differences in top-down and bottom-up processing that appear to be indicated in the spectral recordings are also supported by correlations with behavioral data. Two 8 × 8 correlation matrices (one for the theta band and one for the alpha band) were calculated to test whether the average spectral activity across electrodes in the eight conditions were related to participants' ratings on the amount of time that they focused on the eight different criteria. Although several interesting tendencies occurred, only one of the correlations reached significance; hence, the ratings were not further evaluated. As a result, the following are merely observations rather than published data. In conditions involving abstract art, for example, the theta band power in artists showed a significant positive correlation with ratings on (time spent on) meaning, aesthetic appeal, and emotional impact (although ratings of emotional impact were only correlated in artists with theta during the visual perception of abstract art and not mental imagery). This suggests that when theta power increases in artists during the processing of abstract art, the artists likewise indicated that they spent more time focusing on qualities associated with top-down processes. The alpha band power in nonartists similarly showed positive correlations with ratings on form/shape and color during the processing of abstract art. This suggests that when alpha band power increases in nonartists during the processing of abstract art, they concurrently indicated that they were indeed focusing more on the bottom-up processing of basic visual features. The alpha activity of nonartists during visual perception of both styles of art showed a negative correlation with ratings on emotional impact, further indicating that top-down processing mechanisms are not at work in nonartists. Moreover, in both artists and nonartists, theta and alpha activity during processing of abstract art showed negative correlations with ratings on recognizable objects, as subjects evidently did not spend much time focusing on recognizable objects in abstract pieces.

"Viewing Artworks": Connections to the Work of Cupchik et al. (2009)

Cupchik et al. (2009) conducted a closely related study on the perception of abstract and representational art in which they distinguished perception geared toward aesthetic experience from perception geared toward object identification in everyday perception. The experimental designed was devised to test three factors:

1. Painting "style" (representational vs. abstract paintings)
2. Edge (hard vs. soft "appearance")
3. Mindset/perspective (object identification prompt vs. aesthetic evaluation prompt)

More specifically, subjects were presented with eight blocks of stimuli. Four of the blocks consisted of 8 representational paintings (2 nudes, 2 group portraits, 2 landscapes, and 2 still lifes), and 4 of the blocks consisted of 4 abstract paintings (2 Pollocks and 2 nonfractal paintings by Tsion Avital). Of the 4 representational painting blocks, half were executed in a linear, hard-edge style emphasizing contour and composition, and half were executed in a painterly, soft-edge, and expressive style. In addition, 2 of the representational blocks (1 hard-edge block and 1 painterly block) were preceded by a prompt asking the subject to approach the images in an objective manner and focus on the content of the painting, and 2 blocks (1 hard-edge block and 1 painterly) were preceded by a prompt instructing the subject to approach the paintings in a subjective manner and focus on the emotional impact of the painting and its artistic elements. The 4 blocks of abstract paintings served as a control and did not vary in terms of "edge" or "mindset/perspective." fMRI was used to record BOLD (blood oxygenation level dependent effect), which measures changes in blood flow patterns in the brain that reflect cognitive acitivity. After leaving the scanner, subjects were shown the same 4 blocks of representational paintings and asked to rate how much emotion the paintings elicited based on a 7-point scale.

The experiment revealed that relative to baseline conditions, blocks preceded by a prompt yielded higher activation in the left insula, left cingulated gyrus, left lingual gyrus, and right inferior temporal gyrus (which are often activated whenever subjects engage in tasks relative to baseline conditions; Doenbach et al., 2006) and the bilateral occipital gyri (which may be attributable to a greater load placed on the visual system when processing higher levels of visual detail in representational paintings). Between the two "mindset" conditions, there was more activation in the bilateral insula (BA 13) for the aesthetic-baseline contrast than the pragmatic-baseline contrast, which can be attributed to the experience of emotion while viewing paintings, consistent with the role of the insula in the feeling of emotion (Critchley et al., 2005; Damasio et al., 2000). Studies have shown that the right anterior insula is activated when subjects viewed "beautiful" sculptures compared to ones that were less proportional. In contrast, pragmatic-baseline contrast revealed activation in the right fusiform gyrus (BA 37), which is attributable to object recognition, including faces (Di Dio, 2007; Grill-Spector & Malach, 2004), and the visual and spatial search for imposing situational models on pictorial scenes (Sieborger, Ferstl, & von Cramon, 2007). When directly comparing aesthetic and pragmatic conditions, they observed a higher activation in the left lateral prefrontal cortex (BA 10) for aesthetic conditions, which is attributable to the activation of top-down control in directing perception toward aesthetic orientation (Ridderinkhof et al., 2004) and the maintenance of a main goal while performing concurrent subgoals (Koechlin et al., 1999). Jacobsen et al. (2006) similarly found BA 9/10 to be more active when judging the aesthetic qualities of graphic geometric patterns compared to the symmetry of the patterns. Given the inherently self-referential nature of aesthetic perception, maintaining attention on internally generated cognition may be an important component of the experience. Comparing "edges," they found that the left superior parietal lobule (BA 7) was activated relatively more when subjects viewed soft-edge paintings in the aesthetic orientation than hard-edge paintings in the pragmatic orientation, which may be attributable to the viewers' attempts to resolve the indeterminate forms in soft edge. Behaviorally, there was also a tendency for soft-edge images to receive higher emotion ratings in the context of the aesthetic than pragmatic viewing orientation.

ABSTRACTION AND REPRESENTATION IN ARCHITECTURE: NEW DIRECTIONS IN NEUROAESTHETICS

These insights to the perception of abstract and representational art could be extrapolated to examine the aesthetic perception of other artistic media, such as architecture, and explore the relationship between their aesthetic processing. Exploring these questions in the context of architecture would be particularly relevant especially within the field of art history, as architecture is considered to have both inherently abstract and representational elements. This would be interesting because paintings are inherently an aesthetic object, whereas architecture has more of a dualistic relationship between form and function. Few neuroaesthetic studies, however, have been done in direct relation to architecture. Several studies have found that the parahippocampal place area (PPA) is more strongly activated when viewing spatial layouts than objects and diminishes when the surfaces of the scene are rearranged to disrupt the coherent space (Epstein & Kanwisher, 1998; Kirk et al., 2009). Drawing on our experiment and that of Cupchik et al. (2009), a study involving architecture stimuli could tell us differences in the way that traditional and abstract architecture are perceived. More specifically, it could provide insight to the way that rectilinear architecture is perceived in relation to curvilinear, which is especially interesting in distinguishing linear "abstract" architecture (such as minimalism) from curvilinear abstract architecture (such as the avant-garde forms of Zaha Hadid). This could also provide a direct comparison of the way that architecture and paintings are perceived. It would also provide us with cues in terms of how architecture versus painting elicits certain feelings in us. Is the PPA activated by viewing buildings as aesthetic objects? When people look at "abstract forms of" architecture, is there this differentiation between finding objects and searching from long-term memory (differences in the fusiform gyrus, precuneus, and middle frontal gyrus (MFG) activity, for example), or is this indeterminacy expected, as architecture is inherently abstract? The behavioral data could provide a more explicit evaluation, in terms of how people are approaching the structures, and if the additional "mindset" variable is included, this distinction could be further evaluated.

There are, however, limitations in the amount of information that can be gathered from this experiment. Although the terms *representational* and *abstract* architecture are not descriptive and can encompass a wide range of works, neuroaesthetics and neuroarthistory are nascent fields, and there may not yet be enough data to focus on categories of art that are perhaps more definitive. Moreover, it is a bit reductive to classify minimalist avant-garde architecture as hard edge and more free-form artists as curvilinear. Is it simply enough to show that these differences can be perceived cognitively? Is there some way that these data could be skewed to make a specific theoretical argument? These are questions researchers may soon be addressing.

CONCLUSION

In Batt et al. (2010), results from both FFT analysis and behavioral data indicate significant differences in the way abstract art and representational art are processed at a global, functional level. This was the first study to compare cortical rhythms across these multimodal conditions and correlate them with behavioral data, thus providing one of the only comprehensive overviews of differences in the perception of abstract and representational visual art. At a global processing level, increased theta activity in artists appeared to correspond with the enhanced used top-down processing mechanisms for abstract art, whereas increased alpha activity in nonartists appeared to indicate the extensive bottom-up processing of abstract art. These changes in spectral power are reflected in distinct regions of the brain and correlate with distinct ratings from behavioral data, collectively providing insight to the mechanisms that may underlie the processing of abstract and representational art. Indeed, this study showed that much can be learned about the aesthetic processing of artistic styles through the experience of the perceiver—an idea that has been increasingly explored in the field of neuroaesthetics since the 1990s and will continue to address new and interesting questions about the way we perceive art.

REFERENCES

Aftanas, L. I., Reva, N. V., Varlamov, A. A., Pavlov, S. V., & Makhnev, V. P. (2004). Analysis of evoked EEG synchronization and desynchronization in conditions of emotional activation in humans: Temporal and topographic characteristics. *Neuroscience and Behavioral Physiology, 34*, 859–867.

Arnheim, R. (1954). *Art and visual perception*. Berkeley, CA: University of California Press.

Batt, R., Palmiero, M., Nakatani, C., & van Leeuwen, C. (2010), Style and spectral power: Processing of abstract and representational art in artists and non-artists. *Perception, 39*, 1659–1671.

Berlyne, D. E. (1970). Novelty, complexity, and hedonic value. *Perception and Psychophysics, 8*, 279–286.

Berlyne, D. E. (1971). *Aesthetics and psychobiology*. New York: Appleton-Century-Crofts.

Berlyne, D. E. (1974). *Studies in the new experimental aesthetics*. New York: Taylor & Francis.

Bhattacharya, J. (2009). Increase of universality in human brain during mental imagery from visual perception. *PloS One, 4*, 1–11.

Bhattacharya, J., & Petsche, H. (2002). Shadows of artistry: Cortical synchrony during perception and imagery of visual art. *Cognitive Brain Research, 13*, 179–186.

Bhattacharya, J., & Petsche, H. (2005). Drawing on mind's canvas: Differences in cortical integration patterns between artists and non-artists. *Human Brain Mapping, 26*, 1–14.

Bressler, S. L. (2002). Understanding cognition through large-scale cortical networks. *Current Directions Psychological Science, 12*, 1–47.

Cela-Conde, C., Marty, G., Maestú, F., Ortiz, T., Munar, E., Fernández, A., et al. (2004). Activation of the prefrontal cortex in the human visual aesthetic perception. *Proceedings of the National Academy of Sciences of the United States of America, 101*, 6321–6325.

Critchley, H. D., Rotshtein, P., Nagai, Y., O'Doherty, J., Mathias, C. J., & Colan, R. J. (2005). Activity in the human brain predicting differential heart rate responses to emotional facial expressions. *NeuroImage, 24*, 751–762.

Cupchik, G., Shereck, L., and Spiegel, S. (1994). The effects of textual information on artistic communication. *Visual Arts Research , 20*, 62–78.

Cupchik, G. C., Shereck, L., & Spiegel, S. (2009). The effects of textual information on artistic communication. *Visual Arts Research, 20*, 62–78.

Damasio, A. R., Grabowski, T. J., Bechara, A., Damasio, H., Ponto, L. L., Parvizi, J., et al. (2000). Subcortical and cortical brain activity during the feeling of self-generated emotions. *Nature Neuroscience, 4*, 1049–1056.

Di Dio, C. (2007). The golden beauty: Brain response to classical and Renaissance sculptures. *PloS One, 11*, 1–9.

Dijk, D., Hayes, B., & Czeisler, C. (1993). Dynamics of electroencephalographic sleep spindles and slow wave activity in men: Effect of sleep deprivation. *Brain Research, 626*, 190–199.

Doenbach, N. U., Visscher, K. M., Palmer, E. D., Miezin, F. M., Wenger, K. K., Kang, H. C., et al. (2006). A core system for the implementation of task sets. *Neuron, 50*, 799–812.

Epstein, R., & Kanwisher, N. (1998). A cortical representation of the local visual environment. *Nature, 392*, 598–601.

Fairhall, S., & Ishai, A. (2008). Neural correlates of object indeterminacy in art composition. *Consciousness and Cognition, 17*, 923–932.

Fechner, G. T. (1876). *Preschool of aesthetics*. Leipzig, Germany: Breitkopf & Härtel.

Fitzgibbon, S. P., Pope, K. J., Mackenzie, L., Clark, C. R., & Willoughby, J. O. (2004). Cognitive tasks augment gamma EEG power. *Clinical Neurophysiology, 115,* 1802–1809.

Fokin, V. A., Shelepin, Y. E., Kharauzov, A. K., Trufanov, G. E., Sevost'yanov, A. V., Pronin, S. V., et al. (2008). Location of human cortical areas activated on perception of ordered and chaotic images. *Neuroscience and Behavioral Physiology, 38,* 677–685.

Frith, D., & Nias, D. (1974). What determines aesthetic preferences? *Journal of General Psychology, 91,* 163–173.

Grill-Spector, K., Kushnir, T., Hendler, T., Edelman, S., Itzchak, Y., & Malach, R. (1998). A sequence of object-processing stages revealed by fMRI in the human occipital lobe. *Human Brain Mapping, 6,* 316–328.

Grill-Spector, K., & Malach, R. (2004). The human visual cortex. *Annual Reviews of Neuroscience, 27,* 649–677.

Grillon, C., & Buchsbaum, M. S. (1986). Computer EEG topography of response to visual and auditory stimuli. *Electroencephalography and Clinical Neurophysiology, 63,* 42–53.

Jacobsen, T., Schubotz, R. I., Höfel, L., & von Cramon, D. Y. (2006). Brain correlates of aesthetic judgment of beauty. *NeuroImage, 29,* 276–285.

Jasper, H. H. (1958). Report of the committee on methods of clinical examination in electroencephalography. *Electroencephalography and Clinical Neurophysiology, 10,* 371–375.

Kant, Immanuel. *Critique of Judgment.* Translated by James C. Meredity. Oxford: Clarendon Press, 1911. Originally published as Kritik der Urteilskraft (1790).

Kawabata, H., & Zeki, S. (2004). Neural correlates of beauty. *Journal of Neurophysiology, 91,* 1699–1705.

Kirk, U., Skov, M., Christensen, M. S., & Nygaard, N. (2009). Brain correlates of aesthetic expertise: A parametric fMRI study. *Brain and Cognition, 69,* 306–315.

Koechlin, E., Basso, G., Pietrini, P., Panzer, S., & Grafman, J. (1999). The role of the anterior prefrontal cortex in human cognition. *Nature, 339,* 148–151.

Lane, R. D., Reiman, E. M., Bradley, M. M., Lang, P. J., Ahern, G. L., Davidson, R. J., et al. (1997). Neuroanatomical correlates of pleasant and unpleasant emotion. *Neuropsychologia, 35,* 209–215.

Leder, H., Belke, B., Oeberst, A., & Augustin, D. (2004). A model of aesthetic appreciation and aesthetic judgments. *British Journal of Psychology, 95,* 289–508.

Leder, H., Carbon, C. C., & Ripsas, A. (2006). Entitling art: Influence of difference types of title information on understanding and appreciation of paintings. *Acta Psychologica, 121,* 176–198.

Lengger, P., Fischmeister, F., Leder, H., & Bauer, H. (2007). Functional neuroanatomy of the perception of modern art: A DC-EEG study on the influence of stylistic information on aesthetic experience. *Brain Research, 1158,* 93–102.

Li, Y., Umeno, K., Hori, E., Takakura, H., Urakawa, S., Ono, T., & Nishijo, H. (2009). Global synchronization in the theta band during mental imagery of navigation in humans. *Neuroscience Research, 65,* 44–52.

Locher, P. (2003). An empirical investigation of the visual rightness theory of picture perception. *Acta Psychologica, 114,* 147–164.

Luber, B., Habeck, C., Trott, C., Friedman, D., & Moeller, J. (2004). A ghost of retrieval past: A functional network of alpha EEG related to source memory in elderly humans. *Cognitive Brain Research, 20,* 144–155.

Millis, K. (2001). Making meaning brings pleasure: The influence of titles on aesthetic experiences. *Emotion, 1,* 320–239.

Musial, P., Kublik, E., Panecki, S., & Wróbel, A. (1998). Transient changes of electrical activity in the rat barrell cortex during conditioning. *Brain Research, 786,* 1–10.

Nicki, R. M., & Gale, A. (1977). EEG, measures of complexity, and preference for nonrepresentational works of art. *Perception, 6* 281–286.

Paradiso, S., Johnson, D. L., Anreasen, N. C., O'Leary, D. S., Watkins, G. L., Ponto, L. L. B., et al. (1999). Cerebral blood flow changes associated with attribution of emotional valence to pleasant, unpleasant, and neutral visual stimuli in a PET study of normal subjects. *American Journal of Psychiatry, 156,* 1618–1629.

Parsons, M. J. (1987). *How we understand art: A cognitive developmental account of aesthetic experience.* Cambridge, UK: Cambridge University Press.

Plato. *Hippias Major.* Translated by Dorothy Tarrant. New York: Arno Press, 1976. Originally published circa 390 BC.

Ridderinkhof, K. R., Ullsperger, M., Crone, E. A., & Niewenhuis, S. (2004). The role of the medial frontal cortex in cognitive control. *Science, 306,* 443–447.

Russell, P. A. (2003). Effort after meaning and the hedonic value of paintings. *British Journal of Psychology, 94,* 99–110.

Sauseng, P., Klimesch, W., Doppelmayr, M., Pecherstorfer, T., Greunberger, R., & Hanslmayr, S. (2005). EEG alpha synchronization and functional coupling during top-down processing in a working memory task. *Human Brain Mapping, 26,* 148–155.

Shklovsky, V. (1988). *Modern criticism and theory.* New York: Longman. (Original work published 1917).

Sieborger, F. T., Ferstl, E. C., & von Cramon, D. Y. (2007). Making sense of nonsense: An fMRI study of task induced inference processes during discourse comprehension. *Brain Research, 1166,* 77–91.

Stosnik, P., Krishnan, G., & O'Donnell, B. (2007). The effect of selective attention on the gamma-band auditory stead-state response. *Neuroscience Letters, 420,* 223–228.

Teasdale, J. D., Howard, R. J., Cox, S. G., Ha, Y., Brammer, M. J., Williams, S. C. R., et al. (1999). Functional MRI study of the cognitive generation of affect. *American Journal of Psychiatry, 156,* 209–215.

Vartanian, O., Martindale, C., Podsiadlo, J., Overbay, S., & Borkum, J. (2005). The link between composition and balance in masterworks vs. paintings of lower artistic quality. *British Journal of Psychology, 96,* 493–503.

Vogt, S. (1999). Looking at paintings: Patterns of eye movements in artistically naïve and sophisticated subjects. *Leonardo, 32,* 325.

Vogt, S., & Magnussen, S. (2005). Hemispheric specialization and recognition memory for abstract and realistic pictures: A comparison of painters and laymen. *Brain and Cognition, 58,* 324–333.

Vogt, S., & Magnussen, S. (2007). Expertise in pictorial perception: Eye-movement patterns and visual memory in artists and laymen. *Perception, 36,* 91–100.

Wundt, W. (1874). *Grundzüge der physiologischen Psychologie* [Characteristics of physiological psychology]. Leipzig, Germany: Engelmann.

Zeki, S., & Marini, L. (1998). Three cortical stages of colour processing in the human brain. *Brain, 121,* 1669–1885.

7

Motivation and Construction of Retrospective Opinions

MARCIN SKLAD

INTRODUCTION

Opinions, Attitudes: Conceptualization and Relevance

*T*he importance of the concepts of attitudes and opinions for empirically driven social sciences is hard to overrate. It is a common practice in social survey research to ask respondents about their opinions to determine their attitudes toward various objects. While most theoreticians agree on the multidimensional structure of attitudes (e.g., Manstead & Hewstone, 1995), survey methodologists often treat attitudes and answers to questions about opinions synonymously (e.g., Oppenheim, 2001; Tourangeau, Rips, & Rasinski, 2000). To avoid terminological confusion, I assume that survey questions directly measure opinions rather than attitudes. I use the common language meaning of the term *opinion*, assuming that an opinion is "a personal belief or judgment that is not founded on proof or certainty" (WordNet, 2007). If we define opinions this way, then they seem to be well measured by means of standardized survey questions. At the same time, there is no doubt that they are related to more complex attitudes.

Retrospective Opinions

Personal memories and retrospections allow us to define who we are. They form the foundation of our identity. According to narrativists, memories are part of our private autobiography, defining who we are and how we became who we are (Giddens, 1991). Besides having personal relevance, retrospective opinions also got the interest of social researchers as a useful source of information. Often, researchers are interested not only in the current state of mind of respondents but also in the changes of respondents' views. For this purpose, it is necessary to tap into opinions that respondents held in the past. If such data were not collected in the past, the closest approximation of past answers can be obtained by asking retrospective questions. Replacing the longitudinal design by a retrospective one may serve as a partial remedy to at least some limitations of panel studies. Retrospective design involves lower costs in terms of money, organization, and time than a panel study (e.g., Powers, Goudy, & Keith, 1978); it is affected neither by the selective loss of respondents in consecutive waves, nor by mere measurement at the first wave influencing opinions expressed at later waves of the panel (e.g., Sudman, Bradburn, & Schwarz, 1996). Comparisons of subjective evaluations collected at different points in time often fail to mirror the objective change of circumstances (Diener, Suh, & Oishi, 1997, for review; Diener & Biswas-Diener, 2002; Frederick & Loewenstein, 1999).

It is important to define what is understood by retrospective opinions. There are several types of retrospective questions, of which only one is a logical equivalent to asking the opinion question in the past. As we define an opinion as a subjective judgment, it requires a certain object and a certain standard or procedure according to which the object is judged. An important aspect of the object of an opinion is its relation to the respondent's Self. In most cases, the judgment has evaluative elements, but it can be of any subjective nature (e.g., an estimation of likelihood, brightness, subjective monetary value or importance). Both objects and standards can change in time, and these changes would result in a change of expressed opinion. Therefore, only in the case of retrospective questions in the form, "What *was/would have been* your opinion about the object?" can we consider whether the retrospection is accurate. This is not possible in the case of a question in the form, "What *is* your opinion about the object in the past?" The latter question requires passing on the current judgment of the object as the object was in the past, for instance, "What is your current opinion about the former president?" The same logic applies to comparative questions. For example, the question "Do you think X improved?" is not logically equal to "Did your opinion about X improve?" Only the latter question is logically equivalent to the comparison of two consecutive answers coming from a panel study.

In the next section, we discuss three research paradigms that have been used to analyze retrospective opinions. The section after that consists of an overview of three models that try to explain how retrospective opinions are generated. Then, the focus is on motivational factors in the construction of retrospective opinions.

RESEARCH PARADIGMS

Retrospective opinions were analyzed mainly within three separate research paradigms: methodological studies of validity and accuracy of retrospective reports, cognitive dissonance studies, and hindsight bias studies. The framework proposed in this chapter allows us to integrate the results of these approaches. The three streams of research have been developed separately, but they are concerned with a similar variable (concept). In addition, the results from research carried out within the three paradigms to a certain degree complement each other and overlap.

Validity of Retrospective Opinions as Reflection of Past Opinions

Historically, the oldest of the three paradigms is related to social research methodology. It addressed whether and to which degree retrospective opinions are an accurate reflection of opinions expressed in the past. The assessment of the validity of retrospective opinions as indicators of past opinions has been approached in a few different ways. The first method of assessing the accuracy of retrospective opinions involved the use of a longitudinal study; during the first measurement wave, respondents expressed an opinion on a certain subject, and after some time, during the next wave, they are asked for their retrospective opinions.

The results of research devoted to testing the validity of retrospective opinions as simple reflections of former opinions showed that retrospections were substantially different from recorded past opinions, and that the discrepancy between retrospections and original answers was bigger for attitudinal than for factual questions (e.g., Van der Vaart, Van der Zouwen, & Dijkstra, 1995).

In more recent studies from this tradition, authors tried to find correlates of recall accuracy or bias (e.g., Joslyn, 2003; Kwong & Hamilton, 2004). Unfortunately, predictors of bias used in the research cited here were closely related to the specific subjects of retrospective opinions. Therefore, they cannot predict the accuracy or bias of retrospection of opinions on different issues.

Some authors that used a panel design to estimate the accuracy of recollections requested that respondents would directly indicate whether or to which degree they had changed their opinions, instead of asking respondents to recall their initial opinions recorded in the past. Early research of this kind usually focused on the question of the degree retrospective changes were related to "true" observed changes of opinions. True changes were measured as the computed difference between two recorded expressions of opinion on the same subject, expressed at consecutive points in time (e.g., Lyons & Dickinson, 1973). These two types of indicators correlate moderately at best. The apparent lack of coherence between declared and computed opinion changes, which was originally interpreted as an indication of the lack of validity of the retrospections, may in fact also point to a weakness of serial measures of opinion changes. Retrospective measures seemed to be more sensitive to changes, showing greater effects, and they seemed more related to satisfaction with change (Fischer et al., 1999; Norman, Stratford, & Regehr, 1997). The moderate responsiveness of serial measures to objective changes and their lack of congruence with retrospective reports of changes can be attributed to serial measures being affected by general habituation and adaptation to change.

Finally, the analysis of the accuracy of retrospective opinions was sometimes carried out in absence of records of respondents' initial original opinions. In these studies, researchers estimated the direction and size of directional bias on the aggregate group level. In this type of research, the distribution of answers to retrospective questions of one group of respondents was compared to the distribution of answers given in the past by another equivalent group of respondents (e.g., Smith, 1984).

Moreover, retrospections seem to be generally biased toward currently held opinions (e.g., Levine, 1997). At the same time, results investigating opinion change showed that retrospections are to a certain degree able to capture opinion changes that could be seen by the external observer (e.g., Lyons & Dickinson, 1973). Thus, the retrospections are not just simply current opinions cast back in time. The discrepancy between retrospective changes on the one hand and changes that are computed with the help of past opinions, on the other hand, might also be a sign of the usefulness of retrospections rather than their weakness. A person's current subjective perception of the change might be a better predictor of current and future behavior, thoughts, and feelings than objective changes that were not realized by the individual.

Cognitive Dissonance Paradigm

Results that are relevant for understanding retrospective opinions were also provided by experimental research on attitude change, in particular associated with the concept of cognitive dissonance (Festinger, 1957). In a typical induced compliance schema of a cognitive dissonance experiment, the experimental group is involved in some activity that is in contrast with a certain attitude that they held before the experiment. As a result of the activity, the attitudes of group members change in the direction that makes them more consonant with the action taken. The only difference in methodology between this kind of cognitive dissonance research and the survey studies discussed is the experimental induction of opinion change.

Bem and McConell (1970) were probably the first to include recollections in the classical cognitive dissonance experiment using the paradigm of induced compliance. After measuring initial opinions, the researchers asked students to write a counterattitudinal essay taking the position that students should have little or no control over the choice of courses offered by a university. Then, the subjects were asked to recall their initial opinion and to state their final opinion. The students' recalled estimates of their initial opinions were virtually the same as their final opinions, despite the actual shift of their attitudes caused by the experimental manipulation. In addition, the retrospections were more strongly correlated with final opinions than with initial opinions. In later years, these results were replicated by several studies utilizing retrospections (Leippe & Eisenstadt, 1999).

The results of research carried out in the framework of cognitive dissonance theory confirmed the general bias in retrospections in the direction of overestimation of their consistency with current opinion and the disregard of opinion changes. Nevertheless, caution should be taken since the manipulation causing the opinion shift in these experiments is especially designed to work outside the consciousness of participants. Some researchers (e.g., Nisbett & Wilson, 1977) were even convinced that results obtained in the "insufficient justification" paradigm would not be obtained if participants would realize that they were changing their opinions to fit their behavior. They would realize that their behavior was caused by social pressure and not by their opinions. On the other hand, even if the experiments influenced opinions in a transparent way using simple persuasion, participants still overestimated retrospectively the stability of their opinions (Ross, 1989). The most important advance brought by this stream of research was a shift of focus from simply stating the existence of bias toward explaining it.

Hindsight Bias Paradigm

The third group of research that brought results showing an exaggerated similarity of retrospective opinions to present opinions was related to a phenomenon known as hindsight bias. The hindsight bias in retrospections was demonstrated for the first time by Fischhoff and Beyth (1975). In a classic experimental paradigm introduced by Fischhoff (1975), participants are presented an event that can end with several outcomes. After that, participants are presented with a list of mutually exclusive possible outcomes and informed which of them have actually taken place. Finally, they are asked to estimate what probability they would have given to different outcomes if they did not learn the actual outcome. As a result, participants overestimate the probabilities they would have given to the outcome indicated as actually happening and underestimate the probabilities they would have assigned to other possible outcomes. The existence of hindsight bias has been confirmed in literally hundreds of experimental and observational studies using predictions of a wide variety of outcomes, starting from sport events and diplomatic visits (e.g., Fischhoff & Beyth, 1975) and ending on traffic scenes (Fessel, Epstude, & Roese, 2009).

The results of experiments devoted to hindsight bias can be treated as a particular case of retrospection of past opinions being too similar to current opinions. The only distinguishing element is that opinions recalled in experiments exploring hindsight bias can have an objective verification. The manipulation is based on the underlying assumption that people trust the feedback about the outcome given by the experimenter, indicating which opinion was correct (Hasher, Attig, & Alba, 1981). As a result, participants change their opinions to make them correct—in line with the feedback. As a result of feedback, the current opinion of the participant is that the current post-factum likelihood of the outcome that supposedly happened is 100%, and the subjectively perceived chance that alternative outcomes happened is 0%, assuming the participant does not question the trustworthiness of the source of feedback. Similarly, in the case of almanac questions, subjects should have complete subjective confidence in the correct answer that was just provided to them. At this point, participants are asked to recall or estimate what their estimation of the likelihood of the outcome or subjective confidence was before the feedback was provided. In this respect, likelihood or certainty estimates are no different from any other opinions that one tries to retrospect after they changed.

There is no doubt about the existence of systematic bias in the retrospection of subjective certainty or evaluations of probabilities (for review, Christensen-Szalanski & Willham, 1991; Hawkins & Hastie, 1990). Even though the observed biases suggest that the process in which retrospections of opinions are created is no simple retrieval of past opinions from the memory, the views on how they may come to be are divided.

MODELS OF RETROSPECTIVE OPINION

Retrieval

Since retrospective questions about opinions do not seem to pose special difficulty and most people can answer them fairly easily, respondents may even be convinced that they retrieve their former opinions (Herrmann, 1994). Memories are often accompanied by awareness of remembering, but most of the time people are not able to distinguish what they actually experienced from what was supplemented by their mind (Belli, Schuman, & Jackson, 1997; Loftus, 2003; Neisser, 1981). The lack of introspective insight into our mental processes (Nisbett & Wilson, 1977), causing only their outcome to be present in the consciousness, can let us believe that we can remember our past opinions. Studies showed that opinions that we recall are often very different from what we expressed in the past. Moreover, these differences might be even bigger for retrospections of opinions than of factual questions (e.g., Van der Vaart et al., 1995).

The exaggerated similarity of retrospections to current opinions confirms the hypothesis that recalling of personal history is a process of active reconstruction (Bartlett, 1932) rather than simple retrieval. Currently, memory is rarely depicted as a safe storage where memories wait to be retrieved in a ready form (Bartlett, 1932; Lindsay & Norman, 1972; Taylor & Crocker, 1981). Instead, the recall is an active constructive process (e.g., Aronson & Wieczorkowska, 2001; Dawes, 1988; Schacter, 1996). Remembered facts are reinterpreted, overwritten, and rewritten and missing information is filled in with inferences and guesses. For instance, Schacter (1996) modeled memory as a present act of consciousness, stimulated by a retrieval cue in which the past is reconstructed.

The current state of mind can determine retrieval cues and schemas guiding the recollection process. As a result, we reconstruct internally consistent memories.

The congruency of retrospections with current mood, opinions, expectations, and self-image has been confirmed in multiple studies (Laird, 1989; Matt, Vázquez, & Campbell, 1992; Palfai & Salovey, 1992). According to some theories, the past is reconstructed using not only currently accessible information, but also, in congruence with current needs and desires, people constantly rewrite their personal histories to justify their current opinions, decisions, and actions (Ross & Conway, 1986; Ross, 1989; Schank & Abelson, 1995). Memories are organized in such a way that they explain the presence. Their role is to show how the past determined and led to the present (Fischhoff, 1975; Giddens, 1991; Greenwald, 1980). The bias of retrospections may have its origin before the retrospection takes place. Constructive processes do not appear just at the time of retrieval to fill the gaps in memory. Most of the sensory information is not stored at all; only a few fragments are recorded. Neuropsychological research showed that, already at the encoding stage, details are replaced by generalizations (Schacter, 1996). Trying to solve the dilemma, some researchers of hindsight bias manipulated the depth of information processing and the similarity of feedback to participants' answers. They reached the conclusions that the retrieval errors were small, and the reconstruction errors were responsible for most of the bias (Stahlberg, Eller, Romahn, & Frey, 1993; Stahlberg & Mass, 1998). Many authors believed that cognitive autobiography is constantly rewritten. When an opinion changes, the information structure is reworked, ordered, and adjusted to fit the new point of view. As the new structure literally takes the place of the old, the former structure is gone and inaccessible. Some authors claimed that all opinions are temporary constructions, judgments created on the spot when a question is posed (Schwarz, 2007). In these scenarios, the only possible memories of the old opinion may be reminiscences of expressing it stored in the episodic memory. This view might be supported by results showing smaller hindsight bias in the memory design, in which respondents are actually asked to express their opinion before they learn what is the right thing to think, than in the hypothetical design, in which they never really express their original estimates (e.g., Winman, 1999).

Anchor and Adjust

The first constructive cognitive explanation of the origin of retrospective opinions, which did not refer to memory retrieval, assumed that people reconstruct their former opinions by anchoring on the most accessible current opinion and adjusting it to reflect the past (e.g., Wilson & Ross, 2001). According to this explanation, the fact that this type of adjustment that people make is usually insufficient (Lopes, 1982; Slovic & Lichtenstein, 1971; Tversky & Kahneman, 1974) can explain the observed false consistency of retrospective and current opinions (e.g., Hawkins & Hastie, 1990).

The insufficient adjustment hypothesis was not able to account for situations in which differences between retrospections and current opinions were bigger than differences observed in repeated measurement design (e.g., McFarland, Ross, & Giltrow, 1992). To accommodate for these findings, some researchers (Conway & Ross, 1984; McFarland et al., 1992) claimed that in a process of recalling a past opinion the current opinion is adjusted according to a personal implicit theory of change (or stability), extending the original proposition of Nisbett and Wilson's (1977) that people answering questions about their mental processes make use of a naïve causal theories explaining what stimuli might be a plausible cause of behavior, to the domain of retrospective opinions. Like in the original theory of Nisbett and Wilson (1977), these theories may have various sources, such as cultural beliefs about developmental changes (Ross, 1989), beliefs about population trends (Markus, 1986), or motivation for self-image consistency (e.g., Baumeister, 1995).

The anchor-and-adjust model of retrospective opinions has several limitations. If we agree with the view that most opinions are generated as they are expressed (e.g., Schwarz, 2007), then the strategy in which we first generate the current opinion and then adjust it according to implicit theories would be against the principle of cognitive economy (Fiske & Taylor, 1991). The anchor-and-adjust theory has little predictive value since it hardly indicates under what conditions retrospective opinions can be useful as an opinion research tool and when the change measured by the difference of current and retrospective opinions will be larger and when it will be smaller than the difference between current opinions and those expressed in the past.

The anchor-and-adjust theory did not distinguish between the implicit theory of opinion change and the theory of object change. According to the anchor-and-adjust theory, to compute retrospections, people use their implicit theories of opinion change, whereas most research assesses participants' theories of change of the object of the opinion (e.g., Conway & Ross, 1984; Hirt, Erickson, & McDonald,

1993; McFarland, Ross, & Giltrow, 1992) or even theories of the state of the object in the past (McFarland, Ross, & DeCourville, 1989).

Furthermore, observed correlation between expressed theories of change and the retrospection bias does not imply causation; the theories of change may very well result from biased retrospections of the past and not the other way around. Finally, experiments conducted by Hirt et al. (1993) showed that in the process of creating retrospections of opinions, people also make use of the original information and not only the current opinion and implicit theories of change.

Reconstructed Judgment

At this point, I would like to propose a more robust model. This model can account for the collected data and allows prediction when retrospective opinions would be more or less similar to current opinions than recorded past opinions. Even though the proposed model makes fewer assumptions about what information people use in their retrospections, it offers a bit more insight in the meaning of retrospective opinions and their potential usefulness.

The model assumes that retrospective opinions are generated in the same way as current opinions, by an inference based on any indications or cues that are accessible at the moment (Schwarz, 2007), including beliefs about change. It also allows for rendering judgment at the current time of the object of the opinion as it was remembered from the past. By inferring, we try to access information allowing for the most efficient and valid conclusion about the past opinion. If we agree that there are no mental records of former opinions, the most direct indication of past opinion is a reminiscence of expressing it. Unfortunately, the very reason for collecting retrospective opinions is often the fact that respondents were not asked earlier about their initial opinions. In this situation, people may have at their disposal memories of episodes involving behavior indicating one's past position (Bem, 1972). If no vivid memories of behavioral indicators of our position come to our mind, we can resort to producing retrospection the same way as current opinion. That is, we can produce it by judging the object of the opinion, with the difference that in our retrospection we should try to include only those indications that we would use in the past. The outcome judgment is determined by two main elements: the object and the form of construction process of the judgment. The retrospection of opinion will not match the past opinion when either of the two elements is not reconstructed correctly.

Respondents should have relatively little problem accounting in their retrospections for changes of opinion caused by a change of the object of the opinion. Systematic errors may appear due to omission if respondents do not remember the object in the past and they falsely assume that it was simply the same as it is now. Or, errors may appear if respondents have an incorrect theory concerning how the object was in the past.

It should be harder to accept and take into account changes of an opinion caused by a change in the way we judge the object. We have an inclination to attribute our own opinions to situational rather than dispositional causes (Jones & Nisbett, 1971). Furthermore, we neither have conscious control over our mental processes nor have conscious access to them (e.g., Nisbett & Wilson, 1977). Lack of control over our cognitive processes causes us not to be able to think "as if." Results of different research confirmed that we cannot purposely ignore certain information in our thinking or include some assumption that we know to be false (e.g., Pohl & Hell, 1996). If an opinion was affected by change in the way the judgment is rendered, there is very little chance that these changes would be taken into account and our retrospections would reflect them. Especially, the changes of observed opinions that happened due to changes in the three aspects of judgment (object interpretation, importance of cues, and standard of reference) will tend to render the retrospective opinion different from recorded past opinions.

Every formulation of an object has a certain level of ambiguity. Before we evaluate the object, we have to interpret its meaning (Schwarz, 1996; Sudman et al., 1996). These interpretations can vary in time. The inability to take into account that we ourselves interpreted the object of the opinion differently may be one of the sources of false consistency of our retrospective opinion with current opinions.

To test this hypothesis, we conducted two experiments. Two groups of 27 and 50 undergraduate first-year students expressed their opinion about the attractiveness of a popular brand of cars using a 7-point scale. They were also asked to evaluate in the same way one specific car of this brand. Besides that, they evaluated 16 other brands. Two weeks later, they were asked to recall their initial opinions. Meanwhile, for some of the participants, the context had been changed by replacing some of the other evaluated brands. In both experiments, the retrospection error measured as the absolute size of the difference between initial answer and recollection was significantly bigger for the more vague or unknown brand than for the more specific car, $t_{(26)} = 3.22$, $p < .005$, $\eta^2 = .23$; and $t_{(44)} = 3.14$; $p < .005$, $\eta^2 = .17$. Moreover, in both experiments, there was no significant interaction between the effect of concreteness of the object of the opinion and the manipulation of the context. This indicates that the bigger retrospection errors for the more vaguely defined object were not produced by the manipulation of the standard of reference affecting the brand more than the specific car. However, it indicates that these errors were a product of participants not taking into account changes of object interpretation in their retrospections.

Ignoring the changes in reference standard used to render the judgment (e.g., Sudman et al., 1996; Wedell & Parducci, 1988) can also produce discrepancy between retrospections and past opinions.

In the experiments presented, participants' retrospections were dependent on whether at the time of retrospections the evaluated brand was accompanied by more expensive, cheaper, or the same brands as during the initial expression of the opinion. When the context of retrospection was different from the context of the initial expression of opinions, errors of the retrospection were *bigger* ($M = 1.23$, $SD = 0.68$) than when the contexts were the *same* ($M = 0.84$, $SD = 0.40$). The difference was statistically significant, $F(1, 46) = 5.39$; $p < .025$. Similarly, Higgins and Liberman (1994) conducted an experiment in which subjects recalled their evaluations of severity of a judge. They discovered that the reference context evoked by other judges' verdicts at the time of retrospections had a stronger effect on retrospections than the reference context in which the initial evaluations took place.

In the second study, 432 adult Poles who participated in the Polish General Social Survey (Cichomski & Sawinski, 1995) 9 years earlier were asked to recall their original answers. The analysis concerned three opinions: (a) political system satisfaction; (b) political views (these views were measured by answers to questions about support for socialism and the government role in reducing differences); and (c) family satisfaction. Satisfaction was measured by 6-point Likert scales. The size of the retrospective change was defined as the absolute value of the difference between answers to the question about the current opinion and the retrospection of the past opinion. Analogically, the observed opinion change was defined as the absolute value of the difference between answers to the question about the current opinion and the past opinion from the earlier wave of the panel. The consistency bias was measured by the difference between the retrospective and the observed change of opinion. Respondents whose retrospection was more similar to the current opinion than the past opinion was to the current opinion would show a positive consistency bias. Respondents showing retrospectively a greater magnitude of change than could be observed would have a negative consistency bias.

A repeated measures analysis of variance with the past, retrospective, and current family satisfaction as dependent variables showed the following results (Figure 7.1): The effect of time on family satisfaction was significant, $F(2, 836)$ = 43.59, $p < .001$, Partial η^2 = .094. Post hoc analyses using the Bonferroni post hoc criterion for significance indicated that the average family satisfaction was significantly lower currently than in the past, $t(418)$ = –9.19, $p < .001$. Accordingly, the average family satisfaction was also significantly lower currently than in the retrospections, $t(418)$ = 3.39, p = .002. However, the average family satisfaction was still significantly lower in the retrospections than in the past, $t(418)$ = 5.97, $p < .001$. The average retrospective satisfaction was halfway between the current

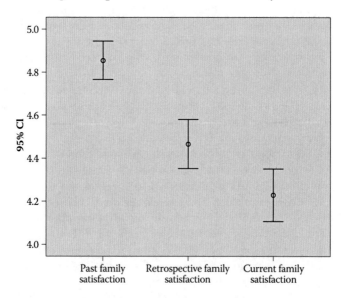

Figure 7.1   Past, retrospective, and current average family satisfaction.

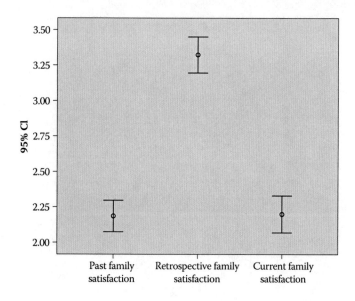

Figure 7.2 Past, retrospective, and current average political system satisfaction.

satisfaction and the past satisfaction. The results of the analysis of the size of the changes indicate that the observed changes of family satisfaction ($M = 1.07$, $SD = 1.08$) were significantly larger than the retrospective changes ($M = 0.92$, $SD = 1.11$), $t(418) = 2.74$, $p = .006$, partial $\eta^2 = .02$.

Similar analyses were carried out for political system satisfaction (Figure 7.2). There was a significant effect of time on political system satisfaction, $F(2, 722) = 178.42$, $p < .001$, partial $\eta^2 = .33$. Post hoc analyses using the Bonferroni post hoc criterion for significance indicated that there was no significant difference in average political system satisfaction between the past and current day, $t(361) = .21$, $p = .99$. Nevertheless, the average political system satisfaction was significantly lower currently than in the retrospections, $t(361) = -15.93$, $p < .001$. Accordingly, the past average political system satisfaction was also significantly lower than retrospections, $t(361) = -16.01$, $p < .001$. Retrospectively, political system satisfaction declined, while there was no significant observed change in satisfaction.

The results of the analysis of the size of the changes indicate that the observed changes of political system satisfaction ($M = 0.9$, $SD = 0.9$) were significantly smaller than the retrospective changes ($M = 1.3$, $SD = 1.16$), $t(418) = 5.22$, $p < .001$, partial $\eta^2 = .07$.

An analysis of variance showed that the effect of time on political views was significant, $F(2, 568) = 34.61$, $p < .001$, partial $\eta^2 = .11$ (Figure 7.3). Post hoc analyses using the Bonferroni post hoc criterion for significance indicated that there was a significant difference in average political views in the past and currently, $t(284) = 7.12$, $p < .001$. Respondents were currently more left-wing oriented than in the past. Accordingly, the average political views were currently also significantly more left wing than in the retrospections, $t(284) = -4.49$, $p < .001$. However, the past average political system satisfaction was still significantly lower than the retrospective

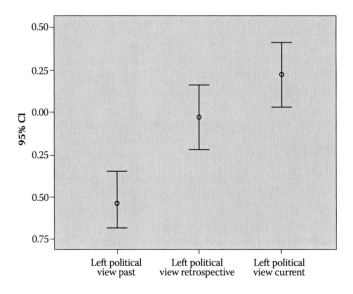

Figure 7.3   Past, retrospective, and current average political views.

political system satisfaction, $t(284)$ = 4.75, p < .001. Respondents retrospectively underestimated how much more right wing their opinions were.

The results of the analysis of the size of the changes indicated that the observed changes of political views (M = 1.46, SD = 1.20) were significantly smaller than the retrospective changes (M = 0.55, SD = 0.84), $t(418)$ = 5.22, p < .001, partial η^2 = .31.

Both studies confirmed the existence of a general consistency bias, with one exception: satisfaction with political system. For this opinion, retrospective changes were bigger than observed changes. This confirms the presented model of the construction of retrospections of opinion. It agrees with the assumption that perceived changes in the object of the opinion can be reflected in retrospective opinions differing from current opinions, while no shift can be observed between actual initial and current records of opinions. The change of the object was accompanied by a parallel shift of evaluation standard. Between the two waves of the study, there was an objective change in the political system of the country. Respondents who were disappointed with it produced retrospections more favorable than their current opinions. However, when they were expressing their opinions in the past, they used different standards. Their opinions expressed in the past were almost exactly as unfavorable as the current opinions expressed 9 years later.

In summary, we can say that our retrospections of opinions are rather current opinions about retrospections of the object. This is a result of our limited ability of taking into account changes of the interpretation of the object, changes in the values assigned to different aspects of it, or changes in our evaluation standards. Whenever any of the mentioned aspects of judgments has changed, the retrospective opinion will not be in line with the opinion expressed in the past. If there has been no change in the way judgment is constructed, retrospections may be accurate as long as the retrospection of the object in the past is accurate. Applying this theory to retrospections of opinions about various objects makes us expect that if a respondent recognizes an objective change of an object's attributes, then the respondent should assume that his or her opinion about the object has changed accordingly. Moreover, the respondent should then produce a retrospection that is different from the current opinion, independently of what the actual expression of the opinion was in the past. In contrast, if the object of an opinion did not change subjectively, for example, because it was abstract (Bergman, 1998), respondents tended to produce retrospections that were identical to their current opinions.

MOTIVATIONAL FACTORS IN CONSTRUCTION OF RETROSPECTIVE OPINIONS

Independent of whether retrospections involve retrieval or are results of inferences based on accessible information, motivation can serve as a filter selecting what information will be used in this process. Retrospective opinions may be affected by the motivation to maintain two aspects of self: self-esteem and self-consistency. To predict how these motives can affect retrospections, it is useful to keep in mind the distinction between the object of opinion and the judgment process as the two motives work differently on these two entities.

Motives Operating on Recall of Object of an Opinion

People attempt to maximize their self-esteem (e.g., Solomon, Greenberg, & Pyszczynski, 1991). In the absence of objective reasons, self-esteem may be enhanced by a set of self-glorification biases (Schlenker & Weigold, 1992). Self-serving judgments can generate positive affect, and people may utilize them to regulate their mood (Roese & Olson, 2007). The motivation to maintain positive self-esteem operates differently on opinions of which the object is an aspect respondent's Self than on opinions about other objects. For example, a different motivation will play a role for an opinion about one's skill than for an opinion about skills of the local government. In the first case, self-esteem maintenance motivation can guide the recollection of the object, allowing for a positive conclusion about oneself. Indeed, multiple research demonstrated our tendency to present the past in too positive a light (e.g., Bahrick, Hall, & Berger, 1996; Field, 1981).

The same motivation can have a completely opposite effect on retrospections when the past self can serve as a reference for the present self. Downward comparisons maintain positive self-esteem. In addition, depreciating the past self can allow one to see an improvement. Results of several studies demonstrated that people indeed tend to report their former self as inferior to the current self (e.g., Karney & Frye, 2002; Wilson & Ross, 2001). For instance, Hagerty (2003), in a meta-analytical study of life satisfaction, demonstrated that in every survey that asks people how happy their own lives are now compared to a moment in the past, a majority say they are happier now than in the past. At the same time, they believe that the quality of life of the average person was better in the past.

The second type of motivation, consistency motivation, also has a special influence on opinions about self. Some researchers contrasted experimentally the self-consistency and self-positivity motives. They showed that people with a negative self-image were ready to deny themselves success to keep their consistent negative self-image (Swann, 1996), and they preferred negative feedback confirming their self-image (Giesler & Swann, 1999). Even though in specially designed studies these two motives were contrasted, in most cases they worked in the same direction. People tended to maintain a positive, slightly exaggerated, self-image as consistently as possible (Baumeister, 1995). They tried to take into account those situations and comparisons that confirmed this image (Linville & Carlston, 1994).

Motives Operating on Reconstruction of Judgment

For retrospections of opinions about objects different from oneself, the object can determine a unique set of motivational forces influencing its retrospection. Not taking into account changes of our opinions that cannot be attributed to changes of its object can also be linked to self-positivity and self-consistency motivation. In this case, both motives seem to go hand in hand, regardless of the level of self-esteem a person has.

Positive Self-Esteem Motivation

First, motivations to be competent and maintain positive self-esteem can make us believe that we have opinions (Bridge, Reeder, Kanouse, Kinder, Nagy, & Judd, 1977). Having no opinion on most subjects is perceived negatively. The results of cognitive dissonance experiments can be attributed to the motivation to maintain positive self-esteem (Steele, 1988; Steele, Spencer, & Lynch, 1993). The motivation to maintain positive self-esteem can also contribute to hindsight bias; by claiming that they "knew it all along," participants may present themselves as wise, knowledgeable, and in control (Campbell & Tesser, 1983), or by claiming that they could never saw it coming, they can avoid assuming responsibility for failure (Pezzo & Pezzo, 2007). The role of motivation in the genesis of hindsight bias was also supported by results showing that the size of hindsight bias depended on the relevance of the outcome (Walster, 1967). Campbell and Tesser (1983) showed a positive correlation between hindsight bias and ego involvement and need for positive self-presentation and social desirability. The retrospections of subjective opinions can be even more susceptible to this kind of self-enhancing bias. Because of its subjective nature, the currently held opinion is always correct. Therefore, admitting to having a different opinion about exactly the same object in the past would mean admitting to have been wrong in the past.

Self-Consistency Motivation

Depending on the theoretical approach, the consistency motivation can be understood as an instrumental or an internal motive. According to most instrumental interpretations, people tend to present themselves as consistent to maintain a positive impression (e.g., Schlenker, 1982; Tedeschi, 1981). Experiments have shown that hindsight bias is positively associated with the desire to maintain a high level of public and private esteem, measured by social desirability and impression management scales (Musch & Wagner, 2007).

The consistency bias may be a product of an internal need to maintain consistency of the self for oneself (Aronson, 1992), not for publicity or social benefit. According to Fabrigar and Krosnick (1995), one's self-esteem may depend to a degree on the belief that one holds correct attitudes.

The most internal type of consistency motivation might be the need to avoid the unpleasant feeling of cognitive dissonance (Festinger, 1957). According to the cognitive explanation of this phenomenon, this feeling is caused by having two inconsistent cognitions that are simultaneously active (e.g., Newby-Clark, McGregor, & Zanna, 2002). This feeling could be experienced when we are confronted with our inconsistent opinions.

All aforementioned motives do not have to lead to retrospective stability of opinion if qualities of the object of opinion have changed subjectively. A respondent remains perfectly consistent if his or her opinion change reflects an objective change of its object. Moreover, a respondent could be perceived as inconsistent if the respondent would not change his or her opinion despite an apparent change of the object of the opinion. For instance, it does not discredit a person if his or her opinion about a certain government changed after it was revealed that members of this government were corrupt. People do not need to keep their opinions stable if they have accessible beliefs about changes of the objects of their opinion. In the language of cognitive dissonance theory, we could refer to this mechanism as resolving the dissonance by addition of a third cognition recovering the balance between inconsistent cognitions (Leippe & Eisenstadt, 1999). If we would like to explain the mechanism in the language of impression management theory (Schlenker, 1982; Tedeschi, 1981) or self-consistency theory (Aronson, 1992), we could note that, if the quality of the political system deteriorated as a result of government change, one is expected to have a more negative opinion about it. Not changing one's opinion in this situation might seem not only inconsistent, but also irrational. Only in the case of stable objects are we consistently motivated to perceive our past opinions as identical to our current opinions.

Determinants of the Strength of Motivation

According to almost all theoretical approaches, the personal relevance of the object of the opinion should affect the strength of the motivation working on the opinion and through it affect the size of consistency bias (e.g., in the framework of the cognitive dissonance theory). The strength of motivation to perceive stability of one's opinion is related to the importance of the opinion and its relation to the self (Aronson, 1999; Thibodeau & Aronson, 1992).

Thus, I hypothesized that if the tendency to retrospect our past opinions as similar to current opinions has motivational sources, then the retrospections of opinions related to the self should be more biased toward current opinions than retrospections of opinions less related to the self.

The first study used the results of the Youth-Parent Socialization Panel Study, 1965–1982 (Jennings, Kent, Markus, & Niemi, 1991). For the analyses that are presented here, the answers of 1,135 offspring and 898 parents, who took part in the second and third wave of the panel, were used. For the first analysis, complete data existed for 456 white parent-child pairs and 38 African American pairs. For the second analysis, complete data existed for 620 parents (245 men and 375 women) and 901 children (439 males and 462 females). During the third wave of the panel, respondents answered a question about their opinion about governmental help for minorities, in particular for the African American minority. The scale of the answers stretched from 1 (the government should help minority groups) to 7 (minority groups should help themselves). Respondents were also asked to recall their opinion about the subject from 9 years before, when they participated in the second wave of the study. The size of the retrospective and observed changes was defined in the same way as in the study previously discussed.

I assumed that governmental help for minorities is more self-relevant for subjects who are minority members than for white Americans. Accordingly, in the first analysis, African Americans, who were considered a high-relevancy group, were compared to white Americans, a low-relevancy group. The results (Figure 7.4) confirmed a general consistency bias: Retrospective changes were significantly smaller than observed changes, $F(1, 492) = 87.33$, $p < .05$, $\eta^2 = .15$. Confirming the hypothesis that there was a significant interaction between the type of change and

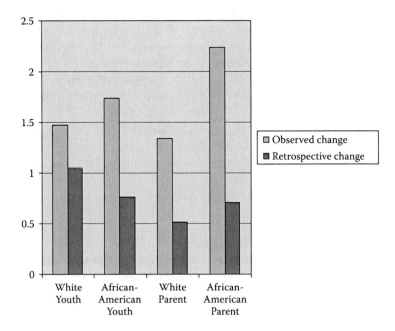

Figure 7.4   Observed and retrospective changes of opinions about governmental help for minorities.

race, $F(1, 492) = 9.9, p < .05, \eta^2 = .02$, African Americans retrospectively under-estimated changes of their opinion more than white Americans. Moreover, there was a significant main effect of race, $F(1, 492) = 6.27, p < .05, \eta^2 = .013$, indicating that African Americans changed their opinions more than white Americans. There was also a significant interaction between the type of change and the age, $F(1, 492) = 6.73, p < .05$, partial $\eta^2 = .013$: The differences between retrospective and observed changes were bigger for parents than for children.

In the second analysis, female and male respondents were compared on their retrospective and observed changes in opinions about women's liberation. The scale for the original questions stretched from 1 (women should have an equal role "in running government, industry, and business") to 7 (a woman's place is in the home). It was assumed that women's rights are a more relevant object for female than for male respondents. Therefore, women were considered a high-relevancy group, while men were a low-relevancy group. Data for parents and children were analyzed separately with a mixed analysis of variance (ANOVA) design with the type of change as a within-subject factor and gender as a between-subject factor (Figure 7.5).

For the youth, there was a weak significant main effect of the type of change, $F(1, 899) = 3.99, p < .05, \eta^2 = .004$. This effect was caused only by female respondents, whose retrospective opinion changes were smaller than observed. The main effect of the type of change was much stronger for parents than for youth $F(1, 618) = 153.81, p < .05$, partial $\eta^2 = .2$. Independent of gender, parents' retrospective opinion changes were smaller than observed. In the youth group, there was a significant

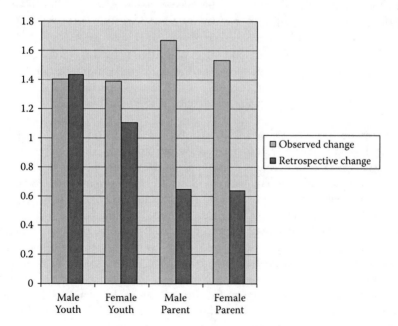

Figure 7.5 Observed and retrospective changes of opinions about equal rights for women.

interaction between the type of change and gender, $F(1, 899) = 5.68$, $p < .05$, partial $\eta^2 = .006$: Young women retrospectively underestimated changes of their opinion about women's role more than young men. For the group of parents, the results were different: There was no significant interaction between the type of change and gender, $F(1, 618) = 0.68$, $p > .05$, partial $\eta^2 = .001$. The consistency bias of mothers was not significantly different from that of fathers. This can be explained by the fact that for male respondents living with their wives, women's liberation might also be a self-relevant issue as it defines their role, whereas for younger male respondents the issue often had as little self-relevance as assumed.

The second analysis also concerned the relationship between gender and retrospective opinion about female emancipation and utilized the earlier sample of Poles presented. The sizes of the observed and retrospective opinion change were measured similar to the prior studies. Among other questions, Polish respondents expressed their opinion about four issues concerning women's emancipation:

A working mother can establish just as warm and secure a relationship with her children as a mother who does not work.

A preschool child is likely to suffer if his or her mother works.

A man's job is to earn money; a woman's job is to look after the home and family.

Women should take care of running their homes and leave running the country up to men.

In the results (Figure 7.6), the general consistency bias was confirmed by a statistically significant main effect of the type of change: Retrospective changes were significantly smaller than observed changes, $F(1, 427) = 234.34$, $p < .001$, $\eta^2 = .35$. There was no significant main effect of gender, $F(1, 427) = 234.34$, $p > .05$, $\eta^2 = .001$. Confirming the hypothesis, there was a significant interaction between the type of change and gender, $F(1, 427) = 4.49$, $p < .05$, partial $\eta^2 = .01$: The differences between retrospective and observed changes were bigger for women than for men.

The results of the statistical analyses confirmed that the relevance to self of the object of the opinion can lead to an increase of stability bias in retrospections of opinions. Retrospective opinions were more similar to current opinions than they should be: Retrospective opinions were closer to current opinions than the true past opinions had been. The exaggeration of the similarity was larger when the object of the opinion was relevant for respondents. People tended to overestimate retrospectively the similarity of their current and past opinions more when the object of the opinion was personally relevant. Nevertheless, this effect was weak. Earlier studies of similar phenomena managed to find only a weak relationship between motivational factors and size of bias (e.g., Campbell & Tesser, 1983). The weakness of the effect may suggest that the consistency bias has mostly cognitive procedural sources. A similar explanation was assumed by Fabrigar and Krosnick (1995), who did not find an effect of attitude importance on the size of false consensus, and Leary (1981), who was not able to find an effect of ego involvement on hindsight bias.

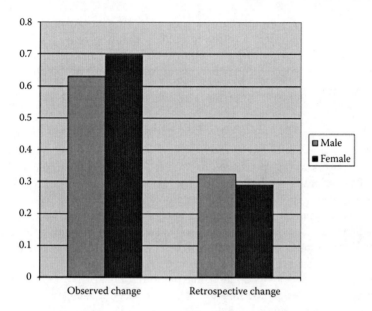

Figure 7.6   Observed and retrospective changes of opinions about women liberation.

Alternative explanations of the weakness of the effect may involve the afore-mentioned change of the object of the opinion. In this research, we took into account opinions about relatively stable, abstract objects (women, minorities). Thus, self-relevance of the object should be related to the tendency to under-estimate the opinion change. However, due to a really long time gap between expressing the initial opinion and the retrospection, some respondents might have believed that even abstract objects such as women or minorities had changed. In certain situations, one can change opinion about something even if the object remains unchanged. For instance, if the opinion that one tries to recall is fairly old, one might believe that one's opinion changed as a result of personal develop-ment. One improved the way of evaluating the object from good to even better. It could happen gradually over a long time or rapidly as a result of sudden enlight-enment. In both cases, a third cognition is being added to the two inconsistent cognitions, resolving the inconsistency in a positive way. In terms of impression management theory, this solution is perfectly acceptable, as long as the explana-tion for opinion change is plausible and presents one in a positive light. Another acceptable reason for changing opinion about an unchanged object might be the acquisition of new information about the object. Even though the object itself did not change, new knowledge about the facts of it became available. The result would be the same as in the case when the object would change: One may change opinion and remain consistent.

The whole study utilized a nonrandomized design, so any obtained results are open to countless alternative interpretations. For example, I assumed that differences in consistency bias between African Americans and white Americans and between women and men were due to higher self-relevance of the object of the opinion for one group than for the other. However, it might just as well be because one group held a different opinion than the other. Only additional research, utilizing a larger variety of opinion objects and an experimental manipulation of self-relevance of the objects could rule out some of the potential alternative explanations.

CONCLUSION

This chapter proposed a model of construction of retrospective opinions understood as answers to questions such as, "What was your opinion about … in the past?" The proposed model draws on the construal theory of attitudes, assuming that expressed opinions are products of judgment processes. According to our proposition, an opinion is a product of a judgment of an object. The outcome can change due to a subjective change in the object and due to changes in the judgment process (interpretation of the meaning of the object, importance attached to different cues or aspects of the object, and reference standards used).

When we try to recall an opinion, due to motivational pressures and the nature of cognitive processes, we are unable to take into account changes in the cognitive processes we used to render the judgment. As a result, retrospections of opinions are current opinions about objects as we recall them rather than recollections of opinions that we expressed in the past. If the process of judgment changed between the initial expression of the opinion and its recollection, retrospections will not be equal to the formerly expressed opinions. The size of the difference between them depends on the amount of change in the process. The direction of the bias is mostly dependent on the type of the object of the opinion. Retrospective opinions about subjectively stable objects are going to show consistency bias, whereas retrospective opinions about objects that subjectively changed may be more different from current opinions than opinions expressed in the past are.

The model has several implications. First is the methodological suggestion that retrospection of opinions cannot be treated as simple replacement of opinions collected in the past, although they might be interesting as predictors of behavior. It might be more useful to ask questions about current opinions about the past straightaway. However, the answers to those questions might also be biased by the motivation to see the change in the object of the opinion (Ross, 1989). This is particularly likely if the object of opinion is Self.

Second, another merit of the proposed model is that it integrates results concerning retrospective opinions collected separately under three different paradigms: attitude measurement, cognitive dissonance, and hindsight bias.

While the model explains well most results, it has been tested only for opinions about some specific objects, which certainly do not form a representative sample of objects of opinion in general. Future research in this direction should be carried out to assess the scope of the theory and to increase the robustness of predictions.

REFERENCES

Aronson, E. (1992). The return of the repressed: Dissonance theory makes a comeback. *Psychological Inquiry, 3*, 303–311.

Aronson, E. (1999). Dissonance, hypocrisy, and the self-concept. In E. Harmon-Jones & J. Mills (Eds.), *Cognitive dissonance: Progress on a pivotal theory in social psychology* (pp. 103–126). Washington, DC: American Psychological Association.

Aronson, E., & Wieczorkowska, G. (2001). Kontrola naszych myśli i uczuć. Warszawa: Santorski.

Bahrick, H. P., Hall, L. K., & Berger, S. (1996). Accuracy and distortion in memory for high school grades. *Psychological Science, 7*(5), 265-271.

Bartlett, F. C. (1932). *Remembering*. Cambridge, UK: Cambridge University Press.

Baumeister, R. F. (1995). Self and identity: An introduction. In A. Tesser (Ed.), *Advanced social psychology* (pp. 51–97). New York: McGraw-Hill.

Belli, R. F., Schuman, H., & Jackson, B. (1997). Autobiographical misremembering: John Dean is not alone. *Applied Cognitive Psychology, 11*, 187–209.

Bem, D. J. (1972). Self-perception theory. In L. Berkowitz (Ed.), *Advances in experimental social psychology* (Vol. 6, pp. 1–62). New York: Academic Press.

Bem, D. J., & McConell, H. K. (1970). Testing the self perception explanation of dissonance phenomena: On the salience of premanipulation attitudes. *Journal of Personality and Social Psychology, 14*, 23–31.

Bergman, M. M. (1998). A theoretical note on the differences between attitudes, opinions, and values. *Swiss Political Science Review, 4*(2), 81–93.

Bridge, R. G., Reeder, L. G., Kanouse, D., Kinder, D. R., Nagy, V. T., & Judd, C. (1977). Interviewing changes attitudes—Sometimes. *Public Opinion Quarterly, 41*, 57-64.

Campbell, J. D., & Tesser, A. (1983). Motivational interpretations of hindsight bias: An individual difference analysis. *Journal of Personality, 51*, 605–620.

Christensen-Szalanski, J. J., & Fobian Willham, C. (1991). The hindsight bias: A meta-analysis. *Organizational Behavior and Human Decision Processes, 48*, 147–168.

Cichomski, B., & Sawinski, Z. (1995). Polish General Social Survey, 1992–1994 [Computer file]. Warsaw, Poland: University of Warsaw, Institute for Social Studies [producer], 1994. Ann Arbor, MI: Inter-university Consortium for Political and Social Research [distributors], 1995.

Conway, M., & Ross, M. (1984). Getting what you want by revising what you had. *Journal of Personality and Social Psychology, 47*, 738–748.

Dawes, R. M. (1988). *Rational choice in an uncertain world*. San Diego, CA: Harcourt, Brace, Jovanovich.

Diener, E., & Biswas-Diener, R. (2002). Will money increase subjective well-being? *Social Indicators Research, 57*, 119–169.

Diener, E., Suh, E., & Oishi, S. (1997). Recent findings on subjective well-being. *Indian Journal of Clinical Psychology, 24*, 25–41.

Fabrigar, L. R., & Krosnick, J. A. (1995). Attitude importance and the false consensus effect. *Personality and Social Psychology Bulletin, 21*, 468–479.

Fessel, F., Epstude, K., & Roese, N. J. (2009). Hindsight bias redefined: It's about time. *Organizational Behavior and Human Decision Processes, 110*, 56–64.

Festinger, L. (1957) *A theory of cognitive dissonance*, Stanford, CA: Stanford University Press.

Field, D. (1981). Retrospective reports by healthy intelligent elderly people of personal events of their adult lives. *International Journal of Behavioral Development, 4*(1), 77–97.

Fischer, D., Stewart A. L., Bloch D. A., Lorig, K., Laurent, D., & Holman, H. (1999). Capturing the patient's view of change as a clinical outcome measure. *Journal of the American Medical Association, 282*, 1157–1162.

Fischhoff, B. (1975). Hindsight not equal to foresight: The effect of outcome knowledge on judgement under uncertainty. *Journal of Experimental Psychology: Human Perception and Performance, 1*, 288–299.

Fischhoff, B., & Beyth, R. 1975. I knew it would happen: Remembered probabilities of once-future things. *Organizational Behavior and Human Performance, 13*, 1–16.

Fiske, S. T., & Taylor, S. E. (1991). *Social cognition* (2nd ed.). New York: McGraw Hill.

Frederick, S., and Loewenstein, G. (1999). Hedonic adaptation. In D. Kahneman, E. Diener, and N. Schwartz (Eds.), *Scientific perspectives on enjoyment, suffering, and well-being* (pp. 302–329). New York: Russell Sage Foundation.

Giesler, R. B., & Swann, W. B., Jr. (1999). Striving for confirmation: The role of self-verification in depression. In T. E. Joiner, Jr. & J. C. Coyne (Eds.), *The interactional nature of depression: Advances in interpersonal approaches* (pp. 189–217). Washington, DC: APA Press.

Giddens, A. (1991). *Modernity and self-identity: Self and society in the late modern age.* Cambridge, UK: Blackwell.

Greenwald, A. G. (1980). The totalitarian ego: Fabrication and revision of personal history. *American Psychologist, 35*, 603–618.

Hagerty, M. R. (2003). Was life better in the good old days? Intertemporal judgments of life satisfaction. *Journal of Happiness Studies, 4*, 115–139.

Hasher, L., Attig, M. S., & Alba, J. W. (1981). I knew it all along: Or, did I? *Journal of Verbal Learning and Verbal Behavior, 20*, 86–96.

Hawkins, S. A., & Hastie, R. (1990). Hindsight: Biased judgments of past events after the outcomes are known. *Psychological Bulletin, 107*, 311–327.

Herrmann, D. J. (1994). The validity of retrospective reports as a function of the directness of the retrieval process. In N. Schwarz & S. Sudman (Eds.), *Autobiographical memory and the validity of retrospective reports* (pp. 21–37). Berlin: Springer-Verlag.

Higgins, E. T., & Liberman, A. (1994). Memory errors from a change of standard: A lack of awareness or of understanding? *Cognitive Psychology, 27*, 227–258.

Hirt, E. R., Erickson, G. A., & McDonald, H. E. (1993). Role of expectancy timing and outcome consistency in expectancy-guided retrieval. *Journal of Personality and Social Psychology, 65*, 640–656.

Jennings, M., Kent, G. B. Markus, & Niemi R. G. (1991). Youth-Parent Socialization Panel Study, 1965–1982: Three waves [Computer file]. Ann Arbor, MI: University Michigan, Center for Political Studies/ Research Center [producers], 1983. Ann Arbor, MI: Inter-university Consortium for Political and Social Research [distributor].

Jones, E. E., & Nisbett, R. E. (1971). *The actor and the observer: Divergent perceptions of the causes of behavior.* New York: General Learning Press.

Joslyn, M. (2003). The determinants and consequences of recall error about Gulf War preferences. *American Journal of Political Science, 47*, 440.

Karney, B. R., & Frye, N. E. (2002). "But we've been getting better lately": Comparing prospective and retrospective views of relationship development. *Journal of Personality and Social Psychology, 82*, 222–238.

Kwong, J. Y. Y., & Hamilton L. V. (2004). Retrospective reports of organizational commitment after Russian military downsizing. *Applied Cognitive Psychology, 18*, 669–681.

Laird, J. D. (1989). Mood affects memory because feelings are cognitions. *Journal of Social Behavior and Personality, 4*(2), 33–38.

Leary, M. R. (1981). The distorted nature of hindsight. *Journal of Social Psychology, 115*, 25–29.

Leippe, M. R., & Eisenstadt, D. (1999). A self-accountability model of dissonance reduction: Multiple modes on a continuum of elaboration. In E. Harmon-Jones & J. Mills (Eds.), *Cognitive dissonance: Progress on a pivotal theory in social psychology* (pp. 201–232). Washington, DC: American Psychological Association.

Levine, L. J. (1997). Reconstructing memory for emotions. *Journal of Experimental Psychology: General, 126*, 165–177.

Lindsay, P. H., & Norman, D. A. (1972). *Human information processing: An introduction to psychology.* New York: Academic Press.

Linville, P. W., & Carlston, D. E. (1994). Social cognition of the self. In P. G. Devine, D. L. Hamilton, & T. M. Ostrom (Eds.), *Social cognition: Impact on social psychology* (pp. 143–193). San Diego, CA: Academic Press.

Loftus, E. F. (2003). Make-believe memories. *American Psychologist, 58*, 864–873.

Lopes, L. L. (1982). *Toward a procedural theory of judgment.* Wisconsin Human Information Processing Program, Technical Report 17, 1–49.

Lyons, T. F., & Dickinson, T. L. (1973). Comparison of perceived and computed change measure over a three year period. *Journal of Applied Psychology, 58*, 318–321.

Manstead, A. S. R., & Hewstone, M. (Eds.). (1995). *The Blackwell encyclopedia of social psychology.* Cambridge, UK: Basil Blackwell.

Markus, G. B. (1986). Stability and change in political attitudes: Observe, recall, and "explain." *Political Behavior, 8*, 21–44.

Matt, G. E., Vázquez, C., & Campbell, W. K. (1992). Mood-congruent recall of affectively toned stimuli: A meta-analytic review. *Clinical Psychology Review, 12*, 227–255.

McFarland, C., Ross, M., & DeCourville, N. (1989). Women's theories of menstruation and biases in recall of menstrual symptoms. *Journal of Personality and Social Psychology, 57*, 522–531.

McFarland, C., Ross, M., & Giltrow, M. (1992). Biased recollection in older adults: The role of implicit theories of ageing. *Journal of Personality and Social Psychology, 62*, 837–850.

Musch, J., & Wagner, T. (2007). Did everybody know it all along? A review of individual differences in hindsight bias. *Social Cognition, 25*, 64–82.

Neisser, U. (1981). John Dean's memory: A case study. *Cognition, 9*, 1–22.

Newby-Clark, I. R., McGregor, I., & Zanna, M. P. (2002). Thinking and caring about cognitive inconsistency: When and for whom does attitudinal ambivalence feel uncomfortable? *Journal of Personality and Social Psychology, 82*, 157–166.

Nisbett, R. E., & Wilson, T. D. (1977). Telling more than we can know: Verbal reports on mental processes. *Psychological Review, 84*, 231–259.

Norman, G. R., Stratford, P., & Regehr, G. (1997). Methodological problems in the retrospective computation of responsiveness to change: The lesson of Cronbach. *Journal of Clinical Epidemiology, 50*, 869–879.

Oppenheim, A. N. (2001) *Questionnaire design, interviewing and attitude measurement.* London: Pinter.

Palfai, T. P., & Salovey, P. (1992). The influence of affect on self-focused attention: Conceptual and methodological issues. *Consciousness and Cognition, 1*, 306–339.

Pezzo, M. V., & Pezzo, S. P. (2007). Making sense of failure: A motivated model of hindsight bias. *Social Cognition, 25*, 147–164.

Pohl, F., & Hell, W. (1996). No reduction in hindsight bias after complete information and repeated testing. *Organizational Behavior and Human Decision Processes, 67*, 49–58.

Powers, E. A., Goudy, W. J., & Keith, P. M. (1978). Congruence between panel and recall data in longitudinal research. *Public Opinion Quarterly, 42*, 380–389.

Roese, N. J., & Olson, J. M. (2007). Better, stronger, faster self-serving judgment, affect regulation, and the optimal vigilance hypothesis. *Perspectives on Psychological Science, 2*, 124–141.

Ross, M. (1989). The relation of implicit theories to the construction of personal histories. *Psychological Review, 96*, 341–357.

Ross, M., & Conway, M. (1986). Remembering one's own past: The construction of personal histories. In R. M. Sorrentino & E. T. Higgins (Eds.), *The handbook of motivation and cognition: Foundations of social behavior* (pp. 341–357). New York: Guilford Press.

Schacter, D. L. (1996). *Searching for memory.* New York: Basic Books.

Schank, R. C., & Abelson, R. P. (1995). Knowledge and memory: The real story. In R. S. Wyer Jr. (Eds.), *Knowledge and memory: The real story* (pp. 1–85). Hillsdale, NJ: Erlbaum.

Schlenker, B. R. (1982). Translating actions into attitudes: An identity-analytic approach to the explanation of social conduct. In L. Berkowitz (Ed.), *Advances in experimental social psychology* (Vol. 15, pp. 193–247). New York: Academic Press.

Schlenker, B. R., & Weigold, M. F. (1992). Interpersonal processes involving impression regulation and management. *Annual Review of Psychology, 43,* 133–168.

Schwarz, N. (1996). *Cognition and communication: Judgmental biases, research methods and the logic of conversation.* Hillsdale, NJ: Erlbaum.

Schwarz, N. (2007). Attitude construction: Evaluation in context. *Social Cognition, 25,* 638–656.

Slovic, P., & Lichtenstein, S. (1971). Comparison of Bayesian and regression approaches in the study of information processing and judgment. *Organizational Behavior and Human Performance, 6,* 649–744.

Smith, T. W. (1984). Recalling attitudes: An analysis of retrospective questions on the 1982 GSS. *Public Opinion Quarterly, 48,* 639–649.

Solomon, S., Greenberg, J., & Pyszczynski, T. (1991). A terror management theory of social behavior: The psychological functions of self-esteem and cultural worldviews. In M. P. Zanna (Ed.), *Advances in experimental social psychology* (Vol. 24, pp. 93–159). New York: Academic Press.

Stahlberg, D., Eller, F., Romahn, A., & Frey, D. (1993). Der Knew-it-all-along-Effekt in Urteilssituationen von hoher und geringer Selbstwertrelevanz. *Zeitschrift für Sozialpsychologie, 24,* 94–102.

Stahlberg, D., & Mass, A. (1998). Hindsight bias: Impaired memory or biased reconstruction? *European Journal of Social Psychology, 8,* 105–132.

Steele, C. M. (1988). The psychology of self-affirmation: Sustaining the integrity of the self. In L. Berkowitz (Ed.), *Advances in experimental social psychology* (Vol. 21, pp. 261–302). New York: Academic Press.

Steele, C. M., Spencer, S. J., & Lynch, M. (1993). Self-image resilience and dissonance: The role of affirmational resources. *Journal of Personality and Social Psychology, 64,* 885–896.

Sudman, S., Bradburn, N., & Schwarz, N. (1996). *Thinking about answers: The application of cognitive processes to survey methodology.* San Francisco, CA: Jossey-Bass.

Swann, W. B., Jr. (1996). *Self-traps: The elusive quest for higher self-esteem.* New York: Freeman.

Taylor, S. E., & Crocker, J. (1981). Schematic bases of social information processing. In E. T. Higgins, C. P. Herman, & M. P. Zanna (Eds.), *Social cognition: The Ontario Symposium* (Vol. 1, pp. 89–134). Hillsdale, NJ: Erlbaum.

Tedeschi, J. T. (Ed.) (1981). *Impression management theory and social psychological research.* New York: Academic Press.

Thibodeau, R., & Aronson, E. (1992). Taking a closer look: Reasserting the role of the self-concept in dissonance theory. *Personality and Social Psychology Bulletin, 18,* 591–602.

Tourangeau, R., Rips, L. J., & Rasinski, K. (2000). *The psychology of survey response.* Cambridge, UK: Cambridge University Press.

Tversky, A., & Kahneman, D. (1974). Judgment under uncertainty: Heuristics and biases. *Science, 185,* 1124–1131.

Van der Vaart, W., Van der Zouwen J., & Dijkstra, W. (1995). Retrospective questions: Data quality, task difficulty, and the use of a checklist. *Quality and Quantity, 29,* 299–315.

Walster, E. (1967). Second guessing important events. *Human Relations, 20,* 239–249.

Wedell, D. H., & Parducci, A. (1988). The category effect in social judgment: Experimental ratings of happiness. *Journal of Personality and Social Psychology, 55,* 341–356.

Wilson, A., & Ross, M. (2001). From chump to champ: People's appraisals of their earlier and present selves. *Journal of Personality and Social Psychology, 80,* 572–584.

Winman, A. (1999). Cognitive processes operating in hindsight. *Scandinavian Journal of Psychology, 40,* 135–145.

WordNet (2007). Opinion. WordNet® 3.0, a lexical database for the English language, Cognitive Science Laboratory, Princeton University. Retrieved July 22, 2007, from http://wordnet.princeton.edu/perl/webwn

8

From Human Creative Cognitive Processes to Adaptable Artificial System Design

GIOVANNA MORGAVI, LUCIA MARCONI,
MAURO MORANDO, and PAOLA CUTUGNO

INTRODUCTION

Since the year 2000, a number of researchers have suggested a developmental perspective on artificial intelligence (AI) and robotics. One of the fundamental methodological assumptions is that cognition is *embodied*, which means that it arises from bodily interactions with the world and that it is continuously meshed with them (Lungarella & Pfeifer, 2001). In other words, thinking emerges from real-life experiences, from sensorimotor coordinated interactions, and from exploration of the surrounding environment (Metta & Fitzpatrick, 2003). Since the complexity of the structure of living beings is much higher than the complexity of actual artifacts, only a few experiments can be done; nevertheless, the increase of this perspective is important. On one hand, psychologists can provide the detailed empirical findings and theoretical generalizations that can guide the implementations of robotic systems capable of cognitive development. On the other hand, these implementations can help clarify, test, and even develop psychological theories, which, due to the complexity of the interaction processes involved, often cannot be exhaustively tested (Berthouze & Prince, 2003). Robots can be used to instantiate and investigate models originating from developmental psychology, and it is necessary to design robotic systems with better autonomy, adaptability, and sociability by applying the insights gained from ontogenetic development studies. Psychological experiments can provide rich and subtle accounts of infant behavior as it changes with age, but it is more difficult to track and describe internal changes.

Robotic models permit us to correlate the changing behaviors of the model in real time and space with all changes in internal representations and processes shown.

The ultimate shared goal among AI researchers seems to be the idea of bootstrapping high-level cognition through a process in which the agent interacts with a real physical environment over extended periods of time (Elman et al., 1996). The next logical step along the road to truly autonomous robots that can be used in unpredictable environments is to investigate how one might design robots capable of "growing up" through experience (Bateson, 2002). A developmental intelligence for robots that grow up must be able to generate autonomously representations for unknown knowledge and skills. Like humans and animals, evolving artifacts must learn in real time while performing "on the fly" (Steels, 1996). Natural systems provide an exceptional source of inspiration for AI. Given the vastness of the information available in nature, the question arises regarding what insights from biology could and should be exploited for designing robots. Simply copying a biological system is either not feasible (even a single neuron is too complicated to be synthesized artificially in every detail) or of little interest (animals have to satisfy multiple constraints that do not apply to robots, such as keeping their metabolism running and getting rid of parasites), or the technological solution is superior to the one available in nature (for example, the biological equivalent of the wheel has yet to be discovered). Rather, working out some principles of biological systems that can in some way be used as inspiration in robot design is important.

Although many challenges remain, concepts from biologically inspired (bioinspired) artifacts can enable researchers to engineer machines for the real world that possess at least some of the desirable properties of biological organisms, such as adaptivity, robustness, versatility, and agility. Biologically motivated intelligent computing has in recent years been successfully applied to solving complex problems. Biological organisms have evolved to perform and survive in a world characterized by rapid changes, high uncertainty, indefinite richness, and limited availability of information. Industrial systems, in contrast, operate in highly controlled environments with no or very little uncertainty. Artifacts having to perform in the real world should be able to cope with uncertain situations and react quickly to changes in the environment. New approaches in which intelligence is not given to the system from outside but is acquired by the system through learning, have proven much more successful. The next logical step along the road to truly autonomous robots that can be used in unpredictable environments is to investigate how one might design robots that are capable of evolving through experience.

Interdisciplinary theory and empirical evidence are used to inform epigenetic robotic models, and these models can be used as theoretical tools to make experimental predictions in developmental psychology and other disciplines studying cognitive development in living systems.

Living systems, starting from a prestructured set of functions, develop competence to better adapt to the environment throughout the life span, from fledging to mature forms or structures. Epigenetic systems, whether natural or artificial, share a prolonged developmental process through which varied and complex cognitive and perceptual structures emerge as a result of the interaction of an embodied system with a physical and social environment.

The Darwinian gradualist concept of evolution considers development as the cumulative result of a large number of very small changes that occur over a long period of time. This gradual, continuous process is driven by the blind process of natural selection. Successful biological adaptation was fueled by a process of random variation and mutation. Highly homogeneous species have limited chances of survival if the environment changes beyond certain bounds. Vested or acquired features keep the system from mutation. This equilibrium lasts until the system is no longer able to assimilate demands for change into its existing structure. A great deal of current research work in robotics and autonomous systems is still focused on getting an agent to learn to do some task such as recognizing an object or going to a specific place. The learning process may be supervised or unsupervised or involve a process of occasional reinforcement, but the whole aim in such work is to get the robot to achieve a task that was predefined by the researcher. The artificial neural network (ANN) models are defined within this paradigm (Rumelhart, Hinton, & Williams, 1986). ANN models are budded from the observation and the simplification of the neuron network in nature. These models allow the optimization of learning specific functions in specific environments (Smith, Ward, & Finke, 1995):

- Supervised ANN models take care of general and conditioning effects of the environment on learning.
- Unsupervised ANNs take care of the internal classification criteria.

Some ANNs are able to generate explicit rules, but none can mime the "cognitive jump" of using something that has been learned as a starting point for reaching a new level of learning, an ability that is common in human beings. In nature, the stage theories of development reflect a discontinuous qualitative change from one stage to another (Kellman & Arterberry, 1998; Ross et al., 2003). Each person develops through a successive, mostly invariant, sequence of stages. Each stage is characterized as more complex than the preceding one and having in its structure subsumed all the cognitive, relational, and organized structures of the previous stages (Thelen & Linda, 1994). In humans, the stage sequence is, in some way, always affordable and flexible: In a later stage, a person can be more able to cope with schematas belonging to an earlier stage.

The transition between stages, denoting the growing-up process, is possible through the assimilation and accommodation dynamic: The assimilation represents the bias of the system to stability. The system maintains itself stable until environment, events, and different circumstances are consistent within its knowledge organization. The sequence of stages derives from the integration of several subprocesses. Each subprocess is unsynchronized with development in other subprocesses (Guastello, 1995). This process called growing up involves, among other things, the processing of perception, knowledge organization, the emotions, the value system, the motivations and drives, the experiences, and the social interactions (Floreano, Mitri, Magnenat, & Keller, 2007).

Literature is confusing on this topic, but many authors clearly endorsed the claim that growing up consists of the same mental processes involved in creative thinking. Many researchers (Finke, Ward, & Smith, 1992) stated that the ability to produce novelty is necessary in common everyday thinking, suggesting that the mechanisms that underlie creative thinking are normal ones. Weisberg (1995) and Ward (1995) emphasized the importance of prior knowledge in creative endeavors; they viewed it from the standpoint of knowledge retrieval and in terms of anteced-ent cognitive structures that underlie idea generation and exploration. Incubation, spreading activation, and contextual fluctuation have been attributed to normal cognitive mechanisms. Dynamical qualities of creative thinking were linked by Freyd and Pantzer (in Smith et al., 1995) to dynamic mental representations that typically give rise to memory distortions. Shank and Cleary (in Smith et al., 1995) defined creative thinking as an "intelligent misuse" of knowledge. Bateson (2002) called it learning to learn.

Everybody agrees that growing up is a fundamental step for adaptation to a new environment, for dealing with a new environment and new experiences, for learning to use what has been learned to reach new goals. In nature, many differ-ent phenomena are similar to what can be called the growing-up process: from insight to abstraction, from learning to learn to change the functional meaning of something that has been already learned. The common definition we can accept is that this process results in a step toward the enlargement of the internal knowl-edge map.

A living artifact grows up when its capabilities and abilities/knowledge shift to a further level of complexity (i.e. the complexity rank of its internal capabilities performs a step forward). Steels (1996) claimed that the new level can "slave" the level or the levels below, or it is possible to see a kind of coevolution toward greater complexity. Models of development can play an important role in specifying the minimal preferences, faculties, and processes needed for a new skill to emerge.

Growing up is an emergent mechanism (Morgavi, Morando, Biorci, & Caviglia, 2005). This means that it cannot be reduced to its parts. In other words, it exists at one level of structure but cannot be fully explained in terms of structure at a lower level. The dynamic systems approach (Ward, Patterson, & Sifonis, 2004) attributes the emergence of complex cognitive skills (e.g., finding objects, imitation, symbol grounding) to basic processes of attention and pattern learning in subsymbolic distributed networks. Robotic models of development can play an important role in specifying the minimal preferences, faculties, and processes needed for a skill to emerge. A better understanding of the growing up mechanism is fundamental for the knowledge of what really is intelligent behavior.

There are many skills that a robot might acquire that are uninteresting or unproductive for observers or even unrecognizable, such as the ability to percept, to classify objects, places, and situations that are not intelligible for human beings. We feel that higher-level skills should be skills that are manifested on appreciably longer timescales than lower-level ones. The ability to recognize a certain location, for example, involves internal and external activity over a longer timescale than the ability to avoid collisions. From the knowledge level (i.e., processing and analysis of input data coming from sensors), growing up introduces a new level of comprehen-sion of objects in relationship to other known objects. The new representation of the world will be more abstract, and it strikes roots in the experience connected to a preceding familiar object (Dreyfus, 2009).

For human beings, the process of abstraction deals with entities belonging to different levels. The abstraction is not something that one experienced at a particular time in the concrete world, but it captures the essence of many concrete experiences. Abstraction results from complex cognitive activities that lead to a growing up in knowledge, in mapping of the environment, in progression to language acquisition and production. Just as a seed transforms into a sprout that emerges from the ground as a plant, an abstract concept can originate from, and be grounded in, perceptual experiences, yet turn into something quite different from anything ever directly perceived. Thus, what was once a constellation of memories of similar experiences organizes itself into an entity whose structure resides primarily at a level that was not present in the constituents from whom it was derived (Knoblock, 1992). In the language research field, abstraction is an example of growing up (Weisberg, 1995). A better understanding of this mechanism could be useful for the knowledge of what really happen in a growing up process.

Let us look at a metaphor as an example of abstraction in the linguistic process. It consists of a relationship among meanings that take the context from one world to another. Abstractions not only are grounded in perceptual experience, retaining something of the "perceptual character" of the experiences from which they were derived, but also are a product or reasoning or creative thought. When we speak about "a sea of troubles," we are interested only in a part of the "sea," its dimension, while all the other meanings and images are discarded. If we are not able to think of the sea as an abstract entity, we will not be able to understand what can be the meaning of a sea of troubles. To reach the meaning, it is necessary to activate our abstraction capability (Morgavi, Biorci, & Martini, 2001). The exploratory behavior seems to "shape" the information flow in various sensory channels. It is easy to imagine which process is involved, but it is difficult to understand how this process starts and evolves.

In sum, our research questions are as follows: How does the process of metaphor understanding happen in nature? Which procedures allow people to bring out the understanding of the metaphor? What mechanisms are triggered?

THE EXPERIMENT

We studied the modalities through which preschool children (4–5 years old) bring out the understanding of metaphor hidden in common idiomatic sentences in their native language. We chose children of this age because of their level of cognitive development. The cognitive development of children of this age does not include the ability of abstraction, but they are able to explain the process they are thinking. We carried out this experiment in an infant school in the Genoese Municipality, Italy, which had a "Sea Laboratory" where children were accustomed to some sea animal names and some of their characteristics, but they were not in touch with the meaning of the idiomatic sentences requiring an abstract act to be understood. Forty-two phrases were proposed to about eight work groups of 9 or 10 children each; the children were asked to provide abstracted meanings for the phrases. The experimenter read a new sentence and asked for help to find its meaning. Children were allowed to talk, to draw, or to move around the classroom as they liked. The experimenter spurred on the meaning search through neutral communication.

The process was recorded, and then we analyzed the answers. Collective speech was analyzed to compensate for individual differences. We collected 6,838 answers and 290 drawings. This output has been analyzed and classified by 4 people. If an answer could be associated with more than one subprocess, each involved subprocess was counted, resulting on 7,230 path instances. Only answers with unanimous classification were accepted; this involved 28 rejections, corresponding to 0.39% of the total instances.

RESULTS

When an unknown new sentence was pointed out, an attention filter selecting only "salient" keywords was activated. This filter shows complex behavior and is connected to motivation, affective relationships, value systems, emotions, experiences, knowledge systems, and so on. When the children realized that in the proposed sentences there were some contradictions in comparison with the script of their concrete knowledge, at first they tried to apply different strategies to reach an acceptable internal configuration. The emotional (affective) state plays an important role in driving the choice of the investigative/creative procedure. Children reach abstraction through a combination/integration of different subprocesses (Figure 8.1).

The procedure applied during this experiment can be summarized as follows:

- When an unknown sentence is suggested, the first procedure is to verify whether the sequence of words can exist within the internal script called to mind.

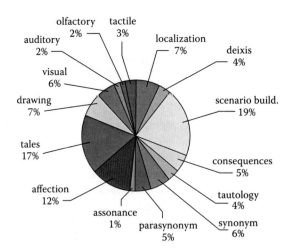

Figure 8.1   Distribution of the interpretation strategies applied by children to interpret metaphors.

- If an input sentence can be led back to the reference script, then it is accepted. The child adapts the new information to the previous knowledge. They propose consequence scenarios, or tautologies, avoiding the cognitive effort of abstraction.
- If within the scripts there are no acceptable solutions, the children carry out many different strategies.
- The children try to solve the current problem using the knowledge structures stored in their working memories. If the problem cannot be solved, the information-processing mechanism backtracking and another set of procedures are tried. If the problem cannot be solved with any possible set of procedures, the children start another set of associations of words.
- This procedure is repeated until a solution is found.

Children used the following mechanisms (see Figure 8.2):

- *Emotional reference*: Children mediated with their affective implications. Their answers were often driven especially by the affective/emotive point of view.
- *Psychomotor answers* (deixis): Ignoring a verbal answer, children tried to express their feeling through gestures or movements. Children tried to represent through the body what they could not interpret verbally.
- *Logical connections:* Children established forced cause–effect connections or tautologies.
- *Contextualization* (contextualization, localization, building scenarios, or tales): Children tried to integrate the unknown situations within their reality or they tried to build a coherent fantastic reality. They built stories that gave meaning to phrases. Drawings were also examples of this subprocess.
- *Sensorial similarities*: Children kept explanations as close as possible to their sensorial perceptions. The most-used sensorial modality was visual, followed by the auditory one. It seems that children have store in their mind most information as images.
- *Knowledge information storage* (parasynonyms, functional similarities, assonance): Sometimes, children chose a word similar to the ones used in the sentence to build an interpretation script. The similarity could be based on parasynonymy, on assonance, or on functional similarity (i.e., *volere il pesce senza lisca,* "to want a boneless fish" or "*to desire something impossible*"). A child said, "The fish could die unless you put new batteries inside its body!" A possible interpretation is that a fish without its *spina* (fishbone) could die unless you promptly put new batteries inside its body. In Italian, *spina* is a homograph that means both fishbone and plug. The connection the child made was that without a plug means without an energy source.

Children tried to find similarities for chosen keywords at a more abstract level of knowledge. They looked for assonance and known synonyms in their vocabulary. They decided that objects with similar functions are equal.

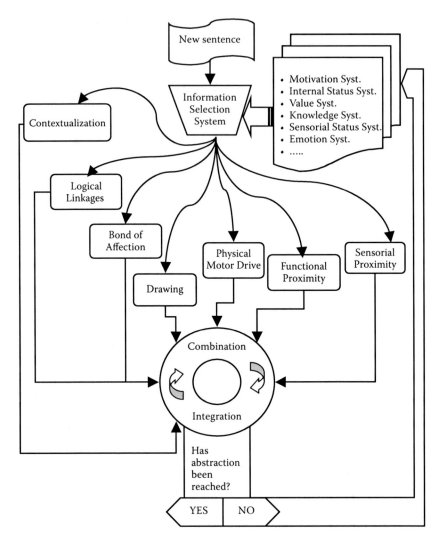

Figure 8.2   Information in the abstraction process in children.

Children tried to give "grammatical" definitions to the novel metaphorical inputs, focusing on the sense of the sentence and not on the referent. The interaction, the nonlinear combination, and the integration of these subprocesses lead to the emergence of abstracted concept learning as shown in Figure 8.2.

SUGGESTION FOR AN ARCHITECTURE FOR A ROBOT THAT GROWS UP

Our experiment resulted in some consideration for the architecture of a robot. As in human beings, an efficient developmental architecture shows a hierarchy of basic parallel paths for processing different aspects of knowledge, to let the growing-up phase emerge; an artificial architecture should be able to parallel process a combination of different paths in an internal representation (see Table 8.1).

To be able to grow up, a robot should have a large set of different sensors. For each set of sensor signals, there should be a number of characteristic extractors (i.e., using different signal-processing techniques like supervised and unsupervised ANNs, isomaps, genetic algorithms, chaotic signal characterization, etc.).

Children scanned memory using images, sound, and emotions as an index. Their memories were elicited from similar characteristics (i.e., colors, shapes, dimensions, positions) or from similar labels. Words with similar sounds were associated with the same meaning. Information in memory should be stored in such a way that the sensorial perspective should be respected. The structure memories work should follow a fuzzy logic. This probably will shorten the time for information retrieval.

Children used different types of memory: short-term memory and long-term memory, procedural memory, episodic memory. They built many cause–effect relationships between stories and words. Also the robot architectures should have some kind of motivational system to maintain a connection between the actual state and the previous and next steps. Only a few studies have evaluated the importance of generating motivational states to simulate future needs and to make possible anticipatory planning (Gulz, 1991).

Only a part of the input was processed. The attention was a function of many variables. Their previous experiences, their mood, their values, their emotions, their motivation systems, their drives, and their goals were fundamental triggers for the choice of the words to be processed.

The emotional world seems to be directing each level, and it seems to be involved in each information-processing box. Some articles on controllers based on emotional learning have shown good robustness and uncertainty-handling properties (Ogden & Richards, 1960).

As confirmed by Balkenius and Moren (1988), whether called emotional control or merely an equivalent version of reinforcement learning with critical (evaluative control), these methods should be increasingly utilized by control engineers, robotic designers, and decision support systems developers and should yield excellent results.

Although for a long time emotion was considered as a negative factor hindering the rational decision-making process, the important role of emotions in human cognitive activities is progressively being documented by other psychologists (Greene, Sommerville, Nystorm, Darley, & Cohen, 2001; Piaget, 1952).

Motivation, drive, value system, and emotions are very difficult to separate; they are strongly related to strong feedback from each other. Motivation is related to some well-known variables, including epistemic needs (needs of structure, for desired outcome), values, goals, and mood. The motivational system maintains a connection between actual state and the next step. Another suggestion from the experiment is that a human being does not act according to the objective situation, but based on a "personal perception of the situation." Since this has a major impact on the resulting behavior, a minimal cognitive apparatus performing characterization or classification using the robot's values should be provided. There is no need

TABLE 8.1   From Child Observation to Robot Design Suggestions

Child Observation	Interpretation Strategies	Mechanism	Robot Design Suggestion
Consequences Tautologies	Cause–effect relationship between stories (memories) and words in the sentence	Logical connections	The motivational system should maintain a connection between actual state and previous and next step.
Assonance Parasynonyms	Children scanned memory looking for similarities in sound or for parasynonyms	Knowledge information storage-functional similarities	The memory logical structure is important in information retrieval. The structure memories work should follow fuzzy logics.
Localization Building scenarios Tales	Different types of memories are used to look for meaning: short-term memory, long-term memory, episodic memory, procedural memory, semantic memory	Contextualization	Situatedness in a physical/social environment. The importance of some law for forgetting/remembering data. The introduction of episodic/procedural memories seems very new for AI field.
Visual proximity Auditory proximity Tactile proximity Olfactory proximity	Research of data stored in memory uses sensorial similarities as keywords	Sensorial proximity	Memories should be organized on similar functional characteristics (i.e., colors, shapes, dimension, and position) or from similar labels. The importance of the embodiment with the presence of a large set of different sensors to be processed in parallel. Feature extraction from different sensors should be connected. Information in memory should be stored in such a way that the sensorial perspective should be respected.
Affective-/emotional-based drive	The emotional and social world seems to be driving each level and to be involved in each information-processing step.	Bond of affection	Need of some kind of "emotional" system to follow the motivational system that is a keystone of the whole growing-up system.
Deixis Imitation	Search for something similar in the concrete past experience	Physical motor drive	Imitation and embodiment are fundamental steps of the growing-up system.

TABLE 8.1 (*Continued*)   From Child Observation to Robot Design Suggestions

Child Observation	Interpretation Strategies	Mechanism	Robot Design Suggestion
Only some input "keywords" were processed	Attention is driven by previous knowledge of motivation, emotion, internal states.	Information selection systems	Information does not need to be entirely processed. The choice of what is important underlines the need for a complex motivation internal system.

to produce a complete worldview by designing a complex ontology; only the most important decision criteria should be provided.

CONCLUSION

In this chapter, we underlined some of the most important characteristics of growing-up behavior, which we think are crucial to the creation of a realistic living artifact that is able to grow up, and we have identified some useful requirements. Some suggestions for the architecture of a new robot confirmed well-known needs, but some characteristics that are often neglected emerged. For instance, the growing-up experiment showed the need for a model of drive connected to the relationship among emotions, goal, and needs; the importance of the procedural memory and of the attention system; and the main influence of the contextualization procedures and of memory storage systems. All these topics are overlooked in AI research, which, for historical reasons, is more focused on other aspects, like embodiment, logical relationships, imitation mechanisms, and feature extractions. All the aspects are important for reaching an adaptive artifact that is able to grow up. This chapter created a reflection on the need for robotics research to be based on observed phenomena.

ACKNOWLEDGMENTS

This research was partially supported by the European Commission's Project "SIGNAL" (Systemic Intelligence for GrowiNg up Artifact that Live) IST-2000-29225. Partners in this project are the University of Bonn (Germany), Napier University Edinburgh (United Kingdom), OFAI Vienna (Austria), and IEIIT CNR Genoa (Italy).

REFERENCES

Balkenius, J., & Moren, A. (1988). Computational model of emotional conditioning in the brain. *Proceedings of the Workshop on Grounding Emotions in Adaptive Systems*, Zurich, Switzerland, August.

Bateson, G. (2002). *Mind and nature—A necessary unity.* New York: Hampton Press.

Berthouze, L., & Prince, C. G. (2003). Introduction. Epigenetic robotics. In C. G. Prince, L. Berthouze, H. Kozima, D. Bullock, G. Stojanov, & C. Balkenius (Eds.), *Proceedings of the Third International Workshop on Epigenetic Robotics: Modeling Cognitive Development in Robotic Systems.* Lund, Sweden: Lund University Cognitive Studies Volume 101.

Dreyfus, S. E. (2009). A modern perspective on creative cognition. *Bulletin of Science Technology Society, 29,* 3–8.

Elman, J., Bates, E., Johnson, M., Karmiloff-Smith, A., Parisi, D., & Plunkett, K. (1996). *Rethinking innateness.* Cambridge, MA: MIT Press.

Finke, R. A., Ward T. B., & Smith, S. M. (1992). *Creative cognition: Theory, research and application.* Cambridge, MA: MIT Press.

Floreano, D., Mitri, S., Magnenat, S., & Keller, L. (2007). Evolutionary conditions for the emergence of communication in robots. *Current Biology, 17,* 514–519.

Greene, J., Sommerville, R. B., Nystorm, L. E., Darley, J. M., & Cohen, J. D. (2001). An fMRI investigation of emotional engagement in moral judgment. *Science, 293,* 2105–2108.

Guastello, J. (1995). *Chaos catastrophe and human affairs.* Hillsdale, NJ: Erlbaum.

Gulz, A. (1991). *The planning of action as a cognitive and biological phenomenon.* Doctoral thesis, Lund University, Lund, Sweden.

Kellman, P., & Arterberry, M. E. (1998). Object perception. In P. Kellman & M. E. Arterberry (Eds.), *The cradle of knowledge: Development of perception in infancy* (Chap. 5). Cambridge, MA: MIT Press.

Knoblock, C. (1992). Automatically generating abstractions for planning. *Artificial Intelligence, 68,* 243–302.

Lungarella, M., & Pfeifer, R. (2001). Robots as cognitive tools: Information theoretic analysis of sensory-motor data. In *Proceedings of the Second IEEE-RAS International Conference on Humanoid Robotics* (pp. 245–252).

Metta, G., & Fitzpatrick, P. (2003). Early integration of vision and manipulation. *Adaptive Behavior, 11,* 109–128.

Morgavi, G., Biorci, G., & Martini, C (2001). Metaphor and neural plasticity: An hypothesis. In *Proceeding of VII simposio Internacional de Comunicacion Social* (pp 237–241). Santiago de Cuba. January 22–26, 2001.

Morgavi, G., Morando, M., Biorci, G., & Caviglia, D. D. (2005). Growing up: Emerging complexity in living being. *Cybernetics and Systems: An International Journal, 36,* 379–395.

Ogden, C. K., & Richards, I. A. (1960). *The meaning of meaning. A study of the influence of language upon thought and of the science of symbolism.* London: Routledge.

Piaget, J. (1952). *Origin of intelligence in children.* New York: Norton.

Ross, P., Hart, E., Lawson, A., Webb, A., Prem, E., Peolz, P., et al. (2003). Requirements for getting a robot to grow up. *Lecture Notes in Computer Science, 2801,* 847–856.

Rumelhart, D. E., Hinton, G. E., & Williams, R. K. (1986). Learning representations by back-propagating errors. *Nature, 323,* 533–536.

Steels, L. (1996). Discovering the competitors. *Adaptive behavior, 4,* 173–199.

Smith, S. M., Ward, T. B., & Finke, R. A. (1995). Cognitive processes in creative contexts. In S. M. Smith, T. B. Ward, & R. A. Finke (Eds.), *The creative cognition approach* (pp. 1–7). Cambridge, MA: MIT Press.

Thelen, E., & Linda, S. (1994). *A dynamical systems approach to the development of cognition and action.* Cambridge, MA: MIT Press.

Ward, T. B. (1995). What's old about new ideas? In S. M. Smith, T. B. Ward, & R. A. Finke (Eds.), *The creative cognition approach* (pp.157-178). Cambridge, MA: MIT Press.

Ward, T. B., Patterson, M. J., & Sifonis, C. M. (2004). The role of specificity and abstraction in creative idea generation. *Creativity Research Journal, 16,* 1–9.

Weisberg, R. W. (1995). Case studies of creative thinking: Reproduction versus restructuring in the real world. In S. M. Smith, T. B. Ward, and R. A. Finke (Eds.), *The creative cognition approach* (pp. 157–178). Cambridge, MA: MIT Press.

Weisberg, R. W. (1995). Prolegomena to theories of insight in problem solving: Definition of terms and a taxonomy of problems. In R. J. Sternberg, & J. E. Davidson (Eds.), *The nature of insight* (pp. 157–196). Cambridge, MA: MIT Press.

9

Euphoria Versus Dysphoria
Differential Cognitive Roles in Religion?

YVAN I. RUSSELL, ROBIN I. M. DUNBAR,
and FERNAND GOBET

INTRODUCTION

*R*eligious believers experience a range of emotions in their religious lives (Kim-Prieto & Diener, 2009; Roberts, 2007; Whitehouse, 2004). Some religious practices create intense feelings of joy and love (Malinar & Basu, 2007; Martin & Runzo, 2007). Other religious practices cause fear and pain (Alcorta & Sosis, 2005; Jackson, 2007; Whitehouse, 2007). Why does religion inspire such a diversity of affect?

In this chapter, we propose a novel hypothesis. Perhaps the extremes of religious affect—euphoria and dysphoria—have a function. What do we mean by function? Niko Tinbergen, the eminent ethologist, pointed out that there are four types of questions that can be asked about any biological phenomenon (Tinbergen, 1963). These are questions about (1) *proximate mechanisms* (the cognitive, physiological, or anatomical mechanisms that support a trait); (2) *phylogenesis* (the historical sequence by which a trait evolved from an ancestral state); (3) *ontogenesis* (how it develops in childhood); and (4) *function* (how the trait allows an organism to maximize its fitness or other short-term goals).

Religion has been studied in all four ways (e.g., evolution: Bulbulia, 2007; development: Oser et al., 2006; psychological mechanisms: Argyle & Beit-Hallahmi, 1997; history: Eliade, 1985). In this chapter, we cite studies of *proximate* mechanism to make inferences about the *functions* of emotion in religion. Traditionally, the psychology of religion has focused on proximate mechanisms, particularly on the effect of religion on various aspects of human psychology (Emmons &

Paloutzian, 2003; Strunk, 1971). With regard to emotion, many researchers have approached this question from a therapeutic angle, investigating the (arguable) claim that religious beliefs are beneficial: They relieve anxiety and promote well-being (e.g., Cohen & Hall, 2009; Kim-Prieto & Diener, 2009; Oser et al., 2006, pp. 982–986; Ross, 1990; Shreve-Neiger & Edelstein, 2004; Urry & Poey, 2008). These studies typically focused on proximate emotion (in other words, how the person is experiencing feelings about which they are fully aware). However, these studies can also be construed from a *functional* perspective. For example, we can speculate that *if* religious belief generates happiness among believers, then perhaps religious beliefs have a function to make people happy (regardless of whether they know it).

In this chapter, we focus on euphoria and dysphoria. *Euphoria* refers to positive emotions, such as joy and elation. *Dysphoria* refers to negative emotion, such as anxiety, fear, and unhappiness. Figure 9.1 illustrates the "circumplex" model of affect (Russell, 1980; Russell et al., 1989). In this model, emotional intensity can be measured in two dimensions on a Cartesian plane. The x-axis (horizontal) is a scale of valence (pleasure-displeasure), and the y-axis (vertical) is a scale of arousal. Horizontally, the leftward areas represent displeasure; the rightward areas represent pleasure. Vertically, the uppermost areas represent high arousal, and the lowermost areas represent low arousal. In this chapter, we ignore the bottom two quadrants ("sleepiness," "depression," etc.). Instead, we focus on the upper left (displeasure + arousal) and the upper right (pleasure + arousal). These represent dysphoria and euphoria, respectively. Obviously, this is only part of the picture. Religions provoke the full range of human affect (e.g., see Alcorta & Sosis, 2005; Kim-Prieto & Diener, 2009; Martin & Runzo, 2007; Miller, 2007; Rubin, 2007), but "high-arousal" situations are particularly interesting because they conspicuously cause differences in cognition and memory.

We review the empirical evidence for these differential affects. Then, we propose that dysphoria is best suited for learning procedural tasks, whereas euphoria

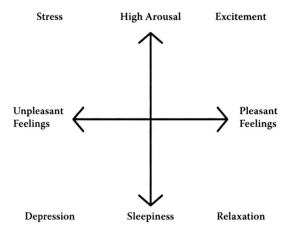

Figure 9.1   Circumplex model of affect.

is better suited for social bonding and creative thinking. First, however, consider some examples of euphoria and dysphoria as they occur in religion.

HIGH AROUSAL AND RELIGIOUS EXPERIENCE

What makes "religious" experience distinct from other types of experience? Stark (1965) defined *religious experience* as those experiences in which the participants perceive themselves to be directly encountering a supernatural realm. There is general agreement about this definition among religious scholars (Wiebe, 2006). Davis (1989) partitioned religious experience into six categories (for a critique, see Wiebe, 2006; cf. Stark, 1965). They are *interpretive* (using a religious framework to interpret actual events); *quasi-sensory* (actual sensory experiences are interpreted as sources of religious information); *revelatory* (sudden changes in religious conviction); *regenerative* (restoration of faith, health, or well-being); *numinous* (awareness of personal limitation compared to eternal supernatural, and desire to connect with supernatural); and *mystical* (perceived comprehension with supernatural "reality," and a feeling of connection with the supernatural realm). In our analysis, we focus on the last two categories—the numinous and mystical—and how they interact with high arousal.

Euphoric arousal in religion occurs in both individual and group situations. Cases of individual arousal have often been cited in the context of *shamanic ecstasy* (Eliade, 1964): Individuals (with a special shamanic status) work themselves into a "trance" state (possibly enhanced by drugs) that involves a perceived journey into the supernatural world, usually for the purposes of truth-seeking, finding inspiration, or physically carrying out a particular task (e.g., healing, exorcism, etc; also see Malinar & Basu, 2007). This kind of shamanism, occurring with multiple variations around the world (see Eliade, 1964), involves interpretive, quasi-sensory, numinous, and mystical forms of experience (cf. Grim, 2006). However, these experiences, as described by Eliade (1964) and others, are not consistently euphoric. They involve a variety of rituals, goals, techniques, and experiences, some of which may be physically demanding (dancing to the point of exhaustion) or have unpleasant side effects (vomiting or, in the case of !Kung San trance dancing, bleeding from the nose). There are many other forms of individual ecstasy (e.g., meditation, see Malinar & Basu, 2007), but the more powerfully euphoric events are those that involve a large group.

One classic example of this is the trance dances of the !Kung San of Namibia and Botswana (Katz, 1982; Lewis-Williams, 2002). These dances (which are often explicitly used to repair community cohesion after relationships have become fractious) entail the men of the community dancing rhythmically in a circle, usually to the beat of clapping and singing by the women, until they collapse with exhaustion and enter a trance state. During the trance state, they experience travels in the spirit world, where they encounter various real and mythical animals or (less commonly) ancestors. On a more familiar everyday level, euphoria and ecstasy are associated with many charismatic sects within Christianity. Well-known examples include the Pentecostal churches (which typically involve a great deal of group singing associated with vigorous rhythmic upper-body movements and hand-clapping) as well as such phenomena as the so-called Toronto blessing. More generally, mystical sects appear in all the main world religions. Among the Abrahamic religions, the various Gnostic sects (including the medieval Cathars) in Christianity, the Sufis in Islam, and the Kabbalah tradition in Judaism are all based on direct experience of God, often mediated through trance-like states. A specific example is provided by the Sufi Mevlevi order in Islam (colloquially known as the "whirling dervishes"), who use a twirling dance to induce a state of trance in adepts.

More extreme examples involve the use of flagellation and other forms of inflicting pain as a means to achieve ecstasy. Perhaps the best known of these are the medieval Christian flagellants, who toured Europe during the period of the Black Death (1347–1348), whipping themselves in public penance for the sins that they believed were responsible for the infliction of this terrible disease. In the Russian Orthodox tradition, the Khlysty ("flagellators") and the Skoptzy ("mutilators") sects aimed to achieve a state of religious ecstasy through self-imposed physical pain. The Khlysty movement had a particularly long history; having first emerged as early as the 1360s, they were still in existence as a semiheretical sect within the Orthodox Church at the end of the 19th century. In Islam, the annual Shia rituals in memory of the martyrdom of the Imam Husain and his family at Kerbala in AD 680 commonly involve individuals whipping or hitting themselves in massed processions.

In contrast, among many of the Eastern world religions (notably Buddhism and the yogic elements in Hinduism), meditation is used to achieve essentially the same ends. Focused attention, relaxation, controlled breathing exercises, and physically taxing positions (or in some forms of yoga, extreme exertion) allow the adept to slip into a trance state. Many Christian saints (e.g., St. Theresa of Avila, St. Francis of Assisi) were well known for their often seemingly spontaneous ecstatic trances. All these are associated to one degree or another with a sense of euphoria, even when pain is inflicted.

Consider now the opposite of euphoria. *Dysphoria* occurs in at least two major contexts. The first concerns ritual ordeals; individuals are subjected to terrifying and physically injurious rituals, often in the context of initiation ceremonies (Eliade, 1964). Whitehouse (2007, p. 260) noted that traumatic rituals occur in every world religion. Some examples that Whitehouse (2007) mentioned include the rituals of the penitents in New Mexico (and similar practices in Mexico and the Philippines); the Sufi performances of mortifications; Opus Dei flagellations; and monastic initiations in Buddhism (especially Zen). Whitehouse (2007) also noted many examples from local cult practices in small-scale traditional societies, which include grisly practices such as the practice of ritual circumcision (mutilation of genitals) among some Aborigine groups. Among the Aranda (central Australia), these ritual practices can be particularly severe, including "sadistic episodes of head-biting, evulsions of their fingernails, showering with red-hot coals, and other agonizing procedures" (Whitehouse, 2007, p. 260). Similar gruesome practices have been found in cult rituals all over the world (Whitehouse, 2007). Initiation ceremonies like these always occur in a particular context (Whitehouse, 2007), where the real-life activities are symbolic of an accompanying supernatural narrative (see numerous examples in Eliade, 1964). The terror described by Whitehouse (2007) is that which comes from firsthand exposure to painful situations.

There is also a second kind of terror in religious life that comes *indirectly*: stories about hell. For example, the Christian version of hell is described as a place of eternal torture (where death never comes). Hell is normally presented as a supernatural place where sinners are justly punished for misdeeds. These stories grew out of ancient writings about a hellish Apocalypse. Kyrtatas (2009) studied an early (proto-Christian) version of hell that comes from the *Oracula Sybillina* (written ca. AD 200–500). As Kyrtatas noted (2009, p. 290), this document tells the story of how a great wall of fire will consume every place at the end of time, wherein the souls of men will burn in the fire and gnash their teeth. Then, they will be resurrected with new souls and new bodies, and they will "pass through the burning river and unquenchable flame" (p. 290). Here, the righteous and good will be saved and the sinners severely punished with flaming whips and unbearable pain and thirst. Furthermore, they will be incapable of dying, forced to suffer the unbearable pain for all of eternity (p. 290).

Similarly gruesome punishments occur in the version of hell in other religions (e.g., see Thomasson, 2009, about Islamic *al-nār*). Followers of these religions learn about hell largely through testimony from their religious orators. For example, Whitehouse (1995) described this process in his ethnographic study of a small religion in Papua New Guinea (called the *Pomio Kivung*, a small modern group with a mix of local and Christian beliefs). Here, the "orators stir up a deep horror of the Devil" (p. 95) by telling of how the sinners are banished into the wilderness, where they will suffer hunger, thirst, loneliness, and fear. These orators speak loudly and with great emotion, speaking "in elaborate and grisly metaphors" (p. 95).

In contrast to ritual ordeals (which are often about surviving a journey), hell is about punishment and justice (Kvanvig, 2007). In some traditions, followers are subject to highly emotional demands to maintain behaviors that allow them to avoid hell (e.g., see Jackson, 2007, about the American hell house tradition). These exhortations are clearly designed to terrify the followers.

THE ROLE OF EMOTION IN RELIGION

What is the relationship between emotion and religion? The question has a long intellectual history (Corrigan, 2007; Davis, 1989; Emmons & Paloutzian, 2003; Kim-Prieto & Diener, 2009; Malinar & Basu, 2007; Oviedo, 2009), but many issues have not yet been studied systematically (e.g., see discussions in Azari & Birnbacher, 2004; Emmons & Paloutzian, 2003). We now review three relevant areas of research for our "differential function" hypothesis. The first area concerns the relationship between emotion and the formation and maintenance of beliefs. The second area concerns the role of emotion in ritual acts. The third area concerns the "power of emotion to bind social collectives" (Corrigan, 2007, p. 7; also see Alcorta & Sosis, 2005; Hayden, 1987).

Consider first the research on beliefs. Azari and Birnbacher (2004) cited two distinct viewpoints about the nature of emotion—cognitive and noncognitive— and described how this influences your view on the relationship between emotion and religion (also see Davis, 1989; Taves, 2008). The *noncognitive* school (i.e., the "James-Lange" view) holds that emotional states are determined precognitively, and that explicit cognition comes afterward (see citations therein). Azari and Birnbacher (2004) compared the different ways that the cognitive and noncognitive views might apply to religion. If we adopt the James-Lange (noncognitive) perspective, then we posit that religious emotions come *before* cognition (Azari & Birnbacher, 2004): They are separate from our thoughts and beliefs, emerging from an unknown source. In other words, the feeling comes first and feeds into our conscious reasoning about specific stimuli and situations. This kind of view is consistent with stories from some indigenous religious traditions in which "revealed knowledge" (spiritual in origin) is regarded as something that can be acquired from direct sensory experiences through "dreams, visions, and intuitions" (Grim, 2006, p. 99).

In contrast, the *cognitive* school (i.e., "attributional" view) holds that the content of an emotion is a cognitive decision in response to a physiological state (see references in Azari & Birnbacher, 2004). In this view, religious emotion comes *after* cognition (Azari & Birnbacher, 2004). Here, a specific stimulus is thought to elicit a causal belief (i.e., that something witnessed was caused by supernatural means), and this leads to religious emotion. Here, the emotion is a consequence of a specific situation. Many researchers appear to support a version of the cognitive view (e.g., Davis, 1989; Roberts, 2007; Taves, 2008). Azari and Birnbacher (2004, p. 902) stated that "emotion affords religious experience its distinctive content and quality." Pyysiäinen (2001, p. 71) wrote that a religious experience "can be understood quite simply as an emotional reaction to religious representations."

Boden and Berenbaum (2010), writing about emotions and belief *in general*, provided a more detailed account. Beliefs consist of two components: *content* (mental representation of a belief) and *conviction* (degree of intensity of that belief). They claimed that there is a bidirectional feedback loop between a person's emotion and the content and conviction of a person's beliefs. Moreover, these feedback loops comprise two separate paths. Belief conviction (how strongly you believe) is linked to emotional arousal (the vertical dimension in Figure 9.1), where belief content (the semantic content of what you believe) is linked to valence (the horizontal dimension in Figure 9.1). Their argument has three premises:

1. The individual has a dual need: to keep his or her emotions in a desirable state (mental distress is avoided) and to make sense of the world. Hence, people might change their beliefs "to regulate their emotions in valued directions" (p. 231).
2. Emotions influence beliefs. If there is increased emotional arousal, then people are motivated to explain to themselves why this arousal has occurred, and this motivation guides their interpretation of new stimuli. If there is a change of valence (pleasant/unpleasant), then this determines the actual content of a belief and which stimuli are considered.
3. Beliefs influence emotion. If there is change in belief conviction, then it links to emotional arousal. If there is a change in the content of a belief, then it links to emotional valence (pleasantness/unpleasantness).

In arguing for this dynamic feedback loop, Boden and Berenbaum (2010) provided a number of examples of empirical studies that supported their claims (see

TABLE 9.1   Six Categories of Ritual, Summarized From Bell (1997)

Category of Ritual	Description
1. Rites of passage	Ceremonies that mark a life transition (birth, coming of age, marriage, death, etc.)
2. Calendrical rites	Ceremonies that mark the periodic renewal of a cycle (e.g., for Christmas, Easter, etc.)
3. Rites of exchange and communion	Offers made to god(s) as a reciprocal exchange for services; Offers might be verbal, material, involve sacrifices, burning, etc.
4. Rites of affliction	Actions to reduce the influence of spirits who might be causing misfortune for a person (e.g., protection, healing, exorcism, purification)
5. Feasting, fasting, and festivals	Collective (simultaneous) performances by a large group of people, in accordance with religious traditions (e.g., dancing, feasting, ritual dramas, Ramadan, etc.)
6. Political rites	Create/reinforce a social order that is congruent with a theological order (e.g., coronation of a divine king)

references therein; for background on cognition and emotion, also see Levenson, 1999; Oser et al., 2006; Storbeck & Clore, 2007; Wyer et al., 1999). This feedback loop will surely function in religious experiences. Situations of high arousal will have an effect on the conviction in a person's religious beliefs (and a minimal level of conviction is required to acquire a belief in the first place). Negative or positive valence will determine how new religious beliefs are selected, existing beliefs are updated, or old beliefs are rejected.

The second relevant area of research concerns the relationship between emotion and religious ritual. Bell (1997) identified six broad categories of ritual. These are shown in Table 9.1. As shown, the definition of *ritual* is extraordinarily broad, denoting some form of action sequence in a variety of domains, both religious and nonreligious (Bell, 1997; Collins, 2009). Bell (1997) also provided six defining *characteristics* of ritual: (1) *formalism* (following rules of convention that preserve the existing social order); (2) *traditionalism* (keeping as closely as possible to traditional methods); (3) *invariance* (elements and ordering of the ritual must be adhered to closely, and innovation is not allowed); (4) *rule-governance* (actions are constrained by predetermined rules); (5) *sacral symbolism* (specific acts/displays that denote a supernatural significance); and (6) *performance* (a theatrical aspect). Many behaviors can be called *ritual-like* (because they have some of these characteristics), but a ritual can only be called *religious* if its actions are thought to have a supernatural significance (for discussion of the definition of religious ritual, see Alcorta & Sosis, 2005; Bell, 1997; Collins, 2009; Hinde, 2004; Klassen, 2007; Turner, 1966; Whitehouse, 2004; for numerous examples of rituals, see Eliade, 1964).

As illustrated, some rituals can impose extreme emotional arousal onto participants. However, this is not true for all rituals. Some rituals are utterly mundane and commonplace. Whitehouse's (2004) *Modes of Religiosity* hypothesis related the emotionality of rituals to the social dynamics of the religious groups (for a critique of this hypothesis, see Hinde, 2004, and Klassen, 2007). Evidently, religions usually occur in two characteristic forms. The *doctrinal* mode is found in the larger institutions, with highly developed theological schemes, bureaucracy, holy writings, and social hierarchies. This category includes the major world religions. In doctrinal traditions, many kinds of rituals exist, but there tends to be heavy *routinization* (i.e., rituals become standardized and routinely encountered). These routinized rituals are "facilitating the storage of elaborate and conceptually complex religious teachings in semantic memory, but also activating implicit memory in the performance of most ritual procedures" (Whitehouse, 2004, pp. 65–66). Doctrinal religions have the characteristics that allow them to spread over wide populations. The most repetitive, commonly occurring rituals tend to be low in emotional arousal. Doctrinal religions *do* have emotional rituals, but these tend to be rarer. The *imagistic* mode of religiosity occurs in the smaller-scale religions, including "the most ancient forms of religious activity" (p. 70), but this form also occurs in modern-day splinter groups and cults (e.g., see Whitehouse, 1995). Here, the religious knowledge tends to be based on episodic memory rather than declarative memory. There is often a lack of holy books and writings, the social organization is minimal, and the groups are small and closely bonded. In imagistic traditions, the ritual procedures are more fluid and less standardized than in doctrinal religions and occur less often. Also—most importantly for our hypothesis—the rituals in imagistic religions tend to be highly emotional events. One of the main themes of *modes theory* is that religions (as individual traditions) tend to take two forms: *low-arousal doctrinal* or *high-arousal imagistic*. The other two possible forms (high-arousal doctrinal and low-arousal imagistic) tend to be unstable (i.e., they tend to change into a more stable form).

One of the predictions of modes theory is that there is an inverse relationship between level of arousal and frequency (Whitehouse, 2004). In other words, high-arousal rituals are far less frequent than low-arousal rituals. Atkinson and Whitehouse (2011) investigated this prediction (among others) by extracting information from the electronic Human Relations Area Files (eHRAF), a very large database of information gathered from ethnographic studies around the world (http://www.yale.edu/hraf/index.html). They analyzed 645 rituals from 74 cultures worldwide. Here, rituals were rated on a scale of 0 to 5 for emotional arousal (0 = no arousal; 5 = extreme arousal), and their frequency was recorded (every day, one day a month, every season, every year, less than every year, once per generation). As predicted, the analysis found a negative correlation between arousal and frequency: Less-arousing rituals happened more often, whereas more-arousing rituals happened less often. This was also true for duration. The longer the ritual, the more emotional it tended to be. When the frequency data were partitioned into *euphoria* and *dysphoria*, the results were interesting. The negative correlation held very strongly for the dysphoric arousal (i.e., the more dysphoric the ritual was and the less frequently it was performed). This was not true for euphoric arousal. Although the inverse correlation still held, the relationship was weaker because the data fit better a quadratic instead of linear pattern. Specifically, rituals that were rated middle-low in arousal (score 1–3) occurred more often than both the highly arousing rituals (score 4–5) and the minimally arousing rituals (score 0–1). Judging from these results, euphoria and dysphoria work in different ways.

The third relevant area of research concerns the relationship between social cohesion and emotion in religion. A century ago, Durkheim (1915) considered in some detail the role of ritual and religion in maintaining community cohesion in traditional societies. He was much struck by the rousing effect that mass religious rituals had in this context, a phenomenon he referred to as "effervescence." Durkheim's view was, in essence, that the rousing effects of dance and other coordinated activities in these contexts created a sense of euphoria that in turn played an important role in mediating community cohesion. Similar views were later developed by Turner (1966), who referred to it as *communitas,* in explicit allusion to the community-bonding processes involved. This seems to arise through an effect of exercise on mood: Harte et al. (1995) found that mood was elevated in both elite runners and experienced meditators, despite the metabolic differences between the two activities (see also Markoff et al., 1982).

In a seminal series of neuroimaging studies, Newberg et al. (2001) have shown that individuals who can achieve a heightened state of religious ecstasy (such as that achieved at the endpoint of meditation) exhibit very specific patterns of brain activation. They have a greatly reduced level of activity in an area in the posterior parietal lobe of the left hemisphere (the area mainly responsible for our sense of spatial self)—and, incidentally, a great deal of generalized activity in the right hemisphere. Based on this evidence, they have argued that carefully orchestrated mental practices (the techniques developed by mystics in all religions) allow adepts to disengage a bundle of neurons in the posterior part of the left parietal lobe of the brain, which, once disengaged from the control of the executive brain centers, release a series of impulses down through the limbic system to the hypothalamus, which then sets up a feedback loop between itself, the attention areas in the frontal cortex (which have been responsible for blocking off the parietal lobe neuron bundles), and the parietal lobe itself. As this cycle builds, it leads to the complete shutdown of the spatial awareness bundles, generating as it does so a burst of ecstatic liberation in which we seem to be united with the "Infinity of Being," often associated with a flash of blinding light.

Synchronized activity (dancing or other rituals) appears to play an important role in ramping up these effects. Simply doing an activity (singing, dancing, the rocking movements associated with pray in some religions) is enough to generate a euphoric effect. However, doing the activity in coordinated synchrony with others seems to massively ramp up this effect. In both cases, the euphoric effect appears to be mediated by the release of endorphins from the hypothalamus. These neuroendocrines are part of the pain control mechanism of the brain and are responsible for the analgesic effect (and hence the euphoria) associated with physical exercise (Belluzzi & Stein 1977; Blalock 1998; Bodnar & Klein, 2006; Boecker et al., 2008; Harbach et al., 2000; Hughes et al., 1975; Nelson & Panksepp 1998; Stephano et al., 2000). Cohen et al. (2009) have tested this synchrony effect using "sweep oar" rowing crews. By comparing endorphin release (assayed using change in before vs. after pain threshold) when individuals rowed alone and when rowing in coordinated synchrony in virtual boats (on ergometric rowing machines), they were able to demonstrate that there was a 100% increase in endorphin output when an activity was carried out in synchrony over and above that generated by physical exercise when working out alone (Cohen et al., 2009). We do not know why this occurs, but it appears to be a direct consequence of behavioral synchrony.

Synchrony, in particular, has been shown to have a significant effect on individuals' willingness to act altruistically toward each other. In a simple experiment, Miles et al. (2009) found that individuals presented with visual or auditory cues of synchrony (and antisynchrony) in the footfalls of a pair of walking people rated the rapport between them as greater than when presented with cues from unsynchronized walkers. These effects appear to have knock-on consequences for prosociality and altruism: Wiltermuth and Heath (2009) were able to show that even simple levels of behavioral synchrony (synchronized vs. unsynchronized arm waving) increased cooperativeness and generosity in public good games.

THE EFFECT OF MOOD ON COGNITIVE PROCESSING

Emotions are not independent from intellect. In fact, there is a large body of literature to show that emotions can influence cognitive processes substantially (Bless et al., 1996; Chepenik et al., 2007; Clore & Huntsinger, 2007; Dolan, 2002; Frederickson & Branigan, 2005; Isen, 1987; Levenson, 1999; Storbeck & Clore, 2007; Wyer et al., 1999). Psychologists divide emotional experience into two distinct states (Boden & Berenbaum, 2010, p. 228): (1) "emotion" and (2) "mood." Whereas an emotion is intense and brief, *mood* refers to a "background" emotional state that "rises and dissipates slowly" (Beedie et al., 2005, p. 871). In contrast to emotion, mood is generally more mild, unfocused, and stable (for discussion, see Beedie et al., 2005; Clore & Huntsinger, 2007; Storbeck & Clore, 2007; Wyer et al., 1999, pp. 5–7).

Mood matters when you process information. According to a burgeoning recent literature, people think differently in a euphoric versus a dysphoric mood (for a review, see Clore & Huntsinger, 2007). In a *euphoric* mood, people adopt a much more global, schematic view. In other words, people in a euphoric mood tend to look at the "big picture." In contrast, people in a *dysphoric* mood tend to be more nonschematic and detail oriented. For example, Bless et al. (1996) found that the participants with an induced positive mood were more likely to falsely recognize an item from a story (when the stimulus was conceptually similar but a different word) than those in a negative mood. Participants in a positive mood appeared to fall back on general semantic knowledge, whereas the ones in negative mood remembered the details better.

Similarly, Gasper and Clore (2002) asked their participants to draw/classify pictures they had seen before and found that participants with an induced positive mood focused on the global characteristics at the expense of the details, while those in a negative mood did the opposite. Beukeboom and Semin (2005) found the same results in a paradigm in which they asked participants to choose appropriate phrases to describe behaviors: those in a good mood thought more about "why" a behavior occurred, and those in a bad mood thought more about "how" a behavior occurred.

Frederickson and Branigan (2005) confirmed the broadening effect of positive mood in a study in which they asked participants to choose which image was the most similar to a previous one. The two choices were appropriate for either a global view (overall shape) or a detailed view (component parts of the overall shape). Those in a good mood chose overall shape more often.

Inspired by this literature, one of our recent studies (Russell et al., submitted) made an attempt to apply these results to the topic of emotion and religion. This was a study of analogical transfer in a ritual-like task. The Tower of Hanoi (TOH) game was used as a proxy (see Simon, 1975) for a religious ritual. Although the TOH lacks many of the features of a real religious ritual, it does have *invariance* and *rule-governance*, which Bell (1997) had defined as two important aspects in the definition of ritual (see Table 9.1). Participants were divided into either a euphoric condition or a dysphoric condition (induced by viewing a humorous and unpleasant video clip, respectively). The same participants were further divided into *expert* and *nonexpert* conditions (creating four conditions: expert euphoric, expert dysphoric, nonexpert euphoric, nonexpert dysphoric). Individuals in the expert condition were first given the TOH game and asked to figure out how to solve the game. Then, they were shown a new game with a drastically different appearance called the Bear God (BG) task, but which was based on the exact same set of rules. Participants were not told that the rules were the same. They simply needed to figure it out for themselves. In the nonexpert condition, participants played a different game (Missionary Cannibal game), which had a different set of rules. In this case, participants played the BG task afterward without having been exposed to the isomorphic TOH task beforehand. This was predicted to be a disadvantage. The other prediction was that the euphoric individuals would be better able to transfer the rules from one game to another (even when they did not know that the rules were the same). This prediction was based on previous research (as cited) showing that euphoria promotes big picture thinking. This was predicted to enable better analogical reasoning, which would result in the euphoric individuals solving more TOH games than dysphoric individuals.

Unexpectedly, the results were opposite to this prediction. The dysphoric group significantly outperformed the euphoric group (measured by number of BG games solved). The other prediction—that the expert group would outperform the nonexpert group—was confirmed. This showed that *dysphoria*—not euphoria—appeared to be an advantage in analogical transfer, but only if there was some extent of background knowledge. In this case, the "background knowledge" consisted of previous exposure to the relevant rules of the game. This result led to rethinking the function of euphoria in religion. Perhaps euphoria is not useful for intense philosophical queries or precise implementation of rituals. Instead, perhaps euphoria is more valuable for motivating participation, stimulating social cohesion, and ensuring continued adherence to the faith.

Two recent studies have provided some insights that might be relevant here. First, Feldman and Kokinov (2009) conducted a study in which participants were asked to generate as many written analogies as possible (within 20 minutes) to support a political position they had just read about (concerning the issue of whether a particular region should be allowed to become an independent country). There were two conditions: *anxiety* and *control*. In the anxiety condition, participants were told that after finishing the analogies, they would be asked to give an unpracticed oral presentation in front of a group of people. In truth, there was no public presentation planned at all. The expectation of public speaking was *itself* the mood induction technique used to create anxiety for the participant. In the *control* group, the participants were not told of any public speaking (hence the anxiety of needing to perform was missing). The results of this study were interesting. The first dependent measure was the number of analogies. Here, the participants in the anxiety condition did not generate significantly fewer analogies. However, in another dependent variable—thematic diversity of analogies— those in the anxiety condition were significantly less diverse. In other words, the participants in the anxiety conditions tended to produce analogies that were only slight variations of their previously produced analogies. In contrast, those in the control condition tended to produce larger variations of their previously produced analogies.

This study (Feldman & Kokinov, 2009) was inspired by an earlier study by Richert et al. (2005), which had a similar design but was designed specifically with a view to study religion. In their two experiments (pp. 133–143), they subjected their participants in low-arousal and high-arousal conditions (this arousal was not specifically negative or positive) to fake religious rituals. Then, they asked participants to generate as many explanations as possible for their experience. In both experiments, those in the high-arousal condition produced more diverse and fuller explanations than those in the low-arousal condition. Why does this appear to contradict the results of Feldman and Kokinov (2009)? The answer might lie in the fact that the Feldman and Kokinov (2009) study was about dysphoric arousal and the Richert et al. (2005) study was (apparently) about euphoric arousal.

Another study from Feldman and colleagues (2010) built on the results of their earlier work. Participants were put into the same anxiety and control conditions as in the previous study (i.e., the expectation of public speaking was used to induce anxiety). However, the task was different. Participants were asked to perform a matching-to-sample task. They would be shown a visual display (B) and then two other visual displays (T1 and T2), which consisted of different geometric shapes. The task was to indicate which of the later visual displays (T1 or T2) better matched the first one (B). In one example (see Figure 2 in Feldman et al., 2010, p. 1455), the first display (B) consisted of three isosceles triangles. The first triangle was on its side (long end pointing left), and the second and third triangles were pointing upward. The second display (T1) had the same three triangles, except that the middle one was on its side (long end pointing left), with the first and third triangles pointing upward. The second display (T2) had three isosceles trapezoids. Mirroring the arrangement of the first display, the first trapezoid was on its side (smaller base facing left), and the second and third trapezoids were right side up (smaller base facing upward). There were two ways to match the samples. In the *superficial* choice, the participant would match the first display (B) to the second display (T1) because both displays consisted of isosceles triangles. In the *relational* choice, the participant would match the first display (B) to the third display (T2) because both displays consisted of the same arrangement (i.e., the first one on its side and the other two upright). The relational choice showed a propensity to reason analogically.

The participants in the anxiety group made the *relational* choice significantly more than the participants in the control group. This mirrors the results from Russell et al. (submitted), for which the participants in the *dysphoric-expert* condition were apparently better at thinking analogically. At first, both of these studies would seem to contradict the body of literature about "narrowing" and "broadening" found in states of dysphoria and euphoria, respectively. However, it could be true that we were not interpreting this research correctly. Perhaps the detail-oriented outlook of a dysphoric individual is what enabled that individual to focus on the *relations* that characterized an analogy. In contrast, the broad outlook of the euphoric individual might be counterproductive for such intellectual demands. Although there might be more big picture thinking in the euphoric cognition, this may come as a sacrifice to the depth of processing.

EUPHORIA VERSUS DYSPHORIA: DIFFERENT FUNCTIONS IN RELIGION?

As noted, euphoria has been described as having a "broadening effect" on cognition (Frederickson & Branigan, 2005) and dysphoria as having a "narrowing effect." In other words, euphoria opens up your attention to the wider array of stimuli, whereas dysphoria restricts one's attention to the most salient details (cf. Clore & Huntsinger, 2007). Does positive affect create a disadvantage? As Frederickson and Branigan (2005) wrote: If "positive emotions do not share with negative emotion this hallmark feature of promoting and supporting specific action, then what good are they?" (p. 314). The answer, they wrote, is that positive affect is probably useful, but for much different purposes than that of dysphoria (cf. Bless et al., 1996; Isen, 1987). Negative affect is useful for the "attack" and "flee" situations, whereas positive attack is about "play, explore, savor and integrate" (Frederickson & Branigan, 2005, p. 314).

Accordingly, it is best to regard euphoria and dysphoria as complementary processes with different purposes. Emotions are valuable because they constitute an "index [of] occurrences of value" (Dolan, 2002, p. 1192): People pay attention to the emotional and remember it better afterward. According to Levenson (1999), the human emotional system (consisting of automatic core processes partially subject to voluntary control) is extremely useful in that it "helps us to engage in adaptive voluntary behaviors" (p. 497; also see Bless et al., 1996; Wyer et al., 1999, §3). Levenson (1999) further claimed that negative emotions "are optimal for the short-term needs of actively dealing with threatening environmental challenges" (p. 492), whereas positive emotions have a "soothing function" (p. 494). Fiedler et al. (2003) concluded that positive moods facilitate "assimilative" tasks (for which you need to think top-down, be creative, and attend to a wide range of stimuli), while negative moods facilitate "accommodative" tasks (for which one needs to think bottom-up and attend closely to the most important stimuli for the task) (also see Spering et al., 2005).

Why is there a cognitive difference between positive and negative affect? According to Isen (1987), the difference might be motivational (people want to escape a sad mood but remain in a happy one) or else structural (happy memories are better integrated than sad memories). A third view (Bless et al., 1996) is that negative mood is a signal of urgency to act in response to a problem, whereas positive mood is nonurgent (for relevant discussion, see Dolan, 2002; Levenson, 1999; Wyer et al., 1999, pp. 38–40).

How does all of this apply to religion? Returning to the topic of *functionality* (Tinbergen, 1963), we can ask: What are the functional consequences of affect in the context of religion? Before answering this question, we need to ask about what the function is *for*. Tinbergen (1963) was referring to function in an evolutionary context. We should note here that, in the cognitive science of religion, the word *evolution* is used in two different ways. The first and more familiar is the Darwinian meaning (Alcorta & Sosis, 2005; Bulbulia, 2007; Kydd, 2008; Rossano, 2006): Questions are asked about the role (if any) that religion may have played in biological evolution. The second and less-familiar meaning of religious *evolution* refers to cultural—not biological—evolution. This view (e.g., Whitehouse, 2004, 2008) pays attention to a different unit of replication. Biological evolution concerns the survivability of the individual organisms and species. In contrast, "religious cultural evolution" concerns the survivability of an individual *religion*. This view of cultural evolution has its intellectual roots in Sperber's "epidemiology of representations" approach (Sperber, 1985), and it is formulated with a recognition that, throughout the history of the human race, there have existed a multiplicity of religious faiths. Each of these religions has had various degrees of success. Many of them have died out, to be replaced by the more successful doctrinal religions that dominate the world today. Theorists such as Whitehouse (2004, 2008) have tried to identify the factors that make some religions successful and some religions not.

Of course, these two definitions of evolution are intertwined. Biological evolution should have produced the religion-seeking human. Cultural processes determine the exact type of religion to which an individual will adhere. An atheist from Sweden and an imam from Saudi Arabia are both human beings—with precisely the same phylogenetic background—but their culture, their locality, their language, and many other factors have caused them to manifest very different ways of looking at the world. When we are asking about the functional significance of mood and emotion in religion, we are asking two different questions. What roles do the emotional facets of religion play in biological evolution? What roles do they play in the successful spread of a religious tradition? These questions require more investigation before we can find definitive answers. In suggesting our differential function hypothesis, our line of reasoning goes this way:

1. Aspects of religion are presumed to have some functional significance.
2. Emotion plays a very important role in religious life.
3. Religious life encompasses a wide diversity of situations for which the emotional tone is on a continuum from extreme euphoria to extreme dysphoria.
4. Cognitive psychology has shown that cognitive processing is influenced by mood.
5. Euphoria is conducive to a broader frame of processing, allowing enhanced creativity and ability to see the big picture.

6. Euphoria plays a role in bonding large groups of individuals.
7. Dysphoria is conducive to a narrower frame of processing, allowing enhanced attention to detail, but with an inhibited ability to see the big picture.
8. We propose that the cognitive sequelae of different affective states have implications for the functional role of these affective states in religious situations.
9. We suggest that euphoria is highly functional for social bonding, which has many beneficial effects for the human species and their religious traditions.
10. We suggest that euphoric emotional arousal is also highly functional for situations involving creativity and lateral thinking in religious settings.
11. We suggest that dysphoria is highly functional for situations for which precision and analogical reasoning are needed in religious settings.

Hence, the typical emotions experienced in a religious setting—whether imagistic or doctrinal—have a meaning that goes beyond the immediate situation. The emotional situations might occur for a reason: They have a "function" that in some way has enhanced the survivability of either the religious tradition itself or the human species that participates in it. Given the staggering diversity of religious experience around the world (Bell, 1997; Davis, 1989; Stark, 1965), it is difficult to generalize. Nonetheless, the evidence is compelling that differential affective states cause differences in transient cognitive abilities (cf. Alcorta & Sosis, 2005, pp. 333–335). Because affect plays a prominent role in religious beliefs, religious ritual, group dynamics, and social bonding, it should also be cogent that different affective states have different functional consequences. This area of research has many questions yet to be answered.

REFERENCES

Alcorta, C. S., & Sosis, R. (2005). Ritual, emotion, and sacred symbols: The evolution of religion as an adaptive complex. *Human Nature, 16*, 323–359.

Argyle, M. J., & Beit-Hallahmi, B. (1997). *The psychology of religious experience, belief and behaviour*. London: Routledge.

Atkinson, Q. D., & Whitehouse, H. (2011). The cultural morphospace of ritual form: Examining modes of religiosity cross-culturally. *Evolution and Human Behaviour, 32*, 50–62.

Azari, N. P., & Birnbacher, D. (2004). The role of cognition and feeling in religious experience. *Zygon, 39*, 901–917.

Beedie, C. J., Terry, P. C., & Lane, A. M. (2005). Distinctions between emotion and mood. *Cognition and Emotion, 19*, 847–878.

Bell, C. (1997). *Ritual: Perspectives and dimensions*. Oxford, UK: Oxford University Press.

Belluzzi, J. D., & Stein, L. (1977). Enkephalin may mediate euphoria and drive-reduction reward. *Nature, 266*, 556–558.

Beukeboom, C. J., & Semin, G. R. (2005). Mood and representations of behaviour: The how and why. *Cognition and Emotion, 19*, 1242–1251.

Blalock, J. E. (1998). β-Endorphin in immune cells. *Immunology Today, 19*, 191–192.

Bless, H., Clore, G. L., Schwarz, N., Golisano, V., Rabe, C., & Wölk, M. (1996). Mood and the use of scripts: Does a happy mood really lead to mindlessness? *Journal of Personality and Social Psychology, 71*, 665–679.

Boden, M. T., & Berenbaum, H. (2010). The bidirectional relations between affect and belief. *Review of General Psychology, 14*, 227–239.

Bodnar, R. J., & Klein, G. E. (2006). Endogenous opiates and behavior: 2005. *Peptides, 27*, 3391–3478.

Boecker, H., Sprenger, T., Spilker, M. E., Henriksen, G., Koppenhoeffer, M., Wagner, K. J., et al. (2008). The runners' high: Opioidergic mechanisms in the human brain. *Cerebral Cortex, 18*, 2523–2531.

Bulbulia, J. A. (2007). The evolution of religion. In R. I. M. Dunbar & L. Barrett (Eds.), *The Oxford handbook of evolutionary psychology* (pp. 621–635). Oxford, UK: Oxford University Press.

Chepenik, L. G., Cornew, L. A., & Farah, M. J. (2007). The influence of sad mood on cognition. *Emotion, 7*, 802–811.

Clore, G. L., & Huntsinger, J. L. (2007). How emotions inform judgement and regulate thought. *Trends in Cognitive Science, 11*, 393–399.

Cohen, A. B., & Hall, D. E. (2009). Existential beliefs, social satisfaction, and well-being among Catholic, Jewish, and Protestant older adults. *The International Journal for the Psychology of Religion, 19*, 39–54.

Cohen, E., Ejsmond-Frey, R., Knight, N., & Dunbar, R. I. M. (2009). Rowers' high: Behavioural synchrony is correlated with elevated pain thresholds. *Biology Letters, 6*, 106–108.

Collins, P. (2009). Religion and ritual: A multi-perspectival approach. In P. Clarke (Ed.), *The Oxford handbook of the sociology of religion* (pp. 671–687). Oxford, UK: Oxford University Press.

Corrigan, J. (2007). Introduction: The study of religion and emotion. In J. Corrigan (Ed.), *The Oxford handbook of religion and emotion* (pp. 3–13). Oxford, UK: Oxford University Press.

Davis, C. F. (1989). *The evidential force of religious experience.* Oxford, UK: Clarendon.

Dolan, R. J. (2002). Emotion, cognition, and behavior. *Science, 298*, 1191–1194.

Durkheim, E. (1915 [1965]). *The elementary forms of religious life.* New York: Free Press.

Eliade, M. (1964). *Shamanism: Archaic techniques of ecstasy.* London: Penguin Arkana.

Eliade, M. (1985). *A history of religious ideas.* Chicago: Chicago University Press.

Emmons, R. A., & Paloutzian, R. F. (2003). The psychology of religion. *Annual Review of Psychology, 54*, 377–402.

Feldman, V., Hristova, P., & Kokinov, B. (2010). How does anxiety influence analogical mapping? In S. Ohlsson & R. Catrambone (Eds.), *Cognition in flux: Proceedings of the 32nd Annual Conference of the Cognitive Science Society* (pp. 1453–1458). Hillsdale, NJ: Erlbaum.

Feldman, V., & Kokinov, B. (2009). Anxiety restricts the analogical search in an analogy generation task. In B. Kokinov, K. Holyoak, & D. Gentner (Eds.), *New frontiers in analogy research* (pp. 117–126). Sofia, Bulgaria: NBU Press.

Fiedler, K., Nickel, S., Asbeck, J., & Pagel, U. (2003). Mood and the generation effect. *Cognition and Emotion, 17*, 585–608.

Frederickson, B. L., & Branigan, C. (2005). Positive emotions broaden the scope of attention and thought-action repertoires. *Cognition and Emotion, 19*, 313–332.

Gasper, K., & Clore, G. L. (2002). Attending to the big picture: Mood and global versus local processing of visual information. *Psychological Science, 13*, 34–40.

Grim, J. (2006). Indigenous lifeways and knowing the world. In P. Clayton & Z. Simpson. (Eds.), *The Oxford handbook of religion and science* (pp. 87–107). Oxford, UK: Oxford University Press.

Harbach, H., Hell, K., Gramsch, C., Katz, N., Hempelmann, G., & Teschemacher, H. (2000). β-Endorphin (1–31) in the plasma of male volunteers undergoing physical exercise. *Psychoneuroendocrinology, 25*, 551–62.

Harte, J. L., Eifert, G. H., & Smith, S. (1995). The effects of running and meditation on beta-endorphin, corticotropin-releasing hormone and cortisol in plasma, and on mood. *Biological Psychology, 40*, 251–265.

Hayden, B. (1987). Alliances and ritual ecstasy: Human responses to resource stress. *Journal for the Scientific Study of Religion, 26*, 81–91.

Hinde, R. A. (2004). Modes theory: Some theoretical considerations. In H. Whitehouse & R. McCauley (Eds.), *Mind and religion: Psychological and cognitive foundations of religiosity* (pp. 31–55). Walnut Creek, CA: AltaMira Press.

Hughes, J., Smith, T. W., Kosterlitz, H. W., Fothergill, L. A., Morgan, B. A., & Morris, H. R. (1975). Identification of two related pentapeptides from the brain with potent opiate agonist activity. *Nature, 258*, 577–579.

Isen, A. M. (1987). Positive affect, cognitive processes, and social behavior. *Advances in Experimental Social Psychology, 20*, 203–253.

Jackson, B. (2007). Jonathan Edward goes to hell (house): Fear appeals in American evangelism. *Rhetoric Review, 26*, 42–59.

Katz, R. (1982). *Boiling energy: Community healing among the Kalahari !Kung*. Cambridge, MA: Harvard University Press.

Kim-Prieto, C., & Diener, E. (2009). Religion as a source of variation in the experience of positive and negative emotions. *Journal of Positive Psychology, 4*, 447–460.

Klassen, P. E. (2007). Ritual. In J. Corrigan (Ed.), *The Oxford handbook of religion and emotion* (pp. 143–161). Oxford, UK: Oxford University Press.

Kvanvig, J. L. (2007). Hell. In J. L. Walls (Ed.), *The Oxford handbook of eschatology* (pp. 413–436). Oxford, UK: Oxford University Press.

Kydd, D. (2008). Supernatural niche construction incubates brilliance and governs the ratchet effect. In J. Bulbulia, R. Sosis, E. Harris, R. Genet, C. Genet, & K. Wyman (Eds.), *The evolution of religion: Studies, theories, critiques* (pp. 93–100). San Margarita, CA: Collins Foundation Press.

Kyrtatas, D. J. (2009). The origins of Christian hell. *Numen: International Review of the History of Religions, 56*, 282–297.

Levenson, R. W. (1999). The intrapersonal function of emotion. *Cognition and Emotion, 13*, 481–504.

Lewis-Williams, J. D. (2002). *A cosmos in stone: Interpreting religion and society through rock art*. New York: Altamira Press.

Malinar, A., & Basu, H. (2007). Ecstasy. In J. Corrigan (Ed.), *The Oxford handbook of religion and emotion* (pp. 241–258). Oxford, UK: Oxford University Press.

Markoff, R. A., Ryan, P., & Young, T. (1982). Endorphins and mood changes in long-distance running. *Medicine and Science in Sports and Exercise, 14*, 11–15.

Martin, N. M., & Runzo, J. (2007). Love. In J. Corrigan (Ed.), *The Oxford handbook of religion and emotion* (pp. 310–332). Oxford, UK: Oxford University Press.

Miles, L. K., Nind, L. K., & Macrae, C. N. (2009). The rhythm of rapport: Interpersonal synchrony and social perception. *Journal of Experimental Social Psychology, 45*, 585–589.

Miller, W. W. (2007). Hope. In J. Corrigan (Ed.), *The Oxford handbook of religion and emotion* (pp. 276–289). Oxford, UK: Oxford University Press.

Nelson, E. E., & Panksepp, J. (1998). Brain structures of infant-mother attachment: Contributions of opioids, oxytocin, and norepinephrine. *Neuroscience and Biobehavioral Reviews, 22*, 437–452.

Newberg, A., d'Aquili, E., & Rause, V. (2001). *Why God won't go away*. New York: Ballantine Books.

Oser, F. K., Scarlett, W. D., & Bucher, A. (2006). Religious and spiritual development throughout the life span. In W. Damon & R. M. Lerner (Eds.), *Handbook of child psychology, Volume 1: Theoretical models of human development* (6th ed., pp. 945–998). Hoboken, NJ: Wiley.

Oviedo, L. (2009). Is religious behavior "internally guided" by religious feelings and needs? In J. R. Feierman (Ed.), *The biology of religious behavior: The evolutionary origins of faith and religion.* Santa Barbara, CA: Praeger.

Pyysiäinen, I. (2001). Cognition, emotion, and religious experience. In J. Andresen (Ed.), *Religion in mind: Cognitive perspectives on religious belief, ritual and experience* (pp. 70–93). Cambridge, UK: Cambridge University Press.

Richert, R. A., Whitehouse, H., & Stewart, E. (2005). Memory and analogical thinking in high-arousal rituals. In H. Whitehouse & R. McCauley (Eds.), *Mind and religion: Psychological and cognitive foundations of religiosity* (pp. 127–145). Walnut Creek, CA: AltaMira Press.

Roberts, R. C. (2007). Emotions research and religious experience. In J. Corrigan (Ed.), *The Oxford handbook of religion and emotion* (pp. 490–506). Oxford, UK: Oxford University Press.

Ross, C. E. (1990). Religion and psychological distress. *Journal for the Scientific Study of Religion, 29,* 236–245.

Rossano, M. (2006). The religious mind and the evolution of religion. *Review of General Psychology, 10,* 346–364.

Rubin, J. (2007). Melancholy. In J. Corrigan (Ed.), *The Oxford handbook of religion and emotion* (pp. 290–309). Oxford, UK: Oxford University Press.

Russell, J. A. (1980). A circumplex model of affect. *Journal of Personality and Social Psychology, 39,* 1161–1178.

Russell, J. A., Weiss, A., & Mendelsohn, G. A. (1989). Affect grid: A single-item scale of pleasure and arousal. *Journal of Personality and Social Psychology, 57,* 493–502.

Russell, Y. I., Gobet, F., & Whitehouse, H. (submitted). *Mood, expertise, and analogy: Implications for religious transmission.* Manuscript submitted for publication.

Shreve-Neiger, A. K., & Edelstein, B. A. (2004). Religion and anxiety: A critical review of the literature. *Clinical Psychology Review, 24,* 379–397.

Simon, H. A. (1975). The functional equivalence of problem solving skills. *Cognitive Psychology, 7,* 268–288.

Sperber, D. (1985). Anthropology and psychology: Towards an epidemiology of representations. *Man, 20,* 73–89.

Spering, M., Wagener, D., & Funke, J. (2005). The role of emotions in complex problem solving. *Cognition and Emotion, 19,* 1252–1261.

Stark, R. (1965). A taxonomy of religious experiences. *Journal for the Scientific Study of Religion, 5,* 97–116.

Stephano, G., Goumon, Y., Casares, F., Cadet, P., Fricchione, G., Rialas, C., et al. (2000). Endogenous morphine. *Trends in Neuroscience, 23,* 436–442.

Storbeck, J., & Clore, G. L. (2007). On the interdependence of cognition and emotion. *Cognition and Emotion, 21,* 1212–1237.

Strunk, O., Jr. (Ed.). (1971). *Psychology of religion: Historical and interpretive readings.* Nashville, TN: Abingdon Press.

Taves, A. (2008). "Religious experience" and the brain. In J. Bulbulia, R. Sosis, E. Harris, R. Genet, C. Genet, & K. Wyman (Eds.), *The evolution of religion: Studies, theories, critiques* (pp. 211–218). San Margarita, CA: Collins Foundation Press.

Thomasson, E. (2009). Islamic hell. *Numen: International Review of the History of Religions, 56,* 401–416.

Tinbergen, N. (1963). On aims and methods in ethology. *Zeitschrift für Tierpsychologie, 20,* 410–433.

Turner, V. (1966). *The ritual process: Structure and anti-structure.* Ithaca, NY: Cornell University Press.

Urry, H. L., & Poey, A. P. (2008). How religious/spiritual practices contribute to well-being: The role of emotion regulation. In R. M. Lerner, R. Roeser, & E. Phelps (Eds.), *Positive youth development and spirituality: From theory to research* (pp. 145–163). West Conshohocken, PA: Templeton Foundation Press.

Whitehouse, H. (1995). *Inside the cult: Religious innovation and transmission in Papua New Guinea.* Oxford, UK: Clarendon/Oxford University Press.

Whitehouse, H. (2004). *Modes of religiosity: A cognitive theory of religious transmission.* Walnut Creek, CA: AltaMira Press.

Whitehouse, H. (2007). Terror. In J. Corrigan (Ed.), *The Oxford handbook of religion and emotion* (pp. 259–275). Oxford, UK: Oxford University Press.

Whitehouse, H. (2008). Cognitive evolution and religion: Cognition and religious evolution. In J. Bulbulia, R. Sosis, E. Harris, R. Genet, C. Genet, & K. Wyman (Eds.), *The evolution of religion: Studies, theories, critiques* (pp. 31–41). San Margarita, CA: Collins Foundation Press.

Wiebe, P. H. (2006). Religious experience, cognitive science, and the future of religion. In P. Clayton & Z. Simpson (Eds.), *The Oxford handbook of religion and science* (pp. 503–522). Oxford, UK: Oxford University Press.

Wiltermuth, S. S., & Heath, C. (2009). Synchrony and cooperation. *Psychological Science, 20,* 1–5.

Wyer, R. S., Jr., Clore, G. L., & Isbell, L. M. (1999). Affect and information processing. *Advances in Experimental Social Psychology, 31,* 1–77.

Section *III*

The Role of Emotion and Motivation in Human Performance

10

Is It Possible to Solve a Problem Without Emotion?

EVELYNE CLÉMENT

INTRODUCTION

Anyone who has solved a difficult problem is well aware of the different emotions experienced while performing the task. Surprisingly, in the framework of thinking and reasoning research, emotions are still neglected. For instance, in *The Cambridge Handbook of Thinking and Reasoning*, edited in 2005 by Holyoak and Morisson, with the exception of one chapter focused on the motivational aspects of cognition (Molden & Higgins, 2005), no chapter is dedicated to the reciprocal relationship between cognition and emotion.

The models and theories developed in a classical cognitive approach have allowed an increasingly fine understanding of human cognition like memory, perception, learning, and reasoning. The greater part of the scientific community agrees with the idea that modeling cognitive processes is necessary to test a broad range of human psychological theories. Yet, most of the cognitive models do not take into account the emotional component of a flexible cognition, which is a prerequisite condition for adaptation and evolution. Therefore, the classical approach is frequently defined as a "cold cognition" approach because, in this conception, emotion is implicitly considered as different and sometimes opposed to rational behavior. However, for instance, experimental evidence from neurobiological research (e.g., Damasio, 1994) had shown that damage to emotion-responsible areas of the brain impairs what is generally called rational behavior. The well-known case of Phinéas Gage is a good illustration of the intrinsic links between emotion and cognition.

This is not to say that emotion and cognition were not considered together and that the study of their links is a new interest in the cognitive community. Actually, for decades some cognitive investigators have contributed to a highly important aspect of emotion theory by integrating it into a cognitive science framework. For instance, as long ago as 1967, Simon (1967) claimed the necessity to develop a general theory of thinking and problem solving that incorporates motivation and emotion. Simon considered emotion and motivation as the two instances that control cognition by interrupting the system and allowing the processor to respond to urgent needs in real time. From this point of view, the function of emotion is to regulate the system by allowing it to abandon the current goal and to substitute a new goal more suitable for the constraints of the environment. In this case, emotion drives attention. In the same vein, Oatley and Johnson-Laird (1987) claimed that emotions have important cognitive functions and are central to the organization of cognitive processing. The authors proposed a theory in which "emotions have important cognitive functions. … They are part of [a] management system to co-ordinate each individual's multiple plans and goals under constraints of time and other limited resources" (p. 31). They considered that the function of emotion is to accomplish and maintain a transition between plans when the evaluation of success in a plan changes.

In the present chapter, I first briefly expose the evolution of the psychological theories on the links between cognition and emotion, then discuss some current approaches that formalize the interactions between cognition and emotion. I especially develop the appraisal theories according to which the subjective (conscious or unconscious) interpretation of the situation may trigger emotion. These approaches are of great interest because they allow interpreting the emotional manifestations associated with critical events of the problem-solving activity. To illustrate this last point, some experimental evidence from the research on problem-solving puzzles is discussed and interpreted in this framework. In conclusion, the challenge of modeling the links between emotion and problem-solving activity is addressed, and grasping the physiological and expressive changes to appraisal dimensions in problem solving is analyzed as a relevant means to integrate the emotional components that accompany such a goal-directed activity in a general model of problem solving.

ARE COGNITION AND EMOTION TWO SEPARATE SYSTEMS?

What are the links between cognition and emotion? Does emotion imply cognitive processing? Does cognition need emotion? Is it more suitable to speak of the motivational and emotional roots of cognition and action or conversely to consider the cognitive elicitors of emotion? These core issues, which have given rise to much controversy, are rooted in antiquity (see Scherer & Sangsue, 2004, for a critical approach to the Platonic conception) and more recently in the famous controversy between James (1884) and Cannon (1927) with regard to the peripheral or central origin of emotion. According to the peripheral theory of James, the changes in physiology and the body are the crucial and the primary cause of the emotional processes. It is the perception of these changes in response to an emotional stimulus that triggers subjective feeling. In other words, it is because we tremble that we are frightened. Thus, the subjective feeling is closely linked with the body's changes and does not need any cognitive appraisal of the event. In the same approach, Lange (1885/1912) postulated that the emotions are differentiated based on the peripheral responses of the system, each emotion corresponding to a specific physiological pattern. On the contrary, according to Cannon, because the physiological patterns are not sufficiently differentiated, the origin of the emotion is located in the central nervous system. More precisely, the thalamus was considered by the author as the center of the organization of the emotions. At the peripheral level, the thalamus would guide the physiological changes, and on the other hand, at the cortical level, it would elicit subjective feeling.

Schachter and Singer (1962) proposed that the emotional processes involve both the physiological and cognitive activities. According to the authors, the physiological responses are a necessary but not a sufficient condition for triggering subjective feeling. The body's reactions would have a significant meaning as long as the physical and social context of their expression is evaluated.

Mandler (1984), who conceived a conflict theory of emotion, has developed this idea. In his theory, it is the evaluation of the gap between the situation and the expectations based on cognitive schemas that produces emotions. When the expectations are congruent with the situation, positive emotion may occur; conversely, discrepancies between the situation and the anticipations would entail negative emotions. This position has been strongly criticized by Zajonc (1980), who claimed a direct link between behavioral responses and subjective feeling without any mediation of the cognition or the consciousness of the emotional processes.

Another important issue in the debate that has gone through the theories of emotion is that of the effects of emotion on cognition. For a long time, a shared conception was that emotion disrupts rational and adaptive behavior.

EMOTION AS A DISTURBANCE IN A RATIONAL THOUGHT OR AS AN ADAPTIVE COMPONENT?

Do emotions disrupt rational and intelligent behavior? Conversely, do emotions allow a flexible adaptation to the unpredictable changes of our environment? These issues have dominated the debates in psychology for a long time and have given rise to many contrasting positions. The answers to these issues come under two antagonist approaches of the role of the emotion in the expression of an adaptive behavior. On the one hand, emotions are considered as a disorder that inevitably leads to the expression of irrational and unsuited behaviors. This conception has largely influenced experimental psychology and has been supported by psychophysiologists' work in the first decades of 20th century (Hebb, 1949; Lindsley, 1951; Magoun, 1960; see Fraisse, 1975, for a review). In the framework of the activation theory, emotion was defined as an extreme of a continuum of different levels of arousal. By progressively stimulating the reticular formation in the brain stem in animals, different levels of arousal were observed, from sleep to hyperexcitation. From this point of view, the works on the relation between the level of activation and performance have shown that beyond a critical threshold of activation, performance decreases even when the level of arousal increases. Performance decreases precisely when emotion occurs (Bloch, 1973). Therefore, when the intensity of the stimulation is too high, the activity seems to be disorganized and uncontrolled.

In other respects, research focused on motivation and performance has shown that emotion appears when the discrepancy between the motivation and the ability to face the situation is too important (see Nuttin, 1975, for a review). For instance, Yerkes and Dodson (1908) studied debilitation in performance and its relation to increased stimulation strength. Their pioneer work on the links between discrimination learning and performance in rats showed that the speed of learning depends on the intensity of the stimulus (electric shock associated with mistake). The manipulation of the strength of the electric shock from weak to medium and strong had dramatic effects on performance: The intensive stimulation (strong shock) yielded poor performance, and the best learning occurred under the medium stimulus (referred to as the Yerkes-Dodson inverted-U curve). From these pioneer research endeavors, widely influenced by the Platonic and Cartesian viewpoints, the negative facet of emotions was highlighted (e.g., Piéron, 1959), and emotion was too often reduced to the notion of stress.

In contrast, from a more recent point of view, it is claimed that emotions play a crucial role in social, adaptive, and intelligent behavior. Actually, several studies in cognitive psychology, neuropsychology, and the neurosciences demonstrated that emotions modulate cognitive processes in an adaptive way by driving selective attention (e.g., Öhman, Flykt, & Esteves, 2001; Öhman & Mineka, 2003); guiding goals management (e.g., Oatley & Johnson-Laird, 1987); allowing selection between alternatives (e.g., Bechara, Damasio, Damasio, & Anderson, 1994); and preparing the organism for action (e.g., Frijda, 1987). In this way, Cacioppo and Gardner (1999) wrote the following:

> The notion that emotions are a disruptive force in rational thought and adaptive action was shown to be a gross oversimplification (e.g., Bernston et al., 1993). Although the obstacles of a civilized world still occasionally call forth blind rages, emotions are increasingly recognized for the constructive role they play in higher forms of human experience. (p. 194)

For the authors, both the neurological cases reported by Damasio (1994) and work on emotional intelligence (Goleman, 1995; Mayer & Salovey, 1993) are strong arguments in favor of the beneficial contribution of emotions to a fulfilling life.

To summarize the historical debates on the relationship between cognition and emotion, controversial issues such as the origin and the nature of the emotion, the independence of the cognitive and the emotional systems, and the negative effect of emotion on cognition have gone through scrutiny under the philosophical as well as the psychological framework. As several contemporary authors noted, some of these debates have been overtaken because they were based on different meanings of cognition and emotion. For instance, cognition does not imply solely rational and explicit thought and may not be confused with reason. In this way, the interpretation of the situation as an emotional event may be under control of conscious or unconscious processes. Therefore, the debate on the sequence of the eliciting factors that give rise to emotion (e.g., the primacy of emotion, Zajonc,

1980; or the primacy of cognition, Lazarus, 1984) was considered a false debate (e.g., Leventhal & Scherer, 1987). On the other hand, the concept of emotion suffered from a lack of a precise definition, and certain confusion was prevalent in the meanings of emotion, mood, affect, passion, and feeling. Nevertheless, these different approaches are the basis of the contemporary theories of emotion.

THE CONTEMPORARY THEORIES THAT FORMALIZE THE RELATIONSHIP BETWEEN COGNITION AND EMOTION

As suggested by Philippot (2004), the main influential theories of emotion may be classified into two broad categories: the *biological* theories and the *cognitive* theories. In the line of the Darwinian conception, the former conceive emotions as specific response patterns to prototypical situations, constituting a set of pre-programmed automatic processes of adaptation to the environment and requiring a minimum of cognitive processing (Ekman, 1972; Izard, 1971; Tomkins, 1962, 1963). This set of processes constitutes the evolutionarily evolved *affect program,* including preprogrammed response patterns from visceral to muscular, expressive, and subjective levels. These theories postulate a limited number of evolutionarily continuous basic or discrete emotions that are triggered by high eliciting situations and that are innate and universal. Therefore, the protagonists of these theories characterize emotion as automatic specific response patterns, especially prototypical facial expressions, even if in recent years they take into account the importance of the effects of the environment and culture on emotional development and highlight the interactions between cognitive and affective processes (Ekman, 1994; Izard, 1992, 1993).

The later influential theories on the emotion research, referred to as the *appraisal* theories, rightly stressed the importance of the evaluation of the personal significance of events as the central antecedent of emotional experience. Following the pioneer works of Arnold (1960) and Lazarus (1966), modern appraisal theories conceived emotions as the result of a set of processes covering both the evaluation of the event according to its consequences for the well-being of the organism *(appraisal)* and the evaluation of the individual's adjustment potential *(coping potential)* that guides the responses according to the person's evaluation of his or her capacity to control the event and its consequences (Frijda, 1986; Lazarus, 1991; Ortony, Clore, & Collins, 1988; Scherer, 1984, 2001a; Smith & Lazarus, 1990, 1993). From this point of view, the cognitive evaluation triggers an emotional episode, which in turn informs the system and takes part in elaborating an adaptive response. The appraisal theories of emotion predict the elicitation and differentiation of emotions based on a set of appraisal dimensions. Despite some divergent approaches developed in this framework, the protagonists came to an agreement about a set of appraisal criteria (see Scherer & Sangsue, 2004, for a comparison of the appraisal criteria proposed by the different theories). These criteria include the perception of change in environment requiring deployment of attention (novelty, expectancy); the intrinsic pleasantness (valence, pleasantness); the relevance of the event to one's goals and needs (relevance, conduciveness, motive consistency); the attribution of agency and intention (responsibility, locus of causality);

the evaluation of one's ability to cope with the event (controllability, power, potential coping); and the evaluation of the normative significance (internal and external standards) (e.g., Roseman & Smith, 2001; Sander, Grandjean, & Scherer, 2005; Scherer, 2001b). Because of their theoretical interest in predicting and interpreting emotional responses in problem-solving situations, we develop in more detail Scherer's (1984, 2001a) component process model (CPM) and the theory of Smith and Lazarus (1990, 1993).

SCHERER'S COMPONENT PROCESS MODEL

In the initial version of his theory, Scherer highlighted the limits in conceiving emotion as an interruption mechanism followed by a capture of the subject's attention on the causes of the interruption (Hebb, 1949; Mandler, 1975; Pribram, 1967; Simon, 1967). He claimed that emotion may also contribute to stimulate the organism: "Whether emotional process interrupt, disturb or adaptively support cognitive or behavioral sequences depends on the respective situation, the nature of the task, degree of arousal and other factors, but does not constitute a specific criterion for describing emotion" (Scherer, 1982, p. 556). In this way, emotion is considered as an interface between the organism and its environment mediating the constant changes of the environment and the individual's responses. Because of its evolutionary and adaptive function, emotion allows decoupling stimulus and response and thus creating a delay to elaborate a flexible and adaptive response to environmental contingencies.

According to Scherer, emotion consists of five components providing five distinct functions. The cognitive component evaluates the objects and events; the peripheral efference component regulates the system; the motivational component prepares and guides the actions; the motor expression component expresses communication of reaction and behavioral intention; and the subjective feeling component monitors the internal state and environment interaction (Scherer, 2001a). In this framework, Sander et al. (2005) described emotion "as an episode of interrelated, synchronized changes in the states of all or most the five organismic subsystems in response to the evaluation of an external or internal stimulus event as relevant to major concerns of the organism" (p. 318). The organismic subsystem (and its major substrata) consists of the following: information processing (central nervous system, CNS); support (CNS, neuroendocrine system, autonomic nervous system); executive (CNS); action (somatic nervous system); monitor (CNS). According to Scherer, the differentiation of elicited emotions is based on a fast succession of stimulus-processing sequences (the *stimulus evaluation checks*). Four appraisal criteria constitute these checks: the *relevance detection* of an event, including novelty, intrinsic pleasantness, goal/need relevance checks; *its implication assessment* with causal attribution, outcome probability, discrepancy from expectation, goal/need conduciveness, and urgency checks; *the individual's coping potential,* comprised of control, power, and adjustment checks; and finally *the normative significance evaluation* of the event corresponding to internal and external standards checks (for a detail description, see Sander et al., 2005). These stimulus evaluation checks occur at three different levels: from the sensorimotor level, to the schematic level, and to the conceptual level (Leventhal & Scherer, 1987). At the sensorimotor level, these checks are supposed to be mostly genetically determined and based on matching mechanisms. At the schematic level, the evaluation is founded on social learning processes, and much of the processing occurs without consciousness. Finally, on the conceptual level, the cortical associative areas process the evaluations that imply cultural meaning systems. In other respects, this model postulates that changes in one subsystem will tend to elicit related changes in other subsystems.

SMITH AND LAZARUS'S APPROACH

Smith and Lazarus (1990, 1993) developed in more detail than Scherer the adaptive strategies and more precisely the appraisal of the coping potential. Emotion was conceptualized as a control system governed by two steps. The first one consists of the evaluation of the relationship between the person and the person's physical and social environment (*appraisal*). The second one corresponds to the strategies for maintaining or altering this relationship (*coping*). According to the authors, the cognitive processes intervene in both of the two steps of processing. On the one hand, they take part in elaborating the individual's interpretation of the relations between the external events and his or her goals and desires, and on the other hand, they guide the adjustment strategies either by motivating actions that change the environment, *problem-focused coping*, or by changing the interpretation of these relations, *emotion-focused coping* (Lazarus, 1991). For instance, problem-focused coping may involve the person in active coping by trying to remove or circumvent the stressor even when emotion-focused coping may correspond to a behavioral disengagement that implies a reduction of effort. Depending on how the events and coping potential are appraised, adjustments may differ. In other words, the estimated ability to face the event and its consequence determines motivational aspects of the activity. For example, an event appraised as undesirable but controllable may motivate planning how to cope and to develop strategies that reverse negative circumstances of the event. In contrast, an event appraised as undesirable but not under control may lead to an avoiding reaction or resignation. In this way, behavior would emerge from the interaction between both the cognitive and emotional processes and the adjustment responses.

Although the appraisal theories have been developed in parallel, they share many common assumptions. The protagonists of these theories agreed on the role of emotions in the expression of adaptive and flexible behavior. In addition, there is a high degree of convergence with respect to the appraisal criteria postulated by the different theories. However, the fixed sequence of the appraisal processes has been the subject of controversy. According to Scherer (1984), on the three levels depicted in the preceding section (sensorimotor, schematic, and conceptual levels), the stimulus evaluation checks are processed in the following fixed order: from the relevance of the event to its implication for the organism, then the coping potential determination and the normative significance evaluation. In contrast, Smith and Lazarus (1990) postulated certain flexibility according to environmental contingencies. The authors claimed:

> It is not necessary to think of the appraisal process as a fixed or pre-defined sequence, since the full appraisal meaning associated with the past experience(s) can be activated in a single step. ... Although conceptual processing of appraisal components perhaps could follow predefined sequences, as Scherer (1984) has suggested, we are wary of a stage theory, since whatever issues and aspects of the encounter seem especially salient may well pre-empt attention at any given moment. (pp. 629–630)

However, some recent experimental evidence supports Scherer's view of the sequential nature of the appraisal hypothesis, at least in the context of psychophysiological responding between the stimulus relevance detection and the goal conduciveness appraisal (Aue, Flykt, & Scherer, 2007).

To summarize, even if at first sight appraisal theories may be perceived as a *cold* and too *cognitivistic* approach to emotion (see Scherer, 2001b, for a rebuttal of these criticisms), they provide a solid theoretical framework allowing predictions on changes of emotional states (diagnosed by the changes of the physiological and expressive responses) based on the evaluation of the event and its consequences. Actually, the fact that the emotions are accompanied by various adaptive responses in the automatic and somatic nervous systems and that both the evaluation of the events and the coping potential appraisal organize the response components, such as physiology and expressive behavior, are now well established (e.g., Frijda, 1986; Johnstone & Scherer, 2000; Lazarus, 1991; Öhman, 1994; Pecchinenda & Smith, 1996; Scherer, 1984; Smith, 1989).

PROBLEM SOLVING AND APPRAISAL THEORIES

The appraisal theories are of great interest and well suited to grasp the elicitation of emotion in goal-directed activity such as problem solving.

Problem-solving activity is generally described by two phases: the exploratory phase and the planning phase (Kotovsky, Hayes, & Simon, 1985). In the exploratory phase, the participant learns how to make a move to reach the goal and is engaged in the construction of the relevant interpretation of the situation. In this phase, the rhythm of actions is slow, there are many interruptions between actions, and perseverative behaviors, reiterating the inefficient sequence of actions, are observed. In the planning phase, the adequate representation of the situation is constructed, and planning activities may occur. In this final phase, there is no interruption between actions and no perseveration, and the rhythm of actions is fast.

In the exploratory phase, two broad types of critical events may be supposed to be emotionally relevant because of their conduciveness to performing well in solving the problem at hand: *impasse* situations and *subgoal achievements*. According to the theoretical framework proposed by Richard and his colleagues (Richard, Poitrenaud, & Tijus, 1993), it is assumed that problem solving consists of elaborating an adequate representation of how the problem has to be solved, by dropping misconceptions (inappropriate interpretations and irrelevant goals generated by these misconceptions) and building increasingly sophisticated goal structures that lead to a planning activity. The impasse situations are states of the problem in which the current representation leads to the feeling that all the ways to the solution are blocked. Three behavioral signals may accompany these subjective impasses: the interruption of the activity without any action, the looking back that undoes the previous action, and the rules violation that consists of making an illegal action. The subgoal achievements are states that objectively draw nearer the goal. In the constraints model (Richard et al., 1993), these events are supposed to be the opportunity for changing the representation (when the first representation leads to impasse) and the current goal (both when the first representation leads to impasse and when a subgoal is achieved). In spite of the great interest of this model because it allows describing the two phases depicted by Kotovsky et al. (1985) and simulating the participant's behavior by identifying the impasse situations and the subgoal achievements, this model remains a "cold" model of cognition. Therefore, a general aim of research conducted in our laboratory (Duvallet, 2007; Duvallet & Clément, 2005) was to integrate, in a foreseeable future, the relationships between cognition and emotion into a general model of problem solving such as the constraints model of Richard et al.

PSYCHOPHYSIOLOGICAL AND EXPRESSIVE RESPONSES TO APPRAISAL DIMENSIONS IN DIFFICULT PROBLEM SOLVING

A preliminary aim of the present research was to examine whether problem-solving events that are contingent with specific appraisal conditions (the impasse situations and the subgoal achievements) would also show specific physiological and expressive response patterns. Actually, in the framework of the appraisal theories, some general hypothesis with respect to both the appraisal of goal conduciveness of critical events and the appraisal of the ability to cope with these events may be formulated. More precisely, it was expected that the appraisal of goal conduciveness would cause changes in both physiological and expressive patterns.

This hypothesis was tested using a difficult problem-solving puzzle, the five disks version of the Tower of Hanoi problem. This relatively difficult problem for adults was chosen because it is supposed to be difficult enough to motivate the participant to perform the task without exceeding his or her own objective ability to solve the problem (Anzai & Simon, 1979). In a series of experiments, two kinds of response components were recorded continuously during the activity: the physiological (skin conductance activity) and the expressive (facial expressions) components. The skin conductance activity, a measure that reflects sympathetic autonomic nervous system arousal, is considered to reflect a process related to *energy regulation* or *mobilization*, particularly an effortful allocation of attentional resources to the task (Dawson, Schell, & Filion, 2000). In the framework of the appraisal theories, the changes of this physiological response are interpreted as a marker of the appraisal process (e.g., Kappas & Pecchinenda, 1999; Pecchinenda & Smith, 1996; Smith, 1989; van Reekum et al., 2004). On the other hand, facial expressions were chosen because facial expressiveness is generally considered a component of emotion, a function of which is to communicate to someone his or her own internal states (e.g., Ekman, 1994; Izard, 1994; Kaiser & Wehrle, 2001; Lee & Wagner, 2002; Wagner, Lewis, Ramsay, & Krediet, 1992). Moreover, it has been assumed that facial expressions reveal the person's appraisals and the action tendencies (Frijda, 1987; Frijda & Tcherkassof, 1997; Scherer & Ellgring, 2007; Smith, 1989). As Scherer and Ellgring (2007, p. 115) wrote, "Facial expressions express components of emotion process, as patterned by the results of appraisal."

To identify the impasse situations and the subgoal achievements and to match the emotional responses and the cognitive events, an individual protocol analysis of the solver's behavior was conducted in the framework of the constraint model. Based on the recording of the behavioral, expressive, and physiological data (Figure 10.1 shows how the different data were recorded during the activity), a first analysis was conducted between the exploratory phase and the planning phase depicted by Kotovsky et al. (1985).

Then, within the exploratory phase, another comparison was conducted between the impasse situations and the subgoal achievements. During the exploratory phase, the sequences of actions were recorded as follows: A sequence guided by the same subgoal constituting a step in the final goal defined an episode. For instance, the current subgoal of the participant may be to release Disk 5 (the largest) to put it on the right peg (at its final place) by moving the smallest disks (Disks 4, 3, 2, 1) from the top of Disk 5. It was assumed that the goal pursued guided the solver's choice between alternative actions (two or three depending on the current state). Second, for each sequence of actions defined in this way, the cognitive events that occurred were recorded. During a sequence of actions, an interruption between two consecutive actions, a rule violation, or a perseverative behavior was coded as an impasse situation. The sequences of actions that were efficient in subgoal achievement were coded as a subgoal achievement. A subgoal achievement was defined by the fact that the participant reached a state that achieved the current subgoal of the sequence of actions.

Two measures of the skin conductance activity were computed for each period of interest. First, the number of spontaneous responses higher than 0.05 microsiemens initiated within the period of interest and expressed as a rate per minute. Then, the maximum amplitude of such responses was scored by computing the difference between their maximum and minimum values. Concerning the facial expressions, the number of positive and negative facial expressions per minute was also computed.

As predicted, the main results showed that the appraisal of goal conduciveness causes changes in both physiological and expressive patterns. On the one hand, comparisons between the exploratory phase and the planning phase showed that in the planning phase there were significantly more spontaneous skin conductance responses (SCRs) than in the exploratory phase, although concerning the maximum amplitude of the responses, no significant differences were observed. Concerning the facial expressions, there were significantly more positive facial expressions during the planning phase than in the exploratory phase and significantly more negative facial expressions in the exploratory phase than in the planning phase. On the other hand, comparisons in the exploratory phase showed the following patterns: There were significantly more responses in the subgoal achievements

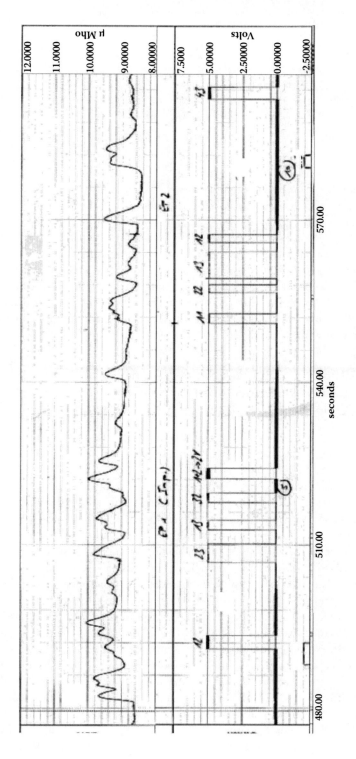

Figure 10.1 Emotional response components and behavioral data were recorded online. In the first track, the skin conductance activity was reported. On the second track, both the actions made by the participant and the facial expressions were reported. All the actions were coded as follows: For instance, 12 means that the participant moved the smallest disk from its current place to the middle. The temporal dimension of the activity is reported on the abscissa axis.

TABLE 10.1   Synthesis of the Results

Exploratory Phase	Compared to	Planning Phase
Facial expressions	Positive facial expressions rate	< °°
	Negative facial expressions rate	> °
Electrodermal activity	Skin conductance response rate	< °°
	Maximum amplitude of the responses	NS
Impasses Situations	**Compared to**	**Subgoal Achievements**
Facial expressions	Positive facial expressions rate	NS
	Negative facial expressions rate	> °
Electrodermal activity	Skin conductance response rate	< °°
	Maximum amplitude of the responses	> °

°° $p < .0001$; ° $p < .01$; NS, no significant differences.

than in the impasse situations, and the maximum amplitude of the responses was significantly higher during the impasse situations than during the subgoal achievements. Concerning the positive facial expressions, there were no significant differences between the impasse situations and the subgoal achievements even when there were significantly more negative facial expressions in the impasse situations. Table 10.1 presents a synthesis of the results.

PSYCHOPHYSIOLOGICAL AND EXPRESSIVE RESPONSES TO APPRAISAL DIMENSIONS IN PROBLEM SOLVING: DISCUSSION AND CONCLUSION

At an aggregate level, as predicted, different patterns of physiological and expressive emotional manifestations were associated with the critical events of problem solving. These results suggest that, as hypothesized, the events are emotionally relevant according to their appraised conduciveness in achieving the goal. Nonetheless, with respect to the physiological component, the two measures showed two paradoxically different patterns. Even though the SCR rate was higher in the subgoal achievements supposed to be appraised as conductive events, the maximum amplitude of the responses was higher in the impasse situations supposed to be appraised as obstructive events. These results may be interpreted in the following way: The SCR rate as well as the facial expression may reflect the coping potential appraisals. In this case, achieving a subgoal could increase the motivation, and confidence would be indicated by the increase of both spontaneous skin conductance responses and positive facial expressions. In return, in the impasse situations, the estimated ability to face the problem might be low. This low potential coping appraisal would be associated with the decrease of the spontaneous skin conductance responses and the increase of the negative facial expressions. This interpretation is in line with studies that focused on the physiological components of coping potential appraisals and have shown positive correlations between the skin conductance responses and coping potential appraisals (Pecchinenda & Smith, 1996; see Pecchinenda, 2001, for review). Nevertheless, with respect to the facial expressions, an alternative but not exclusive explanation could be related to social demands with the experimental situation (e.g., Lee & Wagner, 2002). This alternative explanation was tested in one of the experiments conducted by Duvallet (2007) by manipulating the social presence factor. It was predicted that results would show changes in facial expressions depending on the presence of the experimenter.

On the other hand, with regard to the amplitude of the responses, the higher phasic skin conductance activity observed in response to the impasse situations was consistent with results reported in the literature that concentrated on the physiological response changes to appraisal dimensions in a computer game. For instance, it was shown that the magnitude of the skin conductance responses was higher in the obstructive events than in the conductive events of a video game (e.g., van Reekum et al., 2004). This set of results supports the interpretation that the amplitude of the responses reflects emotional arousal and an effortful allocation of attentional resources.

Yet, some limitations and design of future studies have to be highlighted. In these experiments, the coping potential appraisal was not directly assessed but inferred on the basis of the facial expressions and the skin conductance spontaneous responses. It may be reasonable to hypothesize that in the impasse situations, individual differences may lead to different appraisals of the individual's ability to deal with the obstructive event. In these obstructive events, one may predict that, depending on the participants' appraisals, the potential coping appraisal may be high or low. Some future experiments would be conducted to measure directly the potential coping appraisal. For instance, in an off-line processing, using verbal reports on the participants' subjective feelings while they encountered impasse situations would convey direct information on the coping potential appraisal. In that way, it would be possible to test the post hoc hypothesis of the emotional significance of the SCR rate.

Another limitation of this research is the coding of the facial expressions. Although the use of a rigorous method adapted from the facial expression coding system (FACES) technique of Kring and Sloan (1991), the valence of the facial expressions may appear as an oversimplified measure. According to the authors (Kring & Sloan, 2007), the correlation between self-report and FACES scores for negative emotion are low to medium, indicating that the method is not to be used on its own as a reliable measure of emotional response. In other respects, several studies focused on the facial expressive component used the facial affect coding system of Ekman and Friesen (1978). This technique allows a fine description of the facial action units (AUs) and some predictions of the facial movement as result of individual appraisal checks (Scherer & Ellgring, 2007).

Nevertheless, this set of research studies was a first attempt to find links between appraisals and changes in physiological and expressive behavior in the field of the problem-solving puzzle. In addition, as mentioned, this work was a first experimental step to integrate the relationships between cognition and emotion into a general model of problem solving. In line with this work, some new research was developed on modeling children's behavior when solving an arithmetic problem (Mahboub, Clément, Bertelle, & Jay, 2009).

GENERAL CONCLUSIONS

As noted in the introduction to this chapter, emotion is too often neglected in the contemporary models of thinking and problem solving (e.g., Anderson & Lebiere, 1998, Lovett & Anderson, 2005; Richard et al., 1993), although it is becoming evident that cognitive models should take emotion into account. Actually, as experimental evidence from different fields, such as cognitive psychology, neuropsychology, and the neurosciences, has shown, the reciprocal relationships between emotion and cognition are well established. In this way, it was demonstrated that emotion is closely related to such cognitive processes as learning, decision making, attention, and memory (e.g., Bechara, Damasio, & Damasio, 2000; Corson & Verrier, 2007; Isen, 1999; Öhman et al., 2001).

As pointed out by Sander and Koening (2002), the neglect of emotion may be due to two reasons. First, emotions were considered too complex, and then "the dominant mode of thinking, deeply marked by a scientifically-correct cartesianism, was to conceive the cognitive system as the 'incarnation of reason.' Therefore, emotions were traditionally considered as a trouble of the (cognitive) mind" (p. 250). In this classical point of view, the answer to the provocative title of the present chapter would be that, yes, it is possible to solve a problem without emotion.

Still, the richness and the consistency of the findings emerging from contemporary research on emotion allow us to envisage the development of a general theory of thinking and problem solving that incorporates emotion. Moreover, there have been some attempts to model emotion within a computational perspective (e.g., Belavkin, 2001; Gratch & Marsella, 2004; Sander et al., 2005). Modeling the links between emotion and problem solving is a challenge that now seems to be faced by integrating the assumptions of appraisal theories in a general framework of the activity.

Finally, tracking physiological and expressive responses to the appraised events during the course of the problem-solving activity seems to be a relevant means to attain this objective. Compared to previous studies focused on the influence of the affect on strategies that employ more classical and passive induction methods, (e.g., Ashby, Isen, & Turken, 1999; Isen, 1998), identifying the physiological and expressive components while the participant is actively engaged in the task allows researchers to directly measure the influence of the evaluation processes on these components. In other respects, because of the temporal dynamic of the problem-solving activity, it is necessary to conduct individual protocol analysis in the framework of a general model of the activity. It is only under this condition that it is possible to identify the events that are appraised as obstructive or conductive to the goal and to match them with the different physiological and expressive responses.

To conclude, studying how the relevant cognitive events of the problem-solving activity are emotionally relevant also is a way to both grasp the relationships between cognition and emotion and support the idea that cognition and emotion are not two separate systems. This approach is in line with the assumption that emotion and cognition have to be considered and formalized in integrated models of the activity.

REFERENCES

Anderson, J. R., & Lebiere, C. (1998). *The atomic components of thought*. Mahwah, NJ: Erlbaum.

Anzai, Y., & Simon, H. A. (1979). The theory of learning by doing. *Psychological Review, 86, 2,* 124–140.

Arnold, M. B. (1960). *Emotion and personality: Psychological aspects* (Vol. 1). New York: Columbia University Press.

Ashby, F. G., Isen, A. M., & Turken, U. (1999). A neuropsychological theory of positive affect and its influence on cognition. *Psychological Review, 106,* 529–550.

Aue, T., Flykt, A., & Scherer, K. R. (2007). First evidence for differential and sequential efferent effects of stimulus and goal conduciveness appraisal. *Biological Psychology, 74,* 347–357.

Bechara, A., Damasio A. R., Damasio, H., & Anderson, S. W. (1994). Insensitivity to future consequences following damage to human prefrontal cortex. *Cognition, 50,* 7–15.

Bechara, A., Damasio, H., & Damasio A. R. (2000). Emotion, decision making and the orbitofrontal cortex. *Cerebral Cortex, 10,* 295–307.

Belavkin, R. V. (2001). The role of emotion in problem solving. In C. Johnson (Ed.), *Proceedings of the AISB'01 Symposium on Emotion, Cognition and Affective Computing* (pp. 49–57). Helsington, York, England.

Bernston, G. G., Boysen, S. T., & Cacioppo, J. T. (1993). Neurobehavioral organization and the cardinal principle of evaluative bivalence. *Annals of the New York Academy of Science, 702,* 75–102.

Bloch, V. (1973). Les niveaux de vigilance et l'attention. In P. Fraisse & J. Piaget (Eds), Traité de psychologie expérimentale, Tome 3 (pp. 83–128). Paris: Presses Universitaires de France.

Cacioppo, J. T., & Gardner, W. L. (1999). Emotion. *Annual Review of Psychology, 50,* 191–214.

Cannon, W. B. (1927). The James-Lange theory of emotions: A critical examination and an alternative theory. *American Journal of Psychology, 39,* 106–124.

Corson, Y., & Verrier, N. (2007). Emotions and false memories: Valence or arousal? *Psychological Science, 18,* 208–211.

Damasio, A. R. (1994). *Descartes' error: Emotion, reason, and the human brain*. New York: Grosset Putnam.

Dawson, M. E., Schell, A. M., & Filion, D. L. (2000). The electrodermal system. In J. T. Cacioppo, L. G. Tassinary, & G. G. Bernstson (Eds.), *Handbook of psychophysiology* (2nd ed., pp. 200–223). New York: Cambridge University Press.

Duvallet, D. (2007). *Emotion, cognition, action: Étude des manifestations émotionnelles dans le décours de la résolution de problème* [Emotion, cognition, action: Study of the emotional manifestations during problem-solving activity]. PhD thesis, University of Rouen, Rouen, France.

Duvallet, D., & Clément, E. (2005). Experimental study of emotional manifestations during a problem-solving activity. In C. Johnson (Ed.), *Proceedings of the AISB'05 Symposium on Agents That Want and Like: Motivational and Emotional Roots of Cognition and Action* (pp. 41–44). University of Hertfordshire, Hatfield, England, April 12–15, 2005.

Ekman, P. (1972). Universals and cultural differences in facial expression of emotion. In J. R. Cole (Ed.), *Nebraska Symposium on Motivation* (Vol. 19, pp. 207–283). Lincoln: University of Nebraska Press.

Ekman, P. (1994). Moods, emotions, and traits. In P. Ekman & R. J. Davidson (Eds.), *The nature of emotion: Fundamental questions* (pp. 56–58). New York: Oxford University Press.

Ekman, P., & Friesen, W. V. (1978). *The Facial Action Coding System: A technique for the measurement of facial movement.* Palo Alto, CA: Consulting Psychologists Press.

Fraisse, P. (1975). Les émotions. In P. Fraisse & J. Piaget (Eds.), *Traité de Psychologie Expérimentale, fascicule V, 2e éd. Motivation, émotion et personnalité* (pp. 97–181). Paris: PUF.

Frijda, N. (1986). *The emotions.* Cambridge, UK: Cambridge University Press.

Frijda, N. (1987). Emotion, cognitive structure and action tendency. *Cognition and Emotion, 1,* 115–143.

Frijda, N., & Tcherkassof, A. (1997). Facial expressions as modes of action readiness. In J. A. Russell & J. M. Fernandez-Dols (Eds.), *The psychology of facial expression* (pp. 57–77). Cambridge, UK: Cambridge University Press.

Goleman, D. (1995). *Emotional intelligence.* New York: Bantam.

Gratch, J., & Marsella, S. (2004). A domain-independent framework for modelling emotion. *Cognitive Systems Research, 5,* 269–306.

Hebb, D. O. (1949). *The Organization of behavior.* New York: Wiley.

Holyoak, K. J., & Morrison, R. G. (2005). *The Cambridge handbook of thinking and reasoning.* New York: Cambridge University Press.

Isen, A. M. (1998). On the relationship between affect and creative problem-solving. In S. W. Russ (Ed.), *Affect, creative experience and psychological adjustment* (pp. 3–17). Philadelphia: Brunner/Mazel.

Isen, A. M. (1999). Positive affect. In T. Dalgleish & M. J. Power (Eds.), *Handbook of cognition and emotion* (pp. 521–540). Chichester, UK: Wiley.

Izard, C. E. (1971). *The face of emotion.* New York: Appleton-Century-Crofts.

Izard, C. E. (1992). Basic emotions, relations among emotions, and emotion-cognition relations. *Psychological Review, 99,* 561–565.

Izard, C. E. (1993). Four systems for emotion activation: Cognitive and noncognitive processes. *Psychological Review, 100,* 68–90.

Izard, C. E. (1994). Innate and universal facial expressions: Evidence from developmental and cross-cultural research. *Psychological Bulletin, 115,* 288–299.

James, W. (1884). What is an emotion? *Mind, 9,* 188–205.

Johnstone, T., & Scherer K. R. (2000). Vocal communication of emotion. In M. Lewis & J. Haviland (Eds.), *The handbook of emotion* (pp. 220–235). New York: Guilford.

Kaiser, S., & Wehrle, T. (2001). Facial expressions as indicators of appraisal processes. In K. R. Scherer, A. Schorr, & T. Johnstone (Eds.), *Appraisal processes in emotion: Theory, methods, research* (pp. 285–300). New York: Oxford University Press.

Kappas, A., & Pecchinenda, A. (1999). Don't wait for the monsters to get you: A video game task to manipulate appraisals in real time. *Cognition and Emotion, 13,* 119–124.

Kotovsky, K., Hayes, J. R., & Simon, H. A. (1985). Why are some problems hard? Evidence from Tower of Hanoi. *Cognitive Psychology, 17,* 248–294.

Kring, A. M., & Sloan, D. (1991). *The facial expression coding system (FACES): A users guide.* Unpublished manuscript.

Kring, A. M., & Sloan, D. (2007). The facial expression coding system (FACES): Development, validation, and utility. *Psychological Assessment, 19,* 210–224.

Lange, C. G. (1912). The Classical Psychologists (pp. 672–684). (B. Rand, Trans.) Boston: Houghton Mifflin. (Original work published 1885) Download available from http://psychclassics.yorku.ca/Lange

Lazarus, R. S. (1966). *Psychological stress and the coping process.* New York: McGraw-Hill.

Lazarus, R. S. (1984). On the primacy of cognition. *American Psychologist, 39,* 124–129.

Lazarus, R. S. (1991). *Emotion and adaptation.* New York: Oxford University Press.

Lee, V., & Wagner, H. (2002). The effect of social presence on the facial and verbal expression of emotion and the interrelationships among emotion components. *Journal of Nonverbal Behavior, 26*(1), 2–25.

Leventhal, H., & Scherer, K. (1987). The relationship of emotion to cognition: A functional approach to a semantic controversy. *Cognition and Emotion, 1*, 3–28.

Lindsley, D. B. (1951). Emotion. In S. S. Stevens (Ed.), *Handbook of experimental psychology* (pp. 473–516). New York: Wiley.

Lovett, M. C., & Anderson, J. R. (2005). Thinking as a production system. In K. J. Holyoak & R. G. Morrison (Eds.), *The Cambridge handbook of thinking and reasoning* (pp. 401–429). New York: Cambridge University Press.

Magoun, H. W. (1960). *Le Cerveau Éveillé*. Paris: PUF.

Mahboub, K., Clément, E. Bertelle, C, & Jay V. (2009). Emotion: Appraisal-coping model for the "Cascades" problem. In M. A. Aziz-Alaoui & C. Bertelle (Eds.), *From system complexity to emergent properties* (pp. 311–319). Berlin: Springer-Verlag.

Mandler, G. (1975). *Mind and emotions*. New York: Wiley.

Mandler, G. (1984). *Mind and body: Psychology of emotion and stress*. New York: Norton.

Mayer, J. D., & Salovey, P. (1993). The intelligence of emotional intelligence. *Intelligence, 17*, 433–442.

Molden, D. C., & Higgins, E. T. (2005). Motivated thinking. In K. J. Holyoak & R. G. Morrison (Eds.), *The Cambridge handbook of thinking and reasoning* (pp. 295–317). New York: Cambridge University Press.

Nuttin, J. (1975). La motivation. In P. Fraisse & J. Piaget (Eds.), *Traité de Psychologie Expérimentale, fascicule V, 2e éd. Motivation, émotion et personnalité* (pp. 6–96). Paris: PUF.

Oatley, K., & Johnson-Laird, P. N. (1987). Towards a cognitive theory of emotions. *Cognition and Emotion, 1*, 29–50.

Öhman, A. (1994). The psychophysiology of emotion: Evolutionary and non-conscious origins. In G. d'Ydewalle, P. Eelen, & P. Bertelson (Eds.), *International perspectives on psychological science: Vol. 2. the state of the art* (pp. 197–227). Hove, UK: Erlbaum.

Öhman, A., Flykt, A., & Esteves, F. (2001). Emotion drives attention: Detecting a snake in the grass. *Journal of Experimental Psychology: General, 130*, 466–478.

Öhman, A., & Mineka, S. (2003). The malicious serpent: Snakes as a prototypical stimulus for an evolved module of fear. *Current Directions in Psychological Science, 12*, 5–9.

Ortony, A., Clore, G. L., & Collins, A. (1988). *The cognitive structure of emotions*. New York: Cambridge University Press.

Pecchinenda, A. (2001). The psychophysiology of appraisals. In K. R. Scherer, A. Schorr, & T. Johnstone (Eds.), *Appraisal processes in emotion: Theory, methods, research* (pp. 301–315). New York: Oxford University Press.

Pecchinenda, A., & Smith, C. A. (1996). The affective significance of skin conductance activity during a difficult problem-solving task. *Cognition and Emotion, 10*, 481–503.

Philippot, P. (2004). Facteurs cognitifs et réactions corporelles dans le processus émotionnel. In G. Kirouac (Ed.), *Cognition et émotions* (pp. 37–56). Coimbra, Portugal: Imprensa da Universidade.

Piéron, H. (1959). *De l'actinie à l'homme*. Paris: PUF

Pribram, K. H. (1967). Emotion: Steps towards a neurophysiological theory. In D. C. Glass (Ed.), *Neurophysiology and emotion* (pp. 2–40). New York: Rockefeller University Press and Russell Sage Foundation.

Richard, J.-F., Poitrenaud, S., & Tijus, C. A. (1993). Problem-solving restructuration: Elimination of implicit constraints. *Cognitive Science, 17*, 497–529.

Roseman, I., & Smith, C. A. (2001). Appraisal theory: Overview, assumptions, varieties, controversies. In K. R. Scherer, A. Schorr, & T. Johnstone (Eds.), *Appraisal processes in emotion: Theory, methods, research* (pp. 3–19). New York: Oxford University Press.

Sander, D., Grandjean, D., & Scherer, K. R. (2005). A system approach to appraisal mechanisms in emotion. *Neural Networks, 18*, 317–352.

Sander, D., & Koenig, O. (2002). No inferiority complex in the study of emotion complexity: A cognitive neuroscience computational architecture of emotion. *Cognitive Science Quarterly, 2*, 249–272.

Schachter, S., & Singer, J. E. (1962). Cognitive, social and physiological determinants of emotional states. *Psychological Review, 69*, 378–399.

Scherer, K. R. (1982). Emotion as a process: Function, origin and regulation. *Social Science Information, 21*, 555–570.

Scherer, K. R. (1984). On the nature and function of emotion: A component process approach. In K. R. Scherer & P. Ekman (Eds.), *Approaches to emotion* (pp. 293–317). Hillsdale, NJ: Erlbaum.

Scherer, K. R. (2001a). Appraisal considered as a process of multi-level sequential checking. In K. R. Scherer, A. Schorr, & T. Johnstone (Eds.), *Appraisal processes in emotion: Theory, methods, research* (pp. 92–120). New York: Oxford University Press.

Scherer, K. R. (2001b). The nature and study of appraisal: A review of the issues. In K. R. Scherer, A. Schorr, & T. Johnstone (Eds.), *Appraisal processes in emotion: Theory, methods, research* (pp. 369–391). New York: Oxford University Press.

Scherer, K. R., & Ellgring, H. (2007). Are facial expressions of emotion produced by categorical affect programs or dynamically driven by appraisal? *Emotion, 7*, 113–130.

Scherer, K. R., & Sangsue, J. (2004). Le système mental en tant que composant de l'émotion. In G. Kirouac (Ed.), *Cognition et émotions* (pp. 11–36). Coimbra, Portugal: Imprensa da Universidade.

Simon, H. A. (1967). Motivational and emotional controls of cognition. *Psychological Review, 74*, 29–39.

Smith, C. A. (1989). Dimensions of appraisal and physiological in emotion. *Journal of Personality and Social Psychology, 56*, 339–353.

Smith, C. A., & Lazarus, R. S. (1990). Emotion and adaptation. In L. A. Pervin (Ed.), *Handbook of personality: Theory and research* (pp. 609–637). New York: Guilford.

Smith, C. A., & Lazarus, R. S. (1993). Appraisal components, core relational themes and the emotions. *Cognition and Emotion, 7*, 233–269.

Tomkins, S. S. (1962). *Affect, imagery, consciousness: Vol. 1. The positive affects*. New York: Springer.

Tomkins, S. S. (1963). *Affect, imagery, consciousness: Vol. 2. The negative affects*. New York: Springer.

van Reekum, C. M., Johnstone, T, Banse, R., Etter, A., Wehrle, T., & Scherer K. R. (2004). Psychophysiological responses to appraisal dimensions in a computer game. *Cognition and Emotion, 18*, 663–688.

Wagner, H., Lewis, H., Ramsay, S., & Krediet, I. (1992). Prediction of facial displays from knowledge of norms of emotional expressiveness. *Motivation and Emotion, 16*, 347–362.

Yerkes, R. M., & Dodson, J. D. (1908). The relation of strength of stimulus to rapidity of habit formation. *Journal of Comparative Neurology and Psychology, 18*, 459–482.

Zajonc, R. B. (1980). Feeling and thinking. Preferences need no inferences. *American Psychologist, 35*, 151–175.

11

Cognition and Emotion in Creative Design

NATHALIE BONNARDEL

EMOTION, COGNITION, AND CREATIVE DESIGN

Emotion and Cognition

Although emotion is not as well understood as cognition, both of them can be considered as information-processing systems (Ellsworth & Scherer, 2003), but with different functions and operating parameters. Cognition would allow an interpretation of the world and make it meaningful to the person, whereas emotions would be more judgmental, assigning positive and negative valences to the environment (Norman, 2002b, 2004a; Russell, 2003). Scherer (2005) described various affective states and especially proposed distinguishing utilitarian emotions and aesthetical emotions. These two kinds of emotions result from an appraisal of environmental or proprioceptive information, but they have different functions. Utilitarian emotions, such as anger or fear, allow the adaptation to events that may have important consequences for individuals. These adaptive functions consist, for instance, of the preparation of actions (such as confrontation or escape) or the recuperation and reorientation of work. In contrast, aesthetical emotions are not related to the necessity to satisfy vital and mandatory needs. For instance, a person can be impressed or fascinated or show admiration. Such diffuse sensations highly differ from the felt excitation and orientation of behaviors in the case of utilitarian emotions. In this chapter, we focus on emotions that are conveyed by images or words and that could be related, to such an extent, to aesthetical emotions. More precisely, we analyze their effect on cognitive treatments performed by designers during creative design problem solving.

Discussions have been conducted about the relationships between emotions and cognition. Opposite points of view were adopted by authors such as Zajonc (1980), who argued that emotional and cognitive systems are distinct, and authors

187

such as Mandler (1984), who considered cognition an integral part of the emotional process. According to Murphy and Zajonc (1993), there is an "affective primacy," and emotional reactions would occur before cognitive processes. In contrast, according to Mandler (1984), individuals analyze their environment with regard to their expectations or to cognitive schemata corresponding to the natural process of actions or thinking. The intensity and the valence of emotions would depend on the differences between the current situation and expectations based on activated schemata. In line with these views, according to Musch and Klauer (2003), a cognitive evaluation would occur in all emotional experiences.

Several studies showed that emotions and affects have an impact on the cognitive functioning of individuals engaged in complex tasks (Isen, 2003; Niedenthal, Krauth-Gruber, & Ric, 2006). According to Norman (2004a), emotions could even make us smart. Especially, different from negative affects, positive affects could make difficult tasks easier to perform and would make people more tolerant of minor difficulties and more flexible (Norman, 2002a). In this chapter, in accordance with this view, we explore whether positive affects will broaden the thought processes of designers and whether they could enhance the emergence of creative ideas for designing new products or objects. Toward this end, we present studies in which positive versus negative affects are conveyed by words versus by images. To point out the purposes of such studies from both theoretical and applied points of view, we now describe the main characteristics of design problem solving.

Design Problem Solving

In cognitive psychology, design activities are described as *problem-solving* situations: Designers have to produce an artifact, which should fit a specific function and satisfy different requirements (Malhotra, Thomas, Carroll, & Miller, 1980). These requirements define to some extent the goal to reach, but designers have to construct their mental representation of the design problem since these problems are considered as *ill structured* or *ill defined* (Eastman, 1969; Reitman, 1964; Simon, 1973). Indeed, the designer's initial mental representation is incomplete and imprecise. Therefore, the research space of ideas and potential solutions is, at the beginning, relatively large. Then, the designer's mental representation evolves as the problem solving progresses, and the research space of potential solutions is progressively constrained until the designer reaches a design solution that is considered to satisfy certain criteria. Thus, a *coevolution of problem and solution spaces* can be described (Dorst & Cross, 2001).

This specificity of design problems has also been described as based on an iterative dialectic between problem framing and problem solving (Rittel & Webber, 1984; Simon, 1995). During problem framing, designers refine design goals and specifications and thus refine their mental representation of the problem and evoke sources of inspiration that are useful for elaborating design solutions. Due to relationships between problem framing and problem solving, designers can elaborate solutions and evaluate these solutions with respect to various criteria and constraints, which guide the designers in performing subsequent stages of design problem solving (see Bonnardel, 2000). Therefore, designers' mental representations evolve until they reach a design solution that is considered satisfying, and their evocation processes play a main role in design problem solving (Bonnardel & Marmèche, 2004).

The dynamic of creative design appears also through what is called an *opportunistic activity* (Guindon, 1990; Hayes-Roth & Hayes-Roth 1979; Visser, 1990, 1994). Design activities are characterized as opportunistic because "each decision is motivated by one or two immediately preceding decisions, rather than by some high-level executive program" (Hayes-Roth & Hayes-Roth, 1979, p. 381), although they possibly include hierarchical episodes. This leads to reconsidering previous decisions or postponing certain decisions. This dynamic is facilitated by a process of "externalization," which corresponds to the creation and modification of external representations of the object to be designed, such as drawing or sketches. These representations are useful for the designers themselves since a "reflective conversation" is established between them and their drawings (Schön, 1983). This reflexive conversation allows designers to reach a better understanding of the design problem and to adopt new points of view about the object to be designed. Thus, different designers dealing with the same problem evoke different sources of inspiration, develop different ideas, and reach different solutions, materialized especially by drawings. Therefore, design problems are also considered to be *open ended* since there is usually no single correct solution for a given problem but instead a variety of potential solutions, which satisfy different criteria or constraints to varying degrees (see Bonnardel & Sumner, 1996; Simon, 1995).

Creative Design Activities

In the case of creative design, the solution to be reached has to be both new and respectful of certain constraints and criteria. According to Ward's structured imagination framework (Ward & Sifonis, 1997; Ward, Smith, & Vaid, 1997), people who are engaged in creative or "generative cognitive" activities have to extend the boundaries of a conceptual domain by mentally crafting novel instances of the concept. This is in line with the theory of conceptual blending (Fauconnier & Turner, 1998), which proposes that the process of thought involves "moving" between mental spaces that organize our knowledge of the world. Creativity can be conceived as the combination (or conceptual blending) of two, or more, conceptual spaces. In line with these descriptions, the A-CM (analogy and constraint management) model (Bonnardel, 2000, 2006) highlights the role of two main cognitive processes, which continuously interact during the design activity and can have opposite effects:

- *analogy making*, which may lead designers to extend or "open up" their "space of research" of new ideas and thus can lead to creative design solutions
- the *management of constraints*, which orients design problem solving and allows designers to progressively delimit their research space and assess ideas or solutions until they find a design solution that is both new and adapted to various constraints

Therefore, such processes contribute to both divergent and convergent thinking. The generative phase of design is thus highly based on analogical reasoning (Blanchette & Dunbar, 2000; Bonnardel & Marmèche, 2004, 2005; Kryssanov, Tamaki, & Kitamura, 2001). In this case, the originality of the design ideas or solutions may come from the creative distance between the conceptual domain of the object to be designed and conceptual domains from which analogies are extracted. Especially, the more the participants move away from the first evoked ideas or sources (Ward, Patterson, Sifonis, Dodds, & Saunders, 2002), the more their ideas are creative and original. In addition, there is a positive correlation between the number of ideas produced during the design process and the novelty of the design concepts (Srinivasan & Chakrabarti, 2010). However, when faced with a new design problem, designers may tend to reproduce solution approaches they used in past designs and may not consider alternative and more effective design solutions. A way to influence people in developing ideas is to provide them with suggestions or examples. Thus, several experiments were conducted, in the case of "cognitive generative tasks," to determine the impact of the presentation of examples on participants' productions. Experimental tasks were defined in various areas: to design technical artifacts, such as spill-proof mugs or bicycle racks (Jansson & Smith, 1991; Purcell & Gero, 1992), to design novel space creatures to inhabit a distant planet, and to provide novel ideas for reducing traffic accidents (Marsh, Landau, & Hicks, 1996; Smith, Ward, & Schumacher, 1993; Ward & Sifonis, 1997). Whatever the final objective, mainly similar results were observed: When they were provided with examples, participants' productions conformed to experimenter-provided examples. Such an effect has been called the *design fixation effect* in the case of design activities (Jansson & Smith, 1991). This type of effect appears, to a certain extent, similar to phenomena described for years in psychology under the terms *functional fixedness* and *mechanization of thought* (see Duncker, 1945; Luchins, 1942; Maier, 1931; Weisberg, 1988).

In contrast to these results, we argue that it is possible to enhance the evocation of new ideas by providing designers with specific kinds of words or images, which will exploit relationships between cognition and emotion. To develop a reflection on this topic, we present two exploratory studies that contributed to an analysis and characterization of the conditions necessary for enhancing designers' evocation processes.

THE IMPACT OF WORDS AND IMAGES CONVEYING AFFECTS

Hypotheses

In line with research conducted by Isen (2003), which showed that a positive affect has an enhancing effect on cognitive flexibility, our main hypothesis is that words and images conveying a positive affect will increase the emergence of new sources of inspiration, which are used by designers for reaching new ideas, contrary to words and images conveying a negative affect.

In addition, two opposite hypotheses can be expressed about the effect of the two formats of presentation: words versus images. On the one hand, we could expect that objects playing the role of sources of inspiration that are suggested through images could increasingly limit the space of research than suggesting the same objects as words. Indeed, images could lead participants to focus their attention on specific surface features and thus limit the extent of new ideas, whereas words could allow the evocation of a larger set of samples of the specified category and therefore the activation of more various ideas. On the other hand, since designers have to both evoke ideas and represent them on the basis of sketches, we could also argue that the benefits resulting from the suggestion of images will be higher than those of words since features observed on images could be more easily transferred to the object to be designed.

In addition, we analyzed the impact on the designers' evocation processes of the distance between words or images that are suggested and the object to be designed. Indeed, words and images can be directly related to the object to be designed when they belong to the same conceptual domain as the object to design (called *intradomain* words or images), or on the contrary, they can belong to a different conceptual domain (called *interdomain* words or images). In accordance with previous results (Bonnardel & Marmèche, 2004), a complementary hypothesis is that designers who will be provided with interdomain sources of inspiration will extend their research space of ideas more than those provided with intradomain sources. Indeed, the suggestion of interdomain words or images could stimulate the designers to develop evocation processes and, especially, a reflection based on principles underlying these interdomain words or images since they have been trained to make use of analogies during studies in design schools.

The Effect of the Suggestion of Words

Experimental Framework   To study the effect of the suggestion of words on designers' activities, a first issue consisted of defining the experimental material that will be suggested to designers. Therefore, a prestudy was necessary to select words that were judged as conveying positive versus negative affects. To this end, 20 participants were provided with 24 words that were either intra- or interdomain and were chosen to convey either positive or negative affects. For each of these words, the participants had to give a score from –5 ("very bad feeling") to +5 ("very good feeling"). Statistical tests were then conducted on the gathered data to select words that obtained the higher mean scores and to check that there was a significant difference between the words that were judged as conveying positive versus negative affects. Based on this evaluation, 8 words were selected: 2 conveyed a positive affect and were intradomain ("relaxing deckchair" and "relaxing armchair"); 2 conveyed a positive affect and were interdomain ("hot tub" and "flying carpet"); 2 conveyed a negative affect and were intradomain ("electric chair" and "wheelchair"); and 2 conveyed a negative affect and were interdomain ("guillotine" and "deathbed").

Then, we asked 16 designers to participate in the experimental study. They were all students who had been in the same design school for 5 years and were in their last year in this school. After being trained to perform verbalizations simultaneous to their activity, these participants had to perform a design task while thinking aloud. This design task consisted of creating a new seat for a cyber-café in accordance with the following design brief:

> The object to be designed will be used in a Parisian "cyber-café." It should be a particular seat with a contemporary design in order to be attractive for young customers. Such seats should allow the user to have a good sitting position, holding the back upright. Towards this end, the users should put their knees on a support intended to this function. In addition, these seats should allow the users to relax, by offering them the possibility to rock.

According to the experimental conditions, these participants were provided with two words selected on the basis of the prestudy that both belonged to one of the following categories: intradomain words conveying positive affects, intradomain words conveying negative affects, interdomain words conveying positive affects, and interdomain words conveying negative affects.

Participants individually solved this design problem by being given as much time as they wished while video recorded, which allowed us to gather both their verbalizations and the evolution of their drawings. Then, the designers' verbalizations were transcribed to analyze the sources of inspiration evoked by the participants. To this end, we counted each object mentioned by them that appeared to be inspiring for designing the specified object (i.e., the new seat). Such a role was identified based on designers' verbalizations in relationship to the sketches they were producing. In addition, this account of new sources of inspiration was performed on *newly* evoked sources and not on the suggested ones to determine whether designers were able to extend their research space of sources of inspiration or ideas.

Since we focused on the participants' evocation processes, another issue consisted of defining relevant indicators for characterizing the cognitive treatments that were performed. Three indicators were taken into account: the mean duration of the design task, the number of *new* sources of inspiration evoked by the participants during the design activity, and the nature of these new sources of inspiration. The sources considered "new" were the ones that corresponded to objects that were *not* suggested to participants since we wished to explore the effect of the experimental factors on the research space of ideas. To determine the nature of these new sources of inspiration, two people independently categorized the evoked sources to distinguish whether they were intradomain (if they belonged to the conceptual domain of the seats) or interdomain (if they belonged to another conceptual domain), and a high degree of agreement was obtained (.95).

Results   Concerning the mean duration of the design task, we observed no significant effect of the intra- versus interdomain nature of the words. However, we observed a significant effect of the valence of the words: The designers needed less time for performing the design task when they were provided with words conveying positive affects than with words conveying negative affects (respectively, 6.50 versus 11.50 minutes, $p < .01$).

Although the participants took more time to perform the design task in the case of words conveying negative affects, we observed no effect of the experimental conditions on the number or the nature of the new sources of inspiration evoked by the designers.

To determine whether images exerted more effects on designers' cognitive treatment, a second and complementary experiment was conducted.

The Effect of the Suggestion of Images

Experimental Framework   As for the previous study, a prestudy was necessary to select images that would be suggested to designers. To this end, 20 participants, different from the ones involved in the prestudy conducted for the first study, were provided with 26 images. These images were adapted from the experimental material used in a previous study (Bonnardel & Marmèche, 2004) to add positive or negative affects to them. Thus, the participants in this prestudy were provided with either intradomain or interdomain images that conveyed either positive or negative affects. We asked them to give a score, from –5 ("very bad feeling") to +5 ("very good feeling") to each of the images to indicate whether they judged them as conveying positive or negative feelings. Then, we selected the images that obtained the higher mean scores (either positive or negative) and performed statistical analyses to check that there was a significant difference between images judged as conveying positive versus negative affects. On this basis, we selected 8 images: 2 were intradomain and conveyed positive affects (see example on Figure 11.1), 2 were intradomain and conveyed negative affects, 2 were interdomain and conveyed positive affects, 2 were interdomain and conveyed negative affects.

Then, 12 designers participated in this second study. Similar to participants in the first experiment, they had been studying for 5 years at the same design school and were in their last year in this school.

The procedure was also similar to the one used in the first study, except that these participants were provided with images instead of words; after a training to

Figure 11.1   Example of intradomain image conveying positive affects.

perform simultaneous verbalizations, they had to perform the same design task as in the first study while thinking aloud. According to the experimental conditions, participants were provided with two images that both belonged to one of the following categories: intradomain images conveying positive affect, intradomain images conveying negative affect, interdomain images conveying positive affect, and interdomain images conveying negative affect. As with the first study, these participants individually solved the design problem by being given as much time as they wished while video recorded, which allowed us to gather their verbalizations and the evolution of their drawings.

The designers' verbalizations were transcribed to analyze the *new* sources of inspiration evoked by the participants, in accordance with the analysis method used in the first study. We again took into account the mean duration of the design task, the number of new sources of inspiration evoked in the participants, and the nature of these new sources, which were independently categorized by two people (with a degree of agreement of .95).

Results   First, no significant difference was observed about the mean duration of the design task depending on the experimental conditions.

Second, concerning the number of new sources of inspiration evoked by participants in the different experimental conditions, no significant effect of the affect conveyed by images was observed. However, the designers demonstrated significantly more new sources of inspiration when they were provided with interdomain images than with intradomain images ($p = .009$; see Table 11.1). In addition, we observed a significant interaction between the valence (positive vs. negative) of the images and their nature (intra- vs. interdomain): The designers demonstrated the most new sources of inspiration when they were provided with interdomain and positive images ($p = .03$).

To complement these results, we also analyzed the nature of the sources of inspiration that were evoked by the participants (see Table 11.2). Thus, we

TABLE 11.1   Mean Number of New Sources of Inspiration Evoked by Designers According to the Valence and the Nature of Images

	Positive Affect		Negative Affect	
Images	Intradomain	Interdomain	Intradomain	Interdomain
Participants	2	10	2.66	5.66

TABLE 11.2   Nature of the New Sources of Inspiration Evoked by Designers According to the Valence and the Nature of Images

		Positive Affect		Negative Affect	
	Images	Interdomain	Intradomain	Interdomain	Intradomain
Evoked	Intradomain	2	1	3.33	1
sources	Interdomain	8	1	2.33	1.66
	Total	10	2	5.66	2.66

observed that most of the new sources of inspiration the designers demonstrated when they were provided with interdomain and positive images were themselves interdomain.

Discussion

These two exploratory studies highlight several interesting findings. First, the suggestion of images seems to exert more effects on designers' evocation processes than the suggestion of words. Indeed, when participants were provided with words (the first study), the only influence was observed on the duration of the design task, while when participants were provided with images (the second study), we observed effects on both the number and the nature of the new sources of inspiration evoked by the designers. Thus, students in their last year of design school seemed to be more sensitive to the presentation of images than to presentation of words. This could be due to their training, which could be more focused on works realized on the basis of graphical materials. However, another interpretation is related to the nature of the design activities. As pointed out in the discussion of theory, designers express or "externalize" their ideas through sketches, and a "reflective conversation" occurs between the designer and his or her sketches (Schön, 1983). Therefore, designers are used to making inferences from the external representations they realize. This ability is probably also exploited to make inferences from images they are provided, as suggested by results of the second study. Thus, sources of inspiration demonstrated on the basis of images could enhance inferences as well as the adoption of new points of view by the designers.

Concerning the impact of the valence of the suggested sources, we observed in the first study that designers took less time to perform the task when they were provided with words conveying positive affects. Results obtained in the second study showed that it is possible to exert an influence on the designers' evocation processes since designers evoked more new sources of inspiration when they were provided with images conveying positive affects and, especially, when the images were both interdomain and with positive affects. Contrary to numerous studies that showed a "design fixation effect" (e.g., Jansson & Smith, 1991; Purcell & Gero, 1992), the second study indicates that it is possible to lead designers to extend their research space of ideas. Indeed, we identified conditions that lead designers to generate the most new sources of inspiration and that stimulate them to enhance the evocation of new interdomain sources. Therefore, although a small number of designers participated in these studies, the obtained results tend to show that designers' evocation processes were enhanced when they were provided with interdomain images conveying positive affects.

COMPLEMENTARY RESEARCH PERSPECTIVES

Several perspectives of research can be envisioned for exploring relationships between emotion and cognition in the context of creative design. At least, four ways of analyzing these relationships can be defined:

- First, complementary studies should be conducted to analyze the impact of stimuli conveying emotions (or affects) on designers' activities and cognitive processes. Especially, we plan to reproduce studies, such as the ones presented in this chapter, with professional designers with several years of experience and who could be more efficient in making analogies.
- Second, studies could be performed on designers' verbalizations to analyze the emotions that they express while solving a creative design problem. Such analyses can be conducted using the EMOTAIX tool (Piolat & Bannour, 2009a, 2009b), as done in a previous study (Bannour, Piolat, & Bonnardel, 2007).
- Third, studies can be performed to analyze emotions conveyed to end users by the objects or products resulting from creative design activities. This is especially the objective of research conducted on "emotional design" (Norman, 2004a). Indeed, a current challenge in human–computer interaction is to design systems not only usable but also attractive and pleasant for users. Thus, usability is no longer the ultimate goal for designers of products, objects, or systems. New systems must also bring "beauty" (or a feeling of aesthetics), pleasure, and fun to people's lives (Norman, 2004b). However, classical ergonomic recommendations mainly focused on cognitive and perceptivomotor capacities of users without considering their feelings while interacting with a system. In contrast, now human beings and their interactions with systems are beginning to be considered at three levels: knowing, doing, and feeling (Overbeeke, Djajadiningrat, Hummels, & Wensveen, 2000). This last level of "feeling" is therefore the topic of increasing research in cognitive sciences and in the science of design (Norman, 2002a, 2004a; Shneiderman, 2004).
- Fourth, research can be conducted in the area of "affective computing," that is, "computing that relates to, arises from, or deliberately influences emotion or other affective phenomena" (Picard, 1997, 2010). Such research works pursue several objectives, such as (a) designing new ways for people to communicate affective-cognitive states (e.g., through the creation of novel sensors and learning algorithms that jointly analyze multimodal channels of information); (b) designing new techniques to assess frustration, stress, and mood (through natural interaction and conversation); (c) designing computers that would be more emotionally intelligent and could respond to a person's frustration in a way that reduces negative feelings; and (d) designing personal technologies for improving self-awareness of affective state and its selective communication to others.

These different ways of exploring relationships between emotion and cognition, in the context of creative design, present both fundamental and applied interests. Results from the first kind of studies can be used to develop computational design systems that aim to facilitate designers' cognitive processes and enhance their creativity (see Bonnardel, 2009; Bonnardel & Zenasni, 2010). Indeed, the use of computational supports seems particularly adapted to professional designers because, due to constraints of time, it is difficult for them to be engaged in continuing education. In contrast, the introduction in their working environment of design support systems, which would trigger emotions, sounds particularly convenient since most professional designers already use computational systems in their usual activities. Thus, based on the results we described in this chapter, affects or emotions could be associated with images and exploited to enhance designers' creativity. For instance, while interacting with a system such as TRENDS (Bouchard, Omhover, Mougenot, Aoussat, & Westerman, 2008), designers could be provided with images conveying positive affects, which would play the role of sources of inspiration for solving a design problem. Therefore, new studies could be conducted to analyze the impact of both the nature and the valence of the images during human–computer interactions and, possibly, in professional contexts.

The second kind of research could contribute to a better understanding of the evolution of designers' emotions according to progress in design problem solving as well to characterization of designers' conative and emotional factors, related for instance to personality and emotional features specific to each designer. On such bases, it is possible to fit the support provided by a computational system to designers' specific profiles.

The third kind of research is concretely used for developing objects considered attractive for consumers or end users, for instance, in the context of the design of Web sites (see, for instance, Bonnardel, Piolat, Alpe, & Scotto di Liguori, 2006). It is also useful for an approach emergent in Europe and more mature in Asia, called "kansei engineering" (Bouchard & Aoussat, 2003; Nagamashi, 2002). This approach aims to formalize and explicate, in industrial design contexts, relationships between feelings or emotions of designers or end users and the characteristics of the design solutions or products.

The fourth and last kind of research we envisioned presents multiple applied interests, such as the ones previously evoked (see Picard, 1997, 2010).

In summary, exploring and exploiting relationships between emotion and cognition in the context of creative design should motivate crucial future research, which will lead to both fundamental and applied benefits for our society.

ACKNOWLEDGMENTS

We wish to thank students from the International Design School of Toulon (France) who participated in the two experimental studies as well as Jonathan Lazarini and Michael Said for their precious contributions to these studies.

REFERENCES

Bannour, R., Piolat, A., & Bonnardel, N. (2007). EMOTAIX: Un outil d'identification automatique des émotions, sentiments et affects exprimés en situations professionnelles. In A. Naceur & S. Masmoudi (Eds.), *Cognition, emotion and motivation: Intégrer, mieux expliquer la performance* (p. 75). Tunis: CNP.

Blanchette, I., & Dunbar, K. (2000). How analogies are generated: The roles of structural and superficial similarity. *Memory and Cognition, 28*, 108–124.

Bonnardel, N. (2000). Towards understanding and supporting creativity in design: Analogies in a constrained cognitive environment. *Knowledge-Based Systems, 13*, 505–513.

Bonnardel, N. (2006). *Créativité et conception: Approches cognitives et ergonomiques* [Creativity and design: Cognitive and ergonomics approaches]. Marseille, France: Solal.

Bonnardel, N. (2009). Activités de conception et créativité: De l'analyse des facteurs cognitifs à l'assistance aux activités de conception créatives. *Le Travail Humain, 72*, 5–22.

Bonnardel, N., & Marmèche, E. (2004). Evocation processes by novice and expert designers: Towards stimulating analogical thinking. *Creativity and Innovation Management, 13*, 176–186.

Bonnardel, N., & Marmèche, E. (2005). Towards supporting evocation processes in creative design: A cognitive approach. *International Journal of Human–Computer Studies, 63*, 442–435.

Bonnardel, N., Piolat, A., Alpe, V., & Scotto Di Liguori, A. (2006). Conception d'une page d'accueil: Esthétique et/ou informativité ? In A. Piolat (Ed.), *Lire, écrire, communiquer et apprendre avec Internet* (pp. 313–344). Marseille, France: Solal.

Bonnardel, N., & Sumner, T. (1996). Supporting evaluation in design. *Acta Psychologica, 91*, 221–244.

Bonnardel, N., & Zenasni, F. (2010). The impact of technology on creativity in design: An enhancement? *Creativity and Innovation Management, 19*, 180–191.

Bouchard, C. & Aoussat, A. (2010). Development of a Kansei Engineering System for industrial design. Identification of input data for KES. *Journal of the Asian Design International Conference.* Tsukuba, Japan: Asian Society for the Science of Design.

Bouchard, C., Omhover, J.-F., Mougenot, C., Aoussat, A., & Westerman, S. (2008). Trends: A content-based information retrieval system for designers. In J. S. Gero & A. Goel (Eds.), *Design Computing and Cognition '08* (DCC '08). New York: Springer.

Dorst, K., & Cross, N. (2001). Creativity in the design process: Co-evolution of problem-solution. *Design Studies, 22*, 425–437.

Duncker, K. (1945). On problem solving [entire issue]. *Psychological Monographs, 270.*

Eastman, C. M. (1969). Cognitive processes and ill-defined problems: A case study from design. In *Proceedings of the First Joint International Conference on IA* (pp. 669–690). Washington, DC.

Ellsworth, P. C., & Scherer, K. R. (2003). *Appraisal processes in emotion.* New York: Oxford University Press.

Fauconnier, G., & Turner, M. (1998). Conceptual integration networks. *Cognitive Science, 22*, 133–187.

Guindon, R. (1990). Designing the design process: Exploiting opportunistic thoughts. *Human–Computer Interaction, 5*, 305–344.

Hayes-Roth, B., & Hayes-Roth, F. (1979). A cognitive model of planning. *Cognitive Science, 3*, 275–310.

Isen, A. M. (2003). Positive affect as a source of human strength. In L. Aspinwall & U. Staudinger (Eds.), *A psychology of human strengths* (pp. 179–195). Washington, DC: American Psychology Association.

Jansson, D. G., & Smith, S. M. (1991). Design fixation. *Design Studies, 12*, 3–11.

Kryssanov, V. V., Tamaki, H., & Kitamura, S. (2001). Understanding design fundamentals: How synthesis and analysis drive creativity, resulting in emergence. *Artificial Intelligence in Engineering, 15*, 329–342.

Luchins, A. S. (1942). Mechanization in problem-solving [entire issue]. *Psychological Monographs, 248.*

Maier, N. R. F. (1931). Reasoning in humans: II. The solution of a problem and its appearance in consciousness. *Journal of Comparative Psychology, 12,* 181–194.

Malhotra, A., Thomas, J. C., Carroll, J. M., & Miller, L. A. (1980). Cognitive processes in design. *International Journal of Man-Machine Studies, 12,* 119–140.

Mandler, G. (1984). *Mind and body: Psychology of emotion and stress.* New York: Norton.

Marsh, R. L., Landau, J. D., & Hicks, J. L. (1996). How examples may (and may not) constrain creativity, *Memory and Cognition, 24,* 669–680.

Murphy, S. T., & Zajonc, R. B. (1993). Affect, cognition and awareness: Affective priming with optimal and suboptimal stimulus exposure. *Journal of Personality and Social Psychology, 5,* 123–139.

Musch, J., & Klauer, K. C. (2003). *The psychology of evaluation.* Mahwah, NJ: Erlbaum.

Nagamashi, M. (2002). Kansei engineering as a powerful consumer-oriented technology for product development. *Applied Ergonomics, 33,* 289–294.

Niedenthal, P. M., Krauth-Gruber, S., & Ric, F. (Eds.). (2006). *Psychology of emotion. Interpersonal, experiential, and cognitive approaches.* New York: Psychology Press.

Norman, D. A. (2002a). *The design of everyday things.* New York: Basic Books

Norman, D. A. (2002b). Emotion and design: Attractive things work better. *Interactions Magazine, 9*(4), 36–42.

Norman, D. A. (2004a). *Emotional design: Why we love (or hate) everyday things.* New York: Basic Books.

Norman, D. A. (2004b). Introduction to the special section on beauty, goodness, and usability. *Human–Computer Interaction, 19,* 311–318.

Overbeeke, K., Djajadiningrat, T., Hummels, C., & Wensveen, S. (2000). Beauty in usability: Forget about ease of use! Retrieved June 6, 2008, from http://studiolab.io.tudelft.nl/static/gems/publications/00OverPleBeau.pdf

Picard, R. (1997). *Affective computing.* Cambridge, MA: MIT Press.

Picard, R. (2010). Emotion research by the people, for the people. *Emotion Review, 2,* 250–254.

Piolat, A., & Bannour, R. (2009a). EMOTAIX: Un Scénario de Tropes pour l'identification automatisée du lexique émotionnel et affectif. *L'Année Psychologique, 109,* 657–700.

Piolat, A., & Bannour, R. (2009b). An example of text analysis software (EMOTAIX-Tropes) use: The influence of anxiety on expressive writing. *Current Psychology Letters. Brain, Behavior and Cognition, 5*(2). *Retrieved from http://cpl.revues.org/index4878.html*

Purcell, A. T., & Gero, J. S. (1992). The effects of examples on the results of a design activity, *Knowledge-Based Systems, 5,* 82–91.

Reitman, W. (1964). Heuristic decision procedures, open constraints, and the structure of ill-defined problems. In M. W. Shelley & G. L. Bryan (Eds.), *Human judgements and optimality.* New York: Wiley.

Rittel, H., & Webber, M. M. (1984). Planning problems are wicked problems. In N. Cross (Ed.), *Developments in design methodology* (pp. 135–144). New York: Wiley.

Russell, J. A. (2003). Core affect and the psychological construction of emotion. *Psychological Review, 110,* 145–172.

Scherer, K. R. (2005). What are emotions? And how can they be measured? *Social Science Information, 44,* 693–727.

Schön, D. A. (1983). *The reflective practitioner: How professionals think in action.* New York: Basic Books.

Shneiderman, B. (2004, September–October). Designing for fun: How can we design user interfaces to be more fun? *Interactions,* pp. 48–50.

Simon, H. A. (1973). The structure of ill structured problems. *Artificial Intelligence, 4,* 181–201.

Simon, H. A. (1995). Problem forming, problem finding and problem solving in design. In A. Collen & W. Gasparski (Eds.), *Design and systems* (pp. 245–257). New Brunswick, NJ: Transaction.

Smith, S. M., Ward, T. B., & Schumacher, J. S. (1993). Constraining effects of examples in a creative generation task. *Memory and Cognition, 21,* 837–845.

Srinivasan, V., & Chakrabarti, A. (2010). Investigating novelty-outcome relationship in engineering design. *Artificial Intelligence for Engineering Design, Analysis and Manufacturing, 24*(2), doi: http://dx.doi.org/10.1017/S089006041000003X.

Visser, W. (1990). More or less following a plan during design: Opportunistic deviations in specification. *International Journal of Man-Machine Studies, 33,* 247–278.

Visser, W. (1994). Organisation of design activities: Opportunistic with hierarchical episodes. *Interacting with Computers, 6,* 235–238.

Ward, T. B., Patterson, M. J., Sifonis, C. M., Dodds, R. A., & Saunders, K. N. (2002). The role of graded category structure in imaginative thought. *Memory and Cognition, 30,* 199–216.

Ward, T. B., & Sifonis, C. (1997). Task demands and generative thinking: What changes and what remains the same? *Journal of Creative Behavior, 31,* 245–259.

Ward, T. B., Smith, S. M., & Vaid, J. (1997). Conceptual structures and processes in creative thought. In T. B. Ward, S. M. Smith, & J. Vaid (Eds.), *Creative thought: An investigation of conceptual structures and processes* (pp. 1–27). Washington, DC: American Psychological Association.

Weisberg, R. W. (1988). Problem solving and creativity. In R. J. Sternberg (Ed.), *The nature of creativity: Contemporary psychological perspectives* (pp. 148–176). Cambridge, UK: Cambridge University Press.

Zajonc, R. B. (1980). Feeling and thinking. Preferences need no inferences. *American Psychologist, 35,* 151–175.

12

The Decision Process Is by Definition Irrational

SLIM MASMOUDI

THE SUBJECT MATTER

*P*icasso said, "If you know exactly what you are going to do, what is the good in doing it?" How many times have you thought of doing something and you did something else? How many times have you planned, for example, to go to a Web site and you have seen a Web site quite different? How many times were you talking about shopping on Sunday and instead preferred having a coffee with friends? These questions and others may be asked in addressing the relationship between reason and decision, questions that take us back to our everyday moments involving more or less important decisions. Are our decisions rational or irrational? This is a question whose answer seems obvious to anyone who thinks that decision and reason go together, who believes that affect (feeling) cannot have an effect on the rational. However, recent works in cognitive neuroscience and cognitive psychology on decision making tend to give counterintuitive answers. In his book, *Emotion and Reason: The Cognitive Neuroscience of Decision Making*, Berthoz (2006) shed light on the neural bases of the decisional processes and choice-related behaviors. In the first section of this book, rightly titled "Is Decision-Making Rational or Irrational?" Berthoz reports the current controversy on the account of the decision-making process as a probabilistic accounting of gains and losses. It thus appears that emotion and motivation interfere in the rational decision-making process, yielding a personal and subjective decision process (instead of logical rules) that endows it with a more adapted enactive characteristic to the social and personal needs. But, how is this possible? Would this diminish the value of the decision and reduce its cognitive and adaptive roles for the individual?

INTRODUCTION

Decision making is one of the cognitive activities that have caught more attention from researchers in different disciplines, particularly since the year 2000. A new field has even emerged to focus the studies of this activity around a central unified issue: the "decision sciences" field. This is a multidisciplinary field involving cognitive sciences, economics, social and psychological sciences, and philosophy. Decision-making activity encompasses, in fact, a wide range of situations, ranging from a quick-and-easy choice to go left or right in a traffic jam on the road or to eat a croissant or a bagel or donut for breakfast, to the crucial choice to accept or reject a job offer or to get married. A psychologist makes decisions throughout the course of his or her career, being faced with different and dynamic psychological phenomena. A physician daily copes with various pathologies that sometimes require urgent solutions and demand crucial decisions. A student equally faces the challenge of making decisions in solving a problem or trying to answer a question raised by a teacher. We thus see that our lives and their quality depend on decisions we make every day. In the same vein, most recent work has drawn attention to a strong relationship between one's well-being and decision making and judgment (Diener, Helliwell, & Kahneman, 2010).

Decision making brings together the cognitive processes that allow us to select an option or an action among the alternatives available to us incidentally, by coincidence of natural or artificial circumstances, or intentionally. The conditions under which we make decisions are often uncertain, unclear, if information is incomplete, making it difficult to make sound decisions. So, the decision process seems to be based on a concentrated blending of our cognitive resources, including our previous knowledge of different structures, our perceptual processes that allow us to represent the situation with its components, and our affective and motivational resources that allow us to have a feeling and a motivation to do something.

Three approaches in the study of decision making can be identified: normative, descriptive, and prescriptive (see, e.g., Shafir, 1999). The normative approach provides a rational framework for decision making in which the decision maker has well-defined preferences according to rational axioms. This approach is based on theoretical considerations rather than empirical ones. Developed in economic sciences by von Neumann and Morgenstern (1947) and Savage (1954), this approach is strongly challenged in cognitive science because of several contradictions (Binmore, 1987a, 1987b; Campbell & Sowdon, 1985; Eells, 1982; Gauthier, 1988/1989; Gibbard & Harper, 1985; Kavka, 1983; Lewis, 1985; McClennen, 1989; Nozick, 1969, 1993; Rosenthal, 1982). Indeed, empirical observations seem to inspire models that are developed in cognitive science, favoring heuristic and contextual approaches that take into account personal characteristics in decision making over neutral and rational ones. The descriptive approach is based on the experimental study of decision-making behaviors, including the psychological components in the decisional process. The advantages of this approach include highlighting the role of objective and subjective dimensions in decision making, particularly the role of heuristics (Kahneman & Tversky, 1972). The prescriptive approach emphasizes the importance of methods and techniques defined in improving decision making and the skills associated with it (Fong, Krantz, & Nisbett, 1986; Schoemaker, 1979).

The contemporary study of decision making incorporates it in the study of planning (Ananda & Herath, 2009; Falzer, 2004; Galotti et al., 2006); problem solving (Blanchard-Fields & Mienaltowski, 2007; Boddy, Rezgui, Wetherill, & Cooper, 2007; Darabi, Nelson, & Seel, 2009); psychophysics (Philiastides & Heekeren, 2009; Rao, 2009; Ratcliff & Smith, 2010); memory (Cho & Jeantet, 2010; Dickerson, 2010; Hilbig, Erdfelder, & Pohl, 2010); and social cognition (Abele & Stasser, 2008; Alter & Kwan, 2009; Bos, Dijksterhuis, & Baaren, 2008). The contemporary study of decision making is basically based on behavioral experiments, not without methodological difficulties encountered by the researchers in different fields of decision sciences. It includes techniques for process tracing and verbal protocols (see Ericsson & Simon, 1984; Masmoudi, 2000), knowledge acquisition and elicitation techniques (see Payne, Bettman, & Johnson, 1993), and eye-tracking techniques (i.e., eye movement tracking; see Russo & Dosher, 1983). Research findings indicated that people's choices are influenced by a variety of elements (a nonexhaustive list): conflicting choices, costs incurred by the choices, a possible regret because of the choice, the choice adopted in the past, previous satisfaction generated by a similar choice, and predicted satisfaction of the current choice.

Current work on decision making has revealed its counterintuitive nature and its incompatibility with the normative analysis. The person's characteristics as well as the contextual characteristics conspire to determine the actual production of a decision and the perpetuation of its dynamic and flexible features. In the same vein, cognitive neurosciences offer us some interesting results about the functioning of the brain during a decision-making activity. They show how the frontal lobe, an area functionally dedicated to executive functions and known to be the seat of working memory, is involved most predominantly in decision making. The prefrontal cortex appears to play a decisive role, especially in social contexts.

Researchers from Brown University (Providence, RI) and the University of California–Berkeley (Badre, Hoffman, Cooney, & D'Esposito, 2009) showed that there is a "abstract-concrete" gradient in the frontal lobe that leads to a decisional process functioning on a continuum from abstract decisions (e.g., deciding to prepare a dish of food) to concrete decisions (e.g., choosing the sequence of movements to prepare the dish), respectively, from the front to the rear of the frontal cortex. These results support the idea of a hierarchy of the frontal lobe respective to the degree of the abstraction of the decision. The components of the frontal lobe are involved in the decision-making process to various degrees, depending on the context and nature of the decision. Consider, for example, the role of the orbitofrontal cortex in risk assessment by an individual. We discuss next that strong links bind decision making, emotion, and motivation.

HEURISTICS AND BIASES

How to Solve It (Polya, 1945) is the first book by George Polya, a mathematician at Stanford University (Stanford, CA), in which he used for the first time the term *heuristic*, an adjective used to mean "serving to discover" and applied in mathematics. Heuristic reasoning, according to Polya (1945, p. 115) consists of a "reasoning not regarded as final and strict but as provisional and plausible only, whose purpose is to discover the solution of the present problem." Therefore, a heuristic (the conventional noun) is a useful strategic tool, a method to solve a problem in a shortened and nonalgorithmic way, whose effectiveness is not always guaranteed. To find mentally the result of the arithmetic operation that consists of multiplying 11 by 16, a heuristic (only valid for multiplication by 11) may be to put the sum of the the the two numbers 1 and 6 between them and to read the result, instead of an algorithmic calculation of the result, for example, (16 × 10) + 16. However, this useful heuristic is useless and false as we try to multiply, for example, 11 by 19, an arithmetic operation that needs another heuristic.

Kahneman and Tversky (1972) were the first to use the term *heuristic* to describe (with a descriptive approach) the human judging and decisional processes, outside a normative view, which is far away from cognitive realities. For years, they have attempted to identify the list of heuristics used by humans to make decisions. In their research undertaking, they were able to show that these heuristics can lead to biases in decision making that do not conform to a normative model. These researchers have proposed the "heuristics and bias approach."

The problem with heuristics is that they can turn into a judgment or a decision bias as they do not fit the situation or do not include subsidiary components of this situation. Their advantage is that they can sometimes offer fast, useful, efficient, and well-adapted solutions and thus make decisions humanly more plausible by enlisting intuition, emotion, and motivation. Moreover, biases may play a role in learning and therefore may be a vector for learning, and a factor in improving performance. The work of Tversky and Kahneman (1973, 1974, 1981, 1982, 1983, 1992; Kahneman & Tversky, 1972, 1973, 1982a, 1982b, 1984) has identified at least four heuristics: representativeness, availability, simulation, and anchoring-adjustment. The work of Kahneman and Tversky was somehow and to some extent the first to reveal the noncognitive and irrational dimensions in decision making. Many scholars have adopted these ideas. Because of his contributions to decision theories Daniel Kahneman won the 2002 Nobel Prize in Economics (see Nisbett & Ross, 1980).

The Representativeness Heuristic/Bias

The representativeness heuristic/bias, also known as similarity, consists of making decisions based on the resemblance to stereotypical expectations or knowledge structures in memory, rather than on logical probabilities. If you ask someone to give a random sequence of images in a children's book, then the person will give the sequence that fits what he or she knows better about the images and books for children, not a sequence that corresponds to probabilities calculated logically. The person's decision to give the sequence in an order determined by the personal expectations guarantees a good solution to a certain extent that validates the subject's knowledge and reinforces his or her motives and expectations. This solution does not validate the actual facts. Thanks to such a heuristic, one decides that an animal represents its category as it resembles better the most typical animal in that category and as this most typical animal is what we know best. This heuristic is useful in some situations, such as categorization learning or survival in a threatening context. However, this heuristic may be unnecessary or even wrong, neglecting the salient attributes and determinants of the typical exemplar.

The Availability Heuristic/Bias

Like the example of Kahneman and Tversky (1973, p. 211), what is most likely, to find an English word composed of three letters or to find an English word composed six letters? Most people respond with the first proposition, by thinking about examples of three-letter words, which come to mind more quickly than the six-letter words. Actually, the second proposition is more probable. Thus, people rely on the availability of information in their minds to produce a decision or judgment. They indulge in most cases in a meta-cognitive evaluation of this availability. The frequency is therefore considered on the basis of the activated examples in the mind or the amount of examples that the individual believes he or she has or knows. This heuristic is consistent with the representativeness heuristic. The self-reference, rather than the reference to logical rules, is central to these two heuristics.

The availability of examples, and therefore the resulting heuristic, is affected by mood and emotions. This affects the judgment of frequency and the resulting decisions (Baron, 2008; Johnson & Tversky, 1983).

The Simulation Heuristic/Bias

Who would be the happiest, a student who has an average of 12/20 or a student who has an average of 16/20, knowing that the best of the classroom has an average of 16.5/20? You will probably say "who has an average of 12/20" because the student who has a 16/20 average would say that he or she could be easily be the best of the classroom. Your decision to give this response stems probably from your use of a mental simulation of the minds of the students. This is the simulation heuristic/bias. It is the heuristic that you use when you say that whoever won the bronze medal is happier than whoever won the silver medal at the Olympics. In this heuristic, we simulate the cognitive evaluation, the felt emotion, and the activated motive.

The Anchoring-and-Adjustment Heuristic/Bias

How do you estimate the number of students at the university this year? To give your estimation, you will most likely seek a reference point (e.g., the number of students last year), an anchor around which you make adjustments up or down. Adding other elements to the anchor point will direct the adjustment toward or away from the correct estimation. Biases related to this heuristic have their origins in the wrong choice of the anchor point, the elements to make the adjustment, or both.

The anchoring-adjustment heuristic is useful in social, economic, and even learning contexts. It allows people to make comparisons and thus to discriminate between objects, events, situations, and so on. The frequent use of the adjustment may affect learning, which allows improvement of the individuals' estimation capabilities.

In conclusion, the work of Kahneman and Tversky helped identify crucial aspects of human decision making, shedding light on the irrational and subjective dimension of these processes through the use heuristics that are more or less effective (depending on situations and individuals' characteristics) and in which affective and conative components are injected. We emphasize that although the biases associated with the use of these nonnormative heuristics correspond to misjudgments and decisional errors, they play a critical role in the development of learning decision making. These biases, associated with motivational or emotional states or with other cognitive processes (e.g., creative processes), permit heuristic problem solving and satisfying personal needs.

DECISION IS BASED ON CONCEPTS AND PERCEPTS

Admittedly, the concept of decision has been integrated from the earliest days of the second cognitive revolution (i.e., the emergence of the information-processing model in 1956) with perception, with the signal detection theory (SDT) by John Swets (Swets, Tanner, & Birdsall, 1961; Tanner & Swets, 1954; see also Getty, Swets, Pickett, & Gonthier, 1995, Humphreys & Swets, 1991). He argued that it is not enough to have sensory thresholds for detecting a signal and discriminating this signal from noise, and that we also have a decision criterion by which we decide whether the signal exists (i.e., whether it is significant for us). A wide range of research based on this theory (on memory, perception, language, etc.) was conducted. This decision criterion is strongly related to a person's characteristics and the way the person perceives the consequences of his or her perception activity (e.g., gains and losses; see Markman, 2009).

But, since SDT, have there been changes in the study of decision making? Does a decision remain simply an "output" of the cognitive system, or is it instead fundamentally related to conceptual structures that we build on the world and its functioning and therefore our perceptual experiences online and off-line?

A piece of evidence of the evolution of research on decision making during the decade 2000–2010 is the abundance of studies on this cognitive activity and its integration with conceptual and perceptual processes on the one hand and emotional and motivational processes (MPs) on the other. This decade started with the Nobel Prize for Economics awarded to Daniel Kahneman for his work on decision making and ending by the publication of the *Handbook of Reward and Decision Making* (Dreher & Tremblay, 2009), so the period materialized this evolution and the development of new conceptions of decision making.

One research theme that has greatly influenced the study of decision making and has highlighted the perceptual dimension in decision corresponds to perceptual decision making. This is the whole process to gather information from the sensory systems, combine them, and use them to influence and direct our behavior (Philiastides & Heekeren, 2009). Many studies using methods of brain imaging (functional magnetic resonance imaging [fMRI], electroencephalography [EEG], magnetoencephalography [MEG]) have shown, enriched, or even extended the

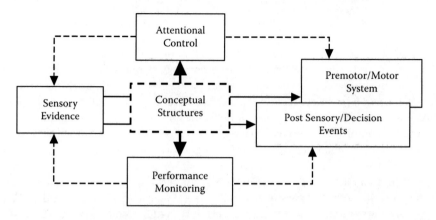

Figure 12.1   Adaptation of the perceptual decision-making theoretical model of Philiastides and Heekeren (2009, p. 187). (Translated from Masmoudi, S. Percept—Concept—Décision, les secrets d'un cheminement émotif et motivé. In S. Masmoudi & A. Naceur (Eds.), *Du percept à la décision: intégration de la cognition, l'émotion et la motivation*. Brussels: Deboeck, 2010, p. 82.)

view of decision making based on three serial stages: representation of sensory evidence; integration of sensory information across time; and comparison of evidence gathered for a decision threshold (Gold & Shadlen, 2007). Philiastides and Heekeren presented a model (2009, p. 187) in which they emphasized the parallel processes of sensory data comparisons and manipulations of decision variables (Figure 12.1). The perceptual uncertainty appeared to play an important role in the activation of attention and recruitment of adequate resources to produce the decision. This model should be improved to successfully take into account the conceptual structures that we believe play a crucial role in the construction of percepts and the guidance of decision making.

A study revealing the links between conceptual knowledge structures and decision making was conducted by Kumaran and his colleagues (Kumaran, Summerfield, Hassabis, & Maguire, 2009) in which neuroimaging techniques were used to trace the emergence of conceptual knowledge in human decision making. The authors show that specific brain structures, the hippocampus and the ventromedial prefrontal cortex, are involved in circuits underlying the emergence of conceptual knowledge that affect choice behavior. The results of this study support the idea that human beings are endowed with remarkable abilities to discover the conceptual structure of perceptual experiences stored in memory and use them for solving decision problems. Other studies (Shea, Krug, & Tobler, 2008) have also shown the role of conceptual structures in decision making.

The adaptation of this model allows for updating the respective roles of attention and conceptual representations built on the world and its working and on self and its functioning.

In an exploratory study of affective and cognitive resources in decision making, used by preadolescents in a school guidance context (Naceur, Masmoudi, & Becher, 2010), we took into consideration the cognitive–emotional osmosis between decisional processes and self-representation, a representation defined as multidimensional, and we tried to see whether preadolescents have the cognitive and emotional resources required to make a school guidance decision. We identified four cognitive dimensions of self-representation: richness/fluency (i.e., to cite a more or less self-descriptive traits); organization (i.e., to consolidate self-descriptors into categories); flexibility (i.e., to classify the descriptors from different perspectives); and decentralization of perception and immediate action (i.e., having an abstract vision of self based on broader values). We defined two affective dimensions of self-representation: the general feeling about oneself (i.e., being happy and self-complacent) and feelings regarding some personal characteristics (i.e., perception of personal academic competence). We studied the decision-making process in terms of its active or passive nature. Three dimensions were selected in this process: whether to use the power of uncertainty (a dimension related to the sense of control of the situation); person's "cognitive engagement" (personal, social) type; and finally presence or absence of an "active mind" (the ability to create new categories, to accept or not new data and multiple perspectives).

For a sample of nine students having to choose between a technical school career and a general education school career, the results of the study using semi-structured interviews as a method of data collection, showed the following:

- Regarding the cognitive component of self-representation, most of the interviewed preadolescents had a undifferentiated self-representation (77.7%); the majority of the interviewed preadolescents showed a lack of disparity between the various descriptive categories of self-images (self-image/social image and real image/ideal image).
- Regarding the affective component of self-representation, 55.5% of the preadolescents did not have a positive "general feeling vis-à-vis oneself," versus 44.5% who clearly had a positive general feeling vis-à-vis oneself.
- The same results were observed for the nature (negative/positive) of academic self-esteem, as 55.6% of preadolescents had negative academic self-esteem.
- Regarding the processing of information related to oneself and regarding the criterion referring to causal attributions for success or academic failure, 77.7% of students recognized an external control of the causes of their success or failure, but 22.3% assumed an internal control.
- Regarding the processing of information related to the decision task, the majority of students used a type of decisional strategy leading to a satisfactory solution, a simplifying decisional bias of the decision task, and a selecting decisional bias of the chosen information; the decision was passive for 88.8% of preadolescents.

The results of this exploratory study supported the idea that preadolescents have not yet the affective and cognitive resources needed to make a decision in choosing a course of instruction (a technical school career or a general education school career), confirming that affective and cognitive dimensions are both involved in decision making, particularly with reference to a person's critical decision for

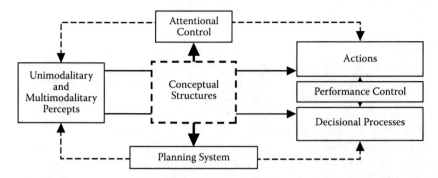

Figure 12.2   Schema of the theoretical paradigm PCD: percept-concept-decision. (Translated from Masmoudi, S. Percept—Concept—Décision, les secrets d'un cheminement émotif et motivé. In S. Masmoudi & A. Naceur (Eds.), *Du percept à la décision: intégration de la cognition, l'émotion et la motivation*. Brussels: Deboeck, 2010, p. 83.)

the future. This exploratory study helped highlight the close links between self-representation, with its cognitive and emotional underpinnings, and the purely decisional processes related to the operations of choice.

In summarizing recent work on the percept–concept, percept–decision, and concept–decision links, the arguments were strongly in favor of a new theoretical paradigm (i.e., a new theoretical model) of the human mind (Figure 12.2). This paradigm integrates perceptual representations, conceptual structures, and decision making in a combined system implementing bidirectional circuits between the various entities. The system makes information processing more dynamic, approximating the abstract from the concrete and connecting the core of the system (concepts) to the connecting components to the environment (percepts and actions) in fruitful interactions, through attentional processes on the one hand and decisional processes on the other. The planning system plays a sequencing role of different processes.

DECISION AND EMOTIONAL AND MOTIVATIONAL PROCESSES

The decisions we make in everyday life or that we make in times of critical choices are far from rational. They deeply depend on our emotions at the moment and our current implicit motives or the current active goal. Thus, the choice of our clothes, the choice of what we eat at a specific time, the choice of the direction we take on the road, the choice of what career we want to embrace, and so on all depend on emotional processes (EPs) and MPs that are engaged (Masmoudi, 2010; Naceur, 2010). In their neural affective decision theory, Litt and his colleagues (Litt, Eliasmith, & Thagard, 2008) identified four operating principles of our decisional processes: (a) affect, the basis for decision making that is fundamentally cognitive-affective, which allows us to make an emotional evaluation of potential actions; (b) brain, the basis for decision making that is essentially neural, which allows us to establish links between the prefrontal cortex and subcortical systems; (c) valuation, a process to differentiate mechanisms for the positive and negative consequences, respectively encoded by dopamine and serotonin; and (d) framing, corresponding to the context and how the elements of choice are presented, which triggers different neural activation patterns. These principles clearly highlight the various interconnections among decision, emotion, and motivation. In the same vein, the interrelationships between reward and decision making have concerned researchers in recent years. These interrelations actually confirm the existence of a cognitive subsystem that can be called "decision-emotion-motivation" and in which the orbitofrontal cortex plays a central role (Frodl et al., 2010; Jollant et al. 2010; Larquet, Coricelli, Opolczynski, & Thibaut, 2010; Shamay-Tsoory, Harari, Aharon-Peretz, & Levkovitz, 2010; Smith, East, & Colombo, 2010).

It seems clear now that the representations of the sensory areas (gustatory, olfactory, somatosensory, visual, and auditory) are transformed into representations related to reward at the orbitofrontal cortex, which plays a role in assigning affective value and generating an emotional experience, then into representations to make decisions and choices based on reward value in areas to which the orbitofrontal cortex is projected (Rolls & Grabenhorst, 2008). Various learning contexts are resources that can build associations in the orbitofrontal cortex between naturally neutral stimuli and primary reinforcers. These associations transform initially neutral stimuli into acquired secondary reinforcers. Different learning situations can make felt emotions more abstract and general, converting them into different motivational patterns, including predetermined choice preferences (e.g., to answer the question to get points or to increase one's grade).

Some recent contributions on the links among decision making, emotion, and motivation can be summarized in a few points. First, it is now confirmed that the representation systems of the physical characteristics of stimuli and the representation systems of their acquired and attributed affective values in learning contexts (reinforcing or inhibitory values) are distinct but highly interconnected. Decisional processes of the orbitofrontal cortex use the information on the identity of the stimulus and associate it with an affective value and a motivational state (i.e., the sought current goal, for example, eating, listening to music). Then, as the emotion and motivation have modulatory effects on decision making, cognitive processes, such as semantic processing, also modulate our emotional and motivational states in the early stages of processing in which an affective value is represented for modification. Subsequently, our decision-making system is strongly linked to the reward value of stimuli/environmental situations and, in the same way, to their emotional valence. This value is assessed on a gradient strongly influenced by the temporal factor. Thus, our decision at the time (to choose Path B because it is shorter or to choose the Path A because it is more beautiful) may change after a few minutes or hours. Finally, our decisional processes are certainly modulated by the reward value but are also determined by objective data processed by reasoning processes, always with more or less emotional valence.

While irrational, our decisions in fact enjoy both of our cognitive resources and our affective resources (see Naceur et al., 2010). While irrational, our decisions can have an adaptive value and respond appropriately and constructively to the

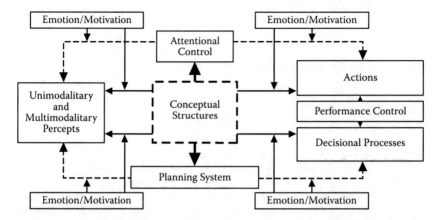

Figure 12.3   PCD paradigm integrating emotion and motivation. (Translated from Masmoudi, S. Percept—Concept—Décision, les secrets d'un cheminement émotif et motivé. In S. Masmoudi & A. Naceur (Eds.), *Du percept à la décision: intégration de la cognition, l'émotion et la motivation.* Brussels: Deboeck, 2010, p. 95.)

needs of the individual. We are far from the days when one considers emotion and motivation as two factors handicapping reason (see Damasio, 1994). I proposed in the *From Percept to Decision: Integration of Cognition, Emotion and Motivation* (Masmoudi & Naceur, 2010) the percept-concept-decision (PCD) paradigm, which is a general theoretical framework connecting decision to percepts and conceptual structures, including the dynamic, reciprocal, and recursive effects of emotion and motivation (Figure 12.3).

This paradigm is proposed based on a critical reading of work done over the past decade in the direction of an integration I would call a horizontal integration (percept-concept-decision) and in the direction of an integration I would call a vertical integration (cognition-emotion-motivation). This model provides a framework for understanding and making empirical studies of a wide range of cognitive phenomena, such as attentional processes, perception, memory, or decision making, and placing the studied phenomena in a global vision in relation to other cognitive, emotional, and motivational components.

CONCLUSION

Decision and reason are effective if and only if they are associated with emotion and motivation. Performance is understood here as the ability to produce an appropriate behavior that meets the needs of the individual and, consequently, as an enactive process that involves mobilizing resources to accomplish a task. Our daily decisions and our important decisions in life tap into our cognitive, affective, and conative resources. At the core of our cognitive resources, we find essentially reasoning. At the core of our affective resources, we find essentially emotion. At the core of our conative resources, we find basically motivation. Recent work in cognitive neuroscience and cognitive psychology tended to confirm that an important basis for deciding is feeling and emotion, rather than merely the rules of logic or reason. One of the current concerns in the decision sciences is to seek ways to improve our decision making, precisely by capitalizing our cognitive, affective, and conative resources, to enable people to produce highly adaptive potential decisions and so optimally meet their needs.

REFERENCES

Abele, S., & Stasser, G. (2008). Coordination success and interpersonal perceptions: Matching versus mismatching. *Journal of Personality and Social Psychology, 95*(3), 576–592.

Alter, A. L., & Kwan, V. S. Y. (2009). Cultural sharing in a global village: Evidence for extracultural cognition in European Americans. *Journal of Personality and Social Psychology, 96*, 742–760.

Ananda, J., & Herath, G. (2009). A critical review of multi-criteria decision making methods with special reference to forest management and planning. *Ecological Economics, 68*, 2535–2548.

Badre, D., Hoffman, J., Cooney, J. W., & D'Esposito, M. (2009). Hierarchical cognitive control deficits following damage to the human frontal lobe. *Nature Neuroscience, 12*, 515–522.

Baron, J. (2008). *Thinking and deciding.* Cambridge: Cambridge University Press.

Berthoz, A. (2006). *Emotion and reason: The cognitive neuroscience of decision making* (G. Weiss, Trans.). Oxford, UK: Oxford University Press, p. 312.

Binmore, K. (1987a). Modeling rational players: Part 1. *Economics and Philosophy, 3*, 9–55.

Binmore, K. (1987b). Modeling rational players: Part 2. *Economics and Philosophy, 4*, 179–214.

Blanchard-Fields, F., & Mienaltowski, A. (2007). Decision making and everyday problem solving. In E. B. James (Ed.), *Encyclopedia of gerontology* (pp. 350–359). New York: Elsevier.

Boddy, S., Rezgui, Y., Wetherill, M., & Cooper, G. (2007). Knowledge informed decision making in the building lifecycle: An application to the design of a water drainage system. *Automation in Construction, 16*, 596–606.

Bos, M. W., Dijksterhuis, A., & Baaren, R. B. V. (2008). On the goal-dependency of unconscious thought. *Journal of Experimental Social Psychology, 44*, 1114–1120.

Campbell, R., & Sowden, L. (Eds) (1985). *Paradoxes of rationality and cooperation: Prisoner's dilemma and Newcomb's problem.* Vancouver, Canada: University of British Columbia Press.

Cho, Y. H., & Jeantet, Y. (2010). Differential involvement of prefrontal cortex, striatum, and hippocampus in DRL performance in mice. *Neurobiology of Learning and Memory, 93*, 85–91.

Damasio, A. R. (1994). *Descartes' error: Emotion, reason, and the human brain.* New York: Putnam.

Darabi, A. A., Nelson, D. W., & Seel, N. M. (2009). Progression of mental models throughout the phases of a computer-based instructional simulation: Supportive information, practice, and performance. *Computers in Human Behavior, 25*, 723–730.

Dickerson, B. C. (2010). Memory loss. In S. B. Mushlin & H. L. Greene II (Eds.), *Decision making in medicine* (3rd ed., pp. 420–423). Philadelphia: Mosby.

Diener, E., Helliwell, J., & Kahneman, D. (2010). *International differences in well-being.* New York: Oxford University Press.

Dreher, J.-C., & Tremblay, L. (2009). *Handbook of reward and decision making.* New York: Academic Press.

Eells, E. (1982). *Rational decision and causality.* Cambridge: Cambridge University Press.

Ericsson, K. A., & Simon, H. A. (1984). *Protocol analysis: Verbal reports as data.* Cambridge, MA: MIT Press.

Falzer, P. R. (2004). Cognitive schema and naturalistic decision making in evidence-based practices. *Journal of Biomedical Informatics, 37*(2), 86–98.

Fong, G. T., Krantz, D. H., & Nisbett, R. E. (1986). The effects of statistical training on thinking about everyday problems. *Cognitive Psychology, 18,* 253–292.

Frodl, T., Bokde, A. L. W., Scheuerecker, J., Lisiecka, D., Schoepf, V., & Hampel, H. (2010). Functional connectivity bias of the orbitofrontal cortex in drug-free patients with major depression. *Biological Psychiatry, 67,* 161–167.

Galotti, K. M., Ciner, E., Altenbaumer, H. E., Geerts, H. J., Rupp, A., & Woulfe, J. (2006). Decision-making styles in a real-life decision: Choosing a college major. *Personality and Individual Differences, 41,* 629–639.

Gauthier, D. (1988/89). In the neighbourhood of the Newcomb-predictor (reflections on rationality). *Proceedings of the Aristotelian Society, 89,* part 3.

Getty, D. J., Swets, J. A., Pickett, R. M., & Gonthier, D. (1995). System operator response to warnings of danger: A laboratory investigation of the effects of the predictive value of a warning on human response time. *Journal of Experimental Psychology: Applied, 1*(1), 19–33.

Gibbard, A., & Harper, W. (1985). Counterfactuals and two kinds of expected utility. In R. Campbell & L. Sowden (Eds.), *Paradoxes of rationality and cooperation: Prisoner's dilemma and Newcomb's problem* (pp. 133–158). Vancouver: University of British Columbia Press.

Gold, J., & Shadlen, M. (2007). The neural basis of decision making. *Annual Review of Neuroscience, 30,* 535–574.

Hilbig, B. E., Erdfelder, E., & Pohl, R. F. (2010). One-reason decision making unveiled: A measurement model of the recognition heuristic. *Journal of Experimental Psychology: Learning, Memory, and Cognition, 36,* 123–134.

Humphreys, L. G., & Swets, J. A. (1991). Comparison of predictive validities measured with biserial correlations and ROCs of signal detection theory. *Journal of Applied Psychology, 76,* 316–321.

Johnson, E. J., & Tversky, A. (1983). Affect, generalization, and the perception of risk. *Journal of Personality and Social Psychology, 45,* 20–31.

Jollant, F., Lawrence, N. S., Olie, E., O'Daly, O., Malafosse, A., & Courtet, P. (2010). Decreased activation of lateral orbitofrontal cortex during risky choices under uncertainty is associated with disadvantageous decision-making and suicidal behavior. *NeuroImage, 51,* 1275–1281.

Kahneman, D., & Tversky, A. (1972). Subjective probability: A judgment of representativeness. *Cognitive Psychology, 3,* 430–454.

Kahneman, D., & Tversky, A. (1973). On the psychology of prediction. *Psychological Review, 80,* 237–251.

Kahneman, D., & Tversky, A. (1982a). Intuitive prediction: Biases and corrective procedures. In D. Kahneman, P. Slovic, & A. Tversky (Eds.), *Judgment under uncertainty: Heuristics and biases* (pp. 414–421). New York: Cambridge University Press.

Kahneman, D., & Tversky, A. (1982b). The psychology of preferences. *Scientific American, 246,* 160–173.

Kahneman, D., & Tversky, A. (1984). Choices, values, and frames. *American Psychologist, 39,* 341–350.

Kavka, G. (1983). The toxin puzzle. *Analysis, 43,* 1.

Kumaran, D., Summerfield, J. J., Hassabis, D., & Maguire, E. A. (2009). Tracking the emergence of conceptual knowledge during human decision making. *Neuron, 63*(6), 889–901.

Larquet, M., Coricelli, G., Opolczynski, G., & Thibaut, F. (2010). Impaired decision making in schizophrenia and orbitofrontal cortex lesion patients. *Schizophrenia Research, 116*, 266–273.

Lewis, D. K. (1985). Prisoner's dilemma is a Newcomb problem. In R. Campbell & L. Sowden (Eds.), *Paradoxes of rationality and cooperation: Prisoner's dilemma and Newcomb's problem* (pp. 251–255). Vancouver, Canada: University of British Columbia Press.

Litt, A., Eliasmith, C., & Thagard, P. (2008). Neural affective decision theory: Choices, brains, and emotions. *Cognitive Systems Research, 9*, 252–273.

Markman, A. (2009, November 2–5). *Emotion, motivation and decision making*. Presentation at Cem09—the Second International Conference on Cognition, Emotion and Motivation, Hammamet, Tunisia.

Masmoudi, S. (2000). *Modélisation cognitive de l'expertise de débogage de systèmes informatiques complexes*. Lille, France: Editions du Septentrion.

Masmoudi, S. (2010). Percept-Concept-Décision, les secrets d'un cheminement émotif et motivé. In S. Masmoudi & A. Naceur (Eds.), *Du percept à la décision: Intégration de la cognition, l'émotion et la motivation* (pp. 55–98). Brussels: Deboeck.

Masmoudi, S., & Naceur, A. (Eds.). (2010). *Du percept à la décision: Intégration de la cognition, l'émotion et la motivation* [From percept to decision: Integration of cognition, emotion and motivation]. Brussels: Deboeck.

McClennen, E. (1989). *Rationality and dynamic choice: Foundational explorations*. Cambridge: Cambridge University Press.

Naceur, A. (2010). Quand l'émotion perçoit et décide, un paradigme se construit. In S. Masmoudi & A. Naceur (Eds.), *Du percept à la décision: Intégration de la cognition, l'émotion et la motivation* (pp. 27–49). Bruxelles: Deboeck.

Naceur, A., Masmoudi, S., & Becher, L. (2010). Ressources cognitives et affectives dans la prise de décision. In S. Masmoudi & A. Naceur (Eds.), *Du percept à la décision: Intégration de la cognition, l'émotion et la motivation* (pp. 307–328). Brussels: Deboeck.

Nisbett, R. E., & Ross, L. (1980). *Human inference: Strategies and shortcomings of social judgment*. Englewood Cliffs, NJ: Prentice-Hall.

Nozick, R. (1969). Newcomb's problem and two principles of choice. In N. Rescher (Ed.), *Essays in honor of Carl G. Hempel* (pp. 114–146). Dordrecht, The Netherlands: Reidel.

Nozick, R. (1993). *The nature of rationality*. Princeton, NJ: Princeton University Press.

Payne, J. W., Bettman, J. R., & Johnson, E. J. (1993). *The adaptive decision maker*. Cambridge: Cambridge University Press.

Philiastides, M. G., & Heekeren, H. R. (2009). Spatiotemporal characteristics of perceptual decision making in the human brain. In D. Jean-Claude & T. Léon (Eds.), *Handbook of reward and decision making* (pp. 185–212). New York: Academic Press.

Polya, G. (1945). *How to solve it: A new aspect of mathematical method*. Princeton, NJ: Princeton University Press.

Rao, R. P. N. (2009). Bayesian cortical models. In R. S. Larry (Ed.), *Encyclopedia of neuroscience* (pp. 119–126). Oxford, UK: Academic Press.

Ratcliff, R., & Smith, P. L. (2010). Perceptual discrimination in static and dynamic noise: The temporal relation between perceptual encoding and decision making. *Journal of Experimental Psychology: General, 139*, 70–94.

Rolls, E. T., & Grabenhorst, F. (2008). The orbitofrontal cortex and beyond: From affect to decision-making. *Progress in Neurobiology, 86*, 216–244.

Rosenthal, R. (1982). Games of perfect information, predatory pricing, and the chain store paradox. *Journal of Economic Theory, 25,* 92–100.

Russo, J. E., & Dosher, B. A. (1983). Strategies for multiattribute binary choice. *Journal of Experimental Psychology: Learning, Memory, and Cognition, 9,* 676–696.

Savage, L. (1954). *The foundations of statistics.* New York: Wiley.

Schoemaker, P. J. H. (1979). The role of statistical knowledge in gambling decisions: Moment versus risk-dimension approaches. *Organizational Behavior and Human Performance, 24,* 1–17.

Shafir, E. (1999). Decision making. In R. Wilson and F. Keil (Eds.), *The MIT encyclopedia of the cognitive sciences* (pp. 220–222). Cambridge, MA: MIT Press.

Shamay-Tsoory, S. G., Harari, H., Aharon-Peretz, J., & Levkovitz, Y. (2010). The role of the orbitofrontal cortex in affective theory of mind deficits in criminal offenders with psychopathic tendencies. *Cortex, 46,* 668–677.

Shea, N., Krug, K., & Tobler, P. N. (2008). Conceptual representations in goal-directed decision making. *Cognitive, Affective, and Behavioral Neuroscience, 8,* 418–428.

Smith, C. A., East, B. S., & Colombo, P. J. (2010). The orbitofrontal cortex is not necessary for acquisition or remote recall of socially transmitted food preferences. *Behavioural Brain Research, 208,* 243–249.

Swets, J. A., Tanner, J. W. P., & Birdsall, T. G. (1961). Decision processes in perception. *Psychological Review, 68,* 301–340.

Tanner, J. W. P., & Swets, J. A. (1954). A decision-making theory of visual detection. *Psychological Review, 61,* 401–409.

Tversky, A., & Kahneman, D. (1973). Availability: A heuristic for judging frequency and probability. *Cognitive Psychology, 5,* 207–232.

Tversky, A., & Kahneman, D. (1974). Judgment under uncertainty: Heuristics and biases. *Science, 185,* 1124–1131.

Tversky, A., & Kahneman, D. (1981). The framing of decisions and the psychology of choice. *Science, 211,* 453–458.

Tversky, A., & Kahneman, D. (1982). Evidential impact of base rates. In D. Kahneman, P. Slovic, & A. Tversky (Eds.), *Judgment under uncertainty: Heuristics and biases* (pp. 153–160). New York: Cambridge University Press.

Tversky, A., & Kahneman, D. (1983). Extensional versus intuitive reasoning: The conjunction fallacy in probability judgment. *Psychological Review, 90,* 293–315.

Tversky, A., & Kahneman, D. (1992). Advances in prospect theory: Cumulative representations of uncertainty. *Journal of Risk and Uncertainty, 5,* 297–323.

Von Neumann, J., & Morgenstern, O. (1947). *Theory of games and economic behavior* (2nd ed.). Princeton, NJ: Princeton University Press.

Epilogue
Where Is the Unity of Attention, Representation, and Performance? A Commentary

DAVID YUN DAI and RON SUN

INTRODUCTION

R esearch reported and summarized in this volume represents a continuing, collective effort to correct a tendency of the cognitive revolution toward an exclusive focus on cognition, leaving emotion and motivation (or affective and conative processes) to obscurity (Hilgard, 1980). In the broader historical scheme of things, it is a reaction to a philosophical and psychological tradition of treating the mind as a disembodied existence, from Descartes' notion of thinking as having its own ontological independence regardless of bodily experiences to Ebbinghaus's disembodied studies of memory capacity (e.g., Damasio, 1994). Integrating emotion and motivation back into cognition is based on an increasing realization that, unlike a rule-based symbol manipulation system, human cognition is adaptive; for better or for worse, emotion and motivation play an important regulatory role in determining how the cognitive system functions (Dai & Sternberg, 2004). Indeed, current efforts in robotics also try to build functions of emotion and motivation into the robots that serve important adaptive and self-directing purposes (see Morgavi et al., Chapter 8). The integration starts with infusing models, in which cognitive processes and functions are seen one way or another regulated by some emotional and motivational states (Bower, 1992), but gradually fully integrative systems of person–environment transactions are developed to account for real-world complex phenomena, such as social cognition (Forgas, 1995), religion practices (Russell et al., Chapter 9), or problem solving. As we move the scale of human behavior to "the foothills of rationality" where much real behavior takes place, according to Newell (1988, p. 428), there is an increasing need for a broad framework to organize integration efforts.

In this commentary, we first introduce CLARION, an architectural model of the mind, as a possible framework with which to understand some of the integration efforts here and organize our discussion of unique contributions of each chapter to the overall understanding of how human systems work. We briefly review the chapters and point out some common threads that connect their efforts. We then discuss some broad issues emergent from this body of research for the sake of benefiting future research.

THE CLARION MODEL OF THE ARCHITECTURE OF MIND

There are several models that propose the functional architecture of the human mind. These architectural models lay out basic, essential assumptions of structural and functional constraints of the mind that can inform cognitive theorizing, modeling, and simulation. CLARION (Sun, 2002, 2006) is one of the few existing models of cognitive architecture that features a distinct role for motivation.

As shown in Figure E.1, The CLARION model has four main components. The cognitive systems are made up of two subsystems: the action-centered subsystem (ACS) with action-centered representations, such as procedural knowledge, and the non-action-centered subsystem (NACS) with non-action-centered representations, such as semantic knowledge, with the NACS supporting the ACS. Each cognitive subsystem has two levels of representation, implicit and explicit, with the former subconceptual (unconscious, implicit) and the latter conceptual (potentially conscious, explicit). The two levels interact by cooperating in action through a combination of the action recommendation from the two levels respectively, as well as cooperating in learning through a bottom-up and a top-down process.

Control and regulation of cognitive systems is realized in the motivation subsystem (MS) and the metacognitive subsystem (MCS). The control and regulation can be a bottom-up process in the sense that the regulatory processes are emotion based, implicit, and impenetrable to conscious awareness and control. The control

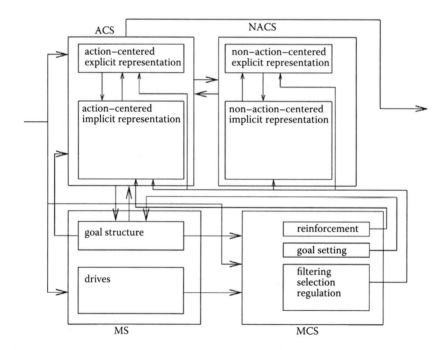

Figure E.1 The CLARION architecture. (From Sun, R. (ed.), *Cognition and multi-agent interaction: From cognitive modeling to social simulation.* New York: Cambridge University Press, 2006.)

and regulation can also be a top-down process in the sense that a particular goal or intention guides the allocation of cognitive processes through the metacognitive control system, which is in charge of managing the implementation of the goal and subgoals and monitoring the effectiveness of performance execution. Adding a motivation component accentuates cognition as serving fundamental adaptive functions to benefit the organism rather than merely a data-crunching machine.

Although emotion is not shown in Figure E.1, CLARION does have some hypotheses regarding emotion, and an emotional appraisal system is being built with existing subsystems. It is also implicated by the structuring of CLARION, especially in the motivation subsystem, which echoes the emotion-motivation system of approach-avoidance (Davidson, 2001). The role of emotion is also implicated as implicit representations in the system; as we shall see, emotions often signal the valence of stimuli without conscious awareness and processing. As implicit representations, emotions can be either a state of mind that alerts the system to the significance of current events or a piece of information to be processed by higher-order ACSs or NACSs.

However, a more interesting part of CLARION is that it is a dynamic, adaptive system; while interacting with the outside world, it continues to learn and change itself as well as change the environment through action. These changes are realized mainly through a top-down and a bottom-up process whereby the perceptual becomes conceptual to facilitate flexible application, and the conceptual becomes perceptual to enhance cognitive efficiency (cf. Masmoudi, Chapter 12, on the interaction between percepts and concepts). One question pertaining to these interactions is how these processes are differentially regulated by motivation and metacognition. For example, the implicit process is more likely emotion related, evocative, fast, and automatic, and explicit processes are more intellectual, deliberate, effortful, and slow (Kahneman, 2003). As a result, motivational and emotional processes that regulate these two kinds of cognitive processes are likely operating at different levels as well. Moreover, if there is a bottom-up process to induct rules and there is a top-down process to make rule-based actions if-then productions, then there must be regulatory forces governing these processes. In addition, CLARION reminds us that, however we define cognition, emotion, or motivation in a particular functional context, it may have different referents and should be understood as such, lest we reify these abstract concepts as having fixed structures and functions irrespective of their specific manifestations. Conversely, with neuroimaging techniques, the neurobiological substrates of specific forms of motivation, cognition, and emotion can be identified, and connectivity of the neuroanatomical structures can be mapped to show their structural and functional relationships and their significance in the organization of human thought and action, which in turn will support or falsify architectural claims.

IMPLICIT PROCESSES BEHIND ATTENTION AND PERCEPTION

Baddeley (Chapter 1) discusses his multicomponent theory of working memory with a focus on infusing the role of emotion in explaining anxiety and depression. He describes the debilitated performance under stress and dangerous conditions. The differential narcosis effect in shallow versus deep water on manual dexterity is an interesting observation in its own right. More pertinent to the focus of this section of the volume, the biased effect of anxiety toward the threat word versus a neutral word (i.e., quicker attention orientation) is consistent with the adaptive function of anxiety in alerting people to imminent danger or threat. Of course, as early research showed, agitated states of emotion and heightened motivation also tend to narrow the range of perceptual field (Bruner, 1994; see also Russell et al., and Gilet & Jallais in this volume). The performance impairment or debilitation under anxiety discussed by Baddeley was computationally simulated using similar assumptions of how stress-related emotions and thoughts affect working memory (Wilson, Sun, & Mathews, 2009, 2010). More interesting but less researched is Baddeley's hypothesis on the origins of depression and how it affects attention. Mood congruence is one of the most researched hypotheses regarding negative and positive mood and attention or memory functions (see Eich, Kihlstrom, Bower, Forgas, & Niedenthal, 2000). What is most interesting from the CLARION point of view is the supposition of the implicit comparison process by which a putative hedonic comparator may malfunction to the point of biasing attentional and cognitive processes, leading to a state of depression. The notion that this process of detecting positive and negative valences can be preattentive and evading the radar scope of conscious awareness entirely is fascinating. Although the hypothesis needs more empirical testing, the implicit comparison process is computationally realizable using the framework and algorithms of CLARION (see Sun, 2006, for details).

Frühholz and Grandjean (Chapter 2) discuss conscious and unconscious processing and advantages of quick detection of emotional information and attentional focus, of changing gears in action or direction, and the role of the amygdala, the bottom-up (limbic) and top-down (frontal) control. Readers will find a good parallel between bidirectional influences in this chapter and what Tucker and Derryberry (1992; Derryberry & Tucker, 1994) delineated about the bottom-up motivated attention and top-down executive functions. What we might find different between the two is that the chapter in this volume provides more updated, detailed neuroscientific evidence to substantiate the neural-level processes of how attention is "motivated" bottom up and top down, consistent with the reciprocal interaction of implicit and explicit representations delineated by the CLARION architecture. For a long time, emotional processing was not amenable to research, as the processes seem too implicit and elusive, subject to neither verbal reports nor observable behavior. Now, we can discuss these processes in a scientifically informed way thanks to neuroimaging techniques. The neuroconnectivity model proposed in this chapter is surely an important step toward a deeper understanding of the implicit processes that regulate attention and processing serving important adaptive purposes.

Mermillod (Chapter 3) continues the discussion of emotional processing in terms of neural substrates and reviews a range of alternative proposals in light of neuroscientific evidence. The most interesting is the comparison he draws between the embodied cognition and associative network theories. Based on a connectionist assumption, the CLARION architecture is receptive to the embodied view that holds that the high-level cognitive processes are rooted within the motor, perceptual, and emotional systems. However, as a computational model, CLARION remains agnostic about how specific mental functions are realized at the neural level. Ultimately, it is an empirical question regarding what type of cognition or representations (even explicit, conceptual ones) should be considered "embodied" and what remains "symbolically" represented, to be activated through an associative network of nodes. The most compelling evidence for embodiment is the evidence for "mirror neurons": Vicariously and directly experienced emotions have the same pattern of brain activation. It not only provides a neural basis for empathy: One literally experiences another person's emotion, be it sadness or excitement; it also validates a broader range of social and observation learning as embodied. Besides the competing models, the careful mapping of structural and functional organization of the brain vis-à-vis complex visual-perceptual processes is interesting, although the author convincingly shows that brain functions are subtle and complex, and structures and functions rarely occur as one-to-one relations. For example, LeDoux's model of the bottom-up route is only one way the emotional system works; Davidson's (2001) approach-avoidance model relies on cortical processing differences, thus operating at a higher level of functional organization of the brain. Although the chapter mainly focused on emotional processing, it has broader implications about the overall organization of the mind and brain functions. Both Frühholz and Grandjean (Chapter 2) and Mermillod (Chapter 3) provide direct evidence against the "stimulus impoverishment" argument in cognitive psychology. It should be clear now that stimulus carries valence information even preattentively; such quick processing has its own adaptive value.

The last chapter in this section by Gil and Droit-Volet (Chapter 4) report a study of perception of time as a function of processing of positive and negative emotions. As shown in the chapter, assessing and understanding variations in time perception itself, an implicit but nevertheless complex process, is no small task. The authors carefully tie time perception to attentional and arousal processes involved in emotional processing and draw some interesting conclusions about why positive and negative emotions tend to "distort" temporal perceptions in a different way. While specific theoretical explanations warrant further research to be conclusive, the study demonstrates how our perception of seemingly neutral, objective properties, such as time, can reflect the mental state of the person. Time, indeed, has a subjective dimension.

BIASED IMPLICIT AND EXPLICIT REPRESENTATIONS

In the CLARION architecture, representations can be both explicitly symbolic and implicitly embodied. Explicit representations are conceptual, analytic, and "crisp," constructed online or activated from long-term memory; implicit representations could be bodily states such as emotions and mental states such as feelings, perceptions, and intuitions, evocative in nature, preanalytic, and often opaque to conscious control. Whatever the case, we endorse Bartlett's (1932) proposition that one has an attitude before constructing a representation. What it means is that representations are not copies of some aspects of the world; rather, as CLARION stipulates, they are fundamentally constructed, organized, and cooperated to assist in human action.

Chapter 5 by Gilet and Jallais tackles a critical issue of how emotion influences memory and cognitive processing: valence or arousal? While there is a line of research suggesting that valence (positive and negative emotions or moods) influences the spread of activation, hence remote or unusual associations, their study of word association using a mood induction paradigm and a 2 × 2 (valence by arousal) design shows that high arousal of both positive and negative valences (happiness and anger) produced significantly more unusual word associations. Determination of effects of valence versus arousal is, of course, a complex matter, depending on the nature of tasks as well as mood induction methods. The authors cited multiple operations of mood induction yielding similar outcomes, thus providing convergent supporting evidence. There is research using similar mood induction methods but drawing different conclusions. For example, Bolte, Goschke, and Kuhl (2003) looked at effects of valence of mood on implicit judgment of semantic coherence and found that positive mood, not a negative one, enhanced coherence judgments. They interpreted the results to mean that positive mood potentiates spread of activation to weak or remote associates in memory, hence better coherence judgment performance, and negative mood restricts spread of activation to close associates and dominant word meanings. Review of this body of research is beyond the scope of this commentary (see Storbeck & Clore, 2008 for a review), but suffice it to say that both valence and arousal have implications for cognitive associations and representations. From a functional perspective, it would be interesting to see when and how these emotional states make cognitive representations more adaptive to real-life situations (Bruner, 1994). For example, high arousal and unusual associations are advantageous when the situation calls for cognitive flexibility and widening the scope of thinking (e.g., writing poetry) but may be disadvantageous when the situation demands precision and sharpened focus (e.g., writing a scientific exposition). This kind of research enriches the CLARION model by providing specific instances of how representations are activated to suggest a particular line of thought and action, for example, through metacognitive regulation on the basis of the arousal states and cognitive appraisals, along the line that Wilson et al. (2009, 2010) suggested.

Batt and van Leeuwen's Chapter 6 deals with a particular kind of representations, visual arts, using an electroencephalographic (EEG) measure. More specifically, they examined two forms, representational and abstract art, with trained experts and untrained laypeople. Perceptions and mental representations of art are rich in aesthetic and emotional qualities, imbued with thematic, formal, and semantic contents, and are therefore a fertile ground for investigation of interaction of cognition and emotion. This specific investigation has two main interests: (a) whether there are differences between representations of representational (depiction of concrete objects) art versus abstract art, which only shows color shades and contours, and dynamics of shapes and lines; and (b) whether there are differences between representations in the mind of experts versus that of novices. For the former, we might consider a bottom-up process whereby paintings of differing styles would trigger or evoke difference reactions and representations. For the latter, we might infer a top-down process whereby there is an effect of "mindset," with artists showing an expert mindset and lay audience an "untrained mind." To examine these two issues, the authors decided to use a global analysis of functional integration rather than discrete measures of localization, namely, capturing activity of brain waves rather than measures (e.g., functional magnetic resonance imaging [fMRI] or positron emission tomography [PET]) more sensitive to spatial location than temporal rhythms. The results showed significant theta band activity for artists, particularly with abstract art, and significant alpha band activity for nonartists. The authors interpreted the increased theta activity during visual perception compared to mental imagery (for both artistic styles) as resulting from the extensive top-down processes required to convert the image from working memory to long-term memory. In contrast, heightened alpha activity shown in nonartists reflected significantly more bottom-up processes, with more focus given to the extraction and organization of discrete visual features when processing abstract art, rather than higher-order meanings and associations. The "expertise" effect is not surprising given the cumulative evidence (see Ericsson, Charness, Feltovich, & Hoffman, 2006), but carefully uncovering its neural substrates and underpinnings is new and warrants continuing efforts. From a CLARION perspective, particularly challenging is not merely describing properties of representations in a static fashion but mapping out how artistic expertise or "neuroasethetics" develops through changing representations at both the perceptual and conceptual levels, and how the two levels of representations reciprocate and interact in the development of appreciative artistry.

Sklad's Chapter 7 deals with a different content and form of representation: the nature and construction of retrospective opinions. The chapter tackles a phenomenon psychological research heavily relies on, and thus has the added importance of elucidating the validity of related research methodology to the understanding the underlying process of constructing these opinions. Most relevant to the theme of this part of the volume is the sources of biases in the construction of retrospective opinions, which may belong to the NACS in CLARION. Retrospective opinions, of course, can be of varied kinds, from the taste of a particular brand of wine to the justification of a political event. Construction of retrospective events involves some form of reasoning, and research shows that invalid inferences are more likely about emotional versus neutral materials (Blanchette & Richards, 2004). In this chapter, the author reviews a range of possible biases built into retrospective opinions, such as hindsight bias. As the author convincingly showed, the sources of biases can be cognitive, emotional, and motivational in nature. The author put forward a new, integrated proposal that treats retrospective opinions as reconstructed judgment. The new model has both a cognitive component and a motivation component. Motivation mainly consists of an effort to maintain self-esteem (or generate positive affect) and self-consistency. Personal relevance of the opinions reconstructed determines the strength of motivation. To broaden the relevance of this line of thinking, we might compare situations asking for retrospective opinions with situations for making social persuasion a process of motivated reasoning (Kunda, 1990) or situations of learning that involve gaining resources (via acquiring skills) as well as maintaining self-esteem and personal resources (Boekaerts, 1993). It seems that representations are biased and motivated to advance personal interests and goals; in other words, treating the human functional system like a data-crunching machine or disinterested bystander has limited utility when explaining real-life phenomena. The author presented several empirical studies along this line. Computationally, modeling these complex processes using CLARION or other models will also be a meaningful way to show how motivations are activated given a particular situation and how they regulate cognitive inferences and conceptualization of a particular issue at hand that has personal and social relevance (as has indeed been under-taken; see, e.g., Sun, 2009).

It can be said that if the traditional modeling of the human cognitive system drew inspirations from workings of a computer, now the endeavor of engineering robots or artificial intelligence (AI) in general tries to mimic human functioning, including its distinct representations of cognition, emotion, and motivation and its self-engendered development (Weng et al., 2001). Morgavi and colleagues (Chapter 8) discuss efforts along this line of AI work. They were particularly interested in building robots capable of autonomous growth through knowledge creative processes, such as changes in functional meaning, increased complexity, expanded the internal knowledge map, abstraction, and insight. To achieve insights into these processes, they sought inspirations from young (preschool, 4–5 years old) children's developing understanding of metaphors. The selection of metaphor makes theoretical sense, as metaphorical use of language reflects the kind of human creativity that is so common and pervasive in daily language and communication (Lakoff & Johnson, 1980/2003) yet proves hard to model in AI research. A finding of their study pertinent to the theme of this section is that emotional processes are involved in every step of the cognitive abstraction and mapping process. Metaphorical understanding is a good challenge for cognitive modeling, and given that it is likely to involve both implicit and explicit representations interacting to produce a metaphor as simple as "she is a tiger mom." CLARION provides a good framework for modeling metaphorical learning and indeed provides algorithms for doing that.

MOTIVATED ACTION AND PERFORMANCE

For the purpose of this volume, human performance is considered as either executing acquired procedures and routines to accomplish a task (e.g., skilled performance) or searching for paths to problem solution or goal attainment (e.g., problem solving). Naturally, it involves directed, selective, focused, and sustained attention, which implicates motivated acts at conscious or unconscious levels. It also involves representations of various kinds, such as action-based (e.g., procedural and strategic knowledge) and non-action-based knowledge (e.g., semantic and episodic knowledge). Activation as well as the nature of these representations can be analyzed in terms of their connections to emotion and motivation. The enactive rather than perceptual and associative nature of performance highlights the function of motivation in terms of the direction, intensity, and duration of the goal-directed action. The process typically involves valued goals to be attained and expectations of the likelihood of achieving the desirable outcomes (Atkinson, 1957). Volitional aspects of motivation (implementation of an intention or goal) also have become a main concern in recent years (Kuhl, 1985). Motivation thus is conceptualized at two levels: anticipation of rewards and implementing an action to attain the reward (Pizzagalli, Sherwood, Henriques, & Davidson, 2005). Alternatively, we might consider implicit drives as primary (e.g., the approach-avoidance emotion-motivation system) and explicit goal strivings as secondary (e.g., the goal commitment for carrying out and sustaining an action) processes of motivation, as prescribed by the CLARION architecture.

Russell, Dunbar, and Gobet (Chapter 9) examine ritualistic practices of religion and their connections to two distinct forms of emotion: euphoria and dysphoria. Their main purpose is to demonstrate how religious practices enlist and evoke intense emotions, positive and negative, to achieve social bonds and sustain religious convictions and commitments. Some of the issues Gilet and Jallais (Chapter 5) focused on, concerning the adaptivity of positive versus negative emotions, high arousal versus serene states, were brought to the forefront again. The authors surveyed religious practices that induce states of ecstasy and those that inflict pain and injuries and evoke fear or horror, and they elucidated the functional utilities of valence and arousal in religious practice in light of the psychological theories and research. While this exposition makes a compelling case, their use of the Tower of Hanoi as an analogous ritualistic task is open to question, despite the authors' claim that it has the same invariance and rule governance as a religious ritual. One can argue that the meanings and goal structures of the tasks as well as emotions experienced in two situations are drastically different. Regardless of the initial impetus of the experiment, it was a typical mood induction (viewing a humorous vs. unpleasant video clip) experiment with problem-solving tasks and transfer as performance criteria. Findings of this study and a couple of others they reviewed echoed those found by Gilet and Jallais, namely, euphoria (positive high arousal) and dysphoria (negative high arousal) serve differential cognitive functions, with the former having a "broadening effect" and the latter a "narrowing effect." They expounded the *differential function hypothesis* with 11 statements. This is a fascinating chapter, consisting of a chain of reasoning and orchestration of supporting evidence, analogous to what Darwin called "a long argument" when describing his own evolutionary theory. However, there still seem to be some loose ends in terms of evidence and warrant.

In comparison, Clément's Chapter 10 tackles a topic that is more circumscribed in scope: Is it possible to solve a problem without emotion? While negative effects of certain emotions such as anxiety in problem solving are well documented (Baddeley, Chapter 1, this volume; Beilock & Carr, 2005) and acknowledged in the chapter, her review attempts to reinstate the adaptive role of emotion; that is, emotion may be necessary to gear problem solving in more promising directions. The connection the author makes between the appraisal aspect of emotion and specific phases of problem solving (e.g., impasse situations and subgoal achievements) reveals the necessity of integrating emotion and opens an opportunity for empirical investigation. The author used a five-disk version of the Tower of Hanoi as a task and facial expressions and skin conductance as measures of emotion. The basic hypothesis is that appraisal of goal conduciveness in particular phases of problem solving would cause changes in facial expressions and the physiological responses. The results support this theoretical prediction, with some discrepancies in the two measures of emotion under impasse and subgoal management conditions. This was a well-conceptualized and well-designed study, albeit the fact that, as the author points out herself, the coping potential appraisal (some form of self-efficacy appraisal) was inferred but not directly measured. Given the enactive nature of problem solving, motivation could be tapped more directly in the experiment. Incidentally, highlighting the adaptive role of emotion (i.e., problem solving entails emotion) does not necessarily mean that emotions are always adaptive, or that the process of appraisal works without the partaking of cognition. There is evidence that activation of higher cognitive processes can mean inhibition of emotional activity (Drevets & Raichle, 1998). It is important to ask when emotion is helpful and how it is helpful for achieving a particular goal. This chapter is exemplary in this regard.

Bonnardel's Chapter 11 deals with a slightly different condition of problem solving: design ideation. Echoing the "broadening effect" of euphoria in Russell et al.'s Chapter 9, this chapter is also concerned with whether a wider range of ideas and inspirations for designing creative products is evoked by positive affective stimuli, particularly those words and images that run across categories (i.e., are interdomain) rather than restricted to one category (i.e., are intradomain). Compared to Tower of Hanoi situations, creative design situations are less constrained and more open ended and ill structured, involving numerous possibilities. The author therefore posited that problem solving starts with an analogical thinking phase and then moves to the phase of management of constraints. The author set up an experiment to address the initial evocation phase and the respective role of positive affect. General findings of these preliminary studies were that images, rather than words, particularly the interdomain ones, have a positive effect on evocation of creative ideation. Using images versus words of various domains to prime for creative ideation has potential for real-life application, which is the main concern of the author. Theoretically, we need to have a better understanding of whether it is positive affect that induces cognitive flexibility, possibly through neurophysiological pathways (e.g., Ashby, Isen, & Turken, 1999; Allman, Hakeem, Erwin, Nimchinsky, & Hof, 2001), or whether it is mainly a cognitive effect of priming for remote association that facilitates analogical mapping in design ideation. More broadly, we might consider different types of problem solving as differentially involving the role of emotion and motivation. Recently, CLARION was used to model the interaction of implicit-explicit knowledge and processes in creative problem solving (Helie & Sun, 2010). How these implicit and explicit representations and processes are evoked, assembled, and controlled via emotional, motivational, and cognitive mechanisms to produce creative ideas warrants further research (see Schawrz & Skurnik, 2003, for a review of the interplay of feeling and thinking in problem solving and creativity).

Masmoudi's Chapter 12 is concerned with the basis of decision making: logic or heuristics? The role of heuristics and affective preference has been uncovered by Tversky and Kahneman for a while. It can be easily extrapolated that implicit and explicit representations are constructed or activated around reward value and opportunity costs. The author tries to provide a general framework that horizontally integrates percepts, concepts, and decisions and vertically integrates cognition, emotion, and motivation. This model in some way echoes the CLARION architecture, such as stipulation of perceptual and conceptual structures, action-centered (ACS) and non-action-centered representations (NACS). Ultimately, non-action-centered representations subserve action-centered representations. Thus, CLARION can be seen as a decision-making model, with its algorithms and equations for determining the strength of activation and propagation, interaction of the four subsystems, and output (i.e., decision). While Masmoudi emphasizes the regulatory role of motivation and emotion in cognition, CLARION also has an explicit representation of motivation influencing cognitive systems directly or through the MCS. Although Masmoudi seems to equate rationality with a system governed by logic and reason, one can argue that emotion and motivation may have their own rationality that reason does not understand (Damasio, 1994), and that implicit processes in general may incorporate many kinds of rational considerations (as indicated by CLARION). It also seems important to distinguish everyday decision making, such as whether to shop at one grocery store versus another, and critical decision making, such as making a big investment in the stock market; in the latter case, deliberation is more common. There are clearly descriptive models that can capture part of how decisions are made, but optimal prescriptive decision theories that maximize chances of success (rationality) are also needed. In such a case, there may be "good" emotions and motivations and "bad" emotions and motivations for particular decision situations. Understanding the differences is also important for optimal human functioning.

At this point, the perusal of the chapters comes full circle. We have taken a journey into the mind's workings, from information uptake through selective attention, to mentally represent and understand complex realities in the service of adaptation and creation, to solving problems, fashioning new products, and making decisions that have personal consequences. Valence, arousal, working memory, appraisal, biases, heuristics, percepts, drives, executive functions, and implicit and explicit processes are but a few of the catchwords that seem to serve us well in carving the mind at its joints. Along with innovative experimental designs, observation of the living brain via neuroimaging techniques helps us literally see the mind at work in a way unimaginable even 20 years ago. This is no small feat.

GENERAL DISCUSSION

In this commentary, we ask: Where is the unity of attention, representation, and performance? To be sure, CLARION is used as a way to "put it all together," to connect seemingly unrelated research programs with their unique foci and research findings that, taken together, might shed light on how the mind works as a whole. Unity here implies a mind that does not work in a fragmentary manner, with numerous modules or selves acting in their own idiosyncratic fashion; rather, there is coordination and communication among various structures, subsystems, and functions in producing behaviors that can serve us well in dealing with life's challenges and living a fulfilling life. This is the initial impetus for integration of cognition, emotion, and motivation. This is also the impetus for incorporating both the implicit, connectionist part of mind's work and the explicit, conceptual, symbolic part so that perceiving, feeling, thinking, and acting interact rather than displaying "autistic" symptoms, only capable of performing monologue. However, the time seems ripe that we can talk about another type of unity: mind-in-context. Rather than seen as having inherent fixed parameters, mind can only be understood in particular functional contexts. For that matter, the real world in which we find ourselves is the best reference.

Tackling Real-Life Phenomena

Developing neat theories in a laboratory is always attractive to researchers, but ultimately ideas and inspirations better come from keen observation of real-life phenomena. In cognitive psychology, Neisser (1967) was among the earliest to emphasize the importance of real-life significance of psychological studies. It was not accidental that he was also among the first to point out the limitations of modeling the human mind after a computer. In an article published in *Science* (Neisser, 1963), he argued that cognition can never be completely dissociated from feeling, and our action often serves not just one but a multitude of motives. Although Simon (1967) tried to reclaim the legitimacy of cognitivism by reinstating the role of motivation and emotion, in hindsight he might have missed the point; complexities of the real-life phenomena demand a more nuanced understanding rather than neat formulations.

Take as an example the issue of valence and arousal, which is brought up in many chapters of this volume (e.g., Gilet & Jallais, Chapter 5; Russell et al., Chapter 9). Cognitive effects of valence and arousal of emotion might well vary in an array of situations, depending on the nature of emotions, cognitive processes, and functional tasks involved. Also, as we move from simple units to complex units of analysis, more complexities and ambiguities will be encountered. Rather than seeking an either-or solution, such an issue has to be tackled in a more complex manner, particularly when we go beyond the static observation of attention and representation as a function of arousal or valence conditions and start to tackle the enactive process of searching for information and making decisions about what to do next (e.g., Clément, Chapter 10). In the latter context, emotion can instigate action or gear one toward a new direction; in other words, it is motivational, not merely evoking certain cognitive processes. What it means is that we cannot figure out the mind in isolation from its action on the world. Affordances and constraints of the environment also structure the way our mind works and grows (Dai, 2010).

Mind-in-context naturally draws our attention to the social dimension of integration efforts. Humans are social creatures, constantly interacting with other human beings. As Gil and Droit-Volet (Chapter 4) convincingly demonstrated, even perception of the physical world (time) can be affected by processing of facial expression, a social encounter for us on a daily, if not hourly, basis. Likewise, much semantic representation carries important social values and valences and thus cannot be studied in a way as if they have invariant properties regardless of social contexts.

The research on stereotype threat (Steele, 1997) can be instructive in that regard. The concept of stereotype threat has origins in social psychology but now is used to understand the subtle but important influence it has on intellectual and academic performance. For example, one study found interesting connections between status, testosterone, and intellectual performance in the context of stereotype threat (Joseph, Newman, Brown, & Beer, 2003). Another study by Italian researchers discovered gender differences in facing stereotype threat (Cadinu, Maass, Rosabianca, & Kiesner, 2005). And still another study found that self-monitoring, a personality character, enhanced intellectual performance under stereotype threat (Inzlicht, Aronson, Good, & McKay, 2005). The situation gets complex as we proceed, but that is the way how real world works. In most situations, human functioning is a not solo show but is best characterized as a multiagent system (Sun, 2006) and should be understood as such.

Honoring Levels of Analysis and Interlevel Interactions

It is always a daunting challenge to face the complexity of real-world phenomena, be it religious practice (Russell et al., Chapter 9), creative problem solving (Bonnardel, Chapter 11), or making life decisions (Masmoudi, Chapter 12). But as the authors of these chapters showed, there is discernible order from the seeming chaos. A useful conceptual tool to disentangle the complexities is levels of analysis. CLARION is a multilevel system. Indeed, any complex system can be seen as a multilevel system (Simon, 1979). When we analyze multilevel systems such as the mind, or even mind-in-context, we inevitably have to deal with the issue of how we describe and explain the dynamic interplay of components sitting at different levels of functioning. One strategy is reductionistic, reducing the complexity of higher-order processes to simpler components. This is the common way experimental psychology conducts its business. It will do no harm if it is not a form of eliminative reductionism (Searle, 2004). Another strategy is to study emergence of higher-order properties as irreducible to lower-level components as they are governed by new organizational principles. This is a strategy Sawyer (1999) used when explaining creative problem solving in various social settings (see Dai, 2005, for more discussion). CLARION sometimes posits implicit and explicit levels of representations and processes as parallel and complementary, and sometimes as reciprocal and interacting (e.g., Sun, Merrill, & Peterson, 2001; Sun, Slusarz, & Terry, 2005). It seems only reasonable to assume that human transactions involve both activation of long-term memory in response to task affordances and constraints and social conditions and online construction of responses and actions that are not readily available. Descriptions of how the human brain works (Baddeley, Chapter 1; Morgavi et al., Chapter 8; Russell et al., Chapter 9, to name a few) give credence to this dynamic portrayal of mind in motion (van Gelder & Port, 1995). In CLARION, complex interactions exist among many components, modules, and subsystems (for cognition, motivations, emotional appraisal, and so on), so that they all affect each other. One point of CLARION is to delineate the exact paths and forms of such interaction.

Integrating the Neurophysiological, Phenomenological, and Functional

Several new movements indicate a trend toward "putting it all together." One is the Human Connectome Project (http://www.humanconnectomeproject.org) of the National Institutes of Health; it aims to use the most advanced neuroimaging technique to map out the connectivity of the brain, structurally and functionally. Another is social cognitive and affective neuroscience (Wilms et al., 2010), aimed at integrating cognitive science, affective science, brain research, and social psychology.

Besides the efforts to seek fundamental understandings of the mind at work, there are also two new movements that are driven by practical needs. One is the AI project on autonomous mental development by robots and animals (Weng et al., 2001). It sets up goals for a new generation of robot programs to have the following properties: not task specific, tasks are unknown, generates a representation of an unknown task, animal-like online learning, and open-ended learning. Morgavi and colleagues' work (Chapter 8) is part of this ongoing effort. Another programming effort is the launch of learning sciences aimed at designing learning environments that optimize human learning and growth for the challenges of the new century (Dai, 2011; Sawyer, 2006), including a particular emphasis on the role of affect in learning, and the importance of social aspects of learning. Integration efforts, therefore, are not merely an intellectual exercise, but a way to solve important problems and improve human conditions.

It is encouraging to see brain research figuring so prominently in this volume. In many ways, it allows us to discuss mental functions such as cognition, emotion, and motivation in a more precise manner, as these functions are not some disembodied mental processes but have their distinct biological substrates. Having said that, we should also point out that the contents of these mental processes cannot be completely explained, or explained away, by neurophysiological processes, as the phenomenology of perceptions, feelings, intuitions, thoughts, and actions is real in its own right, just as seeing an object out there is real and has psychological meaning and functional significance in a context rather than an optical illusion to be explained away by neural activity in the visual-cortical system. We will have the ideal integration when all three dimensions—neurobiological, phenomenological, and functional—come together. This is what Russell and colleagues (Chapter 9) are trying to accomplish on the topic of religion. This is what we should aim at on all fronts of human activity. To be sure, it is going to be a thousand-mile journey, but to complete the Chinese proverb, it starts with one step.

REFERENCES

Allman, J. M., Hakeem, A., Erwin, J. M., Nimchinsky, E., & Hof, P. (2001). The anterior cingulate cortex: The evolution of an interface between emotion and cognition. In A. R. Damasio, A. Harrington, J. Kagan, B. S. McEwen, H. Moss, & R. Shaikh (Eds.), *Unity of knowledge: The convergence of natural and human science* (pp. 107–117). New York: New York Academy of Sciences.

Ashby, F. G., Isen, A. M., & Turken, A. U. (1999). A neuropsychological theory of positive affect and its influence on cognition. *Psychological Review, 106*, 529–550.

Atkinson, J. W. (1957). Motivational determinants of risk taking behavior. *Psychological Review, 64*, 359–372.

Bartlett, F. C. (1932). *Remembering*. Cambridge, UK: Cambridge University Press.

Beilock, S. L., & Carr, T. H. (2005). When high-powered people fail: Working memory and "choking under pressure" in math. *Psychological Science, 16*, 101–105.

Blanchette, I., & Richards, A. (2004). Reasoning about emotional and neutral materials: Is logic affected by emotion? *Psychological Science, 15*, 745–752.

Boekaerts, M. (1993). Being concerned with well-being and with learning. *Educational Psychologist, 28*, 149–167.

Bolte, A., Goschke, T., & Kuhl, J. (2003). Emotion and institution: Effects of positive and negative mood on implicit judgments of semantic coherence. *Psychological Bulletin, 14*, 416–421.

Bower, G. (1992). How might emotions affect learning? In S.-A. Christianson (Ed.), *The handbook of emotion and memory: Research and theory* (pp. 3–32). Hillsdale, NJ: Erlbaum.

Bruner, J. (1994). The view from the heart's eye: A commentary. In P. M. Miedenthal & S. Kitayama (Eds.), *The heart's eye: Emotional influences in perception and attention* (pp. 269–286). San Diego, CA: Academic Press.

Cadinu, M., Maass, A., Rosabianca, A., & Kiesner, J. (2005). Why do women underperform under stereotype threat? *Psychological Science, 16*, 572–578.

Dai, D. Y. (2005). Reductionism versus emergentism: A framework for understanding conceptions of giftedness. *Roeper Review*, 144–151.

Dai, D. Y. (2010). *The nature and nurture of giftedness: A new framework for understanding gifted education*. New York: Teachers College Press.

Dai, D. Y. (Ed.). (2011). *Design research on learning and thinking in educational settings: Enhancing intellectual growth and functioning*. New York: Routledge.

Dai, D. Y., & Sternberg, R. J. (2004). *Motivation, emotion, and cognition: Integrative perspectives on intellectual functioning and development*. Mahwah, NJ: Erlbaum.

Damasio, A. R. (1994). *Descartes' error: Emotion, reason, and the human brain*. New York: Avon Books.

Davidson, R. J. (2001). Toward a biology of personality and emotion. In A. R. Damasio, A. Harrington, J. Kagan, B. S. McEwen, H. Moss, & R. Shaikh (Eds.), *Unity of knowledge: The convergence of natural and human science* (pp. 191–207). New York: New York Academy of Sciences.

Derryberry, D., & Tucker, D. M. (1994). Motivating the focus of attention. In P. M. Miedenthal & S. Kitayama (Eds.), *The heart's eye: Emotional influences in perception and attention* (pp. 167–196). San Diego, CA: Academic Press.

Drevets, W. C., & Raichle, M. E. (1998). Reciprocal suppression of regional cerebral blood flow during emotional versus higher cognitive processes: Implications for interactions between emotion and cognition. *Cognition and Emotion, 12*, 353–385.

Eich, E., Kihlstrom, J. F., Bower, G. H., Forgas, J. P., & Niedenthal, P. M. (2000). *Cognition and emotion*. New York: Oxford University Press.

Ericsson, K. A., Charness, N., Feltovich, P. J., & Hoffman, R. R. (Eds.). (2006). *The Cambridge handbook of expertise and expert performance*. New York: Cambridge University Press.

Forgas, J. P. (1995). Mood and judgment: The affect infusion model (AIM). *Psychological Bulletin, 117*, 39–66.

Helie, S., & Sun, R. (2010). Incubation, insight, and creative problem solving: A unified theory and a connectionist model. *Psychological Review, 117*, 994–1024.

Hilgard, E. R. (1980). The trilogy of mind: Cognition, affection, and conation. *Journal of the History of the Behavioral Sciences, 16,* 107–117.

Inzlicht, M., Aronson, J., Good, C., & McKay, L. (2005). A particular resiliency to threatening environments. *Journal of Experimental Social Psychology, 42,* 323–336.

Joseph, R. A., Newman, M. L., Brown, R. P., & Beer, J. M. (2003). Status, testosterone, and human intellectual performance: Stereotype threat as status concern. *Psychological Science, 14,* 158–163.

Kahneman, D. (2003). A perspective on judgment and choice: Mapping bounded rationality. *American Psychologist, 58,* 697–720.

Kuhl, J. (1985). Volitional mediators of cognition-behavior consistency: Self-regulatory processes and action versus state orientation. In J. Kuhl & J. Beckmann (Eds.), *Action control: From cognition to behavior* (pp. 101–128). Berlin: Springer.

Kunda, Z. (1990). The case for motivated reasoning. *Psychological Bulletin, 108,* 480–498.

Lakoff, G., & Johnson, M. (2003). *Metaphors we live by.* Chicago: University of Chicago Press. (Original work published 1980)

Neisser, U. (1963). The imitation of man by machine. *Science, 139,* 193–197.

Neisser, U. (1967). *Cognitive psychology.* New York: Appleton-Century-Crofts.

Newell, A. (1988). Putting it all together. In D. Klahr & K. Kovovsky (Eds.), *Complex information processing: The impact of Herbert A. Simon* (pp. 399–440). Hillsdale, NJ: Erlbaum.

Pizzagalli, D. A., Sherwood, R. J., Henriques, J. B., & Davidson, R. J. (2005). Frontal brain asymmetry and reward responsiveness. *Psychological Science, 16,* 805–813.

Sawyer, R. K. (1999). The emergence of creativity. *Philosophical Psychology, 12,* 447–469.

Sawyer, R. K. (Ed.). (2006). *The Cambridge handbook of the learning sciences.* Cambridge, UK: Cambridge University Press.

Schawrz, N., & Skurnik, I. (2003). Feeling and thinking: Implications for problem solving. In J. E. Davidson & R. J. Sternberg (Eds.), *The psychology of problem solving* (pp. 263–290). Cambridge, UK: Cambridge University Press.

Searle, J. R. (2004). *Mind: A brief introduction.* New York: Oxford University Press.

Simon, H. A. (1967). Motivational and emotional controls of cognition. *Psychological Review, 74,* 29–39.

Simon, H. A. (1979). Information processing models of cognition. *Annual Review of Psychology, 30,* 363–396.

Steele, C. M. (1997). A threat in the air: How stereotypes shape intellectual identity and performance. *American Psychologist, 52,* 613–629.

Storbeck, J., & Clore, G. L. (2008). Affective arousal as information: How affective arousal influences judgments, learning, and memory. *Social and Personality Psychology Compass, 2,* 1824–1843.

Sun, R. (2002). *Duality of the mind: A bottom-up approach toward cognition.* Mahwah, NJ: Erlbaum.

Sun, R. (Ed.). (2006). *Cognition and multi-agent interaction: From cognitive modeling to social simulation.* New York: Cambridge University Press.

Sun, R. (2009). Motivational representations within a computational cognitive architecture. *Cognitive Computation, 1*(1), 91–103.

Sun, R., Merrill, E., & Peterson, T. (2001). From implicit skills to explicit knowledge: A bottom-up model of skill learning. *Cognitive Science, 25,* 203–244.

Sun, R., Slusarz, P., & Terry, C. (2005). The interaction of the explicit and the implicit in skill learning: A dual-process approach. *Psychological Review, 112,* 159–192.

Tucker, D. M., & Derryberry, D. (1992). Motivated attention: Anxiety and the frontal executive functions. *Neuropsychiatry, Neuropsychology, and Behavioral Neurology, 5,* 233–252.

van Gelder, T., & Port, R. F. (1995). It's about time: An overview of the dynamic approach to cognition. In R. F. Port & T. van Gelder (Eds.), *Mind as motion: Explorations in the dynamics of cognition* (pp. 1–43). Cambridge, MA: MIT Press.

Weng, J., McClelland, J., Pentland, A., Sporns, O., Stockman, I., Sur, M., et al. (2001). Autonomous mental development by robots and animals. *Science, 291*(26), 599–600.

Wilson, N., Sun, R., & Mathews, R. (2009). A motivationally-based simulation of performance degradation under pressure. *Neural Networks, 22*, 502–508.

Wilson, N., Sun, R., & Mathews, R., (2010). A motivationally based computational interpretation of social anxiety induced stereotype bias. In *Proceedings of the 2010 Cognitive Science Society Conference* (pp. 1750–1755). Austin, TX: Cognitive Science Society.

Wilms, M., Schilbach, L., Pfeiffer, U., Bente, G., Fink, G. R., & Vogeley. (2010). It's in your eyes—Using gaze-contingent stimuli to create truly interactive paradigms for social cognitive and affective neuroscience. *Social Cognitive and Affective Neuroscience, 5*, 98–107.

Author Index

Subject Index

A

Abstract architecture, 102
Abstract art, 95, 222
    in architecture, 101–102
    artist/nonartist differences in processing, 97
    right hemispheric activity in processing of, 99
    style and spectral power findings, 95–100
    theta wave dominance in perception of, 98
    viewing artworks findings, 100–101
Abstraction
    correlation with decreased alpha activity, 98
    grounding in perceptual experiences, 137
    and orbitofrontal cortex, 54
    process in children, 140
Action readiness, 61
Activation theory, 171
    valence and, 222
Adaptability, role of emotion in, 171–173
Adaptable artificial system design. *See also*
      Robot design
    children's metaphor interpretations and, 138
    experimental study design, 137–138
    human creative processes and, 133–137
    for robots that grow up, 140–143
    study results, 138–140
Adaptive system design, 219, 224
Adaptivity, 134
Aesthetic experience, 93
    perception geared toward, 100
    self-referential nature of, 101
    visual simplicity and, 94
Aesthetic processing, differences between
      artists and nonartists, 96–98
Aesthetical emotions, 187
Affect, 77
    impact of words and images conveying, 190–195
    religious, 147
Affect program, 173
Affective computing, 196
Affective primacy, 188
Affiliation behaviors, 67
Agility, 134
Alpha wave activity, 223
    in artists *vs.* nonartists, 97, 102
    in right temporoparietal cortex, 99
Amygdala, 34, 51, 55, 220
    in attentional and emotional processing, 20
    as detector of emotionally relevant
      information, 25

direct subcortical pathway to visual system, 48
fast decoding of emotional stimuli by, 34
mediation of fast encoding by, 21
and processing of six primary EFE, 51–52
role in acquisition, storage, expression of
    fear, 50
role in emotional judgment, 13, 26, 47
role in primitive behaviors, 53
sensitivity to anger and fear in vocal
    expressions, 22, 26
sensitivity to human voices, 28
two perceptual routes, 47
Amygdala-cortical network, identification via
    SEM, 30
Amygdala legions, 27
Analogical reasoning, in generative phase of
    design, 190
Analogical transfer, 161
    advantages of dysphoria, 157, 159
Analogy making, 189
Anchor and adjust model, of retrospective
    opinion, 113–114
Anchoring-and-adjustment heuristic/bias,
    205–206
Anger
    amygdala sensitivity to, 22
    approach orientation in, 83
    difference scores, 65
    displacement through depression, 8
    facial expression, 64
    facial expression and overestimation of time,
      67–68
    facilitation of lexical decisions by, 82
    learning to mask, 68
    and unusual word associations, 84, 85
Anterior cingulate cortex, 53
Anterior thalamic nucleus, 46
Antithesis principle, 41
Anxiety, 4, 220
    adaptive function, 220
    and attentional bias, 6
    and cognition, 5–7
    differentiating from depression, 8
    differentiating from fear, 5
    and distraction, 8
    effects on complex cognitive tasks, 6
    effects on nitrogen narcosis, 5
    evolutionary significance, 8
    gastric symptoms in, 9
    role of emotion in, 219

Security, and false memory effect, 84
Self-consistency, as motivation for retrospective
    opinion construction, 120–121
Self-esteem, protective mechanisms, 12
Self-glorification biases, 119
Self-relevance, and opinion change, 125–126
Self-representation
    affective component, 208
    cognitive component, 208
    in decision making, 208, 209
    information processing, 208
Self-serving processes, role in depression, 12
Semantic memory
    impact of arousal, 81–86
    mood's influence on, 77–81
    and positive mood, 80
Sensorial perspective, in robot design, 141
Serenity
    avoidance orientation in, 83
    and unusual word associations, 84, 85
Shame
    difference scores, 66
    facial expression, 64
    as secondary emotion, 69
    underestimation of time and, 69
Shia rituals, 150
Short-term memory, 141
Similarity bias, 204
Simulation heuristic/bias, 205
Skin conductance response (SCR), 181
    in exploratory phase, 180
    in impasse situations, 180
    in problem solving, 179
    in Tower of Hanoi study, 177
Skoptzy tradition, 150
Smith and Lazarus approach, 175–176
Social cohesion, 161
    and emotion in religion, 155
    value of euphoria for, 157, 161
Social contagion, 45
Social interactions, temporal dynamic, 61
Social judgment, impact of negative affect on,
    83
Social research methodology, 109
Social rules, internalization of, 69
Somatic marker hypothesis, 13, 14, 45
Somatosensory cortex, 53
Spatial awareness, religious ecstasy and loss of,
    155
Spectral power, 95–100
SPR-IPO model, xix–xx
Stimulus evaluation checks, 174
    order of, 175
Stimulus impoverishment, 221
Storage capacity
    of hedonic detector, 12
    of hedonic detector mechanism, 11

Structural equation modeling (SEM), amygdala-
    cortical network identification with,
    30
Structural organization, salience of, in art, 93
Stylistic processing, 94
Subcortical structures, and emotions, 50–53
Subgoal achievements, 177, 178
    in problem solving, 176
Subjective feeling, roots of, 170–171
Sufi dancing, 150
Superior temporal sulcus (STS), 31
Supervised ANN, 135
Survey questions, measurement of opinions vs.
    attitudes, 107
Survival behaviors, and emotional expressions,
    41
Symmetry, 93
Synchronized activity
    and altruism, 156
    role in religious ritual, 155
Systematic bias, 111

T

Task disruption, by circuit-breaking system, 30
Task-irrelevant processing, and mood state, 79
Temporal bisection task, 63–64
Temporal information, internal clock
    mechanisms, 62–63
Temporal information-processing model, 62
Thalamus, 51
Theta wave activity, 223
    in artists vs. nonartists, 97–100, 102
    in right frontal lobes, 99
    in right temporoparietal cortex, 99
    and top-down processing, 98–100
Threat, vigilance against, 5
Threat perception, in anxiety and depression, 8
Time distortions, 62, 221
    arousal-based processes in, 62
    attention-based processes in, 62
    difference scores, 65, 66
    disgust expression and, 68–69
    and expressions of anger, fear, happiness,
        sadness, 67–68
    overestimation of time, 67–69
    and subjects' age, 68
    underestimation of time, 69
    variations in, 64
Time perception
    influence of emotional facial expressions
        (EFEs), 61
    in social interactions, 61
Top-down processing, 30, 31, 32, 99, 220
    of attentional processing, 20
    in CLARION model, 219
    and suppression of alpha activity, 99
    theta waves and, 98